MAT®
FOR
DUMMIES®

A Wiley Brand

MAT® FOR DUMMIES®
A Wiley Brand

by Vince Kotchian and Edwin Kotchian

MAT® For Dummies®

Published by
John Wiley & Sons, Inc.
111 River St.
Hoboken, NJ 07030-5774
www.wiley.com

Copyright © 2013 by John Wiley & Sons, Inc., Indianapolis, Indiana

Published by John Wiley & Sons, Inc., Indianapolis, Indiana

Published simultaneously in Canada

For general information on our other products and services, please contact our Customer Care Department within the U.S. at 877-762-2974, outside the U.S. at 317-572-3993, or fax 317-572-4002.

For technical support, please visit www.wiley.com/techsupport.

Wiley also publishes its books in a variety of electronic formats and by print-on-demand. Some content that appears in standard print versions of this book may not be available in other formats. For more information about Wiley products, visit us at www.wiley.com.

Library of Congress Control Number: 2013932107

ISBN 978-1-118-49675-6 (pbk); ISBN 978-1-118-59192-5 (ebk); ISBN 978-1-118-59203-8 (ebk); ISBN 978-1-118-59194-9 (ebk)

Manufactured in the United States of America

10 9 8 7 6 5 4 3 2 1

About the Authors

Vince Kotchian: Vince Kotchian is a full-time test-prep tutor, writer, and admissions consultant who has helped hundreds of students get into the schools of their choice. Originally from Connecticut, Vince graduated from Boston College and now lives in San Diego. In addition to his in-person tutoring, Vince works online with students both throughout the United States and internationally. In his free time, Vince enjoys playing and watching sports, reading and writing fiction, and running (which is enjoyable at least some of the time).

Edwin Kotchian is an MAT tutor and freelance writer who has contributed to a variety of test-prep material. He is also a professional musician and composer.

Abstract of chapter

Dedication

Vince would like to dedicate this book to Julie Melisse.

Authors' Acknowledgments

We would first like to thank Margot Hutchison, our agent, for bringing us this opportunity. We'd also like to thank Tracy Boggier for helping the project get off the ground; Tracy Brown, our project editor, for her organizational guidance; Krista Hansing for her skillful copyediting; and our technical editors, Lisa Tolliver and Jake Fox-Rabinovitz, for their invaluable feedback about the book's content.

Publisher's Acknowledgments

We're proud of this book; please send us your comments at http://dummies.custhelp.com. For other comments, please contact our Customer Care Department within the U.S. at 877-762-2974, outside the U.S. at 317-572-3993, or fax 317-572-4002.

Some of the people who helped bring this book to market include the following:

Acquisitions, Editorial, and Media Development

Project Editor: Tracy Brown Hamilton

Acquisitions Editor: Tracy Boggier

Copy Editor: Krista Hansing

Assistant Editor: David Lutton

Editorial Program Coordinator: Joe Niesen

Technical Editor: Lisa Tolliver and Jake Fox-Rabinovitz

Senior Editorial Manager: Jennifer Ehrlich

Editorial Manager: Carmen Krikorian

Editorial Assistant: Alexa Koschier

Composition Services

Project Coordinator: Sheree Montgomery

Layout and Graphics: Carrie A. Cesavice, Joyce Haughey, Christin Swinford

Proofreaders: Melissa Cossell, Jessica Kramer, Susan Moritz, Shannon Ramsey

Indexer: Claudia Bourbeau

Publishing and Editorial for Consumer Dummies

    Kathleen Nebenhaus, Vice President and Executive Publisher

    Kristin Ferguson-Wagstaffe, Product Development Director

Publishing for Technology Dummies

    Andy Cummings, Vice President and Publisher

Composition Services

    Debbie Stailey, Director of Composition Services

Contents at a Glance

Introduction 1

Part I: Introducing the MAT: Learning about Analogies, Planning, and Test-Taking 5
Chapter 1: All About the MAT 7
Chapter 2: Analogies from A to Z 15
Chapter 3: Types of Analogies and How to Solve Them 25
Chapter 4: Creating a Smart MAT Preparation Plan 41

Part II: Conquering the Content: Reviewing Vocabulary, Knowledge, and Culture 51
Chapter 5: Working with Words and Language 53
Chapter 6: Handling the Humanities 73
Chapter 7: Studying the Social Sciences 97
Chapter 8: Studying Science and Math 117

Part III: MAT Practice Exams 135
Chapter 9: MAT Practice Test #1 137
Chapter 10: Answers to MAT Practice Test #1 149
Chapter 11: MAT Practice Test #2 155
Chapter 12: Answers to MAT Practice Test #2 167
Chapter 13: MAT Practice Test #3 173
Chapter 14: Answers to MAT Practice Test #3 185
Chapter 15: MAT Practice Test #4 191
Chapter 16: Answers to MAT Practice Test #4 203
Chapter 17: MAT Practice Test #5 209
Chapter 18: Answers to MAT Practice Test #5 221
Chapter 19: MAT Practice Test #6 227
Chapter 20: Answers to MAT Practice Test #6 239

Part IV: The Part of Tens 245
Chapter 21: Ten Tried-and-True Test Tips 247
Chapter 22: Ten Ways to Fight off Test-Related Anxiety 251

Part V: The Appendixes 255
Appendix A: Graduate Level Vocabulary 257
Appendix B: Making the MAT Work for You 319

Index 323

Table of Contents

Introduction **1**

About This Book 1
Conventions Used in This Book 2
Foolish Assumptions 2
How This Book Is Organized 2
    Part I: Introducing the MAT: Learning about Analogies, Planning,
       and Test-Taking 2
    Part II: Conquering the Content: Reviewing Vocabulary, Knowledge, and Culture ... 3
    Part III: MAT Practice Exams 3
    Part IV: The Part of Tens 3
    Part V: Appendixes 3
Icons Used in This Book 3
Where to Go from Here 4

Part 1: Introducing the MAT: Learning about
Analogies, Planning, and Test-Taking **5**

Chapter 1: All About the MAT **7**

What Is the MAT? 7
    What the exam looks like 8
    Cultural literacy 9
    Practice makes perfect 9
    Who invented the MAT, anyway? 10
    What does the MAT measure? 10
    The MAT vs. the GRE 10
Registering for the MAT 11
    Paper vs. computer 11
    Score reporting 11
    Accommodations 12
How the MAT Is Scored 12
The After(MAT)h 13

Chapter 2: Analogies from A to Z **15**

Analogical Thinking 101 15
    Why analogical thinking is valued 16
    Analogical thinking in an academic environment 16
    Analogical thinking in the workplace 17
Getting Familiar with MAT Analogy Relationship Categories 18
    Description analogies 18
    Type analogies 19
    Parts analogies 20
    Similar/different analogies 21
    Playful analogies 22
        Wordplay analogies 22
        Grammar change analogies 22
        "Sounds like" analogies 23

Chapter 3: Types of Analogies and How to Solve Them **25**

Understanding 1:2,3:4 Analogies...25
Looking at 1:3,2:4 Analogies 26
Seeing Why 1:4,2:3 Analogies Don't Exist 27
Identifying Analogy Structure 28
Planning Your Attack: Choosing Your Analogy-Cracking Strategy 29
Identifying the structural type 29
Building sentences...30
Checking the choices 31
Practicing your analogy skills 32
Dealing with Tough Questions..33
Skipping tough questions 33
Noticing difficulty level 34
Solving the question when you don't know one or more words 34
Applying the process of elimination 34
Working backward..35
Considering parts of speech...36
Keeping in mind alternate meanings 37
Making educated guesses 37
Avoiding analogy traps 37
Category traps 38
Direction traps...38
Distractor traps 39
Putting it all together..39

Chapter 4: Creating a Smart MAT Preparation Plan **41**

Creating Your MAT Study Plan 41
Knowing where you currently stand...42
Following through with your plan 42
Setting a goal 42
Lights, Camera, Action: Setting Your Plan in Motion..............................43
Setting a deadline and mapping a schedule 43
Making sure you have the right study materials 44
Maximizing your motivation..44
Avoiding procrastination...45
Keeping in mind quality vs. quantity..45
Timing your practice work 45
Duplicating the test environment 46
Taking several practice tests 46
Knowing when you're ready to register 47
Racing the Clock: Tackling MAT Timing 47
Timing each question 48
Developing smart pacing 48
Recovering when you've fallen behind 48
Dealing with Test Anxiety..49
Controlling anxiety 49
Maintaining focus...49
Preparing your body and mind 50

Part II: Conquering the Content: Reviewing Vocabulary, Knowledge, and Culture 51

Chapter 5: Working with Words and Language 53
Looking at Word Roots, Prefixes, and Suffixes 53
    Getting back to your (word) roots 53
    Identifying prefixes 56
    Recognizing suffixes 58
Improving Your Vocabulary 59
Learning Vocabulary Using Mnemonics 60
    Looking at examples of mnemonics 60
    Making your own mnemonics 60
Recognizing Words of a Specific Type 61
    Knowing your –ologies 61
    Identifying collective nouns 62
    Distinguishing commonly confused words 64
Addressing Foreign Words and Alphabets 67
Practicing Words and Language Analogies 69
    Answers 71

Chapter 6: Handling the Humanities 73
Brushing Up on Art 73
    Terms 73
    Artists and works 74
    Museums 76
Building Your Architecture Knowledge 77
    Terms 77
    Architects 78
    Works 78
Naming That Tune: Music 79
    Terms 79
    Composers and musicians 82
    Works 83
Reading Up on Literature 83
    Terms 83
    Authors 85
Thinking Deep Thoughts: Philosophy 89
    Terms 89
    Philosophers 90
    Works 91
Pondering Religion/Mythology 92
    Terms 92
    Religions 92
    Greek/Roman gods 92
    Other gods 93
    Religious figures 93
    Locations 94
    Festivals/holidays 94
    Writings 94
    Places of worship 94
Humanities Analogy Practice 95
    Answers 96

Chapter 7: Studying the Social Sciences..**97**

The Lay of the Land: Getting to Know Geography 97
 Geographical terms 97
Past Is Prelude: Honing Your History Knowledge 100
 Historical terms...100
 Historical figures...102
 Historical events 103
Making Cents of Dollars: Explaining Economics 104
 Economics terms 104
 Economics figures 106
Politically Correct: Polishing Your Political Science 106
 Political Science terms 106
 Political Science figures 107
Freudian Slips: Practicing Psychology..108
 Psychology terms 108
 Psychology figures 109
Sharp Social Skills: Sifting through Sociology..109
 Sociology terms...110
 Sociology figures...111
Be a People Person: Analyzing Anthropology 112
 Anthropology terms 112
 Anthropology figures...113
Social Science Analogy Practice 114
 Answers 115

Chapter 8: Studying Science and Math...................................**117**

Birds and Bees: Biology 117
 Terms 117
 Figures 119
Beyond Bunsen Burners: Chemistry 120
 Terms 120
 Figures 122
Getting Physical: Physics...122
 Terms 122
 Figures 124
And now: Other Sciences...125
 Terms 125
 Figures 126
Staying Classy: Classification 127
 Animals..127
It's Elementary: The Periodic Table 128
Learning about Measurement 129
Mastering Mathematics 130
 Roman numerals 130
 Arithmetic...130
 Algebra 131
 Geometry 131
Science/Math Analogy Practice 133
 Answers...134

Part III: MAT Practice Exams 135

Chapter 9: MAT Practice Test #1 137

Chapter 10: Answers to MAT Practice Test #1 149

Chapter 11: MAT Practice Test #2 155

Chapter 12: Answers to MAT Practice Test #2 167

Chapter 13: MAT Practice Test #3 173

Chapter 14: Answers to MAT Practice Test #3 185

Chapter 15: MAT Practice Test #4 191

Chapter 16: Answers to MAT Practice Test #4 203

Chapter 17: MAT Practice Test #5 209

Chapter 18: Answers to MAT Practice Test #5 221

Chapter 19: MAT Practice Test #6 227

Chapter 20: Answers to MAT Practice Test #6 239

Part IV: The Part of Tens 245

Chapter 21: Ten Tried-and-True Test Tips 247

Exercise Your Body, Not Just Your Brain.................................247
Be Sure You Get Enough Sleep 247
Get Organized the Night Before...247
Be Well Fed...248
On Test Day, Don't Study 248
Warm Up...248
Arrive Early 248
Review How Many Questions You Can Skip...............................249
Write It Down 249
Don't Rush or Second Guess 249

Chapter 22: Ten Ways to Fight off Test-Related Anxiety **251**

Breathe...251
Take a Break..251
Stretch..252
Move Your Pencil...252
Slow Down...252
Skip a Weakness...252
Get Perspective..253
Be Goofy..253
Feel What You're Feeling..253
Use Positive Self-Talk..253

Part V: The Appendixes *255*

Appendix A: Graduate Level Vocabulary.................................**257**

How to Use This Appendix..257
The mnemonics..257

Appendix B: Making the MAT Work for You.............................**319**

Putting Your Scores to Work...319
Retaking the MAT..319
Gearing Up for Graduate Admissions.......................................320
Presenting Your GPA..320
Writing Your Essays...320
Preparing Your Resume..321
Choosing Your Referrals...321
Preparing for Interviews...321

Index.. *323*

Introduction

Whether you're taking the MAT for graduate school admission, a job, or some other reason, you're probably at least somewhat concerned about the test. Something about standardized tests just seems to intimidate many people. And as I'm sure you know, your score will probably matter quite a bit. Or maybe you're so used to taking tests in school that the thought of facing the MAT doesn't faze you, but you figure you may as well read up on it. But no matter what your initial attitude, it's good to take a closer look at what you're up against.

The MAT is probably unlike any test you've ever taken. For starters, it has just one type of question on it: the analogy. You may remember analogies from other standardized tests — they're questions posed in this form:

> Banana is to fruit as carrot is to _____.

You then have to select an answer from four choices, only one of which creates a clear, logical relationship between the terms in the analogy. The right answer to this analogy is *vegetable*: A banana is a type of fruit, just as a carrot is a type of vegetable.

The other unusual characteristic of the MAT is that, unlike most standardized tests, it covers a whole bunch of different topics, ranging from general knowledge to math, to literature, to science. Since it tests your knowledge of so many different areas, the test is extremely difficult to completely master. After all, you're not Wikipedia. Fortunately, you can intelligently prepare for the content the MAT covers by learning the most common terms, people, and concepts in categories such as history, art, and music.

Why is the MAT so weird? Well, studies have consistently shown that if someone can reason the relationships between things, they probably can make connections easily, solve problems, and see patterns — skills that come in handy in most jobs and fields of study. Schools and employers that use the MAT want some evidence that you have the ability to think, and a good score on the MAT is one indication that you do. People with knowledge of lots of different areas may also be intellectually curious, another desirable trait.

As with most tests, the MAT has a time limit: You have just 60 minutes to answer 120 questions. Even if you're a whiz with analogies, you're going to want to employ some intelligent strategies to earn as many points as you can in that hour. Well, the book you're looking at right now is designed to help you do just that.

About This Book

Before you take the MAT, it's a good idea to become as familiar as possible with the test: its format, what it's used for, what it covers, and what tips and tricks you can use to do well on it. In this book, you learn about the MAT, meet analogies and discover how to solve them, master some smart test-taking techniques, tackle the different content areas tested, and take some practice tests. The goal, of course, is to help you get the highest score you possibly can, to improve your chances of being accepted into school or getting the job you want. I recommend that you proceed through the book in the order it is organized, but feel free to skip around, if that works better for you. I also recommend that you take some practice tests before you take the real MAT, no matter which preparation roadmap you decide to follow.

Conventions Used in This Book

To help you make your way through this book, I've used the following conventions:

- ✔ I use *italics* to introduce new terms.

- ✔ **Boldface** shows you the action step in a list of steps or highlights an important point.

- ✔ Monofont indicates an Internet address. If the address is long, it might wrap to the next line in your book, but I don't include extra dashes or type if it starts a new line. In other words, just type the web address as you see it in the book, and it will send you to the right place.

- ✔ From time to time, you're going to see sidebars, or blocks of text in shaded gray boxes. This extra info isn't crucial, but it's usually additional information or stories that can help you make more sense of something. You can always skip these sidebars if you're short on time, but read them if you can.

Foolish Assumptions

As I wrote this book, I made a few important assumptions about you:

- ✔ You're motivated to do well on the MAT, but you're not overwhelmingly pumped up to take the test. That's normal.

- ✔ You have a busy schedule, and adding MAT preparation into your life isn't exactly what you want to be doing with your precious free time. The good news is that I only include things in this book that I think you need to know, since I don't want to waste any of your time.

- ✔ You have some knowledge of some of the content areas (literature, math, science, history, and so on) that the MAT covers. My goal isn't to teach you every possible fact about those areas, but rather to give you the most important facts.

- ✔ You're not a dummy. In fact, I'm assuming that you're a successful, smart person who wants to continue your success. After all, that's probably why you're reading this book.

How This Book Is Organized

I took a lot of care and time in deciding how to organize this book because I want to make sure it works for you. It's set up in a way that I hope will let you find what you're looking for quickly and easily, without distracting you with irrelevant or repetitive information. Here's what you'll find in this book:

Part 1: Introducing the MAT: Learning about Analogies, Planning, and Test-Taking

In this part, you learn about general issues concerning the MAT. You get general information about the MAT, including how to register for it, analogy content and structure, and analogy-solving methods and analogy categories. You'll also find planning advice, study strategies, and time-management tactics. This part gives you a solid foundation for the rest of your MAT preparation.

Part II: Conquering the Content: Reviewing Vocabulary, Knowledge, and Culture

In this part, you learn about the content the MAT covers. Chapters cover words and language, the humanities, social sciences, and natural sciences and math. You'll learn the most important concepts in the areas tested. Each entry includes a brief definition designed to give you the most relevant information about it, and each chapter ends with analogies so you can practice the content.

Part III: MAT Practice Exams

This part contains six full-length MAT practice exams, along with answer keys and answer explanations. Here's where you'll be able to realistically practice on questions that are based on real MAT questions. Each exam has the same number of questions as a real MAT exam and has a similar level and progression of difficulty.

Part IV: The Part of Tens

Every For Dummies book includes a Part of Tens. In this part, you get lists of handy tips to keep in mind during test day, along with some ways to reduce test anxiety.

Part V: The Appendixes

This part contains tips and tricks for conquering graduate level vocabulary and making the MAT work for you.

Icons Used in This Book

Throughout the book, we include icons in the margin that call your attention to really important content. If you notice an icon, check it out — it's worth your time!

✔ **Tip:** This icon points out information to keep in mind about a certain topic. It may highlight a test-taking strategy, so read closely when you see a paragraph accompanied by this icon.

✔ **Warning:** The MAT definitely has its traps in both strategy and content. I use Warning icons to alert you to mistakes many students make when preparing for the MAT, answering questions, or even managing time limits.

✔ **Remember:** Everything in the book is important, but some content is extra important. I put this icon next to content you'll really want to remember for the test. Remember icons also accompany test-taking strategies that you'll want to know for the day of the test.

✔ **Example:** When you notice this icon, it's an indication that you'll be practicing a particular area with a question. Each example question has a corresponding explanation and information on how to best solve questions like it.

Where to Go from Here

Just like every For Dummies book, you don't have to go through this book in order from beginning to end, and you don't even have to read every page. Instead, feel free to skip around as you see fit, spending more time on areas you need the most help with. For example, if you're great at math but weak in the humanities, spend more time analyzing and working on humanities analogies, and perhaps less time poring over the math ones. If you've already spent lots of time learning content, you may just go straight to the analogy-solving section or to the practice exams. You also don't need to take all six of the practice exams, but more practice certainly can't hurt — and will probably help.

Part I

Introducing the MAT: Learning about Analogies, Planning, and Test-Taking

In this part . . .

✔ Get acquainted with the MAT exam and who created it, what topics it covers, and what skills and competencies it measures.

✔ See how the MAT compares with the GRE and discover compelling reasons why the MAT may be a better choice for you and for the program to which you're applying.

✔ Familiarize yourself with analogical thinking and understand what your analogy-solving performance can reveal to admissions boards about how you process information and think.

✔ Understand how to relationships between words are formulated and get to know the five relationship categories covered on the MAT.

✔ Look at various approaches to cracking analogies, such as knowing and identifying analogy structures, building short sentences to express relationships between words, and when it's best to skip a really tough one.

✔ Develop a test-preparation plan that fits your schedule, test-taking style, and anxiety level.

Chapter 1

All About the MAT

In This Chapter

▶ Exploring the MAT

▶ Finding out how to sign up for the MAT

▶ Looking at how the MAT is scored

*I*f you're thinking about going to graduate school, you've probably realized by now that schools don't let you in based on your good looks and charm. Most programs require a standardized test score so the admissions committee can see how you compare to other applicants. If you're reading this book, the program you're interested in probably accepts a MAT score for that very purpose.

Or you may be studying for the MAT because your employer, or prospective employer, wants to see how well you can do on it. You may be applying for financial aid that requires a MAT score. You may even be trying to get into Mensa or another high-IQ club that accepts a high MAT score as a criterion for admission. Whatever your reason for taking the MAT, it's a good idea to learn as much as you can about the test and prepare for it intelligently before taking it.

What Is the MAT?

MAT stands for Miller Analogies Test. Its format is simple. You have 60 minutes to answer 120 questions, all of which are analogies. In each question, part of the analogy is missing. Your job is to pick the correct choice out of four possibilities to complete the analogy. Sounds simple, right? Well, it's a bit more complicated than that. Much like *Trivial Pursuit,* the MAT tests your knowledge of a wide variety of subjects, ranging from astronomy to math, to vocabulary, to zoology — and everything in between.

When you realize just how many subjects the MAT potentially covers, you may be a little discouraged — after all, you're not a walking Wikipedia, nor are you Alex Trebek or the host of any other brainiac TV trivia program (at least, probably not). But don't worry — the MAT doesn't require you to know *everything* about the subjects it covers. If you have some time to prepare, you can significantly increase your knowledge of the subjects you're less familiar with. And you'll be able to learn how to intelligently attack analogy questions.

If you're reading this book, you're off to a great start in preparing to take the MAT. Another good reference for the MAT is the test publisher's website, milleranalogies.com, which has current information about the test. The site has a Candidate Information Booklet that contains much of the info you'll need. Browse as much of the site as you can: As G. I. Joe said, knowing is half the battle. Perhaps most important, the site has a link for purchasing three full-length computer-based MAT practice tests. These tests can (and should) become part of your preparation plan.

What the exam looks like

As I mentioned, the MAT has 120 questions, all of which are analogies. For the purposes of the MAT, an analogy is a relationship between two pairs of terms. For example:

Big is to small as fast is to slow.

The relationship between the terms **big** and **small** is similar to the relationship between the terms **fast** and **slow** — they're both opposites. Several types of relationships between analogy terms show up on the MAT. We discuss some of the more common types in Chapter 2.

If, like most people, you're taking the MAT on a computer, you'll see only one question at a time. Each question looks like the following example:

FISH : SCALES :: BEAR : _____

(A) feathers

(B) fur

(C) spines

(D) wool

This analogy includes four terms: FISH, SCALES, BEAR, and then one of the multiple choices (a. feathers, b. fur, c. spines, d. wool).

The part of the question enclosed in parentheses (a. feathers, b. fur, c. spines, d. wool) can appear as any of the four terms. For example, the question can be rewritten as follows:

_____ : BEAR :: FISH : SCALES

(A) feathers

(B) fur

(C) spines

(D) wool

Your job is to pick the choice that makes the first and second terms have the same relationship to the third and fourth terms, or to make the first and third terms have the same relationship as the second and fourth terms. If you pick Choice B, **fur**, as the missing term, then a logical analogy is formed:

A **fish** is covered with **scales**, like a **bear** is covered with **fur**.

As the MAT progresses, the questions get harder and the topics vary, but you can be sure that analogies will be the only question type you'll encounter.

Cultural literacy

The MAT does more than test your ability to solve analogies. It also tests you on your general knowledge of a variety of topics, similar to the GRE or other standardized test but in a different question format. So preparing for the MAT also means brushing up on your knowledge in the following areas, to name just a few:

- ✔ Anthropology
- ✔ Art
- ✔ Biology
- ✔ Chemistry
- ✔ History
- ✔ Math
- ✔ Music
- ✔ Philosophy
- ✔ Vocabulary

When you realize just how many subjects the MAT can cover, it can seem like you may have to take every course in a college catalog or watch the last 20 years of *Jeopardy!* Of course, you probably can't do either of those things. What you can do is study the lists of terms we've included in this book. If you aren't that knowledgeable about a certain subject, learning some important concepts, terms, and figures can mean getting a few more questions right on the real test. Don't stress out — you don't need to learn everything to do well on the MAT. Learn as much as you can in the time you have, and it will make a difference in your score.

Practice makes perfect

Getting a *perfect* score on the MAT is nearly impossible because of the breadth of the subjects it covers, but in general, the more you practice, the better you'll do. In addition to learning as much as you can about the test's content, we recommend you take every practice test in this book. Also, it's worth purchasing the three practice tests that the MAT's publishers make available. You can buy a year's worth of access to each official practice test on milleranalogies.com. Even though access to each test costs $30 at the time of this book's publication, it's worthwhile since those tests are the closest you can get to the actual MAT exam you'll be faced with on your test date.

Make sure that, no matter how you practice, you come up with a workable, memorable method of approaching analogy questions. In Chapter 3, we outline a step-by-step method designed to maximize your score and help you tackle even tough questions.

Who invented the MAT, anyway?

The MAT is brought to you by the good folks at Pearson Education, Inc. It's been around for more than 60 years as a test of reasoning ability. Analogies have been a part of standardized tests for even longer than that.

What does the MAT measure?

The MAT is marketed as a measure of two main things: your cultural literacy and your reasoning ability. In other words, it claims to measure how much you know about subjects like art, history, science, and math, as well as your ability to make connections between concepts from those subjects. It's also marketed as a good predictor of how you'll do in graduate school.

The MAT's way of measuring your ability is to see how many questions you answer correctly on the test and then compare you to other test takers — in particular, by comparing you to people with your intended major. This data gives graduate programs, or an employer, concrete data with which to help with decisions.

Keep in mind that the MAT isn't an IQ test, nor is it a predictor of your future success. It's certainly true that some people who do well in graduate school scored poorly on the MAT, and some people who fare poorly in graduate school aced the MAT. At the end of the day, your MAT score is an important part of your graduate school application — but it's not the only part.

The MAT vs. the GRE

The graduate program you're interested in may accept a GRE score instead of a MAT score. The GRE test is much different from the MAT. Here's a comparison of the two exams' major differences.

MAT	GRE
60 minutes long	About 4 hours long
1 question type: analogies	2 types of vocabulary questions, several reading comprehension question types, and several types of math questions
Tests cultural knowledge	Doesn't test cultural knowledge
No essays	2 types of essays

If you have a strong vocabulary, you're a skilled reader and writer, and/or you're good at tricky math questions, you may do better on the GRE. On the other hand, if you have a solid foundation of cultural knowledge and you're not excited about doing a lot of math or writing essays, the MAT may be better for you. Another factor that may be important is cost: Taking the GRE is about twice as expensive as taking the MAT. And, don't forget about how long it takes to complete each test. The MAT is a lightweight at one hour, and the GRE tips the scales at more than four hours.

Ultimately, you can take a computer practice test of each and see both which test feels more comfortable and how your scores stack up. You can purchase three official MAT computer tests on www.MillerAnalogies.com. You can download two real computer GRE tests from ets.org, the GRE publisher's website. (As of this book's publication date, the downloadable GRE tests are PC compatible only. Sorry, Mac users.)

Registering for the MAT

When you've made up your mind to take the MAT, you need to find a place to actually take the test. More than 600 CTCs, or Controlled Testing Centers, administer the MAT throughout the U.S. and Canada, and even overseas. Go to milleranalogies.com to find a link (called something like "Find a MAT Testing Center") that provides a list of testing centers by location. If you live more than 100 miles from the nearest center, you can request an alternate site (if you pay an additional fee).

Each one of these Controlled Testing Centers makes up its own schedule for administering the MAT — and has its own fee. As of the publication date of this book, fees average around $90.

Before you sign up for a certain test date, ask the center how long, on average, it takes schools to receive a test-taker's official score report. Then find out your desired graduate school program's admission deadlines so that you can make sure you allow enough time for the official results to be sent to the school. The center where you sign up can tell you more about the dates the MAT is offered, how to register, and what's required when you get to the center. But in general, you have to provide a government-issued photo ID and a supplemental form of identification on test day.

Find out whether you're allowed to bring a watch (highly recommended) and whether you have to supply your own pencils if you're taking the paper version of the MAT.

Paper vs. computer

Each testing center determines whether to offer a computer-based MAT or a pencil-and-paper MAT. The questions on each test are the same — the only difference is the kind of test administration you prefer. Each version allows the test taker to skip back and forth between questions. If you like using computers, you'll probably prefer the computer-based version — especially because you won't have to erase any changed answers. A downside to a computer-based test may be that it takes longer to skip between questions, since you have to click with your mouse each time (as opposed to just looking at the question you'd like to skip to on a paper test).

Score reporting

When you take the MAT, you have the opportunity to send your score to as many as three schools — for free. If you want score reports sent later, each report costs about $25. In addition to seeing your most recent MAT score, these schools will see every one of your

MAT scores within the past five years. If you have a score that's more than five years old, that one isn't reported to schools. The personal score report you receive in the mail isn't an official transcript; schools receive an official transcript of your scores directly from the test publisher.

Accommodations

Most testing centers can offer special accommodations: Braille, audio editions, and so on. Be sure to notify the testing center that you need a certain accommodation several weeks before your test date, and fill out the necessary paperwork from milleranalogies.com.

How the MAT Is Scored

Although the MAT has 120 questions, only 100 of them count. The MAT's publisher uses the other 20 questions for future exams. Since the difficulty level of the MAT's questions increases as the test progresses, the publisher needs to know where to put the difficult questions and where to put the easy ones. Seeing how many people get each experimental question right helps. If most people get a certain experimental question right, that question will appear closer to the beginning of a future MAT. If most people got the question wrong, it will appear closer to the end of a future exam.

The MAT's publisher uses this method so that a MAT given this year has a similar difficulty level to a MAT given last year. It's also a more accurate way of determining which questions are truly hard and which are easy, instead of just having a committee of people vote on each question's difficulty level. So just think, you're helping pave the way for future MAT test takers. Doesn't that make you feel warm and fuzzy? Also keep in mind that you won't know which questions are experimental, so answer them all as if they're real.

One of the most important points to remember about the MAT is that questions left blank are automatically counted as wrong. Unlike some standardized tests, there's no penalty for guessing. Make extra sure you at least answer every question, even if it's a random guess because you're running out of time. It's all too easy to get wrapped up in a question as time is running out and then forget to answer a few questions. Don't let this happen to you! Always save a couple minutes at the end of the test so that you have time to answer every question, even if you have to guess randomly on some of them. Also remember that later questions aren't worth more; every correct answer improves your score by the same amount.

If you really think you failed the MAT after taking it, or if something goes horribly, tragically wrong for you that day, you can exercise what is known as the "no-score" option. This cancels your score — no one will even find out that you took the test. However, you won't get your money back and you won't be able to find out how you did on the test. So use this option only as a last resort.

The After (MAT)h

If you're taking a computer-based MAT, you'll receive a preliminary score right on the screen after you complete the exam. You'll receive your official MAT score in the mail about two weeks after you take the exam. This report will show you the following:

- ✔ Your scaled score, which ranges from 200 to 600 (400 is average)
- ✔ Your percentile rank for your desired major
- ✔ Your percentile rank among all test takers
- ✔ The codes for the schools your scores will be sent to

Note that schools that receive your MAT score will also receive *all* your MAT scores within the last five years. Schools usually consider your highest score, but the fact that they'll see all your scores may motivate you to postpone the test until you're fully confident.

You'll also receive a "Re-Test Admission Ticket" along with your score report, and you'll need to bring the ticket if you want to retake the test. This ticket allows the testing center to make sure they don't give you the exact same MAT you took previously (wouldn't that be nice?) if you decide that your first attempt wasn't good enough. **Be warned:** If you retake the test but don't bring your ticket, your new score will be cancelled.

Remember, if you are taking the MAT for graduate school admission, that it is just one factor graduate schools consider when deciding whether to offer you a place in a program. However, we won't pretend that it's not an important factor. Don't let preparing for the MAT consume your life, but don't underestimate it, either. Intelligent preparation will make you comfortable with the test's format, build your analogy-solving skills, and help you improve the skills you need to get an impressive score.

Chapter 2

Analogies from A to Z

In This Chapter

▶ Getting familiar with analogical thinking

▶ Looking at MAT analogy categories

One of the nice things about the MAT (if you can call a standardized test nice) is that, even though you're facing 120 questions, you have to prepare for only one question type: the analogy. Solving analogies tests your critical thinking skills and vocabulary skills, as well as your understanding of the relationships between analogy terms.

This chapter gives you an overview on analogies and analogical thinking, helps you determine whether the MAT is right for you, and introduces the major MAT analogy relationship categories.

Analogical Thinking 101

People use analogies all the time in everyday speech. Analogies convey meaning by drawing comparisons. For example, you may say, "Trying to change my boss's mind is like banging my head against a brick wall." Banging your head against a wall is painful and futile, which illustrates how you feel about trying to change your boss's mind.

On a standardized test, an analogy is a word problem composed of two different pairs of terms. The word problem is set up to reveal one set of terms first. Those two terms are related to each other in some way. The problem then gives you the first term of the second pair and asks you to choose a second term to complete that pair. This second term must be related to the first term in the same manner in which the first pair of terms is related.

For example:

Black is to white as hot is to _____

(A) great

(B) neutral

(C) cold

(D) gray

This basic analogy is asking you first to recognize the relationship between the terms *black* and *white* and then to pick a term that creates the same relationship. Because black is the opposite of white, the correct answer is Choice (C).

Black is to white as hot is to cold because cold is the opposite of hot.

Why analogical thinking is valued

Your ability to solve analogies offers insight into how you think. Both graduate programs and employers are interested in accepting people who can think, analyze, and reason, and looking at MAT scores is one way they attempt to determine whether an applicant has those abilities.

Analogies help us learn by creating connections in our minds. If I tell a student to answer all the easy questions on a test before attempting any difficult ones, he'll almost certainly understand me. But if I make the analogy that answering the easy questions first is like first grabbing the easiest coins when you're running out of time in *Super Mario Brothers,* he'll have a mental image and create a stronger memory link to the concept.

He'll be able to link it to something he already knows, making it easier to remember and use in the future. In fact, a lot of the learning we do uses analogies, since we often fit new concepts into our existing knowledge by mentally comparing them to things we already know. Analogies aren't bad; they're actually pretty useful. Working on them might even make you smarter.

As with most skills, the more time you spend working on analogies, the better you get at them because your brain gets more used to identifying relationships. When you begin the analogy practice later in this chapter, stick with it. Practice a little every day — before you know it, you'll be able to zero in on most analogy relationships in no time.

Analogical thinking in an academic environment

Standardized tests have included analogies for almost 100 years. Studies have shown that skill with analogies is connected to intelligence, analytical ability, and higher thinking that extends beyond simple memorization. Prospective schools find these traits desirable in their incoming students.

Graduate programs require a standardized test score so that they have some basis for comparing your application to others. Many factors influence grades, so schools use tests like the MAT because they stick to a standard. The MAT you take is most likely the same MAT that someone else across the country took, or at least very similar.

So, for example, if two applicants have the same GPA but different MAT scores, an admissions committee can more easily decide which applicant to accept. Schools also tend to put more stock in concrete data, like a numerical MAT score, than they do subjective data, like a teacher's recommendation letter. After all, you can bribe a teacher to write you a good letter, but you can't bribe the MAT.

Schools like the MAT because it tests your ability to think in terms of analogies. Admission boards want to know that you can think and reason. If you perform well on the MAT, they know you can determine relationships in many different situations.

This skill is particularly valuable in fields like science that often require analogical thinking. For example, if adding acid B to chemical C produces an explosion, then adding acid B to chemical D, which is in the same chemical class as chemical C, will probably also produce an explosion. This inference uses an analogy to predict that a similar situation will produce a similar result. In this example, analogical thinking may save your life!

In a similar vein, schools want to see that you're well rounded. Many programs that accept MAT scores for admission are in education-related fields. If you're going to become an educator, it makes sense that you need a broad spectrum of knowledge, to explain concepts to your future students. A good MAT score most likely means that you have a basic level of knowledge about the humanities, sciences, and so on, making it more likely that you can explain a concept in more than one way. And using analogies is a great way to teach, especially if you can make an analogy using a concept the student is comfortable with.

Analogical thinking in the workplace

You may think that MAT scores are relevant only to getting into a graduate program, but not so. I don't mean to put additional pressure on you, but your scores can follow you far beyond enrolling in the school of your choice.

When you apply for a job, some companies may want to see your scores. Essentially, employers look at your MAT score the same way schools do. If a company asks for a MAT score, it likely wants a standard for comparing you to other applicants. Like schools, companies want to gauge your ability to think and reason, to see if you're well rounded and/ or intellectually curious. People like to base their decisions on facts, and a MAT score is one more fact they can use to consider the strength of your application for the job.

Additionally, companies know that, with the world changing so quickly, they need to hire people who have the ability to adapt. Today's technology will probably be obsolete in ten years. To companies, getting a good score on the MAT may mean that you can think on your feet and apply your current knowledge to solve new problems as they arise.

For example, if you worked at a produce company and were able to recognize that cold-press juicers were selling well in southern California, you could recommend that the company increase its advertising in that area. You'd bring tangible value to the company with your ability to identify relationships.

Determining Your Analogy Aptitude

So how do you find out if you're good with analogies? In general, you're more likely to be good with analogies if one or more of the following applies to you:

- You quickly make connections between concepts and determine whether they're related.

- You're a good teacher, or you're good at explaining concepts in ways others can understand.

- You like learning. You like Googling and researching on the Internet, just for fun.

- You're good with words, you have a good vocabulary, and you enjoy reading.

- You're good with puzzles and figuring things out.

- You're a creative person and enjoy creative expression.

This list isn't comprehensive, but it may help predict whether you'll adapt well to analogical thinking if you're not already good at it. Of course, to really determine whether you're good at analogies, you have to work on a bunch of them and see how you do.

Using this book is a good first step. And after you take the first practice exam that you purchase from the Miller Analogies website, you'll have some hard data about your skill level.

Getting Familiar with MAT Analogy Relationship Categories

If you think about it, we're always formulating relationships between the words we use. If I say any two words to you, like *red* and *car,* you'll probably form a relationship between them — maybe by picturing a shiny red Corvette. MAT analogies are all about relationships, and familiarizing yourself with some of the general categories of relationships on the MAT can make it easier to identify them in questions.

The MAT officially lists four types of relationships: Semantic, Classification, Association, and Logical/Mathematical. The names for these types are not as simple and descriptive as they could be, so I've renamed and expanded the relationship types to make it easier for you to think about them. We can create relationships between words in so many ways that, instead of trying to describe every single possible relationship, I group the MAT analogies into five major categories:

- ✔ Description
- ✔ Type
- ✔ Parts
- ✔ Similar/different
- ✔ Playful

A term occupies one of the four positions in an analogy. Terms can be words, multiple words, letters, or numbers.

It's a good idea to get familiar with these five major categories and how they work by studying the following examples. Then you'll know what's coming on the practice tests and the real MAT. However, don't worry too much about figuring out a category for every single analogy you come across. Some analogies are tough to categorize, and thinking about which category a particular analogy fits into often isn't necessary to solve it.

Description analogies

A verb is a part of speech that expresses existence or action.

Description analogies are quite common on the MAT. In a description analogy, one of the terms in the analogy describes the other term in some way. The description is usually accomplished by a verb, which can be any action. For example:

DOCTOR : HOSPITAL :: FARMER : _____

(A) crop

(B) acre

(C) labor

(D) field

In this 1:2,3:4 analogy, a doctor works in a hospital, as a farmer works in a field, so the right answer is Choice (D). A hospital is a description of where a doctor works, as a field is a description of where a farmer works. The description is accomplished by the word *works.* Here's another description analogy example:

CHICKEN : DOLPHIN :: _____ : CALVE

(A) green

(B) hop

(C) hatch

(D) swim

This analogy is a 1:3,2:4. A baby dolphin leaves its mother's womb through calving, as a baby chicken leaves its protective egg by hatching. The answer is Choice (C). *Calve* is a description of how a dolphin is born, as *hatch* is a description of how a baby chicken is born. In this example, you can think of the description as being accomplished by the word *born*.

Type analogies

Type analogies deal with classifying things and thinking about their types. Here's one example:

_____ : BEAR :: ANACONDA : SNAKE

(A) grizzly

(B) vicious

(C) furry

(D) cunning

In this 1:2,3:4 analogy, an anaconda is a type of snake, as a grizzly is a type of bear. Notice that you can use "type of" to think about the relationship between the terms in this example. Here's another type analogy:

INSECT : MOSQUITO :: SPIDER : _____

(A) crawl

(B) black

(C) black widow

(D) eight

As in the previous analogy, this analogy is also 1:2,3:4. Notice, however, that the direction of the relationship between the related terms is different than in the previous example. A mosquito is a type of insect, as a black widow is a type of spider. It's still a type analogy, though, and thinking about the relationship between related terms using "type of" is still useful. Here's one more type analogy example:

FERRARI : PORSCHE :: DIAL : _____

(A) soap

(B) Ghana

(C) Ivory

(D) number

This 1:2,3:4 analogy also fits into the type category. The first two terms are related because Ferrari and Porsche are both automobile brands, as the second two terms — Dial and the correct answer, Choice (C), Ivory, — are both brands of soap. This example is a bit different than the first two type analogy examples because the related terms fit into the same category. You can still use the phrase "type of" to help you think about the relationships involved.

Parts analogies

In parts analogies, one term is often part of another term, or both related terms are parts of something else. Here's an example of a parts analogy:

CENTIMETER : METER :: OUNCE : _____

(A) pound

(B) liquid

(C) weight

(D) unit

This is another 1:2,3:4 analogy, and the correct answer is Choice (A). A centimeter is part of a meter, as an ounce is part of a pound. Notice that it's handy to use the phrase "part of" to think about the relationship between the related terms.

I could have reversed the relationship direction of the analogy by writing it like this:

METER : CENTIMETER :: _____ : OUNCE

(A) pound

(B) liquid

(C) weight

(D) unit

It's still a 1:2,3:4 analogy and it's still a parts analogy — the only thing that's changed is that the second term is now part of the first term, as the fourth term is part of the third term. (A centimeter is part of a meter, as an ounce is part of a pound.) The answer is still Choice (A) (pound).

Here's another parts analogy example:

SOUTH : DAKOTA :: _____ : VIRGINIA

(A) colonial

(B) coastal

(C) state

(D) west

In this example, the first and second choices (*South* and *Dakota*) are both parts of a whole (the state South Dakota), as the third and fourth choices are both parts of a whole (using Choice [D], they combine to form *West Virginia*). It's a 1:2,3:4 structure. Again, you can think of it in terms of parts; this time, the parts both combine to create a whole.

Similar/different analogies

In a similar/different analogy, the related terms usually are either the same or almost the same, or opposite/very different. Consider an example of a similar/different analogy with a similar relationship:

ANGRY : INCENSED :: _____ : UNIVERSAL

(A) common

(B) barrel

(C) versatile

(D) sharp

In this 1:2,3:4 analogy, the first and second terms, *angry* and *incensed*, are synonyms, as the third and fourth terms, *common* and *universal,* are synonyms. Notice that there is also a difference in intensity or degree between the related terms: *Incensed* means "very angry," just as *universal* means "very common." (The correct answer is Choice [A].)

If the terms in an analogy have a similar relationship, they may just be synonyms without a difference in degree.

Here's another similar/different analogy that falls on the similar side of the fence:

¼ : .25 :: _____ : .2

(A) ½

(B) ⅓

(C) ¼

(D) ⅕

This analogy has a 1:2,3:4 structure. The first two terms, ¼ and .25, are not only similar, they're equivalent. (The fraction ¼ has the same value as the decimal .25). The third and fourth terms are also equivalent. The correct answer is Choice (D): The fraction ⅕ has the same value as the decimal .2.

Here's a similar/different analogy with a "different" relationship:

_____ : ROUGH :: HIGH : LOW

(A) smooth

(B) careful

(C) dangerous

(D) empty

This 1:2,3:4 analogy has a "different" relationship because the first two terms, *smooth* and *rough,* are nearly opposite in meaning, just as the last two terms, *high* and *low,* are opposite. The correct answer is Choice (A): *smooth* is the opposite of *rough,* as *high* is the opposite of *low.*

The following analogy is also of the similar/different type, although in a slightly different way:

EXTANT : EXTINCT :: _____ : PAST

(A) present

(B) fossil

(C) reversal

(D) continuation

This analogy is another 1:2,3:4. *Extant* means "existing," and *extinct* means "not existing." Logically, something is either extant or extinct; it either exists or it doesn't. There's the "different," or either/or, relationship. The correct answer is Choice (A), *present,* because either something is past or it's present or happening later. Therefore, the third and fourth terms have the same "different" relationship — it's an either/or situation.

Playful analogies

I'm not sure how fun you'll find playful analogies to be, but I call them "playful" because they often involve wordplay, grammar changes, and sounds. Another way to think of them is as puzzles. I divide this category into three types: wordplay, grammar changes, and "sounds like."

Be open to looking past the meanings of words so that you can identify playful analogies when they appear.

Wordplay analogies

Wordplay analogies usually play with the order of letters in a word, add or subtract letters, or use other such trickery. The question changes a word's letters in a specific way and then expects you to pick the choice that accomplishes the same change. Examples of wordplay that you may see on the MAT are *anagrams,* which are rearrangements of a word's letters to make a different word, and *palindromes,* which are words that make a word whether they're spelled backward or forward. Here's an example of a wordplay MAT analogy.

WARD: DRAW :: EVIL : _____

(A) live

(B) veil

(C) good

(D) devil

Notice that the word *draw* is *ward* spelled backward. So the analogy is 1:2,3:4. Similarly, the word *live* is *evil* spelled backward. The correct answer is Choice (A).

Grammar change analogies

Grammar change analogies usually involve a verb that changes tense.

Verb tense changes to deal with differences in the time or duration of an action.

For example, the verb *make* is in the present tense as *make* and in the past tense as *made.* Here's an example of how a grammar change analogy may appear on the MAT.

SEE : SAW :: WRITE : _____

(A) wrought

(B) right

(C) rite

(D) wrote

This analogy is a 1:2,3:4 because *saw* is the past tense of *see*. The correct answer is Choice (D): *Wrote* is the past tense of *write*.

"Sounds like" analogies

Unlike wordplay and grammar change analogies, "sounds like" analogies involve only how words sound. The right answer to a "sounds like" analogy usually rhymes with or somehow has a sound similar to its matching term. For example:

FRAY : FREEZE :: BRAY : _____

(A) battle

(B) cold

(C) breeze

(D) brew

This analogy is 1:3,2:4 — *fray* and *bray* rhyme, and no compelling relationship exists between *fray* and *freeze*. Likewise, *freeze* and *breeze* rhyme, so the correct answer is Choice (C).

The relationships you'll see on the MAT may vary somewhat from the five categories I've described here, since again, there are so many ways that words can be related. But instead of trying to describe every possible relationship category (and either bore or confuse you in the process), I picked these five because they give you a good foundation from which to work and help you become more familiar with the test. And remember, you don't have to precisely identify a MAT analogy's relationship category to solve it.

Chapter 3

Types of Analogies and How to Solve Them

. . . .

In This Chapter

▶ Looking at different structures of analogies

▶ Identifying what type of analogy you're dealing with

▶ Choosing an analogy-solving approach

. . . .

When it comes down to it, analogies are pretty simple: They're just relationships between words (and sometimes between numbers). Your job for any MAT analogy question is just to recognize the relationship presented to you and find its match among the answer choices. Easy, right?

The only problem is that sometimes you may not recognize the presented relationship, its match, or even some or all of the terms in the question! (Don't worry, I talk about tough analogy questions and give you some tools to solve them later in the chapter; I also outline a step-by-step process for solving analogies.) The first step in dealing with any MAT analogy is identifying its structure. If you don't correctly determine its structure, you may create a relationship between the wrong terms.

MAT analogies fit into just two structural types: 1:2,3:4 and 1:3,2:4. By "1:2,3:4", I mean that the first and second terms in the question have a relationship, and the third and fourth terms in the question have the same relationship. For 1:3,2:4 analogies, the first and third terms in the question have a relationship, and the second and fourth terms have that same relationship. To help you recognize these two structures, I've presented a few examples here. Take a minute to wrap your head around this notation if it's confusing — it's important to understand before you move on.

Understanding 1:2,3:4 Analogies

Here's a typical 1:2,3:4 analogy (1:2,3:4):

Fitzgerald : literature :: Monet : _____

(A) fishing

(B) philosophy

(C) art

(D) music

The first term in this question, *Fitzgerald,* has a relationship to the second term, *literature*: F. Scott Fitzgerald, a famous American literary figure, created literature — for instance, he authored *The Great Gatsby.* Since the first and second terms are related, the third term, *Monet,* should have a similar relationship to the fourth term, which is one of the answer choices.

You may realize this is a 1:2,3:4 analogy structure instead of a 1:3,2:4 structure, either by recognizing the strong relationship between *Fitzgerald* and *literature* or by reasoning that *Fitzgerald* and *Monet* don't have a clear or compelling relationship. Although you *could* write a sentence linking F. Scott Fitzgerald, a famous American writer, to Claude Monet, a famous French painter, the relationship between the two men is not obvious, other than that they're both famous. The correct answer is Choice (C), *art.* Claude Monet, a famous artist, created art, just as Fitzgerald, a famous writer, created literature.

Looking at 1:3,2:4 Analogies

Here's an example of the second type of analogy structure (1:3,2:4):

Ribosome : pancreas :: cell : _____

(A) body

(B) heart

(C) hormone

(D) molecule

The first term here, *ribosome,* has a relationship to the third term, *cell.* A ribosome is a component of a cell. So the second term, *pancreas,* must have a relationship with the fourth term, which is one of the answer choices. The correct answer is Choice (A), *body,* because the pancreas is a component of a body.

You can determine that the relationship in this analogy is a 1:3,2:4 because the relationship between *ribosome* and *cell* is much stronger than the relationship between *ribosome* and *pancreas.* If you wrote a sentence linking *ribosome* and *pancreas,* the relationship would probably be pretty weak.

It might seem weird at first, but the MAT can put the answer choices in any position in an analogy (1, 2, 3, or 4). For example, a 1:3,2:4 analogy can be written like this:

Ribosome : pancreas :: _____ : body

(A) cell

(B) vitamin

(C) liver

(D) atom

It's still a 1:3,2:4 analogy because the first and third terms and the second and fourth terms have the same kind of clear relationship. The correct answer is Choice (A), *cell.* Again, a ribosome is a component of a cell, and a pancreas is a component of a body.

Alternatively, the answer choices may come first, as in this question:

_____ : body :: ribosome : pancreas

(A) cell

(B) vitamin

(C) blood

(D) atom

Guess what? It's still a 1:3,2:4, since the first and third terms have a clear relationship, as do the second and fourth terms. The right answer is still Choice (A), *cell.*

As you may guess, the test writers can and will put the answer choices in any of the four positions. But no matter where the choices appear, your first task is to identify whether the question in front of you is a 1:2,3:4 analogy or a 1:3,2:4 analogy. The good news is that it doesn't really matter where the answer choices show up — the analogy will always be 1:2,3:4 or 1:3,2:4.

Seeing Why 1:4,2:3 Analogies Don't Exist

A MAT question's structure will *never* be 1:4,2:3, though you sometimes may think you see that type of relationship. For instance, the following question is an attempt to trick you into creating a 1:4,2:3 relationship:

_____ : 6 :: billion : million

(A) 6

(B) 9

(C) 10

(D) 100

You may think about picking Choice (A), reasoning that the first and fourth terms (*6* and *million*) have a similar relationship to the second and third terms (*6* and *billion*). However, MAT analogies can't, don't, and won't have that structure.

Also, there's not much of an argument that the relationship between *6* and *million* can be the same relationship as in *6* and *billion,* and hopefully if you tried to create a sentence for that relationship, you realized it was weak.

The right answer is Choice (B), 9, making the analogy a 1:3,2:4 (a billion has nine zeroes and a million has six zeroes).

Even if, in your mind, the first and fourth or second and third terms of an analogy have the most beautiful relationship in the world, remember that it's not meant to be. 1:4,2:3 relationships don't exist on the MAT.

When you've decided on the analogy's structure, you're ready to move to the next step in the solving process (which we cover in detail later in this chapter).

Identifying Analogy Structure

Identifying which type of analogy a question is presenting is more than half the battle of cracking it. The next MAT-style questions allow you to practice identifying analogy structure. Determining structure is the first step in attacking any analogy question on the MAT. For the following questions, just identify whether the analogy is 1:2,3:4 or 1:3,2:4.

1. Bomb : bombast :: device : _____

    (A) devilish

    (B) speech

    (C) machine

    (D) mechanical

2. Aberrant : abnormal :: _____ : abject

    (A) anonymous

    (B) astute

    (C) abstemious

    (D) abysmal

3. _____ : washboard :: dryer : washing machine

    (A) shirt

    (B) outdoors

    (C) clothesline

    (D) rope

4. _____ : dolphin :: psittaciformes : parrot

    (A) cetacean

    (B) orthoptera

    (C) oceanic

    (D) intelligent

5. –tude : -tion :: _____ : result of

    (A) producing

    (B) capable of

    (C) absence of

    (D) state of

Here are the answers:

1. 1:3,2:4. A bomb is a type of device, as bombast (pompous speech) is a type of speech.

2. 1:2,3:4. Something aberrant (unusual) is abnormal (unusual), as something abysmal (extremely low) is abject (miserable).

3. 1:3,2:4. A dryer is a machine that automates what a clothesline does, as a washing machine automates what a washboard does.

4. 1:2,3:4. In terms of biological classification, a dolphin is a cetacean, as a parrot is a psittaciformes.

5. 1:3,2:4. The suffix *–tude* means "state of," as the suffix *–tion* means "result of."

Planning Your Attack: Choosing Your Analogy-Cracking Strategy

Even if you're already good with analogies and you're scoring well when you practice them, it's wise to have a method. Working on analogies methodically can help you avoid multitasking, which can make it harder to think clearly during the pressure of the real test. It also gives you a process to fall back on if a certain question confuses you. In this section, I present a step-by-step method that you can use to solve MAT analogies.

Identifying the structural type

Again, the first step in solving a MAT analogy is determining what its structural type is: 1:2,3:4 or 1:3,2:4.

In a 1:2,3:4 analogy, the first and second terms have a relationship, and the third and fourth terms have the same relationship.

In a 1:3,2:4 analogy, the first and third terms have a relationship, and the second and fourth terms have the same relationship.

Here's an example of a 1:2,3:4 analogy:

MITTEN : HAND :: _____ : HEAD

(A) toupee

(B) hair

(C) hat

(D) eyeglasses

The first term, *mitten,* has a clear and compelling relationship with the second term, *hand.* A mitten is worn to keep your hand warm. The correct answer is Choice (C) because the same relationship is created between *hat* and *head* (a hat is worn to keep your head warm).

Note that 1:2,3:4 analogies can also be thought of as 2:1,4:3 analogies. The previous example works just as well if you say "A *hand* is warmed by a *mitten* like a *head* is warmed by a *hat*." In some cases, it's easier to make a sentence in that order. For example, check out the following question:

_____ : SKY :: PINK : HOT

(A) plane

(B) cloud

(C) air

(D) blue

The second term, *sky*, goes with the first term, *blue* (Choice D), and the fourth term, *hot*, goes with the third term, *pink*. Sky blue is a color, like hot pink is a color. So the analogy is 1:2,3:4 — it just may be more clear to begin with the second term and think of it as 2:1,4:3.

Here's an example of a 1:3,2:4 analogy.

TIBIA : RADIUS :: LEG : _____

(A) hand

(B) pi

(C) arm

(D) circle

In this example, the first and third terms have a clear and compelling relationship: The tibia is a bone found in your leg. The right answer is Choice (C) because the radius is a bone found in your arm.

So Step 1 is just to determine whether the analogy is 1:2,3:4 or 1:3,2:4.

Building sentences

The next step in the analogy-solving process is building a specific, short sentence to express the relationship between the related terms in the analogy. Keeping your sentences specific is important because, if they're too broad, more than one of the answer choices may seem to work. Keeping your sentences short is smart because longer sentences are more cumbersome to work with and take longer to write down.

Jotting down your sentence on your scratch paper makes it easier to work with and think about because, when written, a sentence has to be concrete — it's not just a vague concept in your mind. Feel free to use shorthand when possible to minimize the amount of writing you'll have to do.

Consider one of the previous analogies again, to practice building a sentence.

MITTEN : HAND :: _____ : HEAD

(A) toupee

(B) hair

(C) hat

(D) eyeglasses

Since the first and second terms in this analogy are given and have a strong relationship, write a sentence that expresses that relationship. Your sentence should look something like:

A mitten warms a hand.

"A mitten warms a hand" is clear and short and nicely expresses the relationship between a mitten and a hand. Now consider these examples of less effective sentences:

A mitten is worn on a hand.

Notice how "A mitten is worn on a hand" doesn't really specify why the mitten is worn on a hand. And notice that, now, more than one answer choice seems to work: Both a toupee and a hat are worn on your head. Keeping your sentence as specific as you reasonably can helps.

Here's another less effective sentence:

> A mitten is shaped like a hand.

"A mitten is shaped like a hand" may be true, but it doesn't really capture the function of a mitten. When in doubt, write a sentence that captures the most common and the clearest relationship between the related terms.

Here's another analogy for practice in building a sentence:

TIBIA : RADIUS :: LEG : _____

(A) hand

(B) pi

(C) arm

(D) circle

This analogy has a 1:3,2:4 relationship, and the first and third terms are given. To express their relationship, you can write something like:

> The tibia is a leg bone.

"The tibia is a leg bone" succinctly describes the major relationship between *tibia* and *leg,* and it helps you complete the final step in the process: checking the choices.

Checking the choices

When you've written a sentence you're happy with, it's time to check the choices to see which answer choice creates a similar relationship to the remaining term.

Make sure you check all the answer choices unless you're completely confident that you've found the right answer.

To practice checking the choices, here's the first analogy again:

MITTEN : HAND :: _____ : HEAD

(A) toupee

(B) hair

(C) hat

(D) eyeglasses

Remembering the analogy's structural type (1:2,3:4) and using your sentence as a guide, see which choice most closely creates a matching relationship. Here's the sentence, for reference:

> A mitten warms a hand.

Looking at the answer choices:

> Does a toupee warm your head? Not really.
>
> Does hair warm your head? Kind of, but it's not clothing like a mitten.
>
> Does a hat warm your head? Usually.
>
> Do eyeglasses warm your head? Not even close.

That's it — pick the choice with the closest relationship to the one you've described in your sentence. You should be able to make a similar sentence with the right answer and its matching term. Since "A hat warms your head" is so similar to "A mitten warms your hand," it's pretty clear that Choice (C) is correct.

Practicing your analogy skills

Here are five example analogies on which you can practice the step-by-step method. Each is from one of the five major MAT analogy relationship categories I describe in Chapter 2. I've kept the difficulty level for each question pretty low so you can focus on your step-by-step technique. Be sure to identify each analogy's type, write a relationship sentence, and then check the choices.

1. JET : AIR :: SUBMARINE : _____

    (A) metal

    (B) pressure

    (C) ocean

    (D) sandwich

2. OSTRICH : BOTTLENOSE :: _____ : DOLPHIN

    (A) sand

    (B) bird

    (C) tall

    (D) feathered

3. _____ : BOTTLE :: LID : CHEST

    (A) cap

    (B) cylinder

    (C) liquid

    (D) neck

4. 3 : _____ :: 27 : 64

    (A) 2

    (B) 4

    (C) 8

    (D) 16

5. USE : ABUSE :: _____ : ACCLAIM

   (A) claim

   (B) clam

   (C) recognition

   (D) mail

Here are the answers:

1. Choice (C) is correct. (1:2,3:4) A jet travels through the air, as a submarine travels through the ocean. This fits the description relationship category.

2. Choice (B) is correct. (1:3,2:4) An ostrich is a type of bird, as a bottlenose is a type of dolphin. This fits the type of relationship category.

3. Choice (A) is correct. (1:2,3:4) A cap is the part of a bottle that covers it, as a lid is the part of the chest that covers it. This fits the parts relationship category.

4. Choice (B) is correct. (1:3,2:4) 3 cubed is 27, as 4 cubed is 64. This fits the similar/different relationship category.

5. Choice (A) is correct. (1:2,3:4) *Abuse* is *use* with two letters added to its beginning, as *acclaim* is *claim* with two letters similarly added. This fits the wordplay relationship category.

Dealing with Tough Questions

Most people are good drivers when it's sunny and traffic is light. But throw a little rain, snow, or rush-hour traffic into the mix, and driving gets a little bit more challenging. The MAT is no different: Certain questions don't immediately lend themselves to the step-by-step analogy solving technique I've described. But fear not — here I give you some techniques for handling tougher MAT analogies.

Skipping tough questions

Before I start talking about how to handle tough questions, here's a crucial piece of advice: As soon as you realize a question will be hard for you, skip it immediately. This decision should be made within a few seconds after seeing the question. Don't fiddle around with it: All the questions on the test count the same towards your score, so never struggle with a tough question when there might be an easier question later. You can always come back to the skipped question if you have time. Of course, make sure to fill in a quick guess (never leave blanks!), and write down the number of the question on your scratch paper so you remember to come back to it.

This is easier said than done. Like any technique in this book, make sure that you practice it consistently if you want to use it efficiently on the real MAT.

Noticing difficulty level

Questions on the MAT range from easy to hard, and luckily, keeping track of the difficulty level is pretty straightforward: Questions get harder as the test goes on. So remember to consider where in the test the question appears when assessing its difficulty level.

Your first instincts are more likely to be correct on easier questions and less likely to be correct on harder ones because hard questions have *unpopular* answers — that's one of the reasons they're hard. In other words, the right answer often doesn't look right at first glance.

The test writers who create the MAT don't just sit around and decide which questions they think are difficult — they actually test them on test takers. That's why 20 of the questions on the MAT don't count toward your score — the test writers use them to see how many students get the question right. If few people get a question right, that question will appear toward the end of a future MAT test. So the questions toward the end of the MAT you take are the ones most previous students got wrong — they're questions with unpopular answers.

Also remember not to overanalyze questions that appear early in the MAT — most people got those questions right!

Solving the question when you don't know one or more words

The most common problem you'll most likely face on the MAT is encountering an analogy with a word — or multiple words — that you don't recognize or can't quite define. The word you don't know may affect your ability to recognize whether the analogy is 1:2,3:4 or your ability to build a sentence. Be careful! Don't make decisions based on information you don't know. Instead, here are a few techniques to use when you don't know one or more terms in a MAT analogy.

Unless you're sure or pretty sure what an analogy term means, don't use its meaning to help figure out a sentence or even an analogy's structural type.

Applying the process of elimination

Process of elimination is a must-have technique when taking the MAT. You don't have to recognize why the right answer is right if you can figure out why the other three choices are wrong. Don't be afraid to pick a word you don't know if you've eliminated everything else!

Here's an example of using process of elimination to get a question right.

BALL : ROUND :: EGG : _____

(A) mystery term

(B) square

(C) triangular

(D) acute

Choice (A) is "mystery term" because, for this exercise, I pretend you don't know that word. First notice that the analogy is 1:2,3:4; a clear relationship exists between *ball* and *round* (and no clear relationship exists between *ball* and *egg*).

Next, build a sentence: "A ball is round." Looking at the answer choices, you can start eliminating some.

Is an egg square? Is it triangular? Acute? No, no, and no. Therefore, the answer must be Choice (A) because you eliminated every other possibility.

You can use process of elimination on most MAT questions to help pick the correct answer.

Working backward

Sometimes when you don't know one of the terms in an analogy, it can work to work backward.

(Mystery term) : HORSE :: CUB : _____

(A) zebra

(B) giraffe

(C) dog

(D) lion

I used the phrase "mystery term" to make sure you don't know what the first term in the analogy is (for the sake of this exercise). But even if you don't know the first term, you may notice that you can make a clear relationship between *cub* and Choice (D), *lion,* since a *cub* is a baby lion. Now you may realize that the analogy is 1:2,3:4 and be able to guess that the "mystery term" probably means a baby horse.

Where the analogy appears in the test matters. Consider difficulty level: Easy questions have more obvious answers; harder questions have less obvious answers.

In this analogy, you'd probably be even more confident you had the right answer if it appeared in the first third of the test (questions 1–40) because easier questions — questions that most test takers answered correctly — appear earlier.

Here's another example of working backward in which I pretend that you don't know either of the first two terms.

(Mystery term) : (Mystery term) :: SMART : _____

(A) hurt

(B) intelligent

(C) confused

(D) brief

Obviously, not knowing two of the terms in an analogy can make answering it tricky. But you can still take an educated guess.

First, think about whether the analogy is 1:2,3:4 or 1:3,2:4. Since both the first and second terms are missing, it's impossible to confirm that the analogy is 1:3,2:4. The only option is to try to make a workable 1:2,3:4 analogy.

Now consider difficulty level. If this analogy appeared early in the test, it would probably make sense to guess Choice (B), reasoning that you could build a sentence like "Smart means intelligent."

If the analogy appeared later in the test, you would probably want to avoid picking Choice (B) — it's too obvious. Instead, you could surmise that most students missed the question because the test writers used a secondary definition of a word, and you could build the sentence "To smart means to hurt" and pick Choice (A).

The MAT writers sometimes choose words with secondary, or less common, meanings.

Considering parts of speech

Sometimes you have to think about parts of speech to get through a tough analogy. Here's a quick review that may bring back memories of elementary school.

Noun: A word that is a person, place, or thing

Verb: A word that means an action or occurrence

Adjective: a descriptive word

Any given MAT analogy contains only two parts of speech, and all the answer choices contain the same part of speech. The correct answer choice will be the same part of speech as its corresponding term in the other pair of terms.

Considering parts of speech can help you solve seemingly confusing analogies on the MAT. Here's an example of an analogy that may look weird at first.

MAN : SHIP :: _____ : POSITION

(A) pose

(B) manipulate

(C) move

(D) staff

As always, the first step is to consider whether the analogy is 1:2,3:4 or 1:3,2:4. It's easier to rule out the 1:3,2:4 type here because the second and fourth terms are given and no clear relationship exists between *ship* and *position*.

But if the analogy is 1:2,3:4, then *man* and *ship* must have a clear relationship. At first, you may build a sentence like "A man travels on water with a ship" but then realize that none of the answer choices can travel in or on a position.

The trick here is to consider alternate parts of speech. If you use *man* as a verb, as in the sentence "Man the battle stations!", you can build a sentence like "One can man a ship." Then you can fit the sentence to Choice (D) because you can staff a position (if *staff* is used as a verb).

On harder questions, be on the lookout for words that can act as different parts of speech.

Keeping in mind alternate meanings

Similarly to MAT analogies that use different parts of speech, some analogies are tough because they use secondary, less common definitions of words — the kind of definitions that are buried most of the way down the word's dictionary entry. If you're watching out for alternate meanings of words on harder questions, you'll be more likely to catch them. For instance, here's an analogy that uses a secondary definition of a word.

DISCRIMINATE : DISTINGUISH :: _____ : DISPARAGE

(A) prejudice

(B) belittle

(C) jest

(D) downplay

Most people think of prejudice and unfair treatment when they see the word *discriminate*. You may mistakenly think this is a 1:3,2:4 analogy and build a sentence like "Discriminate means to prejudice." Hopefully, you'd notice that *distinguish* does not mean "to disparage" and catch your mistake.

If you considered the secondary definition of *discriminate* — to judge between subtle differences — you could correctly identify the analogy as 1:2,3:4 and build a sentence like "Discriminate means to distinguish." Then, you could match it to Choice (B) and the fourth term: "To belittle means to disparage."

Look for alternate meanings to appear more often on questions later in the MAT.

Making educated guesses

When all else fails with a MAT analogy and you're ready to guess and move on, one last strategy is worth trying, to possibly improve your odds. First, consider difficulty level. If the question is early in the test, go with your first instinct and pick the choice with the strongest connection that you recognize. After all, most people before you got the question right.

If the analogy appears later, consider your first instinct or what makes the most sense — and then *don't* pick that choice. Pick anything else. After all, most students got the question wrong for a reason!

Avoiding analogy traps

The test writers are good at composing questions that are subtly designed to trick you by making you think the wrong terms in the analogy are related. In general, the later the question is in the MAT, the more likely it is to contain a trap, since the level of difficulty increases as you go. On the other hand, the earlier in the test a question appears, the less likely it is to contain a trap.

Questions later in the test are ones that most previous test takers answered incorrectly.

Forewarned is forearmed: Now that you know traps await you on the MAT, you'll be less likely to fall for them.

You encounter three main types of analogy traps on the MAT: category traps, direction traps, and distractor traps.

Category traps

Category traps are questions written to try to trick you into misidentifying the analogy's structure category — for example, making you think it's a 1:2,3:4 when it's really a 1:3,2:4, or vice versa. To do this, the test writers often pick terms designed to lead you astray from the question's correct relationship. Check out the following difficult question:

Saturnine: planetary :: gloomy : _____

(A) morose

(B) ebullient

(C) obscured

(D) immense

Quick, is this a 1:2,3:4 or a 1:3,2:4? If you said 1:2,3:4, you fell for the trap. Although *saturnine* and *planetary* may have made you think of Saturn and the planets, these terms aren't related. *Saturnine* means "gloomy," and one meaning of *planetary* is *immense* (huge). This question is made more tricky by the inclusion of *morose* (which means "gloomy") as one of the answer choices, making it even more tempting to categorize the question as 1:2,3:4, compose a sentence like "Saturnine means planetary, and gloomy means morose," and then pick Choice (A).

However, this analogy actually has a 1:3,2:4 structure: The correct answer is Choice (D). Something *saturnine* is also *gloomy,* as something *planetary* is also *immense*. Of course, this question is tougher if you don't know the meanings of all the terms. But even if you *do* know all the terms, be careful. It can be all too easy to miscategorize an analogy's structure if the test writer is trying to mislead you.

Be careful of going too quickly and not taking the time to think of the dictionary definitions of terms. Category traps often prey on people who can't or don't define terms accurately.

Be especially careful of category traps in the last third (questions 81–120) of the MAT. Since the MAT's difficulty level increases as you go, terms that at first seem to be related often are not.

Direction traps

Whether it's a 1:2,3:4 or a 1:3,2:4, an analogy sometimes has a built-in directional trap. Direction traps try to trick you by providing the relationship you want but giving it to you in the wrong direction. Consider the following question:

Candy : gummy bear :: _____ : fruit

(A) food

(B) banana

(C) caramel

(D) seed

It's fairly easy to determine this analogy's structure: It's a 1:2,3:4. But if you picked Choice (B), *banana,* you fell for the trap. We call this a direction trap because picking Choice (B) reverses the analogy relationship's direction. A gummy bear is a type of candy, but fruit is not a type of banana — a banana is a type of fruit. In other words, if the second term is a type of the first term, the fourth term has to be a type of the third term.

The right answer is Choice (A), *food,* because a gummy bear is a type of candy, as fruit is a type of food.

Direction traps are much easier to fall for if you're rushing. When you write down your sentence for the analogy's relationship, take the time to make sure it works in the same direction for both term pairs.

Direction traps aren't particularly hard to avoid if you know they're coming. Since they're not as tricky as category traps, they can and will show up throughout the MAT.

Distractor traps

Distractor traps work by supplying you with an answer choice that, at first glance, may seem to have a lot in common with the term you're pairing it with — but upon closer inspection, it doesn't. Here's an example of a tougher question with a distractor trap:

METICULOUS : EXACTING :: CURRENCY _____

(A) denomination

(B) quarter

(C) mint

(D) acceptance

The analogy is a 1:2,3:4, since *meticulous* means "exacting." Notice that Choices (A), (B), and (C) may be distracting because they all have some relation to the more commonly used definition of *currency* (money). However, if you take the time to make a sentence, you won't get fooled. *Meticulous* means "exacting," as *currency* can mean "acceptance."

Distractor traps are more likely to appear in the latter third (questions 81–120) of the MAT, since, by then, the difficulty level is high.

The bottom line is, if you want to accurately determine an analogy's structure while avoiding any traps, you've got to recognize the relationship being presented to you. Make sure you take the time to consider all the answer choices before deciding whether it's 1:2,3:4 or 1:3,2:4; if you don't categorize it correctly, you're much more likely to get the question wrong.

Putting it all together

It's time to practice your skills! Here are five MAT-style analogies on which to try out some of what you've learned. Answers and sample sentences are provided.

1. _____ : BIPEDS :: HORSES : QUADRUPEDS

(A) humans

(B) chordata

(C) omnivores

(D) fish

2. SURMISED : CONFIRMED :: _____ : KNEW

   (A) inferred

   (B) counterindicated

   (C) commanded

   (D) perceived

3. _____ : MOON :: URANUS : MERCURY

   (A) plane

   (B) cloud

   (C) air

   (D) satellite

4. ROOSEVELT : _____ :: NEW DEAL : DÉTENTE

   (A) Carter

   (B) Nixon

   (C) Reagan

   (D) Ford

5. RUDE : _____ :: SIMPLE : UNCOUTH

   (A) abysmal

   (B) vicious

   (C) nasty

   (D) unrefined

Here are the answers:

1. Choice (A) is correct. (1:2,3:4) *Humans* are *bipeds* (two-footed animals), as *horses* are *quadrupeds* (four-footed animals).

2. Choice (A) is correct. (1:3,2:4) To *surmise* is to *infer* (both mean "to guess"), as to *confirm* is to *know* (both mean "to be certain of something").

3. Choice (D) is correct. (1:2,3:4) A *satellite* and the *moon* both orbit the Earth, as *Uranus* and *Mercury* both orbit the Sun.

4. Choice (B) is correct. (1:3,2:4) *Franklin Roosevelt* was known for creating the *New Deal* policy, as *Richard Nixon* was known for creating the policy of *détente*.

5. Choice (D) is correct. (1:3,2:4) *Rude* means *simple* as *unrefined* means *uncouth*.

Chapter 4

Creating a Smart MAT Preparation Plan

• •

In This Chapter

▶ Optimizing your preparation plan

▶ Tackling MAT timing

▶ Managing test anxiety

• •

*Y*ou know your astrological sign, you probably know your personality type, and you may even know your blood type. But what type of test taker are you?

Often test takers fall into one of two categories. The first category includes people who are a little overconfident about the test. People in this group tend to underprepare for tests and overestimate their ability. Sometimes this type of test taker looks over a few questions to get familiar with a test and then just takes it. As you might guess, people with this test-taking style would perform better if they prepared more and ascertained their ability realistically.

The second category encompasses people with below-average test-taking confidence. They may be so intimidated by the test that they procrastinate on their preparation, double-check even easy questions, and, in general, stress themselves out. This type of test taker will sometimes rush through the test and make careless mistakes, or work too carefully and run out of time. For this type of test taker, timed practice tests are crucial to get used to the pressure.

If you think you lean toward one of these categories, you can adjust your study plan accordingly to find a happy medium. We'll show you how to avoid the pitfalls that can undermine your test-taking preparation and technique, and help you practice intelligently so you can test well.

Fortunately, the MAT presents you with only one type of question — analogies — which I cover from A to Z in Chapter 2. In addition to mastering analogies, you want to develop a comprehensive study plan to boost your test-taking skills and your content knowledge and organize your practice time. You also need to get familiar with what graduate school admissions committees are looking for. The goal of this chapter is to help you develop your own optimal study system to keep you on track as you prepare for the MAT, to ensure that you get the score you need to reach your goals.

Creating Your MAT Study Plan

Preparing for a test as important as the MAT takes time, so it's a good idea to think about the whole process up front instead of randomly plunging into some practice material. You have a lot on the line — your test score is one of many aspects of your graduate school application, but it's a pretty important one and can make the difference between your earning a place in the program of your choice and having to apply all over again next year. Here are some ideas designed to make your preparation more organized, efficient, and effective.

Knowing where you currently stand

If you were training to run a marathon and wanted to set a specific time goal, you'd want to figure out at what pace you could run a few miles, to get a general idea of your potential pace for running 26.2 miles. If you didn't know your current pace, you'd perhaps set an unrealistic goal (and discourage yourself) or set a goal that was too easy and not fulfill your potential. The first step in goal setting is awareness. Being aware of reality allows you to make the most intelligent decisions, regardless of the situation.

For the MAT, it's no different. To develop a realistic goal, you need to know where you stand right now. If you've already taken the MAT, use your most recent score as a baseline. If you haven't, you can take the first practice test (in Chapter 9) and score it. That number is your starting point. Even if the score is lower than you want it to be, at least you have a realistic view of your ability at this point in time.

Following through with your plan

The next step in the planning process is taking responsibility and ensuring that you do the needed work to reach your goal. The fact that you're reading this book means that you've already begun to take responsibility for your MAT preparation, but buying this book — and even reading it — isn't enough to ensure a better score. This book gives you tips, strategies, and plenty of practice opportunity, but, ultimately, you're the one driving the study process.

Taking ownership works just like it does in athletics: An athlete can have the best coach in the world, but if she only relies on the coach and doesn't seek out opportunities to improve even further on her own, she won't maximize her potential. Even if you're using a tutor or taking a class, at the end of the day, you have to be the one to take action, whether it means studying, working on content, or taking a practice test. Recognizing this truth makes it more likely that you'll take the appropriate actions at the right time. Taking ownership of your study plan and seeing it through also entails realizing that, if you don't work hard to stick to your plan, no one else likely will be able to make you work hard on it.

Setting a goal

After you've taken ownership of the process, it's time to decide what score you want. Also decide who's determining your goal: Do you have a personal ambition to get a 600, a perfect score? Or are you aiming for the score range accepted by the school to which you're applying?

A crucial step in the process of deciding what score you want is answering one big question: Why? To answer this question, it's helpful to meditate on what your MAT score will help you obtain. Is it admission to a certain graduate school program? If so, why do you want to go to that particular program? What exactly do you hope to achieve after you complete that program? Write the answers to these questions. The clearer your vision is of where you want to go, the more you'll stoke your motivational fires — and revving up your motivation can make all the difference when you're disciplining yourself to study again and again.

Whatever your goal is, it's important to be realistic. If you got 80 questions correct out of 120, improving to 100 out of 120 is probably more realistic than getting to 115 out of 120, especially since the MAT covers such a broad array of content. The time you'll have to prepare is a factor, too: If you have just a few weeks to prepare, shooting for a modest improvement is a lot more realistic than trying for a major one.

When you're ready to choose a goal score, write the number — the exact number — down, and put it where you can see it every day. Having frequent reminders about your goal will keep you motivated and focused, and making the number concrete will give you a specific target to aim for. Of course, the goal score you write down isn't set in stone; you may make slower or faster progress toward your goal than you initially thought, and that's okay. You can always just set a new goal.

Check in with your goal once you're about a third of the way closer to your test date to see if it needs to be revised.

Write your goal score on a sticky note and post it in places like on your bathroom mirror, your computer monitor, or your refrigerator door, so you see it often.

Lights, Camera, Action: Setting Your Plan in Motion

Of course, studying for the MAT is an active process, but it's a process based on many little actions. Get a pen and a big piece of paper, and write down as many action steps as you can think of that you need to accomplish while studying for the MAT. Here's a sample list:

- ✔ Register and purchase the official tests on www.MillerAnalogies.com.
- ✔ Take one of the official tests, timed, to get a baseline. Record your score and analyze your mistakes.
- ✔ Write down your goal and study plan.
- ✔ Buy content-related books and begin studying content.
- ✔ Take all six *MAT For Dummies* practice tests. Review your mistakes and record your scores.
- ✔ Take all three official practice tests. Review your mistakes and record your scores.

Take the official MAT tests toward the end of your preparation. You'll get more out of them once your skills are at their peak. And, retake the one you took initially for extra practice.

After you've written all the action steps you can possibly think of, start putting them in order. Not all of the steps likely have equal importance. You'll probably find that you need to do some steps, such as reviewing content, on an ongoing basis.

You may need to do other steps, like registering for the MAT, only once. But the process of organizing steps by priority is crucial because you'll more likely begin to tackle the important stuff first. Otherwise, it's sometimes too easy to do all the easy stuff first.

Setting a deadline and mapping a schedule

Getting things done usually progresses more slowly unless you have some sort of time limit. So even if you're not 100% sure about your timeframe for graduate school, set a deadline for completing your studying. If you've already registered for the test, you already have your deadline. If not, you need to think about how much time you need to prepare. This timeline depends on several factors, including your desired program's application deadline, how much free time you have to study, and how familiar you are right now with major content areas.

When in deadline doubt, give yourself a little padding to keep things realistic. Life has a funny way of throwing unforeseen obstacles at you. And it never hurts to give yourself more time to learn content.

Okay, you have all your action steps and your deadline. It's time to schedule everything! Whether you use a notebook planner or schedule everything online doesn't matter — you just need a visual record of your study activity.

If you're not naturally a planner, or if you just like to go with the flow, this step may feel difficult. But persist. Staying organized with a schedule makes completing all your needed study tasks much easier.

Try working backwards from your test date to schedule tasks. For example, what will you do the day before the test and the week before? Then, keep working backward until you're back to the current week.

When you wake up and see MAT studying on the day's schedule, actually doing the studying becomes almost as easy as brushing your teeth and doing your laundry. Okay, maybe that's an exaggeration, but you get the idea. Making MAT preparation part of your routine makes it easier to achieve your goal.

Now that you've planned, set a deadline, and scheduled your practice, only one task remains: As Nike says, "Just Do It."

Making sure you have the right study materials

Okay, you've got a plan and you're working it. But as with any goal, it's important to make sure you're staying on track. New information or circumstances may arise that speed up or set back your deadline or actions.

You may realize that one of the books you're using or a course you're taking doesn't work well for you, or that you need to invest in another. No big deal — just stay flexible. You may discover, for instance, that working with a tutor is more efficient and effective than trying to do everything yourself, or that learning content online works better for you than reading a book.

Check in with your goal, action steps, and deadline once a week to make sure that everything is progressing smoothly and that you don't need to adjust or tinker with anything.

Don't be alarmed if you take a practice test and perform a little worse than the previous test. Improvement isn't always linear, and different practice tests test different content. What you're looking for is a trend of improvement.

Maximizing your motivation

If you've developed a plan (or if you're reading this to figure out how to do so), you've already got some motivation. But how can you increase your current level of drive? Consider a few ideas.

- ✔ **Tell others.** Talk to your close friends about your study plan and graduate school goals, and they'll probably lend you their support.

- ✔ **Schedule a celebration.** After your MAT test date, schedule a get-together or ceremony of some kind to commemorate your achievement.

✔ **Check in with your long-term goal.** Spend time every week visualizing your desired outcome and how good it will feel to get there. Check off tasks as you complete them.

✔ **Stay positive.** Negative thoughts creep into our awareness from time to time. If you catch yourself thinking pessimistically, notice it but don't dwell on the negative. Focus on the benefits of what you're doing instead.

Avoiding procrastination

Procrastination is another tendency you may have to battle as you attack the MAT. A little bit of procrastination or laziness is only human. But if you find yourself continually putting off your scheduled study activities, you're going to have to push yourself a bit harder. Procrastinating also may be a sign that you've bitten off more than you can chew. Adjust your study time downward and try to stick to the revised schedule for a week. Then try ramping up the study time again.

Break down large tasks into discrete action steps. For example, when studying content, assign yourself a manageable number of chapters or pages at a time, and then take a break.

Turn off the technology. With so many distractions in today's world (mobile phones, TV, Internet, tablets, and more), turning off the devices that you know are likely to distract you is simplest. The world will still be there after your study session.

Speaking of distractions, many of us try to do multiple things at once. Some people believe that multitasking can make you more productive. True, you can do more than one thing concurrently, but what about quality? Our brains are designed to focus on one thing at a time. Don't mar your focus by doing too many things at once.

Keeping in mind quality vs. quantity

While we're on the subject of quality, be sure to pay attention to the quality of your studying. You may be the type who can read a novel from start to finish in one sitting, or you may have trouble sitting through a whole movie. Regardless of where you're starting, you'll want to be aware of your attention span and, most likely, gradually increase it.

In the beginning of your studying, be aware of the point when your attention starts to lapse. At that point, try to continue for about five more minutes and then give yourself a quick break. Stand up, move around, and drink some water. Then keep studying. This routine slowly builds your tolerance for studying without letting you spend too long in a state in which you're not concentrating.

Keep your awareness level high. On some days, your ability to study may differ for a variety of factors. No problem — just be careful not to study for too long when you're unable to focus. Better to recognize you're feeling burned out and take a break — or even a nap!

It's usually more efficient to study for an hour or two at a time than to try to study all day.

Timing your practice work

When you're ready to start taking MAT practice tests in earnest, here's a helpful tip: Take the first one or two tests untimed. If I were teaching you how to tie your shoes, I wouldn't time you at first. You'd likely feel nervous and rushed, since you hadn't yet mastered the skill. When you became a pro at shoe tying, *then* I could start speeding you up. If you really want to record your time during your first practice test, go ahead, to build time awareness, but don't worry too much about how long it takes. At this point, building skill is the primary goal. Speed comes with skill.

Of course, after a couple untimed practice tests, you need to start timing yourself. When you're taking a timed test, remember a few points:

✔ **Know how many questions you can ignore for your goal.** Unless you're shooting for a perfect score or close to it, you shouldn't be spending time working on every question, so that you buy yourself more time to get the questions right that you're good at. Quickly guess on harder questions, and know about how many questions you can do this with.

✔ **Don't rush.** Never sacrifice your technique for speed. Your goal on the MAT is to get the questions right that you spend time on.

✔ **Keep question difficulty in mind.** The questions generally get harder as the test goes on. So don't stress out if you don't finish on time — the questions you didn't get to were probably the hardest ones.

There's no penalty for guessing – so don't let the test end without at least guessing on every question.

Do leave a couple minutes at the end of the test to quickly guess on any skipped questions.

Duplicating the test environment

When you take the real MAT, you'll likely be in a quiet room, alone or with other test takers. In the testing environment, you'll experience no pauses, few to no distractions, and lots of heavy silence. In preparing for the test, it's a great idea to get used to testing in this kind of environment. For instance, you'll definitely be sitting at a desk with a straight-backed chair. If you take all your practice tests out on the patio on a chaise lounge with the wind softly caressing your face and a tall glass of iced tea at your elbow, the environment of a typical MAT testing center may feel uncomfortable. Take a few tests in a quiet, isolated room with no distractions. Library study rooms can be good for this type of practice, but any quiet setting in which no one can disturb you works fine. Practicing in this setting will make the real testing environment feel more natural.

Taking several practice tests

Within reason, it's a good idea to take several practice MATs before you attempt the real thing. The best practice tests are the official tests available for purchase from the MAT website (www.milleranalogies.com), simply because they're written by the same people who wrote the MAT that you'll officially take. Buying all three of these tests is absolutely worth it because they expose you to the maximum number of real MAT questions.

Spend a good deal of your time working with the real MAT tests, either alone or with a tutor, because they're as close as you can get to the real thing. Unfortunately, the MAT provides only three tests for purchase, so you'll want to supplement them with the practice tests in this book. I modeled these practice tests on the official MAT practice tests, so they are (in my humble opinion) the closest thing on the market to the real test.

Taking several tests is also important because you see many different questions and content angles. But a quick word or warning is in order: You want to focus on *quality* practice, not *quantity*. You can learn a lot from each practice test you take. Make sure you analyze your mistakes and understand why you missed those questions before you plunge into another new test. Also analyze the questions you guessed on — even those you guessed correctly — to ensure that you understand the best way to answer those items.

Knowing when you're ready to register

If you're applying to graduate school, you may have an admissions deadline. To register for the MAT, you'll need to call one of the testing centers on www.milleranalogies.com. Before you register, check with both the testing center and the programs to which you're applying to find out how long it usually takes for the program to receive the official MAT score. Be sure to allow enough time for the score to reach your program(s).

If your test date is more flexible, you'll need to decide when to register. To be sure you're ready, you'll want to have achieved your goal score on one of the official MAT practice tests, when taken timed. Don't register until you've proven to yourself that you can achieve your goal.

As you take practice tests and score them, you'll get valuable data about your ability. If your scores are increasing according to your study plan, the test date you registered for may make sense. If not, you may want to push back your test date, to give yourself more time to improve.

Make sure you check directly with your testing center to learn about its policies for changing your test date (including any fees that may be involved).

Racing the Clock: Tackling MAT Timing

You likely would love to have unlimited time to think about the analogies you'll see on the MAT, but sadly, you do have to beat the clock. The MAT consists of 120 analogies, and you have only 60 minutes to work on them.

So dividing that equally among the questions, you have only 30 seconds per question, you may be thinking. However, unless you're trying for a perfect score (which you shouldn't be), you don't need to spread those 60 minutes over all 120 questions. Depending on your score goal, you want to spread almost all your time over 90 or 100 of the questions and guess quickly on the last 20 or 30.

If you try to get all 120 questions right, you'll be forced to work too quickly. It doesn't make much sense to rush carelessly on a medium-level question and perhaps get it wrong just so you can get to a harder question (which you may get wrong no matter how much time you spent on it). The bottom line: Don't rush.

Of course, you don't want to work too slowly, either. Even the highest-scoring students can fall behind if they have to double-check everything to make sure it's right. This style of test taking isn't necessary and has the unfortunate side effect of hurting your confidence and slowing you down. The best approach is to work carefully but confidently. Your confidence will grow in proportion to your practice quality and quantity.

Timing each question

To determine about how much time you want to spend per question, it's important to know your goal score. Let's say, for example, that your goal is to get 100 out of 120 questions correct, based on your practice results. That score translates into about 35 seconds per question, keeping in mind that you want to save a couple minutes at the end of the test to randomly guess on the questions you don't have time to analyze. Remember, any unanswered questions are automatically scored as incorrect; you may as well take a guess, even if it's a random one.

Don't underestimate the amount of time it takes to bubble in those random guesses! Err on the side of caution. When you notice 2 or 3 minutes remaining on the clock, abandon your analogy-solving mentality and just start guessing.

When randomly guessing, pick the same letter for every guess. The test makers usually vary the correct answer letters so that test takers don't get weirded out by seeing the same letter come up several times in a row. It doesn't really matter that much, but picking the same letter when guessing may save some time and slightly increase your odds of getting a few of those problems right.

Even a random guess gives you a 1-in-4 chance of answering a MAT question correctly. Leaving it blank give you a 0% chance. There's no penalty for guessing, so give it a shot.

Developing smart pacing

If you know how much time you can allot per question, you can better determine your pacing. Say that, again, you're shooting to work on 100 of the 120 questions. So you can spend 36 seconds on each question, but I round down to 35 seconds here, to leave some extra time for random guesses. However, the clock shows minutes, not seconds, so you have to think in terms of minutes for your pacing goals.

At the minimum, set a halfway goal. For a goal of 100 questions, you want to be on question 50 by the time the clock shows 30 minutes left. You may also want to think about goals in smaller increments: You want to be on question 25 by the time the clock shows 45 minutes, and you want to be on question 75 when the clock shows about 15 minutes.

Don't look at the clock too much, and don't dwell on the time. You need all your mental energy for the analogy in front of you. Staring at the clock can't help you solve it, and it may make you anxious.

Studying under timed conditions helps you develop an efficient pace that's right for you. Try looking at the clock after completing every 10 questions.

Recovering when you've fallen behind

So what do you do if things don't quite go according to plan and you get behind schedule? Let's say that, in the previous scenario, you notice that there's 30 minutes left on the clock, but you're only on question 45 when you'd hoped to be on question 50? Well, first of all, that's not too far off your goal, so don't panic. At this point, you need to start sacrificing questions. The next time a question comes up in a subject area you're weak in, don't think — just randomly guess. Guess what? You just bought yourself some time, and all it cost you was a question you may have gotten wrong anyway. Depending on how far behind schedule you are, you may have to sacrifice a few questions. But wait until you know that it's a hard question for you — there's no sense sacrificing easier questions.

For example, say I know that I'm weaker in questions that test math or science. As soon as I see a question with numbers or scientific terms, I randomly guess. I do this until I feel like I'm close to my desired pace.

Spending much time working on a difficult question is never a great idea. Unfortunately, many test takers sink a lot of time into these questions when they should be doing the opposite. Use your time where it has the highest probability of earning you points: on easy or medium questions.

In terms of order of difficulty, keep two things in mind. One, how late in the test is the question? The later it appears, the harder it is. Second, what are your weaknesses? If math is difficult for you, even an earlier math question may be challenging and, therefore, not worth much of your time. Be aware of your troublesome content categories so you can avoid spending too much time on questions that involve tough topics.

Dealing with Test Anxiety

Chances are, you're probably at least a little anxious about taking the MAT. Feeling anxious is normal. It's probably even a good thing — after all, you care about the outcome. This anxiety can actually be a good thing — it can inspire you to work harder. You *should* respect the MAT. It's not a cakewalk, which is why preparation is a smart idea. But if you're feeling really anxious or you've had trouble with nerves during similar tests, you may want to take stronger measures.

Controlling anxiety

Anxiety before the test often evaporates when the real test opens on the computer screen and your brain kicks into gear to solve the analogies. However, some people feel anxious during the real test as well. If you experience an attack of the nerves, follow these tips:

- ✔ **Accept your anxiety.** Fighting your body and yelling at yourself to calm down probably isn't a great idea. If you're anxious, you're anxious. Acknowledge it.

- ✔ **Take a breath.** Breathing deeply may not completely banish your anxiety, but it helps, and it keeps oxygen going to your brain, which is good!

- ✔ **Focus on the question in front of you and your technique for solving it.** Do something with your pencil. Staying active forces your thoughts away from the anxiety and onto something productive.

- ✔ **Use positive self-talk.** Being negative won't help you feel calmer, but saying encouraging phrases to yourself, like "You can do this," can help. Treat yourself as you would an anxious friend in the same situation. What would you say to your friend? Also, remind yourself that you've prepared intelligently for the test.

Maintaining focus

If you're having trouble focusing and your mind starts wandering during the test, try not to beat yourself up. Go back to the question in front of you and do something active. It's okay if your attention wanders — just catch yourself and go back to the question.

Preparing your body and mind

The expression "An ounce of prevention is worth a pound of cure" isn't an empty saying. Taking several practice tests under realistic testing conditions goes a long way toward reducing anxiety and increasing your focusing power. In addition to focusing on your mental preparation, taking care of your body is a good idea, since your mind and body are closely linked. Try things like:

- ✔ Engaging in aerobic exercise
- ✔ Eating whole foods
- ✔ Staying hydrated
- ✔ Taking time for relaxation, friends, and family

Although your MAT prep is important, you'll do better on the test if you're leading a balanced, healthy life as best you can. Both your body and mind will thank you for it!

Part II

Conquering the Content: Reviewing Vocabulary, Knowledge, and Culture

Five Subjects Covered on the MAT

Words and language　The MAT will test your vocabulary by presenting questions designed to see if you can define graduate-level words like *inchoate* and *guttural*. Also, you'll face questions that test your knowledge of word parts, grammar, and even of word-play like rhymes and patterns.

Humanities　Humanities analogies have terms from noteworthy literature, the fine arts, religion, and philosophy. They often ask you to know things like who created something and what it was that they created.

Social sciences　Social sciences analogies will draw from a broad range of topics, including geography, history, economics, political science, psychology, sociology, anthropology. Studying the famous contributors to these fields along with the most common terms will strengthen your skills.

Natural sciences　Natural science analogies cover sciences like biology, chemistry, physics, and astronomy, as well as classification. You'll need to know the terms used by these fields and some of the scientists who contributed to them.

Mathematics　Math analogies test your numbers knowledge, including measurement and mathematics. Learning about things like Roman numbers and practicing basic arithmetic, algebra, and geometry will help build your number skills.

web extras

Refresh your knowledge of geometry at www.dummies.com/extras/mat.

In this part . . .

✔ Arm yourself with the strategies and memory tricks to conquer the myriad of difficult, obscure (delete obscure – they aren't obscure) words that you'll find in the language section.

✔ Refresh your humanities knowledge to decipher deco from baroque, alto from allegro, Chopin from Stravinksy, Melville from Tolkien, and Plato from Hobbes.

✔ Prepare yourself for analogy questions dealing with social behavior and society without having to earn multiple PhDs with a primer on geography, history, economics, political science, psychology, sociology, and anthropology.

✔ Don't worry if it's been a while since you worked out an algebra equation or memorized the Periodic Table: reviewing the basics of the natural sciences and general arithmetic will get you ready for the math and science section of the MAT.

Chapter 5

Working with Words and Language

In This Chapter

▶ Looking at meanings for common word parts

▶ Using mnemonics to recall word meanings

▶ Recognizing categories of words on the MAT

▶ Practicing with language analogies

The MAT writers love to throw difficult words at you — in fact, if you're having trouble with an analogy, you likely don't know the meaning of one or more of the terms. To gear up for the test, you want to learn as many words as you can between today and test day. But unless you're a robot or you happen to have a photographic memory, you probably need some strategies to learn words efficiently.

This chapter provides the meanings of many word parts, to help you decipher unfamiliar vocabulary, and gives you a method of using memory tricks — mnemonics — to effectively learn word definitions. You'll also find help with learning specific word categories: words that end in *–ology,* foreign words, commonly confused words, and collective nouns. A nice side benefit of working through this chapter is that you'll strengthen your vocabulary, which will help with any reading you have to do in grad school.

Looking at Word Roots, Prefixes, and Suffixes

Word roots, prefixes, and suffixes can all be life preservers if the tough vocabulary in an analogy makes you feel like you're floundering. Knowing your roots, prefixes, and suffixes isn't a cure-all because the English language likes to break its own rules now and then, but it can help you through some tough questions when you just can't recall the word's dictionary definition.

Getting back to your (word) roots

Word roots have nothing to do with genealogy or gardening; they can provide clues to a word's definition.

A word root is a basic unit of a word that contains the most important part of its meaning. For example, the root *circum* means "around" and is the root of words like *circumference* and *circumvent,* both of which have to do with going *around* something.

When studying word roots, it can be useful to make up a memory device that will help you remember the meaning of the root. We'd suggest the following method:

1. Write down the word root and its definition on a piece of paper. The act of writing helps you remember.

2. Below the word root, write a word that uses that root. For example, for the root JECT you might write the word INJECT.

3. Make a creative sentence using the word containing the root. The most memorable sentences are ones that make you imagine something and react emotionally. For example, "I drank so much coffee while studying that I felt as though I'd been given a caffeine INJECTION."

Since there are exceptions to every rule in English, you can't be 100% sure a word means what its root would normally indicate. However, roots work often enough to help you if you otherwise don't know what a word might mean.

The following list is a collection of common English word roots.

ACT: Do; *actuate:* put into action

ALTER: Other; *alternate:* change in turn

AM: Love; *amative:* loving

ANIM: Mind, spirit; *animism:* belief in the soul

ANNU: Year; *annual:* yearly

ARCH: Ruler; *archangel:* principal angel

AUTO: Self; *autograph:* one's signed name

BELL: War; *belligerent:* someone who began a conflict

BEN: Good; *benefaction:* a good act

CAD: Fall; *cadaver:* a deceased human body

CAPIT: Head; *capitol:* the primary building used by government

CEED: Go; *exceed:* go past expectations

CHRONO: Time; *chronograph:* stopwatch

CIS: Cut; *incision:* a cut

CLAIM: Shout; *exclaim:* shout out

CRED: Believe; *credence:* a belief

CUR: Run; *curator:* someone who runs a museum

DEM: People; *demagogue:* a crowd-pleasing speaker

DIC: To say; *dictator:* unquestionable leader

DOC: Teach; *document:* a written statement

DUC: Lead; *conductor:* driver of a train

EU: Well; *eupepsia:* digestion that works well

FAC: To make; *factotum:* someone who does different works

FER: Carry; *ferry:* vessel that carries people across water

FIN: End; *finale:* end of a show

FLECT: Bend; *reflect:* to mirror

FORT: Luck; *fortitude:* ability to withstand hardship

FRAG: Break; *fragile:* breaks with ease

GEN: Race; *genocide:* the killing of a specific people

GRESS: Step; *progress:* moving ahead

JECT: Throw; *inject:* to put into

LEG: Choose; *legible:* able to be read

LOG: Speech; *epilogue:* written at the end of a book

LUM: Light; *luminescence:* giving off light

MAG: Big; *magnum:* a large handgun

MAL: Bad; *malice:* an evil deed

MIT: Send; *transmit:* to send from one to another

MORPH: Shape; *metamorphic:* rock that has changed forms

MUT: Change; *mutate:* to change forms

NAT: Born; *natal:* relating to someone's birth

NOM: Name; *nominate:* to give a name for an election

NOV: New; *novice:* someone new to a skill

OMNI: All; *omnivorous:* eats plants and animals

PATH: Feel; *empathetic:* understanding another's feelings

PED: Foot; *pedicure:* the beautification of the feet

PHIL: Love; *philander:* flirt

PORT: Carry; *porter:* someone who carries luggage

RID: Laugh; *ridicule:* to make someone appear laughable

SCI: Know; *conscious:* being aware

SCRIB: Write; *inscribe:* to write

SENS: Feel; *sensation:* a psychological feeling

SOL: Loosen; *dissolve:* separate into smaller parts

SPEC: Look; *spectacles:* eyeglasses

TAIN: Hold; *abstain:* to avoid doing

TRACT: Pull; *attraction:* feeling drawn to something

VEN: Come; *convention:* a gathering where people come to meet

VER: Truth; *veracity:* truthfulness

VIS: See; *visor:* part of hat that keeps light out of eyes

VIV: Life; *vivify:* bring life to

VOC: Call; *vociferate:* to shout

VOL: Wish; *volition:* an act of free choice

Identifying prefixes

A prefix is letters attached to the front of a word that alter its definition. Some prefixes are so common and well known that they've actually become words in their own right. For example, the prefix ULTRA-, which means "beyond", can be used as an adjective (she's ultra-cool). The word *prefix* itself has a prefix, *pre–*, which means "comes before."

An example of a prefix in action is found in the word anti-inflammatory. The prefix *anti–* often means "against," and the word *anti-inflammatory* means "against inflammation."

Just like word roots, prefixes don't always make a word mean what their definitions below indicate, but they're better than nothing when you don't know the meaning of a word.

The method described earlier in the chapter about how to help yourself remember word roots will work well with prefixes, too.

The following is a list of many common prefixes.

ANTE-: Before; *antechamber:* waiting room

ANTI-: Against; *antifreeze:* prevents water from freezing

BE-: Beset with; *befogged:* bewildered

BI-: Two; *bipedal:* walks on two legs

CIRCUM-: Around; *circumvent:* evade by going around

CONTRA-: Opposite; *contradiction:* deny a statement

DE-: Down; *decelerate:* to slow down

DI-: Two; *diverge:* branching off in two or more ways

DIS-: Separate; *discontinue:* stop

EPI-: Upon; *epitaph:* inscription on a tombstone

EX-: Former; *ex-wife:* one's former, living wife

EXTRA-: Outside; *extraneous:* not needed

HYPER-: Over; *hyperventilate:* breathing faster than normal

HYPO-: Low; *hypothermia:* when body temperature drops below normal

IM-: Not; *impossible:* unachievable

IN-: Into; *incarcerate:* put in prison

INTER-: Between; *intersection:* where two roads meet

INTRA-: Within; *intrados:* the inside of an arch

META-: Beyond; *metaphysics:* abstract philosophy

MIS-: Wrong; *misinformed:* believing incorrect information

MONO-: One; *monolith:* one independent rock

MULTI-: Many; *multipurpose:* having many uses

NON-: Not; *nonissue:* irrelevant

PARA-: Beside; *paragon:* an example of excellence

PER-: Through; *pervasive:* reaching throughout all

POLY-: Many; *polygraph:* method of lie detection measuring several bodily reactions

POST-: After; *postlude:* song played after the main event

PRE-: Before; *prelude:* song played before the main event

PRO-: For; *pro-equality:* in favor of equal treatment for men and women

RE-: Again; *reactivate:* to start again

SEMI-: Half; *semicircle:* a half-circle

SUB-: Under; *subway:* trains below ground

SUPER-: Above; *supervision:* watching over

TELE-: From a distance; *telephone:* device used to talk from great distances

TRANS-: Across; *translating:* deciphering another language

ULTRA-: Beyond; *ultrasound:* sound wave with frequency higher than humans can hear

UN-: Not; *unfair:* not just

UNI-: One; *unicycle:* vehicle with one wheel

WITH-: Against; *without:* lacking

Recognizing suffixes

The opposite of a prefix is a suffix, which is letters attached to the end of a word that alter its definition. For example, the suffix *–ology* means "the study of." The word *biology* means "the study of life." The following list gets you up to speed on many common suffixes.

Like word roots and prefixes, suffixes don't automatically make a word mean what their definitions normally indicate. But that doesn't mean you shouldn't try to use them to help figure out words, especially if you can't otherwise define the words.

The method described earlier in the chapter about how to help yourself remember word roots will work well with suffixes, too.

-ABLE: Being doable; *dissolvable:* able to be dissolved

-ACY: State; *normalcy:* condition of being normal

-AL: Relating to; *musical:* relating to music

-ANT: Performs an action; *reactant:* part of a chemical reaction

-ARY: Associated with; *adversary:* enemy

-ATE: Make; *decimate:* destroy

-DOM: State of being; *serfdom:* the state of being a serf

-EN: Become; *sharpen:* become sharp

-ENCE: Quality of: *prevalence:* being prevalent

-ER: Someone who; *painter:* one who paints

-ESQUE: Similar to; *statuesque:* like a statue

-FUL: Full of; *vengeful:* full of vengeance

-HOOD: A state of being; *adulthood:* the time being an adult

-IAN: Relating to; *magician:* someone who performs magic tricks

-IC: Pertaining to; *rhythmic:* relating to rhythms

-IFY: Make; *beautify:* to make beautiful

-ILE: Relating to; *futile:* pointless

-ISH: Similar; *boyish:* like a boy

-ISM: System; *socialism:* capital owned by government

-IST: One who uses; *machinist:* someone who works with machines

-IVE: Having quality of; *talkative:* talking a lot

-IZE: Forms verbs; *harmonize:* to play in harmony with

-LESS: Lacking; *jobless:* without a job

-LY: Makes adjectives or adverbs from nouns; *beastly:* like a beast

-MENT: Makes nouns from verbs; *punishment:* penalty

-NESS: Makes nouns from adjectives; *thoughtfulness:* being thoughtful

-OR: Someone who; *collector:* one who collects

-OSE: Abounding in; *religiose:* very religious

-OUS: Relating to; *poisonous:* being full of poison

-SHIP: Relationship held; *friendship:* relationship between friends

-TION: Result of a verb; *translation:* result of being translated

-TUDE: Makes nouns from adjectives; *gratitude:* thankfulness

-TY: Quality of; *scarcity:* being

-Y: Quality of; *shiny:* something that shines

Improving Your Vocabulary

If someone you were attracted to called you *mesmeric*, would you run or ask for his number? Having a big vocabulary is a powerful thing. It can help you understand what's going on around you, and it can help you more precisely — and impressively — convey meaning. On top of all that, the bigger your vocabulary, the better you'll probably do on the MAT. The trouble is, thousands upon thousands of words might show up on the MAT, so learning them all isn't a realistic option. But learning some words every day can at least make a dent.

When you select words to memorize, it's a good idea to use a source like a GRE vocabulary book; after all, you want to know graduate level vocabulary.

These kinds of books usually have selected the most commonly tested words and don't have too many obscure or easy words in them. (I've included an appendix in this book with definitions for many commonly tested graduate-level words.)

Learning Vocabulary Using Mnemonics

Mnemonics sound like a sort of sci-fi mind trick, and indeed they are powerful tools. When you're learning vocabulary, unless you give your brain a way to hold on to the words you learn, it will probably have a harder time remembering them when they appear on the MAT. In the appendix, I've designed sentences to help you remember the words through a variety of associations — using mnemonics.

Looking at examples of mnemonics

A mnemonic is just a memory device. It works by creating a link in your brain to something else so that recalling one thing helps recall the other. You can use mnemonics in many ways, but the strongest links are through senses and emotions.

Consider this example:

Quash (verb): to completely stop from happening.

Think: squash

The best way to QUASH an invasion of ants in your kitchen is simple: SQUASH them.

Now your brain has a link from the word *quash* (which it may not have known) to the word *squash* (which it probably knows). Both words sound and look the same, so creating a visual and aural link is easy. If you picture someone squashing ants (and maybe get grossed out), you have another visual link and an emotional link.

Here's another example:

Eschew (verb): to avoid.

Think: Ah-choo!

ESCHEW people who say "AH-CHOO!" unless you want to catch their colds

The word *eschew* sounds similar to someone sneezing *(ah-choo!)*, so your brain links the two sounds. If you picture yourself avoiding someone who is about to sneeze in your face, even better!

The more connections you make in your brain to the new word, the easier it is to recall it.

Making your own mnemonics

When you have a chance to check out some of the words in the appendix, you're ready to make your own mnemonics for words. Have fun with this — be creative in the connections you make, but above all, be sure your mnemonics are memorable for you. Think about another word that looks like either your vocabulary word or a word that rhymes with it. Then try to make a creative, vivid, and/or funny sentence that links the vocabulary word to the word you already know.

Creating a link from something you don't know to something you do know is the key, as is making it emotional and vivid.

Recognizing Words of a Specific Type

To make life a little easier for you when learning about words that often pop up on the MAT, I've also identified specific words on the exam that can be grouped into particular categories. Understanding these categories and recognizing which words belong with each can help you find the meaning of words, even if you haven't encountered them. I've selected the following categories of words: *–ologies,* collective nouns, commonly confused words, and foreign words.

Knowing your –ologies

It's pretty tough to get through high school or college without encountering an "-ology" or two: Biology, Psychology, Sociology, etc. What are *–ologies*? They're words that mean "the study of" — and they're simply words that end in the suffix *–ology*. For example, *astrology* is the study of the stars and planets. The following list has examples of common *–ology* words; each word means "the study of" the word that follows it.

Alology: Algae

Anthropology: Humans

Archaeology: Past human activity

Axiology: Values

Bacteriology: Bacteria

Biology: Life

Cardiology: Heart

Cosmology: Origin and laws of the universe

Cryptology: Codes

Cytology: Cells

Deontology: Ethics

Enology: Wine

Entomology: Insects

Epidemiology: Disease

Epistemology: Knowledge

Eschatology: End of time

Ethology: Animal behavior

Etiology: Causation and origination

Geology: Earth

Gerontology: Aging

Hagiology: Saints

Herpetology: Amphibians and reptiles

Histology: Tissues of plants and animals

Horology: Measuring time

Ichthyology: Fish

Kinesiology: Human movement

Limnology: Fresh inland water

Mammalogy: Mammals

Morphology: Form of organisms

Mycology: Fungi

Numismatology: Currency

Oncology: Tumors

Ontology: Reality

Ophthalmology: Eye

Ornithology: Birds

Paleontology: Fossils

Pathology: Diseases

Philology: Language

Physiology: Functions of organisms

Psychology: Mental functions and behaviors

Teleology: Final causes

Thanatology: Dying and death

Virology: Viruses

Zoology: Animals

Identifying collective nouns

One of the most creative types of words in English is collective nouns. Ever heard of a MURDER of crows, for instance? "Murder" is the collective noun for a group of crows. Collective nouns are just words that stand for groups of things. The following list covers some common collective nouns. The word in CAPITALS is the collective noun for the group of the word that follows it. For example, in the entry "BED of flowers," BED is the collective noun for flower.

Collective nouns are often words with multiple meanings. For example, BED can mean a bed of flowers or a bed you sleep in. Keep an open mind as to what a word means if you see one that has multiple definitions.

ALBUM of photographs

ATLAS of maps

BAND of men

BATTERY of guns

BED of flowers

BELT of asteroids

BEVY of beauties

BOARD of directors

BUNCH of bananas

CACHE of jewels

CAST of actors

CLUTCH of eggs

COLONY of fungi

CONGREGATION of churchgoers

COVEN of witches

CROWD of people

CULTURE of bacteria

DECK of cards

DEN of thieves

FLEET of cars

FLIGHT of stairs

FLOCK of sheep

FOREST of trees

GAGGLE of girls

HERD of cattle

HOST of angels

LIBRARY of books

LITTER of kittens

LOCK of hair

ORCHESTRA of musicians

PAIR of shoes

PANEL of experts

PEAL of bells

POSSE of sheriffs

QUIVER of arrows

RANGE of mountains

REAM of paper

SHOAL of fish

SLATE of candidates

STRING of pearls

TEAM of athletes

TRIBE of natives

TROUPE of dancers

WEALTH of information

WING of aircraft

YOKE of oxen

Distinguishing commonly confused words

Quick: When do you use "affect" vs. "effect"? If you have trouble remembering which one of these commonly confused words to use, you're not alone. Commonly confused words are pairs of similarly spelled words with different definitions that are notorious for tripping people up, like *compliment* and *complement*. The following list is designed to help you keep any troublesome words straight.

Accept: Agree to receive

Except: Not including

Adapt: Adjust

Adopt: Start to use

Advice: Guidance

Advise: To give guidance

Affect: Make a difference

Effect: The result

Altar: Table used for rituals

Alter: Change

Allusion: A reference

Illusion: A deceptive appearance

Appraise: To assess the value of

Apprise: To inform

Ascent: The journey up

Assent: Agreement

Capital: The city where government is located

Capitol: The principal building where government is located

Cite: To reference

Site: A location

Complement: Goes well with

Compliment: Kind words of approval

Confident: Assuredness

Confidant: A trusted person

Council: A group that advises

Counsel: To give suggestion

Currant: A dried grape

Current: Happening at the present

Dependant: Someone who relies on another

Dependent: Contingent on

Desert: Dry landscape

Dessert: The sweet course at the end of a meal

Discreet: Careful, sly

Discrete: Separate

Elicit: Draw forth

Illicit: Illegal

Ensure: To make sure of

Insure: To arrange for compensation

Eminent: Famous

Imminent: Very soon

Faint: Barely perceptible

Feint: A deceptive move

Farther: A larger distance away

Further: More

Foreword: The beginning of a book before the first chapter

Forward: Ahead

Grisly: Gruesome

Grizzly: A brown bear

Hoard: A stockpile

Horde: A large group

Incite: Stir up

Insight: Understanding

Ingenious: Very smart

Ingenuous: Unsuspecting

Lie: To rest horizontally

Lay: To put down

Loose: Unsecured

Lose: To misplace

Palate: The roof of the mouth

Palette: Colors used by an artist

Passed: To have moved by

Past: From a time gone by

Pore: Study carefully

Pour: Cause a flow from a container

Persecute: To annoy and harass

Prosecute: Bring legal action upon

Principal: Head of a school

Principle: A governing belief

Stationary: Not moving

Stationery: Paper to write on

Vain: Conceited

Vane: Device to measure wind direction

Venal: Corrupt

Venial: Pardonable

Wreath: Circular decoration of plants

Wreathe: To surround

Addressing Foreign Words and Alphabets

As if the English words on the MAT weren't challenging enough, the writers decided to have their test include some foreign words. But before you get out your high school Spanish book, keep in mind that the foreign words on the MAT are words that are so commonly used in English that they've become part of the English lexicon and are defined in most English dictionaries. The following list includes some common foreign words that may be tested on the MAT.

A priori: Based on deduction, not fact

Ad hoc: For a definite purpose

Ad nauseum: continuing to a disgusting degree

Alfresco: Outdoors

Alter ego: An alternate identity

Bête noire: Something disliked

Bona fide: The real thing

Carpe diem: Seize the day

Carte blanche: Blank check, freedom; having discretion and authority

Casus belli: Justification for war

Caveat emptor: Buyer beware

Comme il faut: Like it should be

Corpus delicti: Evidence of a crime

Coup de grace: A deathblow

De facto: Actual reality

De jure: Truth by technicality

Déjà vu: A feeling that a new experience has happened before

Deus ex machina: Implausible answer to a problem

Doppelgänger: The ghostly or physical double of a person

Enfant terrible: Misbehaving child

Ex cathedra: Absolute authority

Fait accompli: Completed deed

Faux pas: Mistake made socially

Fiasco: A ludicrous failure

Idée fixe: An idea one obsesses on

In extremis: Near death

In loco parentis: Acting in a parent's stead

In vino veritas: Truth is found in wine

Ipso facto: In and of itself

Joie de vivre: Joy of living

Mea culpa: My fault

Modus operandi: Way of working

Noblesse oblige: The way nobility must behave

Nolo contendere: No contest

Nom de plume: A pen name; an alias

Non sequitur: Doesn't follow logically

Per se: By or in itself

Persona non grata: Someone disliked

Prima facie: At first look

Pro bono: Work done without payment

Pro forma: Done as a formality

Quid pro quo: An exchange

Raison d'être: Reason for being

Rara avis: Rare example

Sangfroid: Cool under pressure

Schadenfreude: Satisfaction from another's misery

Sine qua non: Very important

Status quo: The existing condition

Sui generis: Unique

Tête-à-tête: A private conversation

Veni, vidi, vici: I came, I saw, I conquered

Verboten: Forbidden

Vis-à-vis: In relation to

Weltschmerz: Sadness because of the world's evils

Zeitgeist: Popular opinion of the time

Practicing Words and Language Analogies

Okay, time for some more practice! After all, you're ultimately here to learn how to solve MAT analogies. The following ten MAT-style questions all will test your words and language skills. Remember to use good technique, take your time, and write down what you need to. Good luck!

1. MYCOLOGY : FUNGI :: ONCOLOGY : _____

   (A) tumors

   (B) mushrooms

   (C) reptiles

   (D) oceans

2. _____ : HAIR :: CULTURE : BACTERIA

   (A) key

   (B) lock

   (C) strand

   (D) fur

3. CASTLE : _____ :: CAPITOL : CAPITAL

   (A) cattle

   (B) king

   (C) town hall

   (D) kingdom

4. CARTE BLANCHE : ALFRESCO :: TABULA RASA : _____

   (A) indoors

   (B) mea culpa

   (C) outdoors

   (D) pro forma

5. CYTOLOGY : DEONTOLOGY :: CELLS : _____

   (A) teeth

   (B) ethics

   (C) religion

   (D) mountains

6. DEN : THIEVES :: _____ : CARDS

   (A) deck

   (B) dent

   (C) cave

   (D) stationery

7. _____ : UNIQUE :: MEA CULPA : SUI GENERIS

   (A) no contest

   (B) near death

   (C) my fault

   (D) buyer beware

8. ADVISE : ADVICE :: GRATITUDE : _____

   (A) gratuity

   (B) adverse

   (C) device

   (D) thanks

9. INTRADOS : LINING :: ARCH : _____

    (A) pyramid

    (B) road

    (C) jacket

    (D) computer

10. BELL : WAR :: CLAIM : _____

    (A) shout

    (B) ring

    (C) death

    (D) take

Answers

1. Choice (A) is correct. (1:2,3:4) Mycology is the study of fungi, and oncology is the study of tumors.

2. Choice (B) is correct. (1:2,3:4) A lock is a collection of hair, and a culture is a collection of bacteria.

3. Choice (D) is correct. (1:2,3:4) A castle houses the government in a kingdom, and a capitol houses the government in a capital.

4. Choice (C) is correct. (1:3,2:4) *Carte blanche* and *tabula rasa* both mean "blank slate." *Alfresco* means "outdoors."

5. Choice (B) is correct. (1:3,2:4) Cytology is the study of cells, and deontology is the study of ethics.

6. Choice (A) is correct. (1:2,3:4) A den is a collection of thieves, and a deck is a collection of cards.

7. Choice (C) is correct. (1:3,2:4) *Mea culpa* means "my fault," and *sui generis* means "unique."

8. Choice (D) is correct. (1:2,3:4) Advising is giving advice; gratitude is giving thanks.

9. Choice (C) is correct. (1:3,2:4) The intrados is the inside of an arch, and the lining is the inside of a jacket.

10. Choice (A) is correct. (1:2,3:4) *Bell* is a prefix meaning "war"; *claim* is a prefix meaning "shout."

Chapter 6

Handling the Humanities

$\bullet \bullet$

In This Chapter

▶ Getting familiar with humanities terms

▶ Introducing important humanities figures

▶ Exploring significant humanities works

$\bullet \bullet$

The *humanities* refer to works that deal with people and the nature of being human — topics like music, art, literature, and philosophy. This chapter lists the works, creations, and ideas of some of the most brilliant and creative minds in history. Not only does this knowledge give you a leg up on the MAT, but it also will come in handy if you ever wind up on *Jeopardy!* or want to challenge a buddy in Trivial Pursuit.

Learning a basic fact or two about any of the entries in this chapter will help build your knowledge of potential MAT topics. These study lists are designed to give you the most important information about the entry in a short, easy-to-remember way. Of course, this chapter can't cover every single thing the MAT may test, but it will definitely bolster your humanities foundation. To further build your humanities knowledge, if you have time, it may be a good idea to explore areas below that interest you by doing more reading about them.

Brushing Up on Art

You don't have to be a snobby art critic to do well with art content on the MAT. You just need to know the major developments, works, and people of art history. Even if you've never taken an art class before, you can get familiar with some of the artists, terms, and art movements that may show up on the MAT. The following entries cover visual art terms, artists, works of art, and famous museums.

Terms

Art Deco: Style popular in the 1920s and 1930s, known for its symmetry and bold colors

Baroque: Elaborate and decorative style

Bauhaus: German school of design and art

Caricature: A portrait with exaggerated features

Carving: Using tools to shape an object by shaving off parts of it

Classicism: Art based on Greek or Roman influences

Cubism: Style that uses geometrical forms; Pablo Picasso produced works in the cubist style

Dada: Anti-establishment art style

Etching: Using acid to create art in metal

Expressionism: Style that expressed emotion as opposed to realistic representation; Vincent van Gogh produced works in the expressionist style

Fresco: A painting on plaster, usually done as a mural; Leonardo da Vinci's *The Last Supper* is a well-known fresco

Graffiti: Pictures or writing illegally placed on property

Impressionism: Style showing the artist's impression of the subject rather than a realistic one; Claude Monet produced works in the impressionist style

Mosaic: Work of art made of many small pieces joined together

Motif: Repeated theme or pattern in a work

Mural: A painting that covers a wall or ceiling

Paper Mache: A crafting material made of paper and an adhesive

Pointillism: Painting style that uses many tiny dots to form an image

Portrait: A piece of art focusing on the face of a person

Primary colors: Red, blue, and yellow; they can be combined to make all the other colors

Realism: Art genre that depicts things as they are in reality

Sculpture: Three-dimensional art made by carving or assembling

Still Life: A piece of art that focuses on inanimate objects

Surrealism: Art style with bizarre or surprising imagery

Tempera: Paint made with egg yolks

Whittling: Carving wood or bone with a knife

Artists and works

Angelico, Fra: Italian painter known for *Deposition of Christ*

Bosch, Hieronymus: Dutch painter best known for *The Garden of Earthly Delights*

Botticelli, Sandro: Italian painter famous for *The Birth of Venus*

Calder, Alexander: American sculptor known for his mobiles and wire sculptures

Caravaggio: Italian painter known for *Calling of Saint Matthew*

Cezanne, Paul: French painter known for *The Card Players*

Chagall, Marc: Russian painter famous for his stained glass work and modernist style

da Vinci, Leonardo: Italian painter and sculptor famous for painting the *Mona Lisa*

Dali, Salvador: Spanish painter who worked in the surrealist style; One of his best-known works is *The Persistence of Memory*

Daumier, Honoré: French artist best known for his political caricatures

De Kooning, Willem: Dutch expressionist artist known for *Easter Monday*

Degas, Edgar: French artist famous for his paintings of dancers

Donatello: Italian sculptor known for his bas-relief sculpture

Gaugin, Paul: French painter known for his paintings of Tahitian subjects

Giacometti, Alberto: Swiss sculptor who worked in bronze

Goya, Francisco: Spanish painter known for *Black Paintings*

Homer, Winslow: American painter known for his marine paintings and landscapes

Hopper, Edward: American realist painter; one of his famous works is *Chop Suey*

Johns, Jasper: American pop art painter; one of his famous works is *Three Flags*

Klee, Paul: Swiss/German painter known for *Twittering Machine*

Klimt, Gustav: Austrian painter known for *The Kiss*

Lichtenstein, Roy: American pop artist famous for his art in the style of comic strips

Manet, Edouard: French painter, known for *Olympia*

Matisse, Henri: French painter famous for his bold use of color; one of his greatest works is *La Danse*

Michelangelo: Italian painter and sculptor known for his sculpture *David* and for his paintings in the Sistine Chapel

Miró, Joan: Spanish painter who worked in the surrealist style

Mona Lisa: Famous painting by Leonardo da Vinci; displayed in the Louvre

Mondrian, Piet: Dutch painter famous for his abstract works using primary colors

Monet, Claude: French impressionist painter known for *Haystacks*

Munch, Edvard: Norweigan painter most famous for *The Scream*

Nast, Thomas: German-born caricaturist; created the Republican Party elephant

O'Keeffe, Georgia: American artist who lived in the Southwest; most famous for her paintings of flowers

Picasso, Pablo: Spanish painter; one of his famous works is *Guernica*

Pollock, Jackson: American painter known for his technique of dripping paint onto canvas

Rembrandt: Dutch portrait painter

Renoir, Pierre-Auguste: French impressionist painter

Rodin, Auguste: French sculptor of *The Thinker*

Rubens, Peter Paul: Flemish painter who worked in the baroque style

Sargent, John Singer: American portrait painter known for *Portrait of Madame X*

Titian: Italian painter known for his use of color

Van Gogh, Vincent: Dutch painter; one of his famous works is *Starry Night*

Venus de Milo: Greek statue of the goddess Venus, located in the Louvre

Warhol, Andy: American pop artist known for his Campbell's soup cans paintings

Wood, Grant: American artist who painted *American Gothic*

Wyeth, Andrew: American realist painter; one of his famous works is *Christina's World*

Museums

British Museum: Museum located in London

Guggenheim: Modern art museum located in New York City

Hermitage Museum: A museum of art and culture in Saint Petersburg

Lascaux: Site in France where prehistoric cave paintings were discovered

Louvre: French art museum located in Paris

The Metropolitan Museum of Art: Art museum located in New York City

MOMA: Modern art museum located in New York City

Pergamon: German art museum located in Berlin

Pompidou Centre: A complex in Paris that houses a public library, art museum, and music research facility

Prado: Spanish art museum located in Madrid

Rijksmuseum: Dedicated to arts, crafts, and history — located in Amsterdam

Tate Modern: A modern art gallery in London

Uffizi: Italian art museum located in Florence

Vatican Museums: Located in Vatican City, they display the collection of the Roman Catholic Church

Building Your Architecture Knowledge

Architecture: the art of building things. You're probably already familiar with some of the most famous examples of architecture — like the Roman Colosseum. Architecture isn't as big of a category as art on the MAT, so covering the bases can be a little easier. The following lists familiarize you with some of history's most important architecture and architects and give you the building blocks of architectural terminology.

Terms

Amphitheatre: An open-air venue for performances

Aqueduct: Pipeline that carries water

Atrium: Roman entrance chamber

Bas-relief: Type of sculpture in which the shape protrudes slightly from its background

Cameo: Raised carving; opposite of intaglio

Catacombs: underground burial chambers

Corinthian Order: Greek style of architecture that was very ornate featuring leaves and scrolls

Doric Order: Greek style of architecture where the columns were close together and not on a base

Façade: Front of a building

Gargoyle: Human or animal statue placed on the roof of a building

Gothic Architecture: Style of architecture characterized by high arches and flying buttresses

Hieroglyphs: Egyptian language that uses pictorial characters

Intaglio: Indented carving; opposite of cameo

Ionic Order: Greek style of architecture that prominently features volutes

Odeon: Ancient Greek and Roman building for musical purposes

Pagoda: Buddhist shrine or tomb

Rococo: Ornate, playful, asymmetric architectural style

Ziggurat: Mesopotamian pyramid made of bricks

Architects

Gaudi, Antoni: Spanish architect best known for the incomplete Sagrada Familia

Gehry, Frank: Designer of the Spanish Guggenheim museum

Jefferson, Thomas: American president who designed *Monticello*

Le Corbusier: Swiss-French pioneer of modern architecture

Mies van der Rohe, Ludwig: German-American pioneer of modern architecture; known for his simplicity

Mills, Robert: American architect who designed the Washington Monument

Pei, I. M.: Chinese-American architect who designed many skyscrapers

Sinan, Mimar: Ottoman architect who designed mosques

Sullivan, Louis: American creator of the modern skyscraper

Wren, Christopher: English architect who rebuilt many churches in London after the Great Fire

Wright, Frank Lloyd: American architect who merged buildings with the landscapes in which they were built

Works

Capitol: Government building in Washington, D.C., that houses the U.S. legislature

Colosseum: Roman amphitheatre in which gladiatorial contests took place

Great Sphinx: Statue at the pyramids of Giza in the shape of a lion with a man's head

Hagia Sophia: Church in Istanbul, Turkey

Notre Dame: Cathedral in Paris, France

Pantheon: Roman temple

Parthenon: Greek temple to the goddess Athena built on the acropolis in Athens

St. Peter's Basilica: Roman Catholic church in the Vatican

Stonehenge: Group of stones forming a monument in England

Taj Mahal: Famous Indian mausoleum

Versailles: French palace built by Louis XIV

Naming That Tune: Music

Learning about the musical rock stars of their respective eras is important to do well on the MAT. You have to know the most important musicians and composers throughout history and be familiar with their major works. These lists keep you in tune with musical terms, major musicians and composers, and the most important musical works.

Terms

A cappella: Style of singing without any instruments accompanying the voice(s)

Accelerando: Gradually speeding up

Accent: Marking placed on a note to indicate significance

Adagio: Slow speed for a song

Allegretto: Moderately fast speed for a song

Allegro: Fast speed for a song

Altissimo: Very high range of notes

Alto: Lowest boy's/woman's vocal range

Andante: Relaxed speed for a song, like walking

Appoggiatura: Grace notes that take some of the following note's duration

Arpeggio: Notes of a chord played individually

A tempo: Indicates a return to the original speed of a song

Bass: Lowest male vocal range (or) tones of low frequency. Opposite of treble

Beat: Continued rhythm of a song

Bend: Sliding a note up or down a little in jazz

Brass: Instruments like trumpets, tubas, and trombones

Bridge: Section of a song that differs from the refrain or verse

Cadenza: Solo section of a song

Canon: Musical theme that is repeated and layered

Carol: A festive, usually religious song

Chord: Group of notes played simultaneously

Clef: Symbol on the staff to define note range (for example, G clef, bass clef)

Coda: Final section of a song

Coloratura: Ornamentation of a vocal part

Contralto: Lowest female vocal range

Countertenor: Highest male vocal range

Crescendo: Gradually increasing the volume

Decelerando: Gradually slowing down

Decrescendo: Gradually decreasing the volume

Dirge: A song expressing grief; commonly heard at funerals

Dynamics: Indications of volume in a song

Encore: Another song played at the end of a concert by request

Falsetto: Vocal range above the normal, especially in men

Fermata: Marking to indicate holding a note longer than usual

Fine: The end

Flat: Marking indicating that a note should be lowered by one tone

Forte: Loud

Fortissimo: Very loud

Harmony: The use of multiple notes simultaneously to create chords

Hymn: Song praising a deity

Intro: Beginning of a song

Key: One of the 12 notes that a song can be based on

Largo: Slowly

Legato: Smoothly, connected

Marcato: Every note accented

Measure: Short unit of a song comprising a cycle of beats

Medley: Song made up of parts of other songs

Melisma: Changing the note during one syllable

Meter: The rhythmic beat of a song

Metronome: Timekeeping device that produces regular beats

Mezzo-forte: Moderately loud

Mezzo-piano: Moderately soft

Motif: A short musical idea that repeats itself in songs

Natural: Marking that cancels an existing sharp or flat

Octave: The eight notes comprising a scale

Oratorio: Large musical composition, like an opera

Percussion: Instruments that are struck like drums or bells

Pianissimo: Very soft

Piano: Soft

Pitch: The ordering of musical tones based on frequency

Poco: A little

Prelude: Musical introduction

Presto: Quickly

Rest: A period of silence in a song

Ritard: Slowing down

Rondo: A form of a song where the theme is alternated between other sections

Rubato: Flexible speed, not like a metronome

Scale: A sequence of notes all either ascending or descending

Semitone: Half-step. The smallest interval between notes

Sforzando: Suddenly loud and accented

Sharp: Marking indicating that a note should be raised by one tone

Soprano: Highest female vocal range

Staccato: Making each note very short

Staff: The five lines on which notes are placed

Subito: Suddenly

Syncopation: Style with emphasis on the upbeats

Tacet: Silent

Tempo: Speed of a song

Tenor: High male vocal range

Tenuto: Marking that indicates holding a note slightly longer

Tessitura: Middle or most comfortable part of a note range

Treble: Tones of high frequency; Opposite of bass

Trill: Quickly alternating between two notes

Tutti: All

Vibrato: Note wavering up and down

Woodwinds: Instruments including flutes, oboes, and saxophones

Composers and musicians

Armstrong, Louis: Famous American jazz trumpeter and singer

Bach, Johann Sebastian: Baroque German composer known for his *Mass in B Minor*

Beethoven, Ludwig van: German pianist and composer of the classical and romantic eras

Brahms, Johannes: Romantic German composer known for piano works

Caruso, Enrico: Italian tenor opera singer

Chopin, Frederic: Polish composer known for piano works

Copland, Aaron: American composer who wrote *Billy the Kid*

Debussy, Claude: French composer who wrote impressionist music

Ellington, Duke: American composer and big-band leader

Gershwin, George: American composer and pianist who wrote *Porgy and Bess*

Gilbert and Sullivan: English comic opera composers who wrote *The Pirates of Penzance*

Handel, George Frideric: German composer famous for operas and *The Messiah*

Haydn, Joseph: Austrian composer called the "Father of the Symphony"

Mendelssohn, Felix: German composer who wrote the *Italian Symphony*

Mozart, Wolfgang Amadeus: Austrian composer who wrote *The Magic Flute*

Puccini, Giacomo: Italian opera composer who wrote *La Bohème*

Purcell, Henry: Baroque English composer

Schubert, Franz: Austrian composer known for his *Lieder* and symphonies

Sousa, John Philip: American composer who wrote *The Stars and Stripes Forever*

Strauss, Richard: German composer known for the opera *Salome*

Stravinsky, Igor: Russian ballet composer who wrote *The Firebird*

Tchaikovsky, Pyotr Ilyich: Russian composer who wrote *The Queen of Spades*

Verdi, Giuseppe: Italian opera composer who wrote *Rigoletto*

Vivaldi, Antonio: Venetian composer known for violin works

Works

Amazing Grace: Christian hymn by Englishman John Newton

America: Patriotic American song; lyrics by Samuel Francis Smith

America the Beautiful: Patriotic American song by Samuel A. Ward and Katharine Lee Bates

Auld Lang Syne: Scots poem–based folk song used to celebrate the New Year

Carmen: Opera by the French composer Georges Bizet

Don Giovanni: Opera by Mozart

Frère Jacques: French nursery melody sung in a round

God Bless America: American patriotic song by Irving Berlin

Greensleeves: English folk song and tune

Madame Butterfly: Opera by Giacomo Puccini

The Messiah: Oratorio by Handel

The Star-Spangled Banner: National anthem of the United States, by Francis Scott Key

Swan Lake: Ballet by Tchaikovsky

La Traviata: Opera by Giuseppe Verdi

Reading Up on Literature

Books so good that they stand the test of time are eventually dubbed literature. The MAT loves to test authors and their works from the literary canon, the stuff that a college English major has to read. The following lists give you the basics of literary terminology and some quick info about major authors and their most important writings.

Terms

Act: Major part of a play

Allegory: Work in which things represent or stand for other things

Alliteration: Repeated sounds in consecutive words

Allusion: Reference to something

Anachronism: Error in time sequence

Antagonist: Character who opposes the work's hero

Antihero: Main character who lacks heroism

Apostrophe: Direct reference to something that is absent

Assonance: Repetition of vowel sounds

Ballad: Poem that tells a tale and is usually meant to be sung

Bildungsroman: Autobiographical novel

Canto: Division of a long poem

Cliché: An overused, formerly meaningful element in a work

Climax: Point of highest drama in a work

Couplet: Two consecutive lines of verse that rhyme with each other

Denouement: Final part of a work

Doggerel: Bad poetry

Elegy: Poem expressing sadness

Epic: Long heroic poem

Epiphany: A work or section of a work presenting a moment of revelation

Essay: Short work expressing the author's opinion

Fable: Short story containing a moral lesson

Foot: Unit of verse

Foreshadowing: When the author hints at future plot developments

Genre: Type of literature

Haiku: Japanese three-line poem

Hyperbole: Exaggeration

Idiom: A saying that has a figurative meaning

Imagery: When the author uses descriptive words to enhance his meaning

Irony: Something that means the opposite of its literal meaning

Kitsch: Work of poor quality or reputation

Lampoon: Satirical portrayal

Limerick: Five-line humorous poem

Metaphor: Description of something done by comparing it to something else

Meter: A poem's rhythm

Motif: Repeated theme in a work

Onomatopoeia: Word that sounds like what it means

Oxymoron: Term that contradicts itself

Parable: Story with a moral lesson

Paradox: Illogical statements used to create insight

Parody: Work that mocks another work

Pathos: Something used to get sympathy

Personification: Giving human attributes to things that are not human

Plot: Events of a literary work

Prose: Nonpoetic language

Pun: A humorous use of words to suggest alternate meanings

Rhetoric: An art that writers use to be more persuasive

Rhetorical Question: A question that makes a point; no reply is expected

Sarcasm: An ironic statement usually used in a negative way

Satire: Work that makes fun of something

Scene: Part of a play happening in a certain location

Simile: Description accomplished by comparing one thing to another

Sonnet: Fourteen-line poem

Stanza: Part of a poem consisting of a group of lines

Symbol: A representation of an idea

Theme: The core subject that an author is writing about

Thesis: The primary argument in an essay

Tone: The author's attitude towards the subject matter

Verse: Poetry, or a part of a poem

Authors

Aeschylus: Greek dramatist and author of *Prometheus Bound*

Aesop: Greek author of fables (stories with a moral)

Alcott, Louisa May: American author of *Little Women*

Alger, Horatio: American novelist

Alighieri, Dante: Italian author of *The Divine Comedy*

Andersen, Hans Christian: Danish author of fairytales

Angelou, Maya: Black American writer who wrote about growing up in the South

Aristophanes: Greek playwright and author of *The Clouds*

Austen, Jane: British author of *Pride and Prejudice*

Balzac, Honoré de: French writer and author of *La Comédie Humaine*

Baudelaire, Charles: French poet and author of *Les Fleurs du Mal*

Beckett, Samuel: Irish existentialist and author of *Waiting for Godot*

Bellow, Saul: American novelist and author of *Herzog*

Blake, William: British poet and author of *Songs of Innocence*

Bradbury, Ray: American science fiction writer and author of *The Martian Chronicles*

Brontë, Charlotte: British author of *Jane Eyre*

Brontë, Emily: British author of *Wuthering Heights*

Byron, Lord George: Romantic poet and author of *Don Juan*

Camus, Albert: Existentialist French writer and author of *The Stranger*

Caroll, Lewis: British author of *Alice in Wonderland*

Cather, Willa: American author of *Death Comes for the Archbishop*

Cervantes, Miguel de: Spanish author of *Don Quixote*

Chaucer, Geoffrey: English poet and author of *The Canterbury Tales*

Chekov, Anton Pavlovich: Russian playwright and author of *The Cherry Orchard*

Coleridge, Samuel Taylor: British romantic poet and author of *The Rime of the Ancient Mariner*

Conrad, Joseph: British writer and author of *Heart of Darkness*

cummings, e. e.: American poet

Defoe, Daniel: American author of *Robinson Crusoe*

Dickens, Charles: British author of *David Copperfield, Oliver Twist, A Christmas Carol,* and *A Tale of Two Cities*

Dickinson, Emily: American poet

Donne, John: English poet and author of "Death Be Not Proud"

Dostoevsky, Fyodor: Russian novelist and author of *Crime and Punishment*

Dryden, John: English poet and author of *Alexander's Feast*

Eliot, George: English novelist and author of *Middlemarch*

Eliot, T. S.: British poet and author of "The Waste Land"

Ellison, Ralph: American author of *The Invisible Man*

Emerson, Ralph Waldo: American philosopher and writer, and author of "Concord Hymn"

Euripedes: Greek dramatist known for his tragedies

Faulkner, William: American author of *The Sound and the Fury, As I Lay Dying,* and *Light in August*

Fitzgerald, F. Scott: American novelist and author of *The Great Gatsby*

Flaubert, Gustave: French writer and author of *Madame Bovary*

Frost, Robert: American poet and author of "The Road Not Taken"

Ginsberg, Allen: American poet and author of beat poetry, including *Howl*

Goëthe, Johann Wolfgang von: German writer and author of *Faust*

Golding, William: English author of *The Lord of the Flies*

Grimm Brothers: German authors of fairytales

Hardy, Thomas: English writer and author of *Tess of the D'Urbervilles*

Hawthorne, Nathaniel: American author of *The Scarlet Letter*

Hemingway, Ernest: American author of *For Whom the Bell Tolls* and *The Old Man and the Sea*

Hesse, Herman: German writer and author of *Siddhartha*

Homer: Greek poet and author of *The Iliad* and *The Odyssey*

Hughes, Langston: Black American poet who was part of the Harlem Renaissance

Hugo, Victor: French writer and author of *Les Misérables*

Hurston, Zora Neale: Black American author of *Their Eyes Were Watching God* who was part of the Harlem Renaissance

Huxley, Aldous: British author of *Brave New World*

Ibsen, Henrik: Norwegian playwright and author of *A Doll's House*

James, Henry: American writer and author of *The Turn of the Screw*

Joyce, James: Irish author of *Ulysses* and *A Portrait of the Artist As a Young Man*

Kafka, Franz: German author of *The Metamorphosis*

Keats, John: English poet and author of "Ode on a Grecian Urn"

Kerouac, Jack: American poet and author of *On the Road*

Kipling, Rudyard: British author of *The Jungle Book*

Lawrence, D. H.: British author of *Lady Chatterley's Lover*

Lewis, Sinclair: American satirist and author of *Main Street*

London, Jack: American author of *The Call of the Wild*

Longfellow, Henry Wadsworth: American poet and author of *Paul Revere's Ride*

Mann, Thomas: German author of *The Magic Mountain*

Marlowe, Christopher: English playwright and author of *Dr. Faustus*

Melville, Herman: American author of *Moby Dick*

Miller, Arthur: American playwright and author of *The Crucible*

Milton, John: British author of *Paradise Lost*

Morrison, Toni: Black American author of *Beloved*

Nabokov, Vladimir: Russian writer and author of *Lolita*

O'Neill, Eugene: American playwright and author of *A Long Day's Journey into Night*

Orwell, George: English author of *1984* and *Animal Farm*

Ovid: Roman poet and author of *Metamorphoses*

Paine, Thomas: American writer and author of *Common Sense*

Petrarch: Italian Renaissance poet

Plath, Sylvia: American poet and author of *The Bell Jar*

Plutarch: Greek writer and author of *The Parallel Lives*

Poe, Edgar Allan: American author of "The Raven"

Pound, Ezra: American poet

Proust, Marcel: French novelist and author of *Remembrance of Things Past*

Rushdie, Salman: British novelist and author of *The Satanic Verses*

Scott, Sir Walter: Scottish novelist and author of *Ivanhoe*

Seuss, Dr.: American author of children's books, including *The Cat in the Hat* and *The Lorax*

Shakespeare, William: British dramatist and author of *MacBeth* and *The Tempest*

Shaw, George Bernard: Irish playwright and author of *Pygmalion*

Shelley, Mary: English novelist and author of *Frankenstein*

Shelley, Percy Bysshe: English poet and author of *Prometheus Unbound*

Silverstein, Shel: American author of children's poems, including *Where the Sidewalk Ends*

Sinclair, Upton: American writer and author of *The Jungle*

Solzhenitsyn, Aleksander: Russian writer and author of *One Day in the Life of Ivan Denisovich*

Sophocles: Greek playwright and author of *Oedipus Rex*

Spenser, Edmund: English poet and author of *The Faerie Queen*

Steinbeck, John: American author of *The Grapes of Wrath*

Stevenson, Robert Louis: Scottish author of *Treasure Island*

Stowe, Harriet Beecher: American author of *Uncle Tom's Cabin*

Swift, Jonathan: English author of *Gulliver's Travels*

Thoreau, Henry David: American author of *Walden*

Tolkien, J. R. R.: British author of *The Hobbit* and *The Lord of the Rings*

Tolstoy, Leo: Russian author of *Anna Karenina*

Twain, Mark: American author of *The Adventures of Huckleberry Finn* and *The Adventures of Tom Sawyer*

Updike, John: American author of *Rabbit, Run*

Virgil: Roman poet and author of *The Aeineid*

Vonnegut, Kurt: American novelist and author of *Slaughterhouse-Five*

Wharton, Edith: British author of *Ethan Frome*

Whitman, Walt: American poet and author of *Leaves of Grass*

Wilde, Oscar: Irish author of *The Picture of Dorian Gray*

Wilder, Laura Ingalls: American author of *Little House on the Prairie*

Wilder, Thornton: American playwright and author of *Our Town*

Williams, Tennessee: American playwright and author of *A Streetcar Named Desire*

Woolf, Virginia: British novelist and author of *Mrs. Dalloway*

Wordsworth, William: British poet

Yeats, William Butler: Irish playwright and author of *The Winding Stair*

Thinking Deep Thoughts: Philosophy

What *is* the meaning of life, anyway? Don't worry, you won't have to wade through any confusing philosophy texts to do well with philosophy on the MAT. All you need to know are history's major philosophers, their works, and some basic philosophy terms.

Terms

Empiricism: Theory that knowledge comes mainly from sensory perception

Ethics: Moral philosophy, concepts of right and wrong

Existentialism: School of philosophy based on the concept of free will

Idealism: Theory that reality is mentally constructed

Logic: Study and use of reasoning

Logical Positivism: Analytic philosophy that combines empiricism and rationalism

Neoplatonism: Mystical philosophy based on the teachings of Plato

Philosopher: Someone who studies fundamental questions and uses rational argument

Pragmatism: The idea that theory should come from practice

Rationalism: Method that uses deductive reasoning

Transcendentalism: Belief that the spiritual is more important than the material

Philosophers

Aristotle: Greek philosopher and student of Plato; wrote *Poetics*

Bacon, Francis: English philosopher

Bradley, Herbert Francis: British idealist who wrote *Appearance and Reality*

Descartes, René: Frenchman known as the "Father of Modern Philosophy"

Dewey, John: American philosopher concerned with education and social reform

Gandhi, Mahatma: Indian leader who advocated nonviolent civil disobedience

Hobbes, Thomas: English political philosopher; wrote *Leviathan*

Hume, David: Scottish philosopher known for empiricism and skepticism

James, William: American philosopher and psychologist

Kant, Immanuel: German philosopher who wrote *Critique of Pure Reason*

Leibnitz, Gottfried: German philosopher and mathematician

Locke, John: English philosopher and empiricist; wrote *An Essay Concerning Human Understanding*

Macchiavelli, Nicolo: Italian philosopher and author of *The Prince*

Marx, Karl: German philosopher, economist and proponent of communism; wrote *The Communist Manifesto*

Mill, John Stuart: British philosopher and political economist

More, Thomas: English philosopher and humanist who wrote *Utopia*

Nietzsche, Friedrich: German philosopher known for the idea of the death of God; wrote *Beyond Good and Evil*

Peirce, Charles Sanders: American philosopher known as the "Father of Pragmatism"

Plato: Greek writer and author of *The Republic*

Rousseau, Jean-Jacques: Swiss philosopher and author of *The Social Contract*

Schopenhauer, Arthur: Atheist German philosopher who wrote *The World As Will and Representation*

Smith, Adam: Key figure of the Scottish Enlightenment

Socrates: Greek philosopher known for work in ethics and the teacher of Plato; inspired the Socratic Method

Tzu, Sun: Ancient Chinese philosopher and author of *The Art of War*

Voltaire: French philosopher and author of *Candide*

Zedong, Mao: Chinese communist leader

Works

Appearance and Reality: By British idealist Francis Herbert Bradley

An Essay Concerning Human Understanding: By John Locke. Asserts that the mind is a blank slate at birth

The Art of War: Ancient Chinese book by Sun Tzu about military strategy

Beyond Good and Evil: By Nietzsche; criticizes past philosophers on their acceptance of religious principles

Candide: French satire by Voltaire

The Communist Manifesto: Political manuscript by Karl Marx and Friedrich Engels

Critique of Pure Reason: Influential work by Kant in which he describes the relationship between knowledge and experience

Leviathan: By Thomas Hobbes. Focuses on society and government

Poetics: An analysis of tragedy by Aristotle

The Prince: Political work by Machiavelli where he asserts that the truth is more important than an ideal

The Republic: A Socratic dialogue by Plato

The Social Contract: By Rousseau; focuses on political community

The World as Will and Representaion: Primary work of Schopenhauer; he writes that all of nature has a will to life and that suffering comes from the desire for more

Utopia: Fiction and political philosophy by Thomas More

Pondering Religion/Mythology

Ever since the dawn of time, man has tried to understand the universe with religion and myth. To solve religion or mythology analogies on the MAT, you'll need a little information about the world's major religions, history's most famous myths, and religious and mythological terms. This section doesn't cover as much as some of the other humanities sections, so building your foundation is easier here.

Terms

Armageddon: An end-of-the-world scenario

Asceticism: Lifestyle without physical pleasures

Confirmation: A rite of initiation in Christianity

Hajj: Islamic pilgrimage to Mecca

Original sin: State into which humans are born after the fall of man

Phoenix: Mythical bird that burns to death, only to be born again from its ashes

Ramadan: Month of fasting in Islam

Seven deadly sins: Vices against Christianity: wrath, greed, sloth, pride, lust, envy, and gluttony

Sharia: The moral code of Islam

Religions

Agnosticism: The belief that the existence of deities is unknown

Atheism: The belief that there are no deities

Buddhism: Religion based on the teachings of Buddha; practitioners seek nirvana

Christianity: Monotheistic religion based on the teachings of Jesus

Hinduism: Predominant religion of India, based on karma and dharma

Islam: Monotheistic religion based on the Quran

Judaism: Monotheistic religion based on the Hebrew Bible

Sikhism: Monotheistic religion founded in the Punjab region

Greek/Roman gods

Apollo: Greek and Roman sun god, son of Zeus

Aphrodite/Venus: Goddess of love

Ares/Mars: God of war

Athena/Minerva: Warrior goddess of wisdom

Dionysus/Bacchus: God of wine and pleasure

Hades/Pluto: God of the underworld

Hera/Juno: Goddess of marriage and motherhood

Hermes/Mercury: Messenger of the gods

Poseidon/Neptune: God of the ocean

Zeus/Jupiter: God of the sky who rules other gods

Other gods

Allah: Name for God in Islam

Isis: Egyptian goddess of nature and magic, the ideal wife and mother

Osiris: Egyptian god of the underworld and the dead

Ra: Egyptian sun god

Thor: Norse god of thunder and lightning

Religious figures

Adam: First human male, according to the Creation Myth

Buddha, Gautama: Spiritual teacher and founder of Buddhism

Eve: First human female, according to the Creation Myth

Jesus: Central figure in Christianity, the son of God

Job: Character in the Hebrew Bible; prophet in Islam

John the Baptist: Prophet in Christianity and Islam who baptized Jesus

Mary: Virgin mother of Jesus

Moses: Prophet in Judaism who wrote the Torah

Muhammad: Messengers and prophet of God in Islam

Noah: Figure in the Old Testament who built an ark to save a sampling of life on Earth

Satan: Evil entity who corrupts humans

Zoroaster: Persian founder of Zoroastrianism

Locations

Asgard: Capital city of the Norse gods

Hades: The underworld in Ancient Greek mythology; Hades is also the name of the god of this underworld

Jerusalem: Holy city in Israel in Christianity, Judaism, and Islam

Mecca: In Islam, the birthplace of Muhammad and where the Quran was written

Mount Olympus: Home of the 12 Olympian Greek gods

Styx: In Greek mythology, the river that divided Earth from Hades

Valhalla: The hall in Asgard in Norse mythology

Vatican City: Home of Catholicism and the Pope in Rome, Italy

Festivals/holidays

Christmas: Christian holiday celebrating the birth of Jesus

Easter: Christian holiday celebrating the resurrection of Jesus

Eid al-Adha: Muslim holiday at the end of the Hajj

Eid ul-Fitr: Muslim holiday at the end of Ramadan

Hanukkah: Eight-day Jewish holiday known as the Festival of Lights

Rosh Hashanah: Jewish New Year and the first of the High Holy Days

Yom Kippur: Holy Jewish day of atonement and repentance

Writings

Bible: Collection of Christian and Jewish texts

Quran: Central text of Islam, written by Muhammad

Ten Commandments: Principles given to Moses from God on Mount Sinai

Torah: First five books of the Hebrew Bible, written by Moses

Places of worship

Church: Building for Christian worship that is often cross-shaped

Mandir: Hindu temple for worship

Mosque: Place of worship for Muslims

Synagogue: Jewish house of worship

Vihara: Buddhist monastery

Humanities Analogy Practice

Now, it's time to put your newfound humanities knowledge to use on some MAT-style analogies. Be sure to use good technique in the following questions.

1. VAN GOGH: EXPRESSIONISM :: MONET : _____

   (A) impressionism

   (B) classicism

   (C) surrealism

   (D) cubism

2. DA VINCI : CEZANNE :: _____ : THE CARD PLAYERS

   (A) *The Birth of Venus*

   (B) *Virgin of the Rocks*

   (C) *Easter Monday*

   (D) *Deposition of Christ*

3. _____ : MADRID :: UFFIZI : FLORENCE

   (A) Guggenheim

   (B) Louvre

   (C) Pergamon

   (D) Prado

4. INDENTED : RAISED :: _____ : CAMEO

   (A) doric

   (B) gothic

   (C) intaglio

   (D) pagoda

5. VERSAILLES : _____ :: GREAT SPHINX : EGYPT

   (A) France

   (B) South Africa

   (C) Japan

   (D) Belgium

6. _____ : FRENCH HORN :: PERCUSSION : MARIMBA

   (A) strings

   (B) brass

   (C) woodwinds

   (D) tuba

7. ROSH HASHANAH : _____ :: JUDAISM : ISLAM

   (A) Eid ul-Fitr

   (B) Quaran

   (C) Torah

   (D) Allah

8. ASGARD : _____ :: NORSE : GREEK

   (A) River Styx

   (B) Mecca

   (C) Vatican City

   (D) Mount Olympus

9. POSEIDON : NEPTUNE :: _____ : JUNO

   (A) Pluto

   (B) Zeus

   (C) Hera

   (D) Mercury

10. THE SOCIAL CONTRACT: ROUSSEAU :: UTOPIA : _____

   (A) More

   (B) Plato

   (C) Hobbes

   (D) Voltaire

Answers

1. Choice (A) is correct. (1:2,3:4) Expressionism is the style of van Gogh, and impressionism is the style of Monet.

2. Choice (B) is correct. (1:3,2:4) da Vinci painted _Virgin of the Rocks,_ and Cezanne painted _The Card Players._

3. Choice (D) is correct. (1:2,3:4) The Prado museum is in Madrid, and the Uffizi museum is in Florence.

4. Choice (C) is correct. (1:3,2:4) An intaglio is an indented carving; a cameo is a raised carving.

5. Choice (A) is correct. (1:2,3:4) Versailles is an example of famous architecture in France; the Great Sphinx is an example in Egypt.

6. Choice (B) is correct. (1:2,3:4) The French horn is a brass instrument, and the marimba is a percussion instrument.

7. Choice (A) is correct. (1:3,2:4) Rosh Hashanah is a Jewish holiday, and Eid ul-Fitr is a Muslim holiday.

8. Choice (D) is correct. (1:3,2:4) Asgard is the home of the Norse gods, and Mount Olympus is the home of the Greek gods.

9. Choice (C) is correct. (1:2,3:4) Poseidon/Neptune is the Greek/Roman god of the sea; Hera/Juno is the Greek/Roman goddess of marriage and motherhood.

10. Choice (A) is correct. (1:2,3:4) Rousseau wrote _The Social Contract,_ and More wrote _Utopia._

Chapter 7

Studying the Social Sciences

· ·

In This Chapter

▶ Thinking about geography, history, economics, and political science

▶ Getting familiar with psychology, sociology, and anthropology

▶ Practicing with social sciences analogies

· ·

Social sciences unfortunately don't cover the fine art of how to behave at a party, but they do broadly deal with social behavior and society. They cover a variety of areas: geography, history, economics, political science, psychology, sociology, and anthropology. To build your social science analogy muscles, make sure you're familiar with the main people, terms, and events in these fields.

As with much of the content the MAT tests, you don't have to be able to write a Wikipedia entry on a term to get a question involving that term right — you just have to know the most important fact about the term. For each term in this chapter, I give you the essence of what you need to know so you can do just that.

The Lay of the Land: Getting to Know Geography

You don't have to be able to locate all the world's countries to do well with MAT geography analogies, but the more familiar you are with a map of the world or a globe, the better. In fact, you may want to put up a map on the wall of your study room and check it out when you need a break from reading this book. It's impossible for me to define every geographical term in the world, but the following ones get you started.

Geographical terms

38th parallel north: Line of latitude that divided Korea after World War II

Adriatic Sea: Water that separates Italy from the Balkan peninsula

Aegean Sea: Water that separates Greece and Turkey

Alps: Mountain range in Europe; contains Mount Blanc and the Matterhorn

Amazon River: Second-longest river in the world, located in South America; greatest waterflow

Andes: Longest mountain range in the world, located in South America

Antarctic Circle: Line of latitude, south of which experiences a period of 24-hour sunlight

Appalachian Mountains: Mountain range in eastern North America

Arabian Sea: Branch of Indian Ocean between India, the Arabian Peninsula, and Somalia

Arctic Circle: Line of latitude, north of which experiences a period of 24-hour sunlight

Atlas Mountains: Mountain range in northwest Africa

Black Sea: Large sea separating parts of Europe and Asia

Cartography: The making of maps

Caspian Sea: Largest inland body of water, located in Asia

Chesapeake Bay: Largest estuary in the United States, bordered by Maryland and Virginia

Coordinates: A position on a map, specified by latitude and longitude, ex: 41N 73W

Death Valley: Desert in California; hottest and lowest location in North America

El Niño–Southern Oscillation: A climate pattern where the temperature of the tropical Pacific Ocean warms about every five years

English Channel: Water separating France from Great Britain

Equator: Line of latitude on Earth's surface midway between the North Pole and the South Poles

Erie Canal: Completed in 1825; connects the Atlantic Ocean with Lake Erie via the Hudson River through New York and New Jersey

Everglades: Wetlands in Florida

Gaza Strip: Home to many Palestinian refugees; borders Egypt and Israel

Great Lakes: Five freshwater lakes on the U.S.–Canada border: Lake Superior, Lake Michigan, Lake Huron, Lake Erie, and Lake Ontario

Great Salt Lake: Largest saltwater lake in the Western Hemisphere; located in Utah

Himalayas: World's highest mountain range, located in Asia; contains Mount Everest

Hudson River: South-flowing river in New York, forms a barrier between New York and New Jersey at its bottom end

Iberian Peninsula: Region of southwestern Europe containing Spain, Portugal, and Andorra

International Date Line: Invisible line from the North Pole to the South Pole that separates one day from the next

Kalahari Desert: Desert in southern Africa

Kremlin: Moscow residence of the president of Russia

La Niña: A climate pattern where the temperature of the tropical Pacific Ocean cools about every five years

Lake Titicaca: Largest lake in South America

Lake Victoria: Largest lake in Africa

Latitude: The east–west lines on a map that specify north–south position

Longitude: The north–south lines on a map that specify east–west position

Louisiana Purchase: The 1803 sale of the Louisiana Territory from France to the United States

Mediterranean Sea: Sea between Europe and Africa

Mesopotamia: Location of the cradle of civilization; modern-day Iraq

Mississippi River: Largest river system in North America; flows south through the United States

Missouri River: Longest river in North America

Mount Everest: Tallest mountain in the world, on the China–Nepal border

Mount Kilimanjaro: Tallest mountain in Africa (Tanzania)

Mount McKinley: Tallest mountain in North America (Alaska)

Mount Rushmore: Mountainside sculpture of four U.S. presidents in South Dakota

Niagara Falls: Three waterfalls (Horseshoe Falls, American Falls, and Bridal Veil Falls) on the border of Ontario, Canada and New York

Nile: Longest river in the world; flows north through Africa

Oceania: Large portion of the Pacific Ocean containing thousands of islands

Oregon Trail: East-West wagon trail used by emigrants, traders, trappers, explorers, and pioneers, connecting the Missouri River to Oregon

Pacific Ring of Fire: Area around the Pacific Ocean where most earthquakes and volcanic eruptions take place

Panama Canal: Located in the Central American country of Panama, it was completed in 1914; connects the Atlantic and Pacific oceans

Pangaea: An ancient super-continent; from the Greek "pan" meaning entire and "gaea" meaning Earth

Persian Gulf: Part of the Indian Ocean between Iran and the Arabian Peninsula

Prime meridian: The line of longitude set at 0 degrees; goes through Greenwich, England

River Thames: Longest river in England; flows through London

Sahara: Largest desert in the world, located in Africa

Scandinavia: Region of northern Europe containing Denmark, Norway, and Sweden

Siberia: Huge region comprising most of north Asia, location of many Soviet labor camps (Gulag camps)

Strait of Magellan: Connects the Atlantic and Pacific oceans south of mainland South America

Suez Canal: Completed in 1869; connects the Mediterranean Sea to the Red Sea

Tibet: Region of China northeast of the Himalayas

Tropic of Cancer: Line of latitude that is the most northerly place the sun can be overhead

Tropic of Capricorn: Line of latitude that is the most southerly place the sun can be overhead

Volga: Longest river in Europe, it runs through Central Russia

Past Is Prelude: Honing Your History Knowledge

You know the old saying, "Those who did not learn from history are doomed to have it show up on a test", right? Even if it's been a while since you've thought about history, you can brush up on some of history's biggest moments pretty quickly. To prepare for analogies involving history on the MAT, it's best to start with the most important terms, figures, and events — kind of like what you'd pick up from a basic college course in world history. The following terms, figures, and events give you a good history knowledge foundation.

Historical terms

Abolitionism: Movement to get rid of slavery

Allies: Nations that fought the Axis powers in World War II, including the United States, England, and Russia

Apartheid: Racial segregation in South Africa

Axis: Nations that fought the Allies during World War II, including Germany, Japan, and Italy

Bill of Rights: The first ten amendments of the U.S. Constitution

Bourgeoisie: The middle class in France before the revolution

Caste: A hereditary social class in Hinduism

Cold War: Period of tension after WWII between the United States and the Soviet Union

Communism: Economic system in which the people control the means of production

Confederate States of America: Government of the southern states that seceded from the United States during the Civil War; the northern states were known as the Union

Cultural Revolution: Led by Mao Zedong, a social-political movement in which the Chinese military worked to strengthen the ideals of the Chinese Communist Party

Czar (tsar): An emperor of Russia

Emancipation Proclamation: An order given by Abraham Lincoln on January 1, 1863, to free all slaves

Fourteen Points: Speech given by Woodrow Wilson outlining the post–World War I peace plan in Europe

Geneva Conventions: Developed humanitarian laws to be applied in wartime

Glasnost: Introduced by Mikhail Gorbachev, a period of increased openness and freedom in the Soviet Union during the 1980s; often paired with Perestroika

Great Depression: Decade-long worldwide economic recession preceding World War II

Imperialism: The domination of one country over another

***Laissez-faire* capitalism:** Economic system in which the government does not regulate

Magna Carta: Forced upon King John by his subjects to attain liberties, it is the origination of English law; written in 1215

Manifest Destiny: Belief that Americans were destined by heaven to expand westward to the Pacific Ocean

Mayflower Compact: Governing text of Plymouth Colony

NATO (North Atlantic Treaty Organization): Alliance of nations to defend against Soviet threat

New Deal: Economic programs during the Great Depression proposed by Franklin D. Roosevelt

Perestroika: Political movement for restructuring within the Communist Party of the Soviet Union; often paired with glasnost

Prohibition: The sale, manufacture, and transportation of alcohol was outlawed in the United States from 1920 to 1933

Proletariat: The lower, working social class

Republic: Type of government in which the people elect representatives to rule

Suffrage: The right to vote

Trinity: Code name for the first atomic bomb

Historical figures

Anthony, Susan B.: American civil rights leader who worked to get women's suffrage

Bandaranaike, Sirimavo: Ceylon's (now Sri Lanka) and the world's first female head of government

Bonaparte, Napoleon: French emperor who conquered most of Europe and was then exiled to the island of Elba

Burr, Aaron: Vice President of Thomas Jefferson, killed his political rival, Alexander Hamilton, in a duel in 1804

Carnegie, Andrew: Scottish-American industrialist who expanded steel industry

Castro, Fidel: Communist dictator of Cuba

Charlemagne: Founder of the Carolingian Empire in 800, united Western Europe

Churchill, Winston: Prime minister of the United Kingdom during World War II

Cleopatra: She was the last pharaoh of Ancient Egypt, aligned with Mark Antony after the assassination of Julius Caesar

Columbus, Christopher: Italian explorer who sailed for Spain to the Americas and began the Spanish colonization of the New World

Douglass, Frederick: Escaped slave who worked to free all slaves

Gandhi, Indira: India's and the world's second female head of government

Gandhi, Mohatma: Indian leader who opposed British rule of India through nonviolence

Garvey, Marcus: Jamaican political leader and proponent of Black nationalism

Gorbachev, Mikhail: Final head of state of the Soviet Union, introduced glasnost and Perestroika

Grant, Ulysses S.: Union general in the Civil War and U.S. president

Guevara, Che: Communist revolutionary in South America

Hamilton, Alexander: A Founding Father of the United States and its first Secretary of the Treasury, killed by Aaron Burr in a duel in 1804

Henry VIII: King of England who removed the Catholic Church from England and began the Church of England

Hitler, Adolf: Austrian-born German leader of the Nazi Party, led Germany and the Holocaust during WWII

Ho Chi Minh: Vietnamese communist leader who was a key figure in the founding of North Vietnam and the Viet Cong

Jefferson, Thomas: This Founding Father authored the Declaration of Independence and was the third U.S. president

Joan of Arc: French heroine who led the French army to victories in the Hundred Years' War

Kennedy, John Fitzgerald (JFK): Thirty-fifth president of the United States and noted for his handling of the Bay of Pigs Invasion and the Cuban Missile Crisis, assassinated in 1963 by Lee Harvey Oswald

Kennedy, Robert Francis (RFK): United States senator, attorney general, and brother of JFK; assassinated by Sirhan Sirhan in 1968

King, Martin Luther: American civil rights leader who worked for racial equality

Lee, Robert E.: Confederate general during the American Civil War

Lenin, Vladimir: Leader of the Russian Revolution and the Soviet Union

Louis XIV: King of France who believed in the Divine Right of Kings

Magellan, Ferdinand: Portuguese explorer who led the first circumnavigation of the world though he died during the journey

Malcolm X: Muslim minister and human rights activist, preached black supremacy before becoming more moderate

Mandela, Nelson: Former president of South Africa who spent 27 years in prison, prioritized reconciliation, and won Nobel Peace Prize

Marx, Karl: German philosopher who first created the principles of communism

Meir, Golda: Israel's first and the world's third female head of government, known as the "Iron Lady"

Mother Teresa: Roman Catholic nun known for her missionary and charity work

Peter the Great: Russian czar who modernized Russia and expanded the empire

Rockefeller, J. D.: American industrialist who founded Standard Oil

Roosevelt, Franklin D.: President of the United States during World War II

Stalin, Joseph: Leader of the Soviet Union during World War II

Thatcher, Margaret: The longest-serving and only female prime minister of the United Kingdom, her conservative policies are known as Thatcherism

Washington, George: General during the American Revolutionary War and first U.S. president

Historical events

1970s energy crisis: Shortages of petroleum caused by Arab Oil Embargo and Iranian Revolution

American Civil War: Period in 1861–1865 when the North (Union states) and South (Confederate states) fought over slavery and the Confederates' desire to secede from the Union

American Revolution: Thirteen colonies in North America that broke free from British rule

Apollo 11: First manned landing on the moon, in July 1969

Assassination of Abraham Lincoln: April 14, 1865, in Washington DC. Lincoln was shot by John Wilkes Booth

Attack on Pearl Harbor: Surprise Japanese attack on Hawaii, on December 7, 1941, which led to the United States' involvement in WWII

Bay of Pigs Invasion: Failed attempt by the CIA to overthrow Fidel Castro

Chernobyl disaster: Nuclear accident in the Ukraine on April 26, 1986

Crusades: Religious wars by the Catholic Church to take back the Holy Lands

Easter Rising: Irish insurrection in 1916 that tried to end British rule in Ireland

Fall of the Berlin Wall: On November 9, 1989, East Germany announced that citizens could visit West Gemany; this led to German reunification

Holocaust: Genocide of six million Jews and millions of others during World War II in Europe

Hundred Years' War: Conflicts between England and France between 1337 and 1453

Louisiana Purchase: The purchase of the vast Louisiana Territory by the United States from France in 1803

Manhattan Project: The program by the United States, United Kingdom, and Canada that developed the first atomic bomb

Russian Revolution: 1917 revolutions in Russia that ended the Russian Empire

September 11 attacks: Four hijacked planes attacked targets in the New York City and Washington, D.C., areas in 2001

Thirty Years' War: Series of wars fought in Europe between 1618 and 1648, one of the longest and most destructive wars in European history

Making Cents of Dollars: Explaining Economics

Money makes the world go 'round, and economics deals with the study of how people provide goods and services to one another. Here I give you the basic economics terms you need to know, along with some key economics figures, to give you a working knowledge of what the MAT may test.

Economics terms

Bankruptcy: The legal status of a debtor who cannot pay his debts

Capitalism: Private ownership–based economic system

Communism: Economic system in which the people control the means of production

Consumer Price Index (CPI): Measure of changes in the prices of consumer goods

Credit: Acquiring a good or service and paying for it later

Debt: Money owed

Depression: A severe, long-term recession

Expansion: Period of increased economic activity

Federal Deposit Insurance Corporation (FDIC): Guarantees the security of deposits in banks

Federal Reserve Board of Governors: Group that oversees the central banking system of the United States

Federal Trade Commission (FTC): Protects consumers by opposing anticompetitive business methods

Gift economy: A culture in which goods are given without an agreement for reciprocation

Gross National Product (GNP): Value of products and services produced by a country in a year

Heterodox economics: Economic schools of thought that are not mainstream

Inflation: The rise of prices over time

Interest: A fee paid to borrow money, expressed as a percentage of the money borrowed

Labor union: Group of workers united to achieve common goals that would better their conditions of employment, known as a "trade union" in British English

Market: System in which parties exchange with each other

Mass production: Creating great amounts of products on assembly lines

Monopoly: A single entity is the only supplier of a specific good or service

Protectionism: Government regulating trade between countries to promote domestic trade

Recession: Period of a slowdown of economic activity

Socialism: Social ownership–based political system

Old-Age, Survivors, and Disability Insurance (OASDI): Federal program. The original Social Security Act (1935) and the current version of the act, as amended, encompass several social welfare and social insurance programs

Subsidy: Money paid by a government to a business or industry to help it or to encourage specific behavior

Supply and demand: Model for determining prices of goods in a competitive market

Economics figures

Friedman, Milton: American economist who won the Nobel Prize

Greenspan, Alan: American economist who served as Chairman of the Federal Reserve

Keynes, John Maynard: British economist who contributed to modern macroeconomics

Krugman, Paul: American economist who won the Nobel Memorial Prize

Malthus, Thomas: English political economist who theorized about population growth and decline

Marx, Karl: German economist who first created the principles of communism

Smith, Adam: Scottish economist who wrote *The Wealth of Nations*

Politically Correct: Polishing Your Political Science

Whether you love the intricacies of politics or loathe them, it can be interesting to learn more about how what makes the wheels of government turn. Political science deals with governments and politics, as well as with the systems involved with these entities. To prepare for this content area on the MAT, you need to know the basics of the U.S. government and U.S. politics, as well as be familiar with some important political figures from history.

Political Science terms

Amendment: Alteration of a law

Aristocracy: Government ruled by a small group of (usually elite) citizens

Authoritarianism: A government in which authority rests with a small group of politicians and society is generally submissive to that authority

Autocracy: Government in which all political power rests with one person

Cabinet: High-ranking executive branch officials

Conservative: Someone who believes in retaining traditional institutions

Constitutionalism: Government limited by fundamental laws

Democracy: Type of government in which citizens have a say in decisions

Détente: Relaxed political and military tensions during the Cold War

Dictator: Ruler with complete power

Domino theory: Idea that, if one country becomes communist, its neighbors will follow

Election: Process in which voters choose their leaders

Electoral college: People appointed by each state who elect the President of the United States

Fascism: Radical authoritarian political ideology in which people are united by national identity and the state seeks to eradicate foreign influences

Federalism: Government that divides power between a central authority and smaller divisions

Habeas corpus: A person under arrest must be brought before a judge thereby preventing unlawful detention, translation of Latin: "you have the body"

Impeachment: Formal process by which an official is accused of illegal activity

Jury: Group of people who come to a decision in a courtroom trial

Liberal: Someone who believes in increasing freedom and equality

Nationalism: Ideology in which people strongly identify with their country

Pluralism: Nongovernment entities exert influence on the government and have the belief that there should be diverse and competing centers of power in society

Propaganda: Communication that tries to influence people to side with an issue

Red Scare: Two periods of anti-communism in the United States

Separation of powers: Government divided into branches

Totalitarianism: Government that controls every possible aspect of life

War Powers Resolution: Prevents the President of the United States from entering a war without approval from Congress

Political Science figures

Aldrich, John: American political scientist who wrote the book *Why Parties? The Origin and Transformation of Political Parties in America*, it asserts that parties exist for politicians to achieve their personal desires

Allison, Graham: American political scientist who analyzed government decision making in times of crisis

Hartz, Louis: American political scientist and proponent of American exceptionalism — the belief that America is different from other countries and has an obligation to spread democracy around the world

Huntington, Samuel P.: American political scientist who wrote *Clash of Civilizations*, asserts that in the post-Cold War world conflicts will be caused by the cultural and religious beliefs that people identify with

Machiavelli, Niccolò: Italian founder of modern political science; wrote *The Prince*

Sartori, Giovanni: Italian political scientist and expert on comparative politics

Scott, Dred: Slave in the United States who sued for his freedom

Freudian Slips: Practicing Psychology

Psychology is another minor category that can appear on the MAT. Don't worry — I'm not preparing you to open up your own therapy practice. I'm just giving you some common psychological terms and familiarizing you with some people who have made major contributions to the field. The following lists are a selection of important psychology figures and terms.

Psychology terms

Acute stress reaction: Shock; response to a traumatizing event

Alcoholism: Addiction to alcoholic beverages

Alzheimer's disease: Form of dementia; loss of memory

Anorexia nervosa: Eating disorder in which a person does not eat much and believes, falsely, that he is overweight

Archetype: A universally understood model of a personality or behavior

Attention deficit–hyperactivity disorder (ADHD): Behavioral disorder in which the person is inattentive and hyperactive

Behaviorism: Belief that all actions of an organism are influenced by its environment

Bulimia: Eating disorder in which the person binges and purges

Classical conditioning (AKA Pavlovian conditioning or respondent conditioning): Learning method in which a first stimulus signals a second stimulus

Ego: According to Freud, the part of the mind that seeks to meet the needs of the id in reality

Id: According to Freud, the part of the mind that contains basic instincts

Instinct: Innate inclination toward a behavior

IQ (Intelligence Quotient): A score on a standardized test designed to measure intelligence; 100 is average

Operant Conditioning (AKA instrumental conditioning): Learning method in which the consequences of behavior determine whether that behavior will be repeated

Psychiatrist: Doctor who treats mental illnesses and can prescribe medicine

Psychoanalysis: Therapy in which patient verbalizes thoughts and then confronts defense mechanisms

Psychologist: A trained professional who helps others achieve better well-being and reduce dysfunction

Super-ego: According to Freud, the part of the mind that is our conscience; formed by influences from figures of authority

Psychology figures

Adler, Alfred: Austrian doctor who studied the inferiority complex

Binet, Alfred: French psychologist who invented the first IQ test with Théodore Simon

Ekman, Paul: American psychologist who studied facial expression and emotion

Erikson, Erik: American psychologist who theorized on human development

Freud, Sigmund: Austrian founder of psychoanalysis who studied dreams

Gibson, James: American psychologist who worked in the field of visual perception

Jung, Carl: Swiss psychiatrist who defined personality types

Kübler-Ross, Elisabeth: Swiss-American psychiatrist who studied near-death, death, and dying

Maslow, Abraham: American psychologist who created a hierarchy of human needs

Pavlov, Ivan: Russian psychologist who explained the conditioned reflex by ringing a bell and then feeding dogs

Rogers, Carl: American psychologist who was known for his humanistic approach, he helped found psychotherapy

Simon, Théodore: French psychologist who invented first IQ test with Alfred Binet

Skinner, B. F.: American psychologist who studied behavior and reinforcement

Watson, John B.: American psychologist who established behaviorism

Sharp Social Skills: Sifting through Sociology

You have social skills, but what about your sociology skills? Sociology is just the study of modern society, or the way people act in groups. I've defined a bunch of sociology terms you may not know, along with a few important figures from the field.

Sociology terms

Action theory: Talcott Parsons's belief that social science must consider people's motives when studying their actions

Adoption: Legal process in which the parenting rights and responsibilities are transferred from one person to another

Affirmative action: Policies that benefit minorities or special interest groups in business or education

Antipositivism: The belief that social sciences are not subject to the same methods of understanding as the natural sciences

Antisemitism: Discrimination against Jews

Assimilation: Process by which minorities and immigrants become part of the dominant culture

Black Power: Slogan for ideologies promoting the collective interests of blacks

Cohabitation: An unmarried male and female living together

Cultural relativism: The belief of Franz Boas that civilization is relative, not absolute, and that there is not a relationship between culture and race

Demography: The study of living populations

Diffusion: The process of how innovations spread within an organization or social group

Endogamy: Practice of marrying only a person of a certain group or class

Functionalism: View that society's parts work together to create stability

Gemeinschaft and Gesellschaft: Translated as " community and society" are two normal types of human association according to Ferdinand Tönnies

Gentrification: High-income people acquiring property in low-income areas, as a result of which property values increase and lower-income residents are displaced

Hidden curriculum: Lessons learned in the classroom that were not intentionally taught

Institutional racism: System of inequality based on race

Labeling theory: Tendency of majorities to label minorities with a word or phrase

Macrostructure: Large-scale organization of society

Norm: Guideline that determines behavior of society

Overchoice (AKA choice overload): The problem of consumers having too many choices, this can lead to a consumer making a poor choice or no choice at all

Ponerology: Study of social injustice

Positivism: The belief that in the social and natural sciences the only valid truth is scientific truth

Role homogeneity: Multiple community roles performed by one individual

Scapegoat: A person or group that is singled out to receive unwarranted blame

Social capital: The collective benefits resulting from social cooperation between people or groups

Social stigma: Disapproval of someone who differs from social norms

Tertius gaudens: One person gaining from a disagreement between two others

Underclass: The lowest position in a social hierarchy

Vertical mobility: A person's movement up or down the social-status ladder

Xenocentrism: Preference for products and ideas from another culture, this is the opposite of ethnocentrism

Xenophobia: A fear of people or things from a different culture

Sociology figures

Barzun, Jacques: American historian who studied culture

Coleman, James: American sociologist who defined social capital

Comte, Auguste: A founder of sociology and positivism

DuBois, W. E. B.: American sociologist who cofounded the NAACP (National Association for the Advancement of Colored People)

Durkheim, Émile: French father of sociology

Parsons, Talcott: American sociologist who developed action theory

Simmel, Georg: German sociologist and founder of antipositivism

Spencer, Herbert: English sociologist and biologist who coined the term "survival of the fittest" and applied it to humans in a sociology context

Tönnies, Ferdinand: German sociologist who defined Gemeinschaft and Gesellschaft

Veblen, Thorstein: American sociologist who wrote *The Theory of the Leisure Class* — asserts that the division of labor from the feudal system continued into the modern era

Weber, Max: German sociologist who promoted antipositivism

Be a People Person: Analyzing Anthropology

If you've ever wondered about why people act the way they do, you might find anthropology fascinating. Anthropology is the study of humans and their behavior, but it focuses more on all of human history than does sociology. These terms and figures familiarize you with some common anthropology terms.

Anthropology terms

Anthropocentrism (AKA humanocentrism): Belief that humans are the most important creatures in the world

Balanced reciprocity: Exchange of goods in which the value of each good is equal

Caste: A system of dividing society into rigid socio-economic classes

Clan: A group of people united by a real or imagined kinship

Cultural materialism: View that social life is a reaction to the practical problems of a mortal life

Diffusion: Exchange of ideas from one culture to another

Ethnocentrism: Practice of judging another culture based on your own culture's ideals

Focal vocabulary: Set of words to describe something important to a particular group of people

Genealogy: Study of families and their histories

Generalized reciprocity: Exchange of goods in which the value of each good is not exactly calculated but a fair balance is expected over time

Humanism: Belief that humans are of great value and that science is greater than faith

Indigenous: Being native to a specific place

Joint family: Two or more related families living together which are all part of the same extended family

Kinesics: Interpretation of body language and nonverbal communication

Levirate marriage: The brother of a deceased man marrying his widow by obligation

Linguistic relativity (AKA Sapir-Whorf hypothesis): The idea that language affects the way its speakers think

Matriarchy: Society in which women are the leaders

Multiculturalism: Describes communities that contain multiple cultures and the ideologies that promote such communties

Negative reciprocity: Exchange of goods in which each party intends to profit

Nomad (AKA itinerant): Member of a society that moves around instead of settling in one place

Oligarchy: Power in a society resting with only a small number of people

Patriarchy: Society in which men are the leaders

Redistribution: Altering the distribution of goods and wealth based on specific principles

Religious cosmology: A way of explaining the origin of the universe based on mythology

Structuralism: View that each part of a culture cannot be understood without understanding the culture in whole

Third World: Developing countries, mostly in the Southern Hemisphere

Urbanization: Expansion of cities and urban areas

Westernization: Societies adopting aspects of Western culture

Anthropology figures

Benedict, Ruth: American anthropologist who wrote *The Races of Mankind* which uses scientific evidence to challenge racist ideas

Boas, Franz: German-American father of modern anthropology

Geertz, Clifford: American anthropologist who studied symbols

Hurston, Zora Neale: American anthropologist and author during the Harlem Renaissance

Korotayev, Andrey: Russian anthropologist known for cross-cultural studies

Krantz, Grover: American anthropologist who researched Bigfoot

Leach, Edmund: British anthropologist known for ethnographic work

Leaf, Murray: American anthropologist known for South Asia studies

Lévi-Strauss, Claude: French anthropologist who believed that human traits were the same in all geographic locations

Macfarlane, Alan: British anthropologist and expert on the history of England, Nepal, Japan and China

Malinowski, Bronislaw: Polish anthropologist and proponent of participant observation

Mauss, Marcel: French anthropologist and sociologist who analyzed the significance of gift-giving

Mead, Margaret: American anthropologist who promoted a broadening of sexual mores in Western culture

Radcliffe-Brown, Alfred: English anthropologist who developed Structural Functionalism, the belief that society is a system whose parts work together to create stability

Reichel-Dolmatoff, Gerardo: Austrian anthropologist who studied tropical rainforest cultures

Social Science Analogy Practice

Okay, time to try out your new knowledge on some analogies modeled on MAT analogy questions. As always, be sure to practice good technique for each question, as if you're taking a real MAT.

1. MOUNT BLANC : ALPS :: MOUNT EVEREST : _____

   (A) Andes

   (B) Pyrenees

   (C) Himalayas

   (D) Rockies

2. SLAVERY : ALCOHOL :: _____ : PROHIBITION

   (A) abolitionism

   (B) apartheid

   (C) communism

   (D) suffrage

3. RECESSION : _____ :: DEBIT : CREDIT

   (A) depression

   (B) expansion

   (C) inflation

   (D) monopoly

4. _____ : DICTATORSHIP :: NATIONALISM : FASCISM

   (A) Aristocracy

   (B) Democracy

   (C) Republic

   (D) Autocracy

5. BINET : WATSON :: _____ : CRICK

   (A) Simon

   (B) Einstein

   (C) Jung

   (D) Freud

6. ANTISEMITISM : ENDOGAMY :: AFFIRMATIVE ACTION : _____

   (A) institutional racism

   (B) social stigma

   (C) xenocentrism

   (D) labeling theory

7. MISSOURI : _____ :: NORTH AMERICA : EUROPE

   (A) Nile

   (B) Volga

   (C) Amazon

   (D) Danube

8. CARNEGIE : ROCKEFELLER :: STEEL : _____

   (A) oil

   (B) textiles

   (C) automobiles

   (D) radio

9. MARX : COMMUNISM :: KEYNES : _____

   (A) microeconomics

   (B) socialism

   (C) capitalism

   (D) macroeconomics

10. ID: SIBERIA :: _____ : ASIA

    (A) ego

    (B) superego

    (C) mind

    (D) Freud

Answers

1. Choice (C) is correct. (1:2,3:4) Mount Blanc is a mountain in the Alps, and Mount Everest is a mountain in the Himalayas.

2. Choice (A) is correct. (1:3,2:4) Abolitionism is the movement to end slavery, and prohibition is the movement to get rid of alcohol.

3. Choice (B) is correct. (1:2,3:4) A recession is a decrease in economic activity, and an expansion is an increase in economic activity. A debit is an amount owed, and a credit is an amount gained.

4. Choice (D) is correct. (1:2,3:4) In an autocracy and dictatorship, power rests with one person. With nationalism and fascism, people are united by a strong sense of national identity.

5. Choice (A) is correct. (1:3,2:4) Binet and Simon worked together to develop the IQ test. Watson and Crick worked together to discover DNA.

6. Choice (C) is correct. (1:2,3:4) Antisemitism and endogamy are examples of discriminating against those who are different from you. Affirmative action and xenocentrism are ways of appreciating those who are different from you.

7. Choice (B) is correct. (1:3,2:4) The Missouri is the longest river in North America, and the Volga is the longest river in Europe.

8. Choice (A) is correct. (1:3,2:4) Carnegie was a magnate in the steel industry, and Rockefeller was a magnate in the oil industry.

9. Choice (D) is correct. (1:2,3:4) Marx profoundly influenced the theory of communism, and Keynes profoundly influenced the theory of macroeconomics.

10. Choice (C) is correct. (1:3,2:4) The id is a part of the mind, and Siberia is a part of Asia.

Chapter 8

Studying Science and Math

● ●

In This Chapter

▶ Reviewing the basics of the sciences

▶ Mastering basic mathematical knowledge

▶ Practicing with math and science analogies

● ●

Science and math aren't the most prevalent topics on the MAT, but they are tested. Luckily, you don't need to be a math major or a scientist to do well with MAT math and science analogies. You just need to know the basics about the major natural sciences (biology, chemistry, and physics) and know a little bit about numbers. You also want to know how to do basic arithmetic, algebra, and geometry.

The following lists aren't designed to cover every topic under the sun; they're just a selection of the most important concepts in science and math. Memorizing these entries builds your science and math muscles and increases the chances you'll ace those types of MAT analogies.

Birds and Bees: Biology

Biology covers the birds and the bees, plus a whole lot more: It's the study of life. The following lists give you some major biological terms and figures that you'd encounter as a bio major in college. Don't worry — there's no frog dissection required this time.

Terms

Abscission: Process by which an organism sheds a part of itself

Acclimatization: The process in which an organism adjusts to its surroundings

Aerobic organism: Organism that has an oxygen-based metabolism

Amino acid: Building block of proteins

Anatomy: Study of the structure of organisms

Arachnology: Study of arachnids (examples: spiders, scorpions)

Bacteria: Microorganisms without a cell nucleus

Bacteriophage: Virus that infects bacteria

Biochemistry: Study of chemical processes in living things

Biology: Study of life and living things

Botany: Study of plant life

Cell membrane: Barrier between a cell and its environment

Cell nucleus: Organelle in a cell containing genetic information

Chloroplast: Plant organelle that does photosynthesis

Chromosome: DNA and protein in cells, and contains genes

Cytoplasm: The gel inside of a cell that organelles are suspended in

Deciduous: Type of organism that sheds parts of itself

DNA: Nucleic acid with genetic instructions for reproduction

Ecology: Study of the relationship between life and its environment

Ecosystem: Community of living things

Egg: Place where an embryo begins to develop

Embryo: Earliest stage of multicellular life

Endemism: Life unique to a geographical area

Enzyme: Molecule that speeds up chemical reactions

Ethology: Study of animal behavior

Gene: Unit of heredity

Genetics: Science of genes and heredity

Herpetology: Study of amphibians

Histology: Study of microscopic anatomy

Ichthyology: Study of fish

Insulin: Hormone that regulates metabolism

Invertebrate: Animal with no vertebral column

Krebs cycle: Reactions by aerobic life to produce energy

Larva: Young form of animals before metamorphosis

Leukocyte: White blood cell; part of the immune system

Ligament: Tissue that connects bones to other bones

Lipids: Molecules, including fats and waxes

Mammalogy: Study of mammals

Marine biology: Study of ocean-based life

Meiosis: Cell division required for sexual reproduction

Microbiology: Study of microscopic life

Mitosis: Process in which chromosomes split into two identical sets

Mycology: Study of fungi

Neurobiology: Study of the nervous system

Oncology: Study of cancer

Ornithology: Study of birds

Osmosis: Movement of molecules through a membrane

Parasitology: Study of parasites and their hosts

Physiology: Study of the physical functions of organisms

Phytopathology: Study of plant diseases

Transcription: In genetics, the copying of DNA to RNA

Vacuole: Membrane-enclosed organelle in all plant cells

Virology: Study of viruses

Zoology: Study of the animal kingdom

Figures

Crick, Francis: English cofounder of DNA with James Watson

Darwin, Charles: English naturalist who proposed natural selection

Fleming, Alexander: Scottish biologist who discovered penicillin

Goodall, Jane: British expert on chimpanzees

Hippocrates: Ancient Greek father of Western medicine

Lamarck, Jean-Baptiste: French naturalist and proponent of evolution

Lister, Joseph: British surgeon who pioneered antiseptics

Mendel, Gregor: Founder of genetics who worked with pea plants

Pasteur, Louis: French microbiologist who invented pasteurization

Pavlov, Ivan: Russian scientist who worked with dogs to show a conditioned response

Sabin, Albert: American scientist who developed an oral polio vaccine

Salk, Jonas: American scientist who developed the first polio vaccine

Watson, James: American cofounder of DNA with Francis Crick

Beyond Bunsen Burners: Chemistry

Some chemistry terms are familiar because we use them in everyday conversation: "reaction", "catalyst", etc. Others may be a little bit less familiar. Overall, chemistry analogies on the MAT require knowledge of many terms you encounter in a typical high school chemistry class, plus a familiarity with the who's who of chemists throughout history. These lists fill you in on the most important chemistry terms and figures.

Terms

Absolute zero: Theoretical temperature, the coldest possible

Acid: Something that reacts with a base, with a pH of less than 7

Activation energy: Energy that must be overcome for a chemical reaction to occur

Aeration: Process in which air is mixed with a liquid

Anion: Negatively charged ion

Atom: Smallest form of a chemical element, made of protons, neutrons, and electrons

Atomic number: Number of protons in the nucleus of an atom

Barometer: Device used to measure atmospheric pressure

Base: Something that reacts with an acid, with a pH of more than 7

Biochemistry: Study of chemical processes in life forms

Boiling: Phase transition of a liquid rapidly vaporizing

Bond: Attraction between atoms that allows chemicals to form

Catalyst: Substance that changes the rate of a reaction

Cation: Positively charged ion

Centrifuge: Device that uses rotation to separate substances

Chemical reaction: Process that changes one chemical substance to another

Colloid: Mixed substances that are evenly dispersed

Combustion: Burning with fuel, heat, and oxygen

Compound: Pure substance with at least two chemical elements

Condensation: Change from a gas to a liquid

Conductor: Material that allows electricity to flow

Deposition: Settling of particles in a solution

Electrolyte: Electrically conducive substance

Electron: Elementary particle with no charge

Entropy: Even distribution of a system

Freezing: Phase transition of a liquid to a solid

Frequency: Number of events per unit of time

Gas: State of matter in which particles have no definite volume

Geochemistry: Chemistry of the Earth's composition

Indicator: Compound added to a solution that changes color depending on acidity

Inorganic compound: Nonbiological, or lacking carbon and hydrogen

Insulator: Material that resists the flow of electricity

Ion: Atom that has gained or lost an electron

Ionization: Process of converting an atom into an ion

Kinetics: Study of the rates of chemical processes

Lattice: Arrangement of atoms or molecules in a crystal

Liquid: State of matter that has a fixed volume but not shape

Melting: Phase change from a solid to a liquid

Mole: Measurement that contains $6.02x10^{23}$ units

Molecule: Neutral group of atoms held together by bonds

Neutron: Neutral part of an atom's nucleus

Nucleus: Center of an atom, made of protons and electrons

Organic chemistry: Chemistry of carbon-based compounds

pH: Measure of the acidity of a solution

Plasma: State of matter similar to a gas, in which some particles are ionized

Precipitate: Formation of a solid in a solution

Proton: Positive part of an atom's nucleus

Quark: Elementary particle of matter

Reagent: Substance that is added to a system to get a reaction

Sol: Suspension of solids in a liquid

Solid: State of matter in which molecules resist movement

Solute: The part of the solution that is put into the solvent

Solvent: The part of the solution that dissolves the solute

Sublimation: Phase transition from a solid to a gas

Triple point: Temperature and pressure at which three states of matter exist simultaneously

Valence electron: Outermost electrons of an atom

Vaporization: Phase change from a liquid to a gas

Viscosity: Measure of resistance of a fluid, or thickness

Yield: Amount of a product made in a chemical reaction

Figures

Avogadro, Amedeo: Italian scientist who worked in molecular theory

Curie, Marie: French-Polish chemist known for work in radioactivity

Lavoisier, Antoine: French father of modern chemistry

Lewis, Gilbert: American chemist who discovered the covalent bond

McMillan, Edwin: American chemist who first produced the transuranium element

Mendeleev, Dmitri: Russian chemist who invented the periodic table of elements

Mohr, Karl Friedrich: German chemist known for conservation of energy principle

Nobel, Alfred: Swedish chemist and inventor of dynamite

Pauling, Linus: American quantum chemist who won multiple Nobel prizes

Woodward, Robert Burns: American organic chemist

Getting Physical: Physics

Mass, velocity, acceleration — yep, it's time to review all the physics you learned in high school. Getting familiar with physics doesn't entail learning any complicated equations. You just have to remember some physics terms and learn about some famous physicists. These lists help you remember the basics.

Terms

Acceleration: Rate at which velocity changes with time

Acoustics: Science that deals with the study of mechanical waves

Adhesion: Tendency for different types of particles to cling together

Aerodynamics: Study of the motion of air when it interacts with solid objects

Alloy: Metallic mixture of two different elements

Alternating current: Movement of electric charge that reverses direction

Ampere: Unit of electric current

Angstrom: One ten-billionth of a meter

Astronomical unit: Distance from Earth to the sun

Background radiation: Ionizing radiation that is always present in Earth's atmosphere

Big bang: Model that explains the early development of the universe

Binary star: Star system with two stars orbiting around each other

Black hole: Region of space where gravity prevents everything from escaping

Boson: Fundamental particle

Buoyancy: Upward force that opposes the weight of a submerged object

Celsius: Scale and measurement unit for temperature

Centripetal force: Force that makes something follow a curved path

Cohesion: Tendency for like particles to cling together

Density: Mass per volume

Dew point: Temperature at which water vapor condenses to liquid water

Displacement: Fluid moving out of the way when an object is placed in it

Doppler effect: Change in the frequency of a wave when the observer moves

Drag: Air resistance or fluid resistance

Elasticity: Property of an object returning to its original shape after a force is applied

Endothermic: Reaction in which the system absorbs energy from its surroundings

Equilibrium: A system in balance

Exothermic: Reaction in which the system releases energy

Farad: Unit of capacitance

Fission: Process in which the nucleus of an atom splits into smaller parts

Force: Mass times acceleration

Friction: Force resisting the motion of materials sliding against each other

Fusion: Process in which multiple atomic nuclei join to create a larger nucleus

Gamma ray: Electromagnetic radiation of high frequency

General relativity: Einstein's theory of gravitation

Hertz: Unit of frequency, defined as cycles per second

Inertia: Resistance of an object to change in its motion

Joule: Unit of heat

Lever: Simple machine consisting of a beam pivoting on a hinge

Light: Electromagnetic radiation visible to the human eye

Mass: Amount of matter in a body

Matter: Anything that has mass and volume

Momentum: Mass times velocity

Neutrino: Neutral elementary particle

Ohm: Unit of electrical resistance

Pendulum: Suspended weight that can swing on a pivot

Photon: Elementary particle of light

Pneumatics: Application of pressurized gas to affect motion

Pressure: Ratio of force to area

Pulley: Simple machine; a wheel on an axle that moves a cable along its circumference

Quantum mechanics: Physics dealing with atomic and subatomic particles

Supernova: Explosion of a star

Temperature: Physical property that expresses notions of hot and cold

Torque: Tendency of a force to rotate an object on an axis

Transducer: Device that converts energy from one form to another

Uncertainty principle: Principle that the position and momentum of a particle cannot be simultaneously known

Vacuum: Space that is empty of matter

Watt: Unit of power

Figures

Ampere, Andre-Marie: French founder of classical electromagnetism

Archimedes: Ancient Greek scientist known for hydrostatics

Becquerel, Antoine Henri: French physicist who helped discover radioactivity

Bernoulli, Daniel: Swiss physicist who worked on fluid dynamics

Bohr, Niels: Danish physicist who contributed to quantum mechanics

Einstein, Albert: German physicist known for general and special relativity

Faraday, Michael: English scientist known for work in electromagnetism

Fermi, Enrico: Italian-American physicist who developed the nuclear reactor

Galileo: Italian astronomer and father of modern physics

Heisenberg, Werner: German physicist credited for creating quantum mechanics

Newton, Isaac: English physicist who described three laws of motion

Planck, Max: German physicist who came up with quantum theory

Tesla, Nikola: Serbian-American known for contributions to alternating current electricity

And Now: Other Sciences

Science is so broad that there are a variety of sub-disciplines. The MAT also tests sciences like astronomy and ecology, and although these kinds of analogies are more rare, it's still a good idea to memorize the following lists. The good news is that you don't have to know that many terms and figures.

Terms

Acid rain: Precipitation with a low pH that's harmful to life and infrastructure

Amber: Fossilized tree resin

Andromeda galaxy: Galaxy closest to the Milky Way

Asteroid: Small body that orbits the sun

Astronomy: Study of celestial objects (stars, planets, galaxies, and so on)

Comet: Small icy body that shows a coma and tail when close to the sun

Constellation: Pattern of stars in the sky

Distillation: Way of separating the parts of a liquid mixture

Energy: Ability to do work

Galaxy: System of at least 10 million stars held together by gravity

Gravitation: Gravity; bodies attract each other based on their masses

Greenhouse effect: Heat is absorbed by atmospheric gases and redirected back to Earth

Half-life: Time for a quantity to reach half of its starting value

Heliocentric: Model in which the planets revolve around the sun

Igneous rock: Rock formed from cooled lava

Light-year: Unit of length; distance light travels in a year; about 6 trillion miles

Lunar eclipse: The moon covered by Earth's shadow

Metamorphic rock: An igneous or sedimentary rock exposed to heat and pressure

Meteor: Visible path of a meteoroid in the atmosphere

Meteorite: Meteoroid that survives impact on the surface

Meteoroid: Small body in the solar system; smaller than asteroid

Milky Way: Our home galaxy

Orbit: Curved path of an object around another object

Plate tectonics: Theory that describes the motions of Earth's crust

Pulsar: A rotating, magnetized neutron star

Quasar: Very bright nucleus of a distant galaxy

Satellite: A natural or artificial object that orbits another object

Sedimentary rock: Rock formed by deposits in bodies of water

Seismometer: Instrument that measures the motion of the ground

Solar eclipse: The moon passing in front of the sun

Solar system: The sun and all objects (planets, comets, and so on) that orbit it

Sunspot: Dark, relatively cool areas on the sun's surface

Thermodynamics: Study of heat on other forms of energy

Figures

Bell, Alexander Graham: American inventor of the telephone

Copernicus, Nicolaus: Polish astronomer who was the first to propose the heliocentric model

Diesel, Rudolf: German inventor of the diesel engine

Edison, Thomas: American inventor of the light bulb

Franklin, Benjamin: American inventor of bifocal glasses

Kepler, Johannes: German astronomer known for planetary motion laws

Marconi, Guglielmo: Italian inventor of the radio

Morse, Samuel: American coinventor of the telegraph and Morse code

Pascal, Blaise: French inventor of mechanical calculator

Ptolemy: Greek-Roman astronomer who wrote the _Almagest_

Rontgen, Wilhelm: German who detected and produced x-rays

Staying Classy: Classification

There are so many plants and animals that it only makes sense that we came up with a way to sort them all out. Classification of living things is a fairly common MAT topic, so be familiar with the following terms.

Kingdom: One of five major classification units

Phylum: Division of kingdom

Class: Division of phylum

Order: Division of class

Family: Division of order

Genus: Division of family; always italicized, with the first letter capitalized

Species: Division of genus; smallest unit of classification; always italicized, with the first letter lower case

Human example: Animal, Chordate, Vertebrate, Primate, Hominid, *Homo, sapiens*

Animalia kingdom: Humans, dogs, fish, birds, reptiles

Fungi kingdom: Yeasts, molds, mushrooms

Monera kingdom: Unicellular organisms without a cell nucleus

Plantae kingdom: Flowers, trees, ferns, mosses

Protista kingdom: Microorganisms with a cell nucleus

Animals

The MAT has also been known to test animal terms, even obscure ones, so knowing what to call male and female animals, their babies, and a group of that animal can pay off.

(**Animal:** Male, Female, Offspring, Group, Adjective)

Bear: Boar, sow, cub, sleuth, ursine

Bee: Drone, queen, larva, swarm, apian

Cat: Tom, queen, kitten, clowder, feline

Cattle: Bull, cow, calf, herd, bovine

Chicken: Rooster, hen, chick, brood

Deer: Buck, doe, fawn, herd, corvine

Ferret: Hob, jill, kit, business, ferrety

Fox: Dog, vixen, kit, skulk, vulpine

Goat: Billy, nanny, kid, tribe, goatish

Goose: Gander, goose, gosling, gaggle

Horse: Stallion, mare, foal, herd, equine

Kangaroo: Jack, doe, joey, troop

Lion: Lion, lioness, cub, pride, leonine

Pig: Boar, sow, piglet, sounder, porcine

Sheep: Ram, ewe, lamb, flock, ovine

Swan: Cob, pen, cygnet, wedge, swanlike

It's Elementary: The Periodic Table

If you took chemistry in high school, you probably spent a good amount of time staring at the periodic table, a chart that organizes all the known elements according to their properties. Instead of memorizing the whole table, memorize just the following terms.

Actinide: Fifteen metallic elements with the atomic numbers 89–103

Alkali metal: Highly reactive elements; shiny, soft, and silvery

Alkaline earth metal: Moderately reactive natural elements; shiny and silvery white

Atomic mass: Total mass of protons, neutrons, and electrons in an atom

Atomic number: Number of protons in the nucleus of an atom

Chemical symbol: One- or two-letter code for a chemical element

Halogen: Series of very reactive nonmetals

Isotope: Variant of a chemical element; protons are the same, but neutrons vary

Lanthanide: Fifteen metallic elements with the atomic numbers 57–71

Mass number: Total number of protons and neutrons in a nucleus

Metal: Element that is a good conductor of electricity and heat

Metalloid: Elements that are a mix between metals and nonmetals

Noble gas: Six odorless, colorless gases with low reactivity

Nonmetal: Group of elements that are poor conductors of heat and electricity; dull and brittle

Periodic table: Display of the chemical elements

Post-transition metal: Metals to the right of transition elements on the periodic table

Rare earth element: Seventeen elements; lanthanides plus scandium and yttrium

Transition metal: Familiar metals such as iron, nickel, copper, and gold

Learning about Measurement

You'd think that there would be one standard for measuring things by this point in human history — but sadly, that is not the case. The human race has invented so many terms for measuring things that learning them all can seem daunting. These lists give you the most important terms to know for the MAT.

Ampere: Unit of electrical current

Beaufort: Scale that measures wind speed

Bit: Unit in computer engineering; ⅛ of a byte

Byte: Unit in computer engineering; 8 bits

Caliber: Diameter of a bullet or shell

Carat: Measures diamonds or gold

Celsius: Temperature scale on which 0 is freezing and 100 is boiling

Centi-: Metric prefix; ⅟₁₀₀

Cord: 128 cubic feet of timber

Curie: Unit of radioactivity

Deci-: Metric prefix; ⅟₁₀

Decibel: Logarithmic unit that measures sound

Fahrenheit: Temperature scale on which 32 is freezing and 212 is boiling

Fathom: Used for measuring depth; 6 feet

Furlong: Unit of distance; ⅛ of a mile

Hectare: 2.47 acres of land

Hertz: Unit of frequency

Joule: Unit of energy

Kelvin: Temperature scale on which all degrees equal Celsius plus 273

Kilo-: Metric prefix; 1,000

Knot: Unit of speed for ships

League: Unit of distance for ships; 3 miles

Milli-: Metric prefix; ⅟₁₀₀₀

Ohm: Unit of electrical resistance

pH: Scale that measures acids and bases

Richter: Scale that measures movements of the earth

Score: 20

Stone: 14 pounds

Volt: Unit of electricity

Watt: Unit of power

Mastering Mathematics

Math: it really is everywhere, even the MAT. If you don't like math, don't worry: The MAT doesn't require you to do a lot of calculation. But you do have to know a few things about the basic math a high school student would learn, as well as be familiar with numbers, even Roman numerals. These lists help fill in any math gaps you might have.

Roman numerals

Strangely enough, we still use Roman numerals today, even though they're more cumbersome than our normal numbering system. And since the MAT likes to test them, make sure you study the following list to get the basic rules and numbers.

When smaller values precede larger values, the smaller values are subtracted from the larger values.

I: 1

V: 5

X: 10

L: 50

C: 100

D: 500

M: 1,000

Arithmetic

Arithmetic is stuff like adding, subtracting, multiplying, and dividing. These terms are the basics of what you need to know for the MAT.

Addition: Combining numbers

Average: The number you get when you add a set of things and divide it by the number of things

Decimal point: A period that marks the place value for numbers with values less than 1

Denominator: Bottom number of a fraction

Difference: Answer to a subtraction problem

Dividend: The number that is divided in a division problem

Division: Finding out how many times one number can be put into another

Divisor: The number that divides into the dividend

Exponent: A small number placed to the upper right of a number that indicates how many times to multiply that number by itself

Factor: A number being multiplied in a multiplication problem

Fraction: A number that expresses part of a whole number

Multiplication: Adding the same number to itself a certain amount of times

Numerator: The top number of a fraction

Prime number: A number that can be divided only by itself and 1

Product: Answer to a multiplication problem

Quotient: Answer to a division problem

Square root: The original number's square root is a number that, when multiplied by itself, gives you the original number

Subtraction: Taking one number away from another to get a smaller number

Sum: Answer to an addition problem

Algebra

You don't have to know many algebraic terms for the MAT, but you do need to be familiar with a few — and here they are.

Coordinates: Two points that define a position on a line graph

Equation: Statement that two expressions are equal

Parabola: Shape with one curve and two lines going away from it

Geometry

You have to cover a bunch of geometrical terms for the MAT. Use the following lists to relearn anything you've forgotten from that high school geometry class.

Acute angle: An angle that measures less than 90 degrees

Angle: Space between two lines meeting at the same point, measured in degrees

Arc: Part of the circumference of a circle, measured in degrees

Area: Amount of surface a shape has

Circle: Round shape in which all points on the circumference are the same distance from the center

Circumference: Edge of a circle

Congruent: Identical

Degree: Unit of measurement for angles and arcs

Diameter: Line from one point to another on a circle's circumference that passes through its center

Ellipse: Round shape like an oval

Equilateral triangle: Triangle with all sides and angles being equal

Geometry: Study of shapes

Hexagon: Shape with six sides

Hypotenuse: Longest side of a right triangle

Isosceles triangle: Triangle in which two sides and angles are equal

Obtuse angle: Angle that measures more than 90 degrees

Octagon: Shape with eight sides

Parallel: Two lines on the same plane that never cross

Parallelogram: Shape with four sides in which opposite sides are parallel to each other

Pentagon: Shape with five sides

Perimeter: Distance around the edge of a shape

Perpendicular: Two lines that form a 90-degree angle

Pi: Ratio of a circumference to its diameter; approximately 3.14

Polygon: Shape with all straight lines

Radius: Length of a line drawn from the center of a circle to a point on its circumference

Rectangle: Shape with four sides and four right angles

Rhombus: Shape with four sides but no right angles

Right angle: Angle that is exactly 90 degrees

Right triangle: Triangle that contains a right angle

Scalene triangle: Triangle in which no sides are the same length

Square: Shape with four sides of equal length

Trapezoid: Shape with four sides and only two sides that are parallel to each other

Triangle: Shape with three sides

Science/Math Analogy Practice

Time to practice with a few science and math analogies and apply your new knowledge! Remember to use good technique as you work through these MAT-style questions.

1. ABSCISSION : DECIDUOUS :: DIVISION : _____

   (A) dividend

   (B) divisor

   (C) factor

   (D) quotient

2. ISOSCELES TRIANGLE : _____ :: SCALENE TRIANGLE : TRAPEZOID

   (A) right triangle

   (B) line

   (C) rhombus

   (D) pentagon

3. _____ : XXXVI :: 81 : LXXXI

   (A) 34

   (B) 35

   (C) 36

   (D) 360

4. KRYPTON : NOBLE :: _____ : HALOGEN

   (A) planet

   (B) hydrogen

   (C) oxygen

   (D) chlorine

5. FERRET: BUSINESS :: _____ : SOUNDER

   (A) lion

   (B) pig

   (C) giraffe

   (D) antelope

6. PASCAL : MARCONI :: CALCULATOR : _____

   (A) telephone

   (B) telegraph

   (C) television

   (D) radio

7. QUASAR : BLACK HOLE :: CYTOPLASM : _____

  (A) mitochondrion

  (B) nebula

  (C) cilia

  (D) acid

8. GENUS : _____ :: ATOM : QUARK

  (A) order

  (B) family

  (C) species

  (D) kingdom

9. ICHTHYOLOGY : ORNITHOLOGY :: _____ : CARDINAL

  (A) robin

  (B) iguana

  (C) salmon

  (D) newt

10. _____ : x :: 125 : 5

  (A) x

  (B) x2

  (C) x3

  (D) x^4

Answers

1. Choice (A) is correct. (1:2,3:4) *Deciduous* describes a tree that goes through the process of abscission; a dividend is a type of number that goes through the process of division.

2. Choice (C) is correct. (1:3,2:4) Isosceles triangles and scalene triangles are types of three-sided shapes; rhombuses and trapezoids are types of four-sided shapes.

3. Choice (C) is correct. (1:2,3:4) XXXVI is 36, as LXXXI is 81.

4. Choice (D) is correct. (1:2,3:4) Krypton is a noble gas, and chlorine is a halogen.

5. Choice (A) is correct. (1:2,3:4) A business is a group of ferrets, as a sounder is a group of pigs.

6. Choice (D) is correct. (1:3,2:4) Pascal developed the calculator, as Marconi developed the radio.

7. Choice (A) is correct. (1:2,3:4) A quasar contains a black hole, as a cell contains a mitochondrion.

8. Choice (C) is correct. (1:2,3:4) Species are divisions of genera (the plural of genus); quarks are divisions of atoms.

9. Choice (C) is correct. (1:3,2:4) Ichthyology is the study of fish (for example, salmon), and ornithology is the study of birds (for example, cardinals).

10. Choice (C) is correct. (1:2,3:4) x^3 is x cubed, as 125 is 5 cubed.

Part III

MAT Practice Exams

Five Tips for Practice Tests

Prepare like it's the real deal.

Get a good night sleep and have a healthy breakfast before settling in with your practice test. You want to feel at your best.

Relax.

Anxiety is your worst enemy when taking a test, so be sure to breath, stretch your body, sit comfortably, and keep your nerves at bay.

Time yourself.

The MAT is a timed test. Time yourself when taking practice tests to ensure you get as real-world an experience as possible.

Location matters.

Take the practice tests in a quiet environment with no distractions.

Review.

Review your answers carefully so you can identify and conquer your mistakes.

 Find more biology basics at www.dummies.com/extras/mat.

In this part . . .

✔ Flex your test-taking muscles with six practice test, each
loaded with 120 questions that represent the types of analogies
and subjects you can expect on the actual exam.

✔ Time your practice tests to get a sense of the pace you'll keep
on test day, and take the tests in a quiet place to mimic as
closely as possible the actual testing environment.

✔ Check your answers and pay particular attention to identifying
the types of analogies or subject questions that give you the
most trouble.

Chapter 9
MAT Practice Test #1

*I*f you're ready to take a full-length MAT exam, you're in the right place! This exam is similar to a real MAT and helps you get used to the way the MAT poses questions. Remember to use good technique throughout the test as you take it. If you want to make the experience realistic, don't just look through the test. Instead, take it all at once, timed strictly, in a room where you won't be interrupted for an hour.

As you take the test, it's a good idea to circle questions you guessed on — after all, if you get them right, it may just be luck. Review questions you guessed on as carefully as you review questions you got wrong. After taking the test, review your mistakes and guesses as best you can so you learn as much as possible from the experience. Good luck!

1. COMPUTER : SINGER :: _____ : SING

   (A) compute
   (B) song
   (C) printer
   (D) musician

2. AIR : _____ :: HORMONES : ENDOCRINE SYSTEM

   (A) esophagus
   (B) trachea
   (C) oxygen
   (D) glands

3. FOUL : _____ :: SPORT : SOCIAL

   (A) party
   (B) game
   (C) stigma
   (D) referee

4. (6, 8) : 10 :: (7, 24): _____

   (A) 2
   (B) 17
   (C) 13
   (D) 25

5. NEWSPAPER : _____ :: NEWS : SYNONYMS

   (A) headline
   (B) author
   (C) thesaurus
   (D) words

6. CLEAN : _____ :: HAPPY : JUBILANT

   (A) sparkling
   (B) dirty
   (C) sad
   (D) emotion

7. MATHIEU : ROUSSEAU :: ALBERTO : _____

   (A) Smith
   (B) Mikhail
   (C) Peter
   (D) Martinez

8. CARPENTER : MUSICIAN :: PROTRACTOR : _____

   (A) tool
   (B) metronome
   (C) wood
   (D) album

9. DROPPING : HIT :: FLIES : _____

   (A) hay
   (B) swat
   (C) baseball
   (D) drooping

10. BOARD : DIRECTORS :: _____ : STAIRS

    (A) airplane
    (B) movie
    (C) flight
    (D) screening

11. _____ : TRACE :: CLAY : SCULPT

    (A) Stencils
    (B) Crayons
    (C) Paint
    (D) Statue

12. RIFLE : CARTRIDGE :: SLING : _____

    (A) bullet
    (B) stone
    (C) cast
    (D) weapon

13. AFFECTATION : ANATHEMA :: SINCERITY : _____

   (A) asthma

   (B) effected

   (C) genuine

   (D) treasure

14. PRETTY : BEAUTIFUL :: UGLY : _____

   (A) gorgeous

   (B) average

   (C) duckling

   (D) hideous

15. YELLOW : GREEN :: _____ : CALLOW

   (A) red

   (B) blue

   (C) chicken

   (D) broccoli

16. VOLUNTEER : PLEDGE :: SOUP KITCHEN : _____

   (A) fraternity

   (B) allegiance

   (C) church

   (D) chef

17. EGOTISTIC : NARCISSISTIC :: BENEVOLENCE : _____

   (A) altruism

   (B) selfish

   (C) malevolence

   (D) sarcastic

18. (–4, –7) : (7, –4):: (–6, 8) : _____

   (A) (6, 8)

   (B) (–8, -6)

   (C) (–6, 8)

   (D) (–8, 6)

19. _____ : RESIDENCY :: JUDGE : PHYSICIAN

   (A) Intern

   (B) Judge

   (C) Stewardship

   (D) Clerkship

20. _____ : PERCUSSION :: EUPHONIUM : TIMPANI

   (A) Saxophone

   (B) Brass

   (C) Steel

   (D) Triangle

21. LEDERHOSEN : KIMONO :: GERMAN : _____

   (A) Chinese

   (B) Mexican

   (C) Japanese

   (D) Russian

22. TRUNK : BOOT :: HUMOR : _____

   (A) humour

   (B) elephant

   (C) foot

   (D) comedy

23. DOG : _____ :: HAUNCH : LEG

   (A) cat

   (B) paw

   (C) withers

   (D) canine

24. _____ : SYCOPHANT:: CLANDESTINE : INSINCERE

   (A) Barber

   (B) Grocer

   (C) Secretary

   (D) Spy

25. DETAILING : CLEANLINESS :: SERVICING : _____

(A) filthiness
(B) functionality
(C) details
(D) shininess

26. GIVEN NAME : STAGE NAME :: MARSHALL : _____

(A) general
(B) Eminem
(C) Madonna
(D) last name

27. PHYSICS : _____ :: TRIGONOMETRY : ENGINEERING

(A) phonology
(B) entomology
(C) cosmology
(D) sinology

28. DEPRESSION : SADNESS :: AGONY : _____

(A) pain
(B) gladness
(C) hill
(D) irony

29. PTEROPUS : PTERODACTYLUS :: _____ : WREN

(A) dinosaur
(B) flying
(C) terror
(D) wrestle

30. INTEGER : NATURAL :: –4 : _____

(A) [½]
(B) 0.25
(C) 16
(D) –8

31. SOLID : SQUALID :: VALID : _____

(A) dirty
(B) braid
(C) liquid
(D) clean

32. QUIZ : INQUISITION :: CROWN : _____

(A) frown
(B) coronation
(C) irrigation
(D) test

33. PROMOTION : CASTLE :: PAWN : _____

(A) job
(B) sell
(C) king
(D) fortress

34. TRIANGULAR PRISM : 5 :: PENTAGONAL PRISM : _____

(A) 3
(B) 4
(C) 7
(D) 8

35. DEER : SHEEP :: _____ : MUTTON

(A) cow
(B) glutton,
(C) wool
(D) venison

36. DRUGS : _____ :: PHARMACOLOGIST : HYPNOLOGIST

(A) hypnosis
(B) sleep
(C) hydrogen
(D) marijuana

37. ROOD : _____ :: ACRE : SQUARE CHAIN

    (A) perch

    (B) roost

    (C) Acme

    (D) bird

38. WATT : POWER :: NEWTON : _____

    (A) Fig

    (B) amp

    (C) force

    (D) Isaac

39. GRANDMOTHER : GERIATRIC :: _____ : NEONATE

    (A) mother

    (B) great-great-granddaughter

    (C) grandfather

    (D) doctor

40. _____ : BEES :: BOTANY : PLANTS

    (A) Cetology

    (B) Cynology

    (C) Herpetology

    (D) Apiology

41. DIRECT : INDIRECT :: OBLIQUE : _____

    (A) prepositional

    (B) straight

    (C) angle

    (D) obtuse

42. CIRCLE : ELLIPSE :: _____ : PARABOLA

    (A) oval

    (B) vertical

    (C) cone

    (D) geometry

43. _____ : DIAMETER :: ARC : RADIUS

    (A) Diameters

    (B) Circle

    (C) Circumference

    (D) Demeter

44. SQUARE : _____ :: two : three

    (A) sphere

    (B) triangle

    (C) four

    (D) cube

45. NUDGE : PUSH :: _____ : DECIMATE

    (A) damage

    (B) shove

    (C) poke

    (D) decimal

46. GORILLA : GUERRILLA :: PRIMATE : _____

    (A) probate,

    (B) jungle

    (C) soldier

    (D) monkey

47. CAULFIELD : SALINGER :: _____ : SPIELBERG

    (A) Holden

    (B) Neary

    (C) Steven

    (D) Skywalker

48. DAMMING : RESERVOIR :: DIVISION : _____

    (A) quotient

    (B) dividend

    (C) river

    (D) beaver

49. VENOM : _____ :: FORMIC : GLUCONIC

    (A) milk

    (B) water

    (C) honey

    (D) snake

50. 24 IN. : 2 FT. :: 2^4 : _____

    (A) 2

    (B) 6

    (C) 8

    (D) 16

51. CHAPTER : _____ :: NOVEL : OPERA

    (A) act

    (B) section

    (C) classical

    (D) fiction

52. QUINARY : SEPTENARY :: 5 : _____

    (A) 9

    (B) 6

    (C) 1

    (D) 7

53. TRUSS : BUTTRESS :: BRIDGE : _____

    (A) trust

    (B) mattress

    (C) wall

    (D) tunnel

54. TUNER : _____ :: DIMMER : BRIGHTNESS

    (A) light

    (B) frequency

    (C) printer

    (D) switch

55. SENATOR : GOVERNMENT :: _____ : FLORA

    (A) shrub

    (B) Senate

    (C) Capitol

    (D) plants

56. PSYCHOLOGY : ANTHROPOLOGY :: _____ : BIOLOGY

    (A) bacteriology

    (B) oenology

    (C) sinology

    (D) geology

57. _____ : GENE :: CELL : CYTOPLASM

    (A) DNA

    (B) Capillary

    (C) Membrane

    (D) Prison

58. FISH : CARP :: _____ : WOLF

    (A) fang

    (B) spider

    (C) werewolf

    (D) shark

59. SANCTIFICATION : CONSECRATION :: TERMINATION : _____

    (A) contribution

    (B) commencement

    (C) completion

    (D) holy

60. PHYSICS : MEDICINE :: CALCULATIONS : _____

    (A) physician

    (B) physicist

    (C) examinations

    (D) stethoscope

61. _____ : DEER :: VULPINE : FOX

   (A) Bovine

   (B) Fawn

   (C) Doe

   (D) Corvine

62. DORSAL : VENTRAL :: SPINE : _____

   (A) left foot

   (B) right hand

   (C) brain stem

   (D) navel

63. HEPTAGON : 7 :: TETRAHEDRON : _____

   (A) 4

   (B) 5

   (C) 6

   (D) 7

64. _____ : STUMBLE :: SING : WALK

   (A) Serenade

   (B) Skip

   (C) Croak

   (D) March

65. INSECT : _____ :: BUTTERFLY : CATERPILLAR

   (A) pupa

   (B) chrysalis

   (C) cocoon

   (D) larva

66. IGNEOUS : PUMICE :: METAMORPHIC : _____

   (A) obsidian

   (B) marble

   (C) ingenious

   (D) sedimentary

67. BRACELET : EARRING :: BANGLE : _____

   (A) wearing

   (B) necklace

   (C) dangle

   (D) bangs

68. CURSE : BLESSING :: DISEASE : _____

   (A) health

   (B) influenza

   (C) witch

   (D) prayer

69. MONSIGNOR : PRESIDENT :: _____ : CONGRESS

   (A) senator

   (B) conclave

   (C) priest

   (D) Capitol

70. PHYLUM : CLASS :: _____ : FAMILY

   (A) genus

   (B) teacher

   (C) parent

   (D) order

71. _____ : EXCITEMENT :: ENNUI : APATHY

   (A) Ideology

   (B) Boredom

   (C) Effect

   (D) Empathy

72. BIPLANE : JET :: _____ : MOBILE

   (A) airplane

   (B) rotary

   (C) telephone

   (D) engine

73. RAYS : VERTEX :: STREETS : _____
    - (A) lines
    - (B) vortex
    - (C) intersection
    - (D) line segments

74. STAPLES : _____ :: PAPERS : BOARDS
    - (A) paperclips
    - (B) exams
    - (C) trees
    - (D) nails

75. ABSTRACT : NOVELLA :: PAINTING : _____
    - (A) novel
    - (B) book
    - (C) novelette
    - (D) impressionist

76. COMPLAIN : _____ :: CURMUDGEON : DEMAGOGUE
    - (A) whine
    - (B) bludgeon
    - (C) manipulate
    - (D) demigod

77. INUIT : IGLOO :: BACKPACKER : _____
    - (A) hostel
    - (B) ice
    - (C) traveler
    - (D) bookkeeper

78. INCORRIGIBLE : _____ :: PUNCTUAL : TARDINESS
    - (A) patience
    - (B) reformability
    - (C) mischievousness
    - (D) time

79. CONTENTS : _____ :: INDEX : TERMS
    - (A) bibliography
    - (B) author
    - (C) preface
    - (D) titles

80. SEXTET : 6 :: TRIO : _____
    - (A) 2
    - (B) 12
    - (C) 3
    - (D) 4

81. VEHICLE : AUTOGYRO :: _____ : TARTINE
    - (A) motorcycle
    - (B) sandwich
    - (C) bicycle
    - (D) soup

82. SODIUM BICARBONATE : BAKING SODA :: PATELLA : _____
    - (A) kneecap
    - (B) baking powder
    - (C) vinegar
    - (D) shoulder blade

83. _____ : JAILOR :: PRISONER : INMATE
    - (A) Jail
    - (B) Incarceration
    - (C) Turnkey
    - (D) Prison

84. ATOMIC NUMBER : MASS NUMBER :: PROTONS : _____
    - (A) neutrons
    - (B) electrons
    - (C) nuclei
    - (D) nucleons

85. _____ : ARCHIPELAGO :: FJORD : PENINSULA

    (A) Ocean

    (B) Bay

    (C) Ponds

    (D) Atoll

86. ELECTRIC CAPACITANCE : ELECTRIC RESISTANCE :: FARAD : _____

    (A) joule

    (B) ohm

    (C) hertz

    (D) lumen

87. BLAME : BRUSH :: LAME : _____

    (A) rush

    (B) paint

    (C) guilt

    (D) comb

88. MALLEABLE : _____ :: BRITTLE : RUNNY

    (A) viscous

    (B) ductile

    (C) watery

    (D) plasticity

89. MCENROE : BORG :: NICKLAUS : _____

    (A) Connors

    (B) Woods

    (C) Picard

    (D) Palmer

90. EQUINE : OVINE :: CLYDESDALE: _____

    (A) leopard

    (B) Labrador

    (C) Rambouillet

    (D) goat

91. COMEDY : _____ :: ARISTOPHANES : HOMER

    (A) satyr

    (B) epic

    (C) astronomy

    (D) geology

92. AREA : CIRCUMFERENCE :: πr^2 : _____

    (A) diameter

    (B) radius

    (C) πd

    (D) 1

93. WEAK INTERACTION : FERMIONS :: FERROMAGNETISM : _____

    (A) aluminum

    (B) quarks

    (C) strong interaction

    (D) iron

94. SOLAR SYSTEM : PLANETS :: _____ : VEGETABLES

    (A) carrot

    (B) salad

    (C) galaxy

    (D) seeds

95. CRUCIFIX : CHRISTIANITY :: _____ : TAOISM

    (A) Hinduism

    (B) Islam

    (C) yin-yang

    (D) fleur-de-lis

96. ABSTRUSE : FATHOMABLE :: RECONDITE : _____

    (A) comprehensible

    (B) unfathomable

    (C) obtuse

    (D) recondition

97. JOSEPHINE : _____ :: CLEOPATRA : MARK ANTONY

    (A) Lancelot

    (B) Paris

    (C) Paolo

    (D) Napoleon

98. LEAD : RULE :: _____ : SUBJECTS

    (A) Pb

    (B) guideline

    (C) followers

    (D) pipe

99. ALUMNI : _____ :: APPENDICES : APPENDIX

    (A) graduate

    (B) alumnus

    (C) alumnis

    (D) alumnix

100. _____ : 2 :: 99 : 33

    (A) 3

    (B) 22

    (C) 66

    (D) 6

101. _____ : EAGLE :: SING : SCREAM

    (A) Whale

    (B) Hawk

    (C) Karaoke

    (D) Afraid

102. ALVEOLI : BRONCHIOLES :: _____ : PYLORUS

    (A) incus

    (B) ureter

    (C) cardia

    (D) fovea

103. PUJARI : RABBI :: _____ : CROSIER

    (A) priest

    (B) kapala

    (C) paganism

    (D) Pope

104. ABDUCTION : _____ :: EXEMPLAR : EXAMPLES

    (A) adjective

    (B) data

    (C) abductors

    (D) exemplary

105. APOCRYPHAL : AUTHENTICITY :: ASSIDUOUS : _____

    (A) truthfulness

    (B) apothegm

    (C) hardworking

    (D) laziness

106. ORTHONYM : ALIAS :: _____ : PSEUDOSCIENTIFIC

    (A) pseudonym

    (B) orthopedic

    (C) systematic

    (D) metaphysics

107. HARANGUE : LECTURE :: HARDY : _____

    (A) indefatigable

    (B) lectern

    (C) lactulose

    (D) picayune

108. GUSTATORY CALYCULI : TASTE :: OLFACTORY BULB : _____

    (A) sight

    (B) bitter

    (C) umami

    (D) smell

109. 1 DM : 10 CM :: 1 CUBIC METER :
     _____

     (A) 1,000,000 cubic dm

     (B) 10 cubic dm

     (C) 1,000,000 cubic cm

     (D) 10,000 cubic cm

110. TOJO : MACARTHUR :: HINDENBURG :
     _____

     (A) airship

     (B) Pershing

     (C) disaster

     (D) Douglas

111. PHONOGRAPH : _____ :: SPEAKING
     TUBE : TELEPHONE

     (A) cassette deck

     (B) gramophone

     (C) needle

     (D) telegraph

112. _____ : WALLFLOWER :: TIMID : SHY

     (A) Recidivist

     (B) Milquetoast

     (C) Virtuoso

     (D) Sunflower

113. _____ : SPEECH :: APOSTROPHE :
     POSSESSIVE

     (A) Generous

     (B) Guillotine

     (C) Keynote

     (D) Guillemet

114. CHERRY : _____ :: TOMATO :
     SQUASH

     (A) vegetable

     (B) maraschino

     (C) summer

     (D) fruit

115. RATIONAL : IRRATIONAL :: $\sqrt{4}$:
     _____

     (A) $\sqrt{3}$

     (B) 3.5

     (C) 3

     (D) $\sqrt{9}$

116. RUSSIA : FEDERAL SUBJECT :: JAPAN :
     _____

     (A) county

     (B) municipality

     (C) prefecture

     (D) oblast

117. SKATE : _____ :: SIDEWALK : TRAIL

     (A) wheels

     (B) roller

     (C) street

     (D) off-road

118. JUMBLE : HODGEPODGE :: LINEUP :
     _____

     (A) police

     (B) array

     (C) bumble

     (D) hedgehog

119. FREUD : COPERNICUS :: JUNG :
     _____

     (A) Tesla

     (B) Galileo

     (C) Adler

     (D) Curie

120. _____ : 4 FT., 3 IN. :: 5 IN. : 1 FT., 3
     IN.

     (A) 1 ft., 5 in.

     (B) 1 ft., 7 in.

     (C) 2 ft., 3 in.

     (D) 2 ft., 9 in.

Chapter 10

Answers to MAT Practice Test #1

Now that you've finished taking the first practice MAT, make sure that you spend time learning from your mistakes. Also, be sure to take a second look at any questions you guessed on — if you just got lucky, there is probably something to be learned. Your mistakes should be helpful in pointing you toward areas where you need to learn more content, and they may illuminate flaws in your technique.

1. Choice (A) is correct. (1:3,2:4) **Sing** is the verb form of **singer,** and **compute** is the verb form of **computer.**

2. Choice (B) is correct. (1:2,3:4) The trachea has air passing through it, and the endocrine system has hormones passing through it.

3. Choice (C) is correct. (1:3,2:4) A foul is undesirable in sports, and a stigma is undesirable in social settings.

4. Choice (D) is correct. (1:2,3:4) 6 squared + 8 squared = 10 squared. 7 squared + 24 squared = 25 squared.

5. Choice (C) is correct. (1:3,2:4) One finds news in a newspaper and synonyms in a thesaurus.

6. Choice (A) is correct. (1:2,3:4) **Sparkling** means "extremely clean," and **jubilant** means "extremely happy."

7. Choice (D) is correct. (1:2,3:4) **Mathieu** and **Rousseau** are French names; **Alberto** and **Martinez** are Spanish names.

8. Choice (B) is correct. (1:3,2:4) A protractor is a tool that a carpenter uses; a metronome is a tool that a musician uses.

9. Choice (A) is correct. (1:3,2:4) "Dropping like flies" and "hit the hay" are idioms.

10. Choice (C) is correct. (1:2,3:4) A board is a group of directors; a flight is a group of stairs.

11. Choice (A) is correct. (1:2,3:4) One traces with stencils and sculpts with clay.

12. Choice (B) is correct. (1:2,3:4) A rifle fires a cartridge; a sling launches a stone.

13. Choice (D) is correct. (1:3,2:4) **Affectation** and **sincerity** are opposites, as are **anathema** and **treasure.**

14. Choice (D) is correct. (1:2,3:4) **Beautiful** means "very pretty"; **hideous** means "very ugly."

15. Choice (C) is correct. (1:3,2:4) **Yellow** and **chicken** both mean "cowardly"; **green** and **callow** both mean "inexperienced."

16. Choice (A) is correct. (1:3,2:4) One volunteers at a soup kitchen; one pledges at a fraternity.

17. Choice (A) is correct. (1:2,3:4) **Egotistic** and **narcissistic** are synonyms, as are **benevolence** and **altruism.**

18. Choice (B) is correct. (1:2,3:4) With positions (w, x) : (y, z) the numbers in positions w and z should be the same and have the same signs. The numbers in positions x and y should be the same and have opposite signs.

19. Choice (D) is correct. (1:3,2:4) A judge begins his career with a clerkship; a physician begins his career with a residency.

20. Choice (B) is correct. (1:3,2:4) The euphonium is a brass instrument, and the timpani is a percussion instrument.

21. Choice (C) is correct. (1:3,2:4) Lederhosen is a German garment; kimono is a Japanese garment.

22. Choice (A) is correct. (1:2,3:4) Americans call a part of their cars *trunk*; Britons call the same part *boot.* Americans spell **humor** as **humor**; Britons spell it as *humour.*

23. Choice (D) is correct. (1:2,3:4) Dog and canine are synonyms; haunch and leg are also synonyms.

24. Choice (D) is correct. (1:3,2:4) A spy is clandestine. A sycophant is insincere.

25. Choice (B) is correct. (1:2,3:4) Detailing increases a car's cleanliness; servicing improves a car's functionality.

26. Choice (B) is correct. (1:2,3:4) The entertainer Marshall Mathers's given name is Marshall, and his stage name is Eminem.

27. Choice (C) is correct. (1:2,3:4) Physics is used by those who study cosmology. Trigonometry is used by those who study engineering.

28. Choice (A) is correct. (1:2,3:4) Depression is severe sadness; agony is severe pain.

29. Choice (D) is correct. (1:2,3:4) *Pteropus* and *pterodactylus* have the same first two letters, the first of which is silent. *Wrestle* and *wren* have the same first two letters, the first of which is silent.

30. Choice (C) is correct. (1:3,2:4) –4 is an integer, and 16 is a natural number.

31. Choice (A) is correct. (1:3,2:4) *Solid* and *valid* are synonyms; *squalid* and *dirty* are synonyms.

32. Choice (B) is correct. (1:2,3:4) An inquisition is a process that quizzes people; a coronation is a process that crowns someone.

33. Choice (C) is correct. (1:3,2:4) In chess, a promotion is something that a pawn does and castle is something that a king does.

34. Choice (C) is correct. (1:2,3:4) A triangular prism has five faces; a pentagonal prism has seven faces.

35. Choice (D) is correct. (1:3,2:4) Meat from deer is called venison; meat from sheep is called mutton.

36. Choice (B) is correct. (1:3,2:4) A pharmacologist studies drugs, and a hypnologist studies sleep.

37. Choice (A) is correct. (1:2,3:4) Roods and perches are units of area, with roods being larger. Acres and square chains are units of area, with acres being larger.

38. Choice (C) is correct. (1:2,3:4) A watt is a unit of power, and a newton is a unit of force.

39. Choice (B) is correct. (1:2,3:4) A grandmother could be a geriatric, and, of the choices, only a great-great-granddaughter could be a neonate.

40. Choice (D) is correct. (1:2,3:4) Apiology is the study of bees, and botany is the study of plants.

41. Choice (A) is correct. (1:2,3:4) *Direct, indirect, oblique,* and *prepositional* are all types of objects in grammar.

42. Choice (B) is correct. (1:2,3:4) A circle is a type of ellipse; *vertical* is a type of parabola. Both ellipses and parabolas are conic sections.

43. Choice (C) is correct. (1:3,2:4) The circumference and an arc of a circle are both curved. The diameter and radius of a circle are both straight.

44. Choice (D) is correct. (1:2,3:4) A square is two-dimensional, and a cube is three-dimensional.

45. Choice (A) is correct. (1:2,3:4) **Nudge** and **push** are synonyms, with the meaning of **nudge** being weaker. **Damage** and **decimate** are synonyms, with the meaning of **damage** being weaker.

46. Choice (C) is correct. (1:3,2:4) A gorilla is a primate, and a guerrilla is a soldier.

47. Choice (B) is correct. (1:2,3:4) Caulfield is the surname of the protagonist in *The Catcher in the Rye,* by author J. D. Salinger. Neary is the surname of the protagonist in *Close Encounters of the Third Kind,* from writer/director Steven Spielberg.

48. Choice (A) is correct. (1:2,3:4) Damming leads to the creation of a reservoir, and division leads to the creation of a quotient.

49. Choice (C) is correct. (1:3,2:4) Formic acid is found in venom, and gluconic acid is found in honey.

50. Choice (D) is correct. (1:2,3:4) Twenty-four inches is the same as 2 feet; 2^4 is the same as 16.

51. Choice (A) is correct. (1:3,2:4) A chapter is a division of a novel; an act is a division of an opera.

52. Choice (D) is correct. (1:3,2:4) A quinary numeral system has a base of 5; a septenary numeral system has a base of 7.

53. Choice (C) is correct. (1:3,2:4) A truss supports a bridge; a buttress supports a wall.

54. Choice (B) is correct. (1:2,3:4) A tuner controls radio frequency; a dimmer controls the brightness of a light.

55. Choice (A) is correct. (1:2,3:4) A senator belongs to a government; a shrub belongs to the flora of a location.

56. Choice (A) is correct. (1:2,3:4) Anthropology is the study of humans; a branch of that is psychology, the study of human behaviors. Biology is the study of life; a branch of that is bacteriology, the study of bacteria.

57. Choice (A) is correct. (1:2,3:4) DNA contains genes; a cell contains cytoplasm.

58. Choice (B) is correct. (1:2,3:4) Carp is a kind of fish; wolf is a kind of spider.

59. Choice (C) is correct. (1:2,3:4) **Sanctification** and **consecration** are synonyms, as are **termination** and **completion.**

60. Choice (C) is correct. (1:3,2:4) Calculations are commonly done in the field of physics; examinations are commonly done in the field of medicine.

61. Choice (D) is correct. (1:2,3:4) **Corvine** means "relating to deer"; **vulpine** means "relating to foxes."

62. Choice (D) is correct. (1:3,2:4) The spine is on a human's dorsal side; the navel is on a human's ventral side.

63. Choice (A) is correct. (1:2,3:4) A heptagon is a two-dimensional shape with seven sides; a tetrahedron is a three-dimensional shape with four faces.

64. Choice (C) is correct. (1:3,2:4) To croak is to sing poorly; to stumble is to walk poorly.

65. Choice (D) is correct. (1:3,2:4) A butterfly is a type of insect, and a caterpillar is the larva of a butterfly.

66. Choice (B) is correct. (1:2,3:4) Pumice is a type of igneous rock; marble is a type of metamorphic rock.

67. Choice (C) is correct. (1:3,2:4) A bangle is a type of bracelet; a dangle is a type of earring.

68. Choice (A) is correct. (1:3,2:4) Disease is usually considered a curse; health is usually considered a blessing.

69. Choice (B) is correct. (1:3,2:4) A monsignor is a religious figure of authority; a conclave is a council of religious authorities. A president is a political figure of authority; a congress is a council of political authorities.

70. Choice (D) is correct. (1:2,3:4) In taxonomy, classes make up phyla and families make up orders.

71. Choice (A) is correct. (1:2,3:4) One usually needs an ideology to feel excitement; one usually needs to feel ennui to have apathy.

72. Choice (B) is correct. (1:2,3:4) A biplane is an older type of airplane; a jet is a current type of airplane. **Rotary** is an older type of telephone; **mobile** is a newer type of telephone.

73. Choice (C) is correct. (1:2,3:4) Rays come together in a vertex, and streets come together in an intersection.

74. Choice (D) is correct. (1:3,2:4) Staples hold papers together; nails hold boards together.

75. Choice (B) is correct. (1:3,2:4) An abstract is a type of painting; a novella is a type of book.

76. Choice (C) is correct. (1:3,2:4) A curmudgeon is someone who complains a lot; a demagogue is someone who manipulates.

77. Choice (A) is correct. (1:2,3:4) An Inuit sleeps in an igloo; a backpacker sleeps in a hostel.

78. Choice (B) is correct. (1:2,3:4) Someone who is incorrigible is not known for reformability; someone who is punctual is not known for tardiness.

79. Choice (D) is correct. (1:2,3:4) In a book, chapter titles are found in the table of contents; important terms are found in the index.

80. Choice (C) is correct. (1:2,3:4) A sextet is a group of six; a trio is a group of three.

81. Choice (B) is correct. (1:2,3:4) An autogyro is a kind of vehicle; a tartine is a kind of sandwich.

82. Choice (A) is correct. (1:2,3:4) **Sodium bicarbonate** is the scientific name for baking soda; **patella** is the scientific name for the kneecap.

83. Choice (C) is correct. (1:2,3:4) **Turnkey** and **jailor** are synonyms; **prisoner** and **inmate** are also synonyms.

84. Choice (D) is correct. (1:3,2:4) The atomic number is the number of protons in an atom; the mass number is the number of nucleons in an atom.

85. Choice (C) is correct. (1:2,3:4) Ponds are multiple bodies of water surrounded by land; an archipelago is multiple landmasses surrounded by water. A fjord is a body of water mostly surrounded by land; a peninsula is a landmass mostly surrounded by water.

86. Choice (B) is correct. (1:3,2:4) A farad is a unit of electric capacitance; an ohm is a unit of electric resistance.

87. Choice (A) is correct. (1:3,2:4) **Lame** is **blame** without the **b**; **rush** is **brush** without the **b**.

88. Choice (A) is correct. (1:3,2:4) **Malleable** and **brittle** are antonyms; **viscous** and **runny** are also antonyms.

89. Choice (D) is correct. (1:2,3:4) John McEnroe and Björn Borg were great rivals in tennis. Jack Nicklaus and Arnold Palmer were great rivals in golf.

90. Choice (C) is correct. (1:3,2:4) A Clydesdale is a type of horse, which is an equine animal. A Rambouillet is a type of sheep, which is an ovine animal.

91. Choice (B) is correct. (1:3,2:4) Aristophanes was an ancient Greek writer of comedies. Homer was an ancient Greek author of epics.

92. Choice (C) is correct. (1:3,2:4) The formula for the area of a circle is πr^2. The formula for the circumference of a circle is πd.

93. Choice (D) is correct. (1:2,3:4) Weak interaction is a force that acts upon fermions; ferromagnetism is a force that acts upon iron.

94. Choice (B) is correct. (1:2,3:4) Planets make up a solar system; vegetables make up a salad.

95. Choice (C) is correct. (1:2,3:4) The crucifix is the symbol of Christianity; the yin-yang is the symbol of Taoism.

96. Choice (A) is correct. (1:3,2:4) *Abstruse* and *recondite* both mean "hard to understand." *Fathomable* and *comprehensible* both mean "able to understand."

97. Choice (D) is correct. (1:2,3:4) Josephine and Napoleon were a historical couple with great political power. The same can be said of Cleopatra and Mark Antony.

98. Choice (C) is correct. (1:3,2:4) One leads followers; one rules over subjects.

99. Choice (B) is correct. (1:2,3:4) *Alumni* is the plural form of *alumnus. Appendices* is the plural form of *appendix.*

100. Choice (D) is correct. (1:2,3:4) Six is three times more than 2; 99 is three times more than 33.

101. Choice (A) is correct. (1:3,2:4) The sounds that a whale makes are called singing; the sounds that an eagle makes are called screaming.

102. Choice (C) is correct. (1:2,3:4) Alveoli and bronchioles are parts of the lung; the cardia and pylorus are parts of the stomach.

103. Choice (B) is correct. (1:2,3:4) A pujari and a rabbi are both people involved with religious ceremony. A kapala and a crosier are both objects involved with religious ceremony.

104. Choice (B) is correct. (1:2,3:4) Abduction is a type of reasoning that uses data; exemplar is a type of reasoning that uses examples.

105. Choice (D) is correct. (1:2,3:4) If something is apocryphal, it is lacking in authenticity. If someone is assiduous, he is lacking in laziness.

106. Choice (C) is correct. (1:2,3:4) An orthonym is a real name; an alias is a fake name. Real science is done systematically; fake science is pseudoscientific.

107. Choice (A) is correct. (1:2,3:4) *Harangue* and *lecture* are synonyms; *hardy* and *indefatigable* are also synonyms.

108. Choice (D) is correct. (1:2,3:4) The gustatory calyculi (taste buds) detect taste; the olfactory bulb detects smell.

109. Choice (C) is correct. (1:2,3:4) One decimeter equals 10 centimeters; 1 cubic meter equals 1,000,000 cubic centimeters.

110. Choice (B) is correct. (1:2,3:4) Tōjō and MacArthur were opposing commanders in World War II. Hindenburg and Pershing were opposing commanders in World War I.

111. Choice (A) is correct. (1:2,3:4) The phonograph is a device that preceded the cassette deck; both are used to record and play sounds. The speaking tube preceded the telephone; both are used to communicate over distances.

112. Choice (B) is correct. (1:2,3:4) *Milquetoast* and *wallflower* are synonyms, meaning a person who is shy; *timid* and *shy* are synonyms.

113. Choice (D) is correct. (1:2,3:4) Guillemets are punctuation marks that show speech. An apostrophe is a punctuation mark that can show the possessive case.

114. Choice (C) is correct. (1:3,2:4) *Cherry* is a type of tomato; *summer* is a type of squash.

115. Choice (A) is correct. (1:3,2:4) $\sqrt{4}$ is an example of a rational number; $\sqrt{3}$ is an example of an irrational number.

116. Choice (C) is correct. (1:2,3:4) The federal subject is a division of Russia; the prefecture is a division of Japan.

117. Choice (D) is correct. (1:3,2:4) One skates along sidewalks; one off-roads along trails.

118. Choice (B) is correct. (1:2,3:4) *Jumble* and *hodgepodge* are synonyms; *lineup* and *array* are also synonyms.

119. Choice (B) is correct. (1:3,2:4) Freud and Jung were psychiatrists; Copernicus and Galileo were astronomers.

120. Choice (A) is correct. (1:2,3:4) 1 ft., 5 in. is one-third of 4 ft., 3 in; 5 in. is one-third of 1 ft., 3 in.

Chapter 11

MAT Practice Test #2

*Here's the second MAT practice test. Again, this exam is similar to a real MAT and helps you get accustomed to the way the MAT poses questions. Remember to use good technique throughout the test as you take it. If you want to make the experience realistic, then don't just look through the test. Instead, take it all at once, timed strictly, in a room where you won't be interrupted for an hour.

As you take the test, it's a good idea to circle questions you guessed on — after all, if you get them right, it may just be luck. Review questions you guessed on as carefully as you review questions you got wrong. After taking the test, review your mistakes and guesses as best you can so you learn as much as possible from the experience. Good luck!

1. CONFUSE : CONFOUND :: _____ :
CREATE
   (A) coerce
   (B) craft
   (C) choose
   (D) croon

2. PARLOR : PARLOUS :: ROOM :
_____
   (A) dangerous
   (B) shop
   (C) ice cream
   (D) roof

3. _____ : SEA LION :: ARACHNID :
SPIDER
   (A) Struthio
   (B) Squamata
   (C) Pinniped
   (D) Seal

4. _____ : SCREWDRIVER ::
FLASHLIGHT : POWER DRILL
   (A) Phillips
   (B) Hammer
   (C) Moonlight
   (D) Candelabra

5. _____ : DRINK :: CUISINE : FOOD
   (A) Libation
   (B) Kitchen
   (C) Menu
   (D) Bread

6. –CYTE : –ALGIA :: _____ : PAIN
   (A) algae
   (B) cell
   (C) blood
   (D) small

7. TENOR : MALE :: _____ : FEMALE
   (A) bass,
   (B) contralto,
   (C) soprano,
   (D) alto

8. VOUCH : ADVISE :: _____ :
RECOMMEND
   (A) deny
   (B) favorite
   (C) guidance
   (D) certify

9. TEETH : _____ :: WOODWINDS :
SAXOPHONES
   (A) gums
   (B) molars
   (C) jaws
   (D) tongue

10. EISENHOWER : _____ ::
INTERSTATE HIGHWAY SYSTEM : NEW
DEAL
   (A) Roosevelt
   (B) Lincoln
   (C) Ford
   (D) Hoover

11. VOCIFERATE : SUSURRATE :: SHOUT :
_____
   (A) vocalize
   (B) speak
   (C) whisper
   (D) yell

12. POVERTY : _____ :: PENURY :
RECIDIVIST
   (A) destitution
   (B) covertly
   (C) tenure
   (D) criminal

13. REAL NUMBER : IMAGINARY NUMBER :: 16 : _____

    (A) √–16

    (B) 4

    (C) –4

    (D) √16

14. _____ : 9π :: 27 : 81π

    (A) 1

    (B) 3

    (C) 9

    (D) 18

15. SIMILE : _____ :: ALLITERATION : REPEATING

    (A) reiterating

    (B) smile

    (C) comparing

    (D) literate

16. ORBIT : GRAVITATION :: _____ : SOL

    (A) sun

    (B) Milky Way

    (C) Halley's Comet

    (D) black hole

17. _____ : FREQUENCY :: BQ : HZ

    (A) Inductance

    (B) Pressure

    (C) Entropy

    (D) Radioactivity

18. LAMP : PYRE :: _____ : TIMBER

    (A) kerosene

    (B) lumberjack

    (C) light

    (D) fire

19. _____ : PRAISE :: CRITICISM : COMMENDATION

    (A) Denigrate

    (B) Commend

    (C) Award

    (D) Prize

20. _____ : COMPARATIVE :: SUPERMARKET : AUGMENTATIVE

    (A) Worst

    (B) Better

    (C) Best

    (D) Market

21. EVAPORATE : DESECRATE :: WATER : _____

    (A) steam

    (B) condensation,

    (C) shrine,

    (D) waiter

22. LESS : FEWER :: MASS NOUN : _____

    (A) proper noun

    (B) adverb

    (C) more

    (D) count noun

23. DECIDUOUS : _____ :: CONIFEROUS : JUNIPER

    (A) pine

    (B) decide

    (C) Jupiter

    (D) maple

24. FAIN : FAINT :: _____ : WEAK

    (A) feeble

    (B) willingly

    (C) week

    (D) feint

25. _____ : SHIP :: FLOOR : DECK

    (A) Patio

    (B) Ceiling

    (C) Building

    (D) Car

26. INDIGNATION : _____ ::
    CONSTERNATION : TREPIDATION

    (A) umbrage

    (B) jubilation

    (C) indigo

    (D) intaglio

27. CIRCULATORY : _____ AORTA ::
    ENDOCRINE :

    (A) jugular

    (B) brain

    (C) thyroid

    (D) coccyx

28. SEE : SEAL :: _____ : KEEL

    (A) plea

    (B) boat

    (C) eye

    (D) key

29. _____ : BASSOON :: TRUMPET :
    TUBA

    (A) Reed

    (B) Piccolo

    (C) Symphony

    (D) Bocal

30. FEEDBACK : CATALYST :: LAUGHTER :
    _____

    (A) funeral

    (B) joke

    (C) enzyme

    (D) catalyze

31. SEDENARY : _____ :: VIGENARY : 20

    (A) 6

    (B) 7

    (C) 16

    (D) 32

32. ATE : WON :: (3*2+2): _____

    (A) (3*2+2–7)

    (B) (0/1)

    (C) ($\sqrt{10}$)

    (D) (2^1)

33. CAPACIOUS : BANTAM :: REASSURE:
    _____

    (A) dishearten

    (B) reaffirm

    (C) calm

    (D) capricious

34. GENETICS : SPECTROSCOPY :: BIOLOGY :
    _____

    (A) anthropology

    (B) anatomy

    (C) spectroscope

    (D) chemistry

35. TITAN : _____ :: GANYMEDE :
    JUPITER

    (A) Zeus

    (B) Neptune

    (C) Saturn

    (D) Hyperion

36. _____ : MAYOR :: ADMIRAL :
    ENSIGN

    (A) General

    (B) Senator

    (C) Captain

    (D) Selectman

37. SHAWL : CHEETAH :: _____ : PITA
    (A) clothing
    (B) bread
    (C) margarita
    (D) mall

38. KAHLO : _____ :: DALI : SPAIN
    (A) Mexico
    (B) India
    (C) Russia
    (D) Colombia

39. (3,5): 8 :: _____ : 18
    (A) (6,12)
    (B) (3,15)
    (C) (14,4)
    (D) (7,11)

40. JUPITER : _____ :: SATURN : OPS
    (A) Mars
    (B) Earth
    (C) Juno
    (D) Zeus

41. _____ : DIFFERENCE :: DIVIDEND : QUOTIENT
    (A) Divisor
    (B) Minuend
    (C) Subtrahend
    (D) Addend

42. BODY : SKELETON :: VEHICLE : _____
    (A) frame
    (B) wheels
    (C) cabin
    (D) engine

43. PEDESTRIAN : EQUESTRIAN :: FOOT : _____
    (A) boat
    (B) horse
    (C) boot
    (D) orthopedic

44. GENERAL : PRIVATE :: CARDINAL : _____
    (A) bird
    (B) red
    (C) specific
    (D) bishop

45. SCHOOL : MILITARY :: DROPOUT : _____
    (A) recruit
    (B) graduate
    (C) deserter
    (D) rank

46. KILOGRAM : _____ :: MASS : ELECTRIC CURRENT
    (A) candela
    (B) voltage
    (C) electricity
    (D) ampere

47. PREFORMATIONISM : BIOLOGY :: _____ : PHYSICS
    (A) emission theory
    (B) spontaneous generation
    (C) phlogiston theory
    (D) telegony

48. TACHYMETER : _____ :: THERMOMETER : TEMPERATURE
    (A) (temperature, time)
    (B) (speed, distance)
    (C) (time, distance)
    (D) (speed, time)

49. CRASH : CLASH :: _____ : CROWN
   (A) coronate
   (B) clown
   (C) conflict
   (D) tiara

50. NOISOME : _____ :: STINKY : NOSY
   (A) handsome
   (B) snoopy
   (C) noisy
   (D) ugly

51. _____ : CHEESE :: ROTTEN : MOLDY
   (A) Fermented
   (B) Chips
   (C) Eggs
   (D) Wine

52. PRAISE : SUCCESS :: PRIDE : _____
   (A) lions
   (B) failure
   (C) sin
   (D) confidence

53. _____ : VELOCITY :: TIME : MPS
   (A) Speed
   (B) Acceleration
   (C) Timepiece
   (D) Second

54. PUNCTILIOUS : OBSTINATE :: _____ : CANTANKEROUS
   (A) careful
   (B) stubborn
   (C) punctual
   (D) obsolete

55. GAMMA : RADIO :: VIOLET : _____
   (A) omega
   (B) red
   (C) purple
   (D) television

56. _____ : SPECULATE :: SPECIFICATION : SPECULATION
   (A) Hypothesis
   (B) Specify
   (C) Special
   (D) Guess

57. INSPIRE : PLACATE :: CONFIDENCE : _____
   (A) assuredness
   (B) anxiety
   (C) calm
   (D) appease

58. ELEPHANT : 4 :: _____ : 8
   (A) spider
   (B) condor
   (C) stegosaurus
   (D) human

59. _____ : BLADE :: BEACH : GRAIN
   (A) Knife
   (B) Seashore
   (C) Sand
   (D) Meadow

60. 3:10 : ACUTE :: _____ : OBTUSE
   (A) 7:45
   (B) 6:20
   (C) 12:05
   (D) 3:55

61. SAW : _____ :: AXE : TAPE

    (A) video

    (B) abrasive

    (C) glue

    (D) seen

62. AMINO ACIDS : _____ :: FATTY ACIDS : LIPID

    (A) amine

    (B) peptide

    (C) molecule

    (D) aliphatic

63. ORNATE : FLORID :: _____ : GRASPING

    (A) ornament

    (B) greedy

    (C) loose

    (D) decorative

64. ORDER : _____ :: MANDATE : SCHEME

    (A) machination

    (B) chaos

    (C) command

    (D) pyramid

65. ROBORANT : SKULDUGGERY :: _____ : BEHAVIOR

    (A) monster

    (B) mannerism

    (C) robotic

    (D) drug

66. EQUINOX : _____ :: SOLSTICE : SUMMER

    (A) equator

    (B) season

    (C) vernal

    (D) verdant

67. _____ : THE NIGHT WATCH :: MUNCH : THE SCREAM

    (A) Rembrandt

    (B) Bernini

    (C) Pissarro

    (D) Renoir

68. APPROBATION : _____ :: ABSTAIN : AVOID

    (A) affectation

    (B) admiration

    (C) anodyne

    (D) apoplectic

69. SPHERICAL : HOT :: ROLL : _____

    (A) sun

    (B) rotate

    (C) burn

    (D) lukewarm

70. $x^2 + 4x + 4 : x + 2 :: x^2 + 10x + 25 :$ _____

    (A) x + 15

    (B) $^2 + 5$

    (C) $x^2 + 5x + 10$

    (D) x + 5)

71. TESLA : ELECTRICITY :: CURIE : _____

    (A) superconductivity

    (B) radioactivity

    (C) dark matter

    (D) genetics

72. CARPACCIO : BELLINI :: RAW MEAT : _____

    (A) cocktail

    (B) sushi

    (C) salmonella

    (D) appetizer

73. PLANE : PLAIN :: EARN : _____

(A) undistinguished

(B) obtain

(C) urn

(D) yearn

74. LYSOSOME : DIGESTION :: MITOCHONDRION : _____

(A) protein translation

(B) energy

(C) genetics

(D) photosynthesis

75. CIRCLE : _____ :: PI x DIAMETER : SIDE x FOUR

(A) rectangle

(B) perimeter

(C) area

(D) square

76. AMERICAN CIVIL : LINCOLN :: SPANISH-AMERICAN : _____

(A) McKinley

(B) Cleveland

(C) Johnson

(D) Arthur

77. RENAL : KIDNEY :: HEPATIC : _____

(A) hepatitis

(B) spleen

(C) liver

(D) bean

78. ATHEIST : PACIFIST :: GOD : _____

(A) Pacific

(B) war

(C) devil

(D) agnosticism

79. _____ : EISENHOWER :: REVOLUTIONARY WAR : WASHINGTON

(A) World War I

(B) World War II

(C) interstate highway system

(D) Continental Congress

80. JOEY : TROOP :: PIGLET : _____

(A) porcine

(B) army

(C) boar

(D) sounder

81. IMPLORE : BESEECH :: ELUCIDATE : _____

(A) expound

(B) besiege

(C) nourish

(D) strive

82. OVERDRAFT : MORTGAGE :: OPEN-END FUND : _____

(A) financial swap

(B) insurable interest

(C) unit investment trust

(D) certificate of deposit

83. MOZART : ALEXANDROS OF ANTIOCH :: DON GIOVANNI : _____

(A) *Pieta*

(B) *Venus de Milo*

(C) *David*

(D) *The Kiss*

84. MEAL : SONG :: DESSERT : _____

(A) coda

(B) notes

(C) sweet

(D) capo

85. NEAPOLITAN : _____ :: ROMAINE : ICEBERG

(A) Naples

(B) *Titanic*

(C) lazio

(D) glacier

86. CORD : _____ :: FATHOM : WATER

(A) cable

(B) boat

(C) think

(D) wood

87. ZIMBABWE : AUSTRALIA :: RHODESIA : _____

(A) Siam

(B) New Holland

(C) Dahomey

(D) Zaire

88. TONSILS : UTERUS :: IMMUNE : _____

(A) reproductive

(B) digestive

(C) circulatory

(D) endocrine

89. DIFFIDENCE : PLUCKINESS :: LACKADAISICAL : _____

(A) difference

(B) luckiness

(C) enthusiastic

(D) enervated

90. SNOW : ICE :: MAN : _____

(A) woman

(B) Eskimo

(C) chimpanzee

(D) cream

91. KOLACHE : KOLKATA :: PASTRY : _____

(A) river

(B) city

(C) pastille

(D) cookie

92. HOUSE : HUMAN :: _____ : VENTRICLE

(A) sump pump

(B) atrium

(C) chimney

(D) ventriloquist

93. ZOOM : ZEAL :: ZIP : _____

(A) button

(B) zany

(C) tie

(D) fervor

94. PLANE : _____ :: ASCENT : ASSENT

(A) point

(B) descent

(C) jury

(D) helicopter

95. JURASSIC : TRIASSIC :: VICTORIAN : _____

(A) victorious

(B) Edwardian

(C) Mesozoic

(D) triangular

96. CONCISE : _____ :: VERBOSITY : GENEROSITY

(A) penurious

(B) expeditious

(C) profligate

(D) precise

97. RETICENT : FORTHCOMING :: ESOTERIC : _____

   (A) homecoming

   (B) mysterious

   (C) convectional

   (D) conventional

98. SWEET : _____ :: SALTY : PROSCIUTTO

   (A) Calypso

   (B) Volga

   (C) Baumkuchen

   (D) Kamchatka

99. CONVECTION : ADVECTION :: _____ : PHYSICAL TRANSFER

   (A) movement of fluids

   (B) oven

   (C) movement of solids

   (D) metaphysical transfer

100. BODY : _____ :: CORPOREAL : PSYCHOLOGICAL

   (A) psychologist

   (B) mind

   (C) spirit

   (D) anatomy

101. DAMAGE : _____ :: DESTROY : INVULNERABLE

   (A) destruction

   (B) invincible

   (C) vulnerable

   (D) strong

102. CIRCUMFERENCE/DIAMETER : π :: _____ : 3.14

   (A) radius

   (B) area

   (C) 3.14

   (D) 1

103. _____ : WEIGHT :: SPECTROMETER : LIGHT

   (A) Mass

   (B) Scale

   (C) Wait

   (D) eavy

104. INCH : FOOT :: SEMITONE : _____

   (A) octave

   (B) tone

   (C scale

   (D) half-step

105. CALVIN : _____ :: REFORMED TRADITION : LEVIATHAN

   (A) Locke

   (B) Aristotle

   (C) Socrates

   (D) Hobbes

106. NEEDLE : _____ :: SEW : WRITE

   (A) thread

   (B) stitch

   (C) quill

   (D) ink

107. FISH : PLANTS :: AQUARIUM : _____

   (A) greenhouse

   (B) animals

   (C) bamboo

   (D) planetarium

108. _____ : UNDER :: STAKER : WRITER

   (A) Over

   (B) Grub

   (C) Below

   (D) Author

109. EFFULGENT : _____ :: LUMINOUS : INKY

    (A) tenacious

    (B) incandescent

    (C) effusive

    (D) tenebrous

110. PAGE : LEAF :: COLLARBONE : _____

    (A) branch

    (B) skeleton

    (C) clavicle

    (D) calcium

111. SOUTH KOREA : RUSSIA :: WON : _____

    (A) ruble

    (B) North Korea

    (C) World War II

    (D) Putin

112. PLACEBO : NOCEBO :: HELP : _____

    (A) Nocera

    (B) harm

    (C) yelp

    (D) prescription

113. _____ : GNU :: CORN : MAIZE

    (A) Gnome

    (B) Grain

    (C) Labyrinth

    (D) Wildebeest

114. CHARACTERS : WORDS :: CHINESE : _____

    (A) letters

    (B) sentences

    (C) Mandarin

    (D) English

115. STEEL : PREPARE :: OPERATE : _____

    (A) run

    (B) safety

    (C) alloy

    (D) surgery

116. DARWINSIM : CREATIONISM :: _____ :: SUPERNATURAL

    (A) Charles

    (B) spontaneous generation

    (C) evolution

    (D) God

117. BOB : _____ :: HOPE : BALL

    (A) apples

    (B) Lucille

    (C) Camille

    (D) hoop

118. GLUTTONOUS : ORPHAN :: _____ :: PARENTS

    (A) moderation

    (B) indulgence

    (C) food

    (D) sloth

119. ENDEMIC : COSMOPOLITAN :: ISOLATED : _____

    (A) pandemic

    (B) island

    (C) everywhere

    (D) cocktail

120. ROMEO : JULIET :: _____ : CAPULET

    (A) Verona

    (B) Laurence

    (C) Mercutio

    (D) Montague

Chapter 12

Answers to MAT Practice Test #2

• •

*N*ow that you've finished taking the second practice MAT, make sure that you take the time to review any questions on which you guessed or struggled, as well as to review any incorrect answers. Your mistakes should be helpful in pointing you toward areas where you need to learn more content, and they may highlight places where you can use your technique more strictly.

1. Choice (B) is correct. (1:2,3:4) **Confuse** and **confound** are synonyms; **craft** and **create** are also synonyms.

2. Choice (A) is correct. (1:3,2:4) A parlor is a room; **parlous** means "dangerous."

3. Choice (C) is correct. (1:2,3:4) A sea lion is a pinniped; a spider is an arachnid.

4. Choice (D) is correct. (1:3,2:4) Candelabras and flashlights are used to see in the dark; flashlights are more modern. Screwdrivers and power drills are used to turn screws; power drills are more modern.

5. Choice (A) is correct. (1:2,3:4) **Libation** is another word for "drink." **Cuisine** is another word for "food."

6. Choice (B) is correct. (1:3,2:4) **–cyte** is a suffix meaning "cell"; **–algia** is a suffix meaning "pain."

7. Choice (C) is correct. (1:2,3:4) Tenor is the high voice part for males. Soprano is the high voice part for females.

8. Choice (D) is correct. (1:3,2:4) When advising or recommending, one is making a suggestion. When vouching or certifying, one is making a stronger statement of truth.

9. Choice (B) is correct. (1:2,3:4) Molars are a type of teeth; saxophones are a type of woodwind.

10. Choice (A) is correct. (1:3,2:4) The interstate highway system was created during Eisenhower's administration. The New Deal was created during Roosevelt's administration.

11. Choice (C) is correct. (1:3,2:4) **Vociferate** and **shout** are synonyms; **susurrate** and **whisper** are also synonyms.

12. Choice (D) is correct. (1:3,2:4) Penury is a type of poverty; a recidivist is a type of criminal.

13. Choice (A) is correct. (1:3,2:4) The number 16 is an example of a real number; $\sqrt{-16}$ is an example of an imaginary number.

14. Choice (B) is correct. (1:2,3:4) 3π multiplied by 3 equals 9π; 3π multiplied by 27 equals 81π.

15. Choice (C) is correct. (1:2,3:4) A simile is indicated by comparing things that are different. Alliteration is indicated by repeating consonant sounds.

16. Choice (C) is correct. (1:2,3:4) An orbit is a path around a center of gravitation. An example of an orbit is Halley's Comet's path around Sol (the sun).

17. Choice (D) is correct. (1:3,2:4) Bq is the abbreviation for becquerel, which is a unit relating to radioactivity. Hz is the abbreviation for hertz, which is a unit relating to frequency.

18. Choice (A) is correct. (1:3,2:4) A lamp can be fueled by kerosene; a pyre is fueled by timber.

19. Choice (A) is correct. (1:3,2:4) When one denigrates another, it could be called criticism; when one praises another, it could be called commendation.

20. Choice (B) is correct. (1:2,3:4) **Better** is the comparative form of the word **good.** **Supermarket** is the augmentative form of the word **market.**

21. Choice (C) is correct. (1:3,2:4) Water is something that can be evaporated; a shrine is something that can be desecrated.

22. Choice (D) is correct. (1:3,2:4) When talking about words that mean the opposite of **more,** one uses **less** with mass nouns and **fewer** with count nouns.

23. Choice (D) is correct. (1:2,3:4) A maple is a type of deciduous tree; a juniper is a type of coniferous tree.

24. Choice (B) is correct. (1:3,2:4) **Fain** means "willingly"; **faint** means "weak."

25. Choice (C) is correct. (1:3,2:4) The levels of a building are called floors; the levels of a ship are called decks.

26. Choice (A) is correct. (1:2,3:4) **Indignation** and **umbrage** are synonyms; **consternation** and **trepidation** are also synonyms.

27. Choice (C) is correct. (1:2,3:4) The circulatory system includes the aorta; the endocrine system includes the thyroid.

28. Choice (D) is correct. (1:3,2:4) **See** and **key** rhyme; **seal** and **keel** rhyme. **See** and **seal** begin with *s*; **key** and **keel** begin with *k*.

29. Choice (B) is correct. (1:2;3:4) The piccolo is a small woodwind instrument, and the bassoon is a large woodwind instrument. The trumpet is a small brass instrument, and the tuba is a large brass instrument.

30. Choice (B) is correct. (1:2,3:4) A joke, the catalyst, causes laughter, the feedback.

31. Choice (C) is correct. (1:2,3:4) **Sedenary** means "sixteenth"; **vigenary** means "twentieth."

32. Choice (A) is correct. (1:3,2:4) **Ate** sounds the same as **eight**; eight equals (3*2+2). **Won** sounds the same as **one**; one equals (3*2+2-7).

33. Choice (A) is correct. (1:2,3:4) **Capacious** and **bantam** are antonyms; **reassure** and **dishearten** are also antonyms.

34. Choice (D) is correct. (1:3,2:4) Genetics is a subfield of biology; spectroscopy is a subfield of chemistry.

35. Choice (C) is correct. (1:2,3:4) Titan is the largest moon of Saturn; Ganymede is the largest moon of Jupiter.

36. Choice (B) is correct. (1:2,3:4) Senators and mayors are both members of government; senators have more authority. Admirals and ensigns are both members of the Navy; admirals have more authority.

37. Choice (D) is correct. (1:3,2:4) **Shawl** and **mall** rhyme; **cheetah** and **pita** rhyme.

38. Choice (A) is correct. (1:2,3:4) Frida Kahlo was a Mexican painter; Salvador Dalí was a Spanish painter.

39. Choice (D) is correct. (1:2,3:4) 3 + 5 = 8; both 3 and 5 are prime. Although all the choices add to 18 only (7,11) is the choice in which both numbers are prime.

40. Choice (C) is correct. (1:2,3:4) In Roman mythology, Jupiter was married to Juno; Saturn was married to Ops.

41. Choice (B) is correct. (1:2,3:4) In subtraction, the minuend is the larger number from which the subtrahend is subtracted to give you the difference. In division, the dividend is the larger number, which is divided by the divisor to give you the quotient.

42. Choice (A) is correct. (1:2,3:4) A human body is supported by the skeleton; a vehicle is supported by the frame.

43. Choice (B) is correct. (1:3,2:4) A pedestrian travels by foot; an equestrian travels by horse.

44. Choice (D) is correct. (1:2,3:4) **General** and **private** are both ranks in the military. **Cardinal** and **bishop** are both members of clergy.

45. Choice (C) is correct. (1:3,2:4) A dropout is someone who leaves school before completing all requirements. A deserter is someone who leaves the military before completing all requirements.

46. Choice (D) is correct. (1:3,2:4) The kilogram is the SI base unit for mass; the ampere is the SI base unit for electric current.

47. Choice (A) is correct. (1:2,3:4) Preformationism is a now-obsolete idea in biology. Emission theory is a now-obsolete idea in physics.

48. Choice (B) is correct. (1:2,3:4) A tachymeter is used to measure speed or distance. A thermometer is used to measure temperature.

49. Choice (A) is correct. (1:2,3:4) **Crash** and **clash** are synonyms; **coronate** and **crown** are also synonyms.

50. Choice (B) is correct. (1:3,2:4) **Noisome** and **stinky** are synonyms; **snoopy** and **nosy** are also synonyms.

51. Choice (C) is correct. (1:3,2:4) Eggs gone bad are rotten; cheese gone bad is moldy.

52. Choice (D) is correct. (1:3,2:4) Receiving praise usually causes one to have pride; having success usually causes one to have confidence.

53. Choice (D) is correct. (1:3,2:4) Velocity can be expressed in mps, or meters per second. The unit of time in this case is the second.

54. Choice (A) is correct. (1:3,2:4) **Punctilious** and **careful** are synonyms; **obstinate** and **cantankerous** are also synonyms.

55. Choice (B) is correct. (1:2,3:4) In the electromagnetic spectrum, gamma rays have the highest frequency and radio waves have the lowest. In the visible spectrum, violet light has the highest frequency and red light has the lowest.

56. Choice (B) is correct. (1:3,2:4) **Specify** is the verb form of the noun **specification.** **Speculate** is the verb form of the noun **speculation.**

57. Choice (C) is correct. (1:3,2:4) When one inspires someone, one gives confidence. When one placates someone, one gives calm.

58. Choice (A) is correct. (1:2,3:4) An elephant has four legs; a spider has eight legs.

59. Choice (D) is correct. (1:2,3:4) Many blades of grass make up a meadow; many grains of sand make up a beach.

60. Choice (D) is correct. (1:2,3:4) When an analog clock reads 3:10, the hands form an acute angle. When the clock reads 3:55, the hands form an obtuse angle.

61. Choice (C) is correct. (1:3,2:4) Saws and axes are tools used for cutting wood. Glue and tape are used for adhesion.

62. Choice (B) is correct. (1:2,3:4) Amino acids form peptides; fatty acids form lipids.

63. Choice (B) is correct. (1:2,3:4) **Florid** means "very ornate"; **grasping** means "very greedy."

64. Choice (A) is correct. (1:3,2:4) *Order* and *mandate* are synonyms; *machination* and *scheme* are also synonyms.

65. Choice (D) is correct. (1:3,2:4) A roborant is a type of drug; skulduggery is a type of behavior.

66. Choice (C) is correct. (1:2,3:4) The vernal equinox is a type of equinox. The summer solstice is a type of solstice.

67. Choice (A) is correct. (1:2,3:4) *The Night Watch* is a painting by Rembrandt van Rijn; *The Scream* was a painting by Edvard Munch.

68. Choice (B) is correct. (1:2,3:4) *Approbation* and *admiration* are synonyms; *abstain* and *avoid* are also synonyms.

69. Choice (C) is correct. (1:3,2:4) A spherical object can roll; a hot object can burn.

70. Choice (D) is correct. (1:2,3:4) By squaring (x + 2), one gets $x^2 + 4x + 4$. By squaring (x + 5), one gets $x^2 + 10x + 25$.

71. Choice (B) is correct. (1:2,3:4) Nikola Tesla was known for his work with electricity; Marie Curie was known for her work with radioactivity.

72. Choice (A) is correct. (1:3,2:4) Carpaccio is a dish of raw meat; a Bellini is a cocktail.

73. Choice (C) is correct. (1:2,3:4) *Plane* and *plain* sound the same; *earn* and *urn* also sound the same.

74. Choice (B) is correct. (1:2,3:4) In cells, lysosomes handle digestion; mitochondria handle energy production.

75. Choice (D) is correct. (1:3,2:4) Pi times diameter is the formula for the circumference (perimeter) of a circle. Side times 4 is the formula for the perimeter of a square.

76. Choice (A) is correct. (1:2,3:4) Lincoln was the president during the American Civil War. McKinley was the president during the Spanish-American War.

77. Choice (C) is correct. (1:2,3:4) The word *renal* refers to the kidneys; the word *hepatic* refers to the liver.

78. Choice (B) is correct. (1:3,2:4) An atheist opposes the idea of God; a pacifist opposes war.

79. Choice (B) is correct. (1:2,3:4) Eisenhower was a leader in World War II before becoming president. Washington was a leader in the Revolutionary War before becoming president.

80. Choice (D) is correct. (1:2,3:4) A joey is a young kangaroo; a troop is a group of kangaroos. A piglet is a young pig; a sounder is a group of pigs.

81. Choice (A) is correct. (1:2,3:4) *Implore* and *beseech* are synonyms; *elucidate* and *expound* are also synonyms.

82. Choice (C) is correct. (1:2,3:4) Overdrafts and mortgages are types of loans; open-end funds and unit investment trusts are types of mutual funds.

83. Choice (B) is correct. (1:3,2:4) *Don Giovanni* is an opera by Mozart; the *Venus de Milo* is a sculpture by Alexandros of Antioch.

84. Choice (A) is correct. (1:3,2:4) The dessert comes at the end of a meal; the coda comes at the end of a song.

85. Choice (C) is correct. (1:2,3:4) Neapolitan and Lazio are types of pizza; romaine and iceberg are types of lettuce.

86. Choice (D) is correct. (1:2,3:4) The cord is used to measure the volume of wood; the fathom is used to measure the depth of water.

87. Choice (B) is correct. (1:3,2:4) Rhodesia is a former name of Zimbabwe; New Holland is a former name of Australia.

88. Choice (A) is correct. (1:3,2:4) The tonsils are part of the immune system; the uterus is part of the reproductive system.

89. Choice (C) is correct. (1:2,3:4) **Diffidence** and **pluckiness** are antonyms; **lackadaisical** and **enthusiastic** are also antonyms.

90. Choice (D) is correct. (1:3,2:4) In linguistics, **snowman** and **ice cream** are compounds.

91. Choice (B) is correct. (1:3,2:4) Kolache is a pastry; Kolkata is a city.

92. Choice (A) is correct. (1:3,2:4) In a house, the sump pump pumps water; in a human heart, the ventricles pump blood.

93. Choice (D) is correct. (1:3,2:4) **Zoom** and **zip** are synonyms; **zeal** and **fervor** are also synonyms.

94. Choice (C) is correct. (1:3,2:4) A plane's climb is an ascent; a jury's delivery of a verdict is an assent.

95. Choice (B) is correct. (1:2,3:4) The Jurassic and Triassic were periods. The Victorian and Edwardian were eras.

96. Choice (A) is correct. (1:3,2:4) When one is concise, one does not have verbosity; when one is penurious, one does not have generosity.

97. Choice (D) is correct. (1:2,3:4) **Reticent** and **forthcoming** are antonyms; **esoteric** and **conventional** are also antonyms.

98. Choice (C) is correct. (1:2,3:4) Baumkuchen is a sweet food; prosciutto is a salty food.

99. Choice (A) is correct. (1:3,2:4) Convection is a method of heat transfer by the movement of fluids. Advection is a method of heat transfer by the physical transfer of objects.

100. Choice (B) is correct. (1:3,2:4) **Corporeal** means "relating to the body"; **psychological** means "relating to the mind."

101. Choice (D) is correct. (1:3,2:4) To **destroy** means "to damage to the extreme"; to be **invulnerable** means "to be strong to the extreme."

102. Choice (C) is correct. (1:2,3:4) Circumference divided by diameter equals π. Therefore, the relationship between π and π is the same as the relationship between 3.14 and 3.14.

103. Choice (B) is correct. (1:2,3:4) A scale measures weight; a spectrometer measures light.

104. Choice (A) is correct. (1:2,3:4) There are 12 inches in a foot; there are 12 semitones in an octave.

105. Choice (D) is correct. (1:3,2:4) John Calvin is best known for developing Reformed Tradition. Thomas Hobbes is best known for his book *Leviathan*.

106. Choice (C) is correct. (1:3,2:4) One can sew with a needle (the needle requires thread). One can write with a quill (the quill requires ink).

107. Choice (A) is correct. (1:3,2:4) Aquariums contain fish; greenhouses contain plants.

108. Choice (B) is correct. (1:3,2:4) In linguistics, **grubstaker** and **underwriter** are compounds. They are also synonyms.

109. Choice (D) is correct. (1:3,2:4) **Effulgent** and **luminous** are synonyms. **Tenebrous** and **inky** are also synonyms. Both pairs of words are antonyms to each other.

110. Choice (C) is correct. (1:2,3:4) **Page** and **leaf** are synonyms, meaning part of a book. **Collarbone** is the common name for the bone called the clavicle.

111. Choice (A) is correct. (1:3,2:4) The currency of South Korea is the won. The currency of Russia is the ruble.

112. Choice (B) is correct. (1:3,2:4) The placebo effect helps a patient; the nocebo effect harms a patient.

113. Choice (D) is correct. (1:2,3:4) **Gnu** is another name for **wildebeest**; **maize** is another name for **corn.**

114. Choice (D) is correct. (1:3,2:4) In Chinese writing, characters are used much like words are used in English writing.

115. Choice (A) is correct. (1:2,3:4) The verbs **steel** and **prepare** are synonyms. **Operate** and **run** are also synonyms.

116. Choice (C) is correct. (1:3,2:4) Darwinism is the belief that life as we know it came to be by means of evolution. Creationism is the belief that life as we know it came to be by means of a supernatural power.

117. Choice (B) is correct. (1:3,2:4) Bob Hope and Lucille Ball were comedians.

118. Choice (A) is correct. (1:3,2:4) Someone who is gluttonous lacks moderation. Someone who is an orphan lacks parents.

119. Choice (C) is correct. (1:3,2:4) If an organism is endemic, it is isolated in one location. If the distribution of an organism is cosmopolitan, it is found almost everywhere.

120. Choice (D) is correct. (1:3,2:4) Romeo is a Montague; Juliet is a Capulet.

Chapter 13

MAT Practice Test #3

• •

*W*elcome to the third MAT practice test. Like the other exams in this book, this one is modeled on real MAT questions to help you get accustomed to the real test's style. Remember to use good technique throughout the test as you take it. If you want to make the experience realistic, don't just look through the test. Instead, take it all at once, timed strictly, in a room where you won't be interrupted for an hour. Time yourself for 60 minutes; there'll be 120 questions.

As you take the test, it's a good idea to circle questions you guessed on — after all, if you get them right, it may just be luck. Review questions you guessed on as carefully as you would review questions you got wrong. After taking the test, review your mistakes and guesses. If you knew all the terms in the question and still missed it, your analogy-solving technique may need work, and you might benefit from reviewing the solving technique outlined in Chapter 3. If you didn't know one or more of the terms, take the time to look up their definitions. Good luck!

1. IGNITION : APPLAUSE :: :: _____ : APPLAUD
   - (A) ignite
   - (B) rocket
   - (C) audience
   - (D) applauding

2. LYMPHOCYTE : _____ :: BONE : SKELETAL
   - (A) nervous
   - (B) immune
   - (C) muscular
   - (D) digestive

3. EXCOMMUNICATION : _____ :: CATHOLICISM : SCHOOL
   - (A) journalism
   - (B) Christianity
   - (C) detention
   - (D) pope

4. (2,3) : 35 :: (4,5) : _____
   - (A) 67
   - (B) 70
   - (C) 143
   - (D) 189

5. RECIPE : _____ :: INGREDIENTS : DOSAGE
   - (A) prescription
   - (B) cookbook
   - (C) chef
   - (D) dose

6. EXCITED : _____ :: WARM : SCALDING
   - (A) happy
   - (B) ecstatic
   - (C) empathetic
   - (D) angry

7. USA : FBI :: UK : _____
   - (A) CIA
   - (B) DGSE
   - (C) MI6
   - (D) KGB

8. SCRIBE : REFEREE :: PEN : _____
   - (A) paintbrush
   - (B) officiating
   - (C) writing
   - (D) whistle

9. DIME : PIECE :: DOZEN : _____
   - (A) 12
   - (B) coin
   - (C) $1.20
   - (D) cake

10. CRISIS : SYLLABUS :: _____ : SYLLABI
    - (A) crisis
    - (B) crisi
    - (C) crises
    - (D) crisises

11. _____ : TANGO :: LIGHT : SEE
    - (A) mirror
    - (B) partner
    - (C) hear
    - (D) salsa

12. BAZOOKA : ROCKET :: PISTOL : _____
    - (A) round
    - (B) ship
    - (C) gum
    - (D) gun

13. PLAGIARISM : ORIGINALITY :: DENOUEMENT : _____

    (A) denouncement

    (B) creative

    (C) copyright

    (D) beginning

14. GREAT : EXCELLENT :: POOR : _____

    (A) rich

    (B) atrocious

    (C) amazing

    (D) bad

15. PIG : SHEEP :: _____ : FOLLOWER

    (A) disciple

    (B) horse

    (C) glutton

    (D) leader

16. ACT : PLAY :: COMPANY : _____

    (A) orchestra

    (B) business

    (C) scene

    (D) platoon

17. SINISTER : INAUSPICIOUS :: VERACIOUS : _____

    (A) auspicious

    (B) suspicious

    (C) insincerity

    (D) credible

18. $(-9, -13) : (13, -9) :: (-14, 15) :$ _____

    (A) (14, 15)

    (B) (−15, −14)

    (C) (−14, 15)

    (D) (−15, 14)

19. _____ : ACADEMY :: CLERGY : POLICEMEN

    (A) school

    (B) priest

    (C) seminary

    (D) sergeant

20. _____ : BRASS :: CASTANETS : SOUSAPHONE

    (A) Percussion

    (B) Saxophone

    (C) Minuets

    (D) Castellan

21. SASHIMI : OKROSHKA :: JAPAN : _____

    (A) Polish

    (B) Czech

    (C) Turkish

    (D) Russian

22. SALOON : SEDAN :: LABOUR : _____

    (A) room

    (B) labor

    (C) work

    (D) car

23. EMU : _____ :: TALON : CLAW

    (A) flightless

    (B) fang

    (C) ostrich

    (D) egg

24. _____ : ADULATOR :: BASENESS : FLATTERY

    (A) Bully

    (B) Adult

    (C) Victim

    (D) Samaritan

25. POLISH : SHINY :: WASH : _____
    (A) shoe
    (B) chrome
    (C) laundry
    (D) clean

26. REAL MCCOY : SEMBLANCE :: DIAMOND : _____
    (A) ring
    (B) rhinestone
    (C) ruby
    (D) resemblance

27. ANATOMY : _____ :: PHONETICS : LINGUISTICS
    (A) phonics
    (B) chemistry
    (C) biology
    (D) language

28. RAGE : ANGER :: CHAGRIN : _____
    (A) annoyance
    (B) love
    (C) boredom
    (D) excitement

29. PSYCHIC : PSYCHOSIS :: _____ : WRITE
    (A) right
    (B) psychiatrist
    (C) psychologist
    (D) wrong

30. EVEN : PRIME :: 22 : _____
    (A) 21
    (B) 23
    (C) 24
    (D) 25

31. RAW : WAR :: _____ : CONFLICT
    (A) frigid
    (B) broiling
    (C) peace
    (D) battle

32. EXECUTE : LYNCHING :: CELEBRATE : _____
    (A) mob
    (B) celestial
    (C) party
    (D) celibate

33. ROYAL : LOVE :: STRAIGHT : _____
    (A) trey
    (B) deuce
    (C) regal
    (D) arrow

34. TRIANGLE : 180 :: SQUARE : _____
    (A) 240
    (B) 360
    (C) 480
    (D) 720

35. SILK : WOOL :: _____ : SHEEP
    (A) snake
    (B) mink
    (C) flower
    (D) caterpillar

36. INTELLECT : _____ :: NOOLOGIST : DENDROLOGIST
    (A) teeth
    (B) psychology
    (C) trees
    (D) stupidity

37. GALLON : QUART :: QUART : _____
    (A) gallon
    (B) quart
    (C) pint
    (D) cup

38. KELVIN : TEMPERATURE :: AMPERE : _____
    (A) electric current
    (B) radioactivity
    (C) decibels
    (D) heat

39. _____ : STOP :: JADE : GO
    (A) Lavender
    (B) Freeze
    (C) Burn
    (D) Crimson

40. _____ : FUNGI :: CARCINOLOGY : CRUSTACEANS
    (A) Lobsters
    (B) Fontology
    (C) Mycology
    (D) Mushrooms

41. HIATUS : DIAERESIS :: PERFECT QUADRILATERAL : _____
    (A) triangle
    (B) square
    (C) pentagon
    (D) circle

42. GRAPH : AXIS :: MATRIX : _____
    (A) column
    (B) allied
    (C) film
    (D) coordinates

43. _____ : ISOSCELES :: 3 : EQUILATERAL
    (A) 1
    (B) 2
    (C) 3
    (D) 4

44. HEXADECAGON : _____ :: NONAGON : 3
    (A) 2
    (B) 12
    (C) 8
    (D) 4

45. HOP : LEAP :: _____ : SLUMBER
    (A) jump
    (B) rabbit
    (C) nap
    (D) lumber

46. CANVAS : CANVASS :: FABRIC : _____
    (A) easel
    (B) votes
    (C) fabricate
    (D) cloth

47. GATSBY : FITZGERALD :: _____ : CURTIZ
    (A) Blaine
    (B) Carraway
    (C) Michael
    (D) Scott

48. CONSTRUCTION : BUILDING :: MULTIPLICATION : _____
    (A) addition
    (B) house
    (C) multiplicand
    (D) product

49. WINE : _____ :: GRAPES : HONEY

    (A) champagne

    (B) rum

    (C) mead

    (D) ale

50. 27 FEET : 9 YARDS :: 3^3 : _____

    (A) 3

    (B) 9

    (C) 27

    (D) 81

51. SECTION : _____ :: NEWSPAPER : BIBLE

    (A) news

    (B) book

    (C) piece

    (D) religion

52. POPULAR VOTE : ELECTORAL COLLEGE :: DEMOCRACY : _____

    (A) republic

    (B) dictatorship

    (C) communism

    (D) socialism

53. BIZARRE : BAZAAR :: STRANGE : _____

    (A) weird

    (B) syringe

    (C) grange

    (D) market

54. FAUCET : _____ :: AMPLIFIER : VOLUME

    (A) channel

    (B) knob

    (C) flow

    (D) guitar

55. EAGLE : SCOUT :: _____ : EAGLE

    (A) golden

    (B) silver

    (C) cub

    (D) girl

56. BRYOLOGY : BOTANY :: _____ : SOCIOLOGY

    (A) oology

    (B) positivism

    (C) zoology

    (D) nephrology

57. _____ : BILE :: BLADDER : URINE

    (A) Excretory

    (B) Liver

    (C) Gallbladder

    (D) Spleen

58. DOG : DACHSHUND :: _____ : BURMILLA

    (A) city

    (B) canine

    (C) clover

    (D) cat

59. EXASPERATION : PIQUE :: VILIFICATION : _____

    (A) mollification

    (B) calumny

    (C) trepidation

    (D) consternation

60. ARCHITECTURE : MUSIC :: BLUEPRINT : _____

    (A) score

    (B) plan

    (C) melody

    (D) arpeggio

61. _____ : WASP :: BUBALINE : BUFFALO

    (A) Bee

    (B) Bison

    (C) Vespine

    (D) Porcine

62. BASE : APEX :: FOUNDATION : _____

    (A) annex

    (B) spire

    (C) charity

    (D) support

63. CUBE : HEXAHEDRON :: √36 : _____

    (A) 3

    (B) 12

    (C) 24

    (D) 6

64. _____ : CUT :: FALL : SCAR

    (A) Trip

    (B) Balance

    (C) Heal

    (D) Connect

65. BIRD : REPTILE :: CHICK : _____

    (A) larva

    (B) turtle

    (C) hatchling

    (D) amphibian

66. SEDIMENTARY : LIMESTONE :: METAMORPHIC :

    (A) polymorphism

    (B) marble

    (C) igneous

    (D) obsidian

67. HAT : SHOE :: KUFI : _____

    (A) sock

    (B) laces

    (C) kanga

    (D) brogue

68. HIT : PITCH :: SINGLE : _____

    (A) sinker

    (B) black

    (C) double

    (D) married

69. CARDINAL : SENATOR :: _____ : PARLIAMENT

    (A) congressman

    (B) church

    (C) convocation

    (D) pope

70. KINGDOM : PHYLUM :: _____ : ORDER

    (A) life

    (B) class

    (C) chaos

    (D) king

71. _____ : PRIDE :: MISTAKE : SHAME

    (A) Sloth

    (B) Guilt

    (C) Happiness

    (D) Accomplishment

72. QUILL : PEN :: _____ : WATCH

    (A) sundial

    (B) observe

    (C) ink

    (D) abacus

73. INFINITE : LINE :: FINITE : _____
    (A) volume
    (B) point
    (C) line segment
    (D) ray

74. BEEHIVE : _____ :: MOHAWK : BUN
    (A) Indian
    (B) afro
    (C) bread
    (D) honey

75. BEBOP : JITTERBUG :: MUSIC : _____
    (A) insect
    (B) virus
    (C) song
    (D) dance

76. BLUNDER : _____ :: BUNGLER : PUNDIT
    (A) mistake
    (B) ponder
    (C) lecture
    (D) burgle

77. PRINCE : PALACE :: PEON : _____
    (A) shack
    (B) castle
    (C) princess
    (D) peasant

78. IRASCIBLE : _____ :: DISCONSOLATE : JOY
    (A) sadness
    (B) cheer
    (C) surprise
    (D) irate

79. WATER : _____ :: AMMONIA : NITROGEN
    (A) bleach
    (B) vinegar
    (C) carbon
    (D) oxygen

80. GOOGOL : 100 :: 100 : _____
    (A) 10
    (B) 100
    (C) 2
    (D) 1

81. BOAT : SLOOP :: _____ : RAMBUTAN
    (A) fruit
    (B) maritime
    (C) bread
    (D) holiday

82. CALCIUM CARBONATE : CHALK :: SCAPULA : _____
    (A) spatula
    (B) shoulder blade
    (C) kneecap
    (D) board

83. _____ : TYRANT :: SERF : VASSAL
    (A) Peasant
    (B) Wassail
    (C) Despot
    (D) Abecedary

84. SODIUM CHLORIDE : MONOSACCHARIDE :: SALT : _____
    (A) disaccharide
    (B) sodium bicarbonate
    (C) pepper
    (D) sugar

85. _____ : ATOLL :: HILL : BUTTE
    - (A) Island
    - (B) Lagoon
    - (C) Mountain
    - (D) Valley

86. FREQUENCY : PRESSURE :: HERTZ : _____
    - (A) interval
    - (B) pascal
    - (C) Newton
    - (D) decibel

87. BLAZE : BROOM :: LAZE : _____
    - (A) fire
    - (B) loaf
    - (C) room
    - (D) sweep

88. ENCUMBRANCE : _____ :: RELIEF : HELP
    - (A) circumference
    - (B) aid
    - (C) servants
    - (D) onus

89. KARPOV : KASPAROV :: FEDERER : _____
    - (A) Nadal
    - (B) Jordan
    - (C) Woods
    - (D) Carlsen

90. PISCINE : LUPINE :: MACKEREL : _____
    - (A) macaroon
    - (B) gray wolf
    - (C) scrod
    - (D) holy

91. PHILOSOPHY : _____ :: SOCRATES : HESIOD
    - (A) anthropology
    - (B) Plato
    - (C) poetry
    - (D) sculpture

92. SQUARE : CIRCLE :: s^2 : _____
    - (A) π
    - (B) 4s
    - (C) 0
    - (D) πr^2

93. EARTH : IRON :: SUN : _____
    - (A) oxygen
    - (B) hydrogen
    - (C) helium
    - (D) nickel

94. ALPHABET : LETTERS :: _____ : FLOWERS
    - (A) bouquet
    - (B) croquet
    - (C) numbers
    - (D) plants

95. OM : HINDUISM :: _____ : ISLAM
    - (A) Christianity
    - (B) Muslim
    - (C) crescent
    - (D) crucifix

96. CONVIVIAL : STAID :: MIRTHFUL : _____
    - (A) debonair
    - (B) affable
    - (C) genteel
    - (D) demure

97. THE TEMPEST : _____ :: TWELFTH NIGHT : VIOLA

    (A) Prospero

    (B) Theseus

    (C) Othello

    (D) Titania

98. FLY : RUN :: _____ : WORK

    (A) insect

    (B) abscond

    (C) walk

    (D) job

99. DATA : _____ :: FOCI : FOCUS

    (A) datus

    (B) datas

    (C) dati

    (D) datum

100. _____ : 16 :: 8 : 2

    (A) 4

    (B) 32

    (C) 64

    (D) 128

101. _____ : SEAL :: SQUEAK : BARK

    (A) Mouse

    (B) Close

    (C) Oil

    (D) Dog

102. DUODENUM : ILEUM :: _____ : MANDIBLE

    (A) jejunum

    (B) tarsal

    (C) chew

    (D) maxilla

103. EUCHARIST : TABERNACLE :: _____ : BARN

    (A) house

    (B) animals

    (C) farm

    (D) building

104. FALLACY : ERROR :: AXIOM : _____

    (A) premise

    (B) conclusion

    (C) falsity

    (D) axon

105. OBSTREPEROUS : QUIET :: SCINTILLATING : _____

    (A) mean

    (B) kind

    (C) dull

    (D) loud

106. EPITHET : APPELLATION :: _____ : MONIKER

    (A) epitaph

    (B) meretricious

    (C) spurious

    (D) sobriquet

107. ERSATZ : BOGUS :: ERUDITE : _____

    (A) bogey

    (B) educated

    (C) triumphant

    (D) carbonate

108. BAROMETER : PRESSURE :: THEODOLITE : _____

    (A) angles

    (B) temperature

    (C) decibels

    (D) voltage

109. 36 IN. : 1 YD. :: 1 CU. FT. : _____

    (A) 12 cu. in.

    (B) 144 cu. in.

    (C) 1,728 cu. in.

    (D) 36 cu. yd.

110. DEARBORN : PREVOST :: SCOTT :

    _____

    (A) Taylor

    (B) Montojo

    (C) Sampson

    (D) Arista

111. MORTAR : _____ :: CANNON : TREBUCHET

    (A) howitzer

    (B) ballista

    (C) artillery

    (D) arquebus

112. _____ : KILLJOY :: PESSIMISTIC : CYNICAL

    (A) Spoilsport

    (B) Unhappy

    (C) Optimistic

    (D) Naive

113. _____ : SEPARATION :: HYPHEN : JOINING

    (A) Dash

    (B) Plus

    (C) Ampersand

    (D) Interpunct

114. FIRE : _____ :: MAN : FALL

    (A) smoke

    (B) autumn

    (C) water

    (D) woman

115. PI : RADICAL :: π : _____

    (A) Δ

    (B) $\sqrt{\ }$

    (C) $\neq$

    (D) $\approx$

116. BOLIVIA : SPANISH :: CAMBODIA :

    _____

    (A) Mandarin

    (B) Comorian

    (C) Chuukese

    (D) Khmer

117. JUMP : _____ :: TRAMPOLINE : ICE

    (A) skate

    (B) snow

    (C) start

    (D) skip

118. PLOT : _____ :: DRESSER : BUREAU

    (A) clothes

    (B) department

    (C) lot

    (D) drawers

119. ADLER : KEPLER :: BRANDEN :

    _____

    (A) Lennon

    (B) Halley

    (C) Darwin

    (D) Mendel

120. _____ : 1 FT., 6 IN. :: 7 IN. : 1 FT., 2 IN.

    (A) 7in.

    (B) 8in.

    (C) 9in.

    (D) 10in.

Chapter 14

Answers to MAT Practice Test #3

· ·

*P*hew! Now that you've finished taking the third practice MAT, it's time to find out how you did. Make sure you take the time to review any questions on which you guessed or struggled, as well as to review any questions you got wrong. No matter how you fared, pat yourself on the back a little bit: You've just become more familiar with the MAT and increased your scoring potential.

Don't beat yourself up if you made some mistakes. Analyzing your mistakes help point out areas where you need to learn more content, and they may highlight places where you can use your technique more strictly. If you need to brush up on your analogy-solving technique, head back to Chapter 3.

1. Choice (A) is correct. (1:3,2:4) *Ignite* is the verb form of *ignition; applaud* is the verb form of *applause.*

2. Choice (B) is correct. (1:2,3:4) A lymphocyte is part of the immune system; bones are part of the skeletal system.

3. Choice (C) is correct. (1:3,2:4) Excommunication is a punishment used in Catholicism; detention is a punishment used in schools.

4. Choice (D) is correct. (1:2,3:4) $2^3 + 3^3 = 35$; $4^3 + 5^3 = 189$

5. Choice (A) is correct. (1:3,2:4) In cooking, a recipe provides information about ingredients. In medicine, a prescription provides information about dosage.

6. Choice (B) is correct. (1:2,3:4) *Ecstatic* is "extremely excited"; *scalding* is "extremely warm."

7. Choice (C) is correct. (1:2,3:4) The FBI is an intelligence agency in the United States of America; MI6 is an intelligence agency in the United Kingdom.

8. Choice (D) is correct. (1:3,2:4) A scribe uses a pen to work; a referee uses a whistle to work.

9. Choice (D) is correct. (1:3,2:4) "A dime a dozen" and "a piece of cake" are idioms.

10. Choice (C) is correct. (1:3,2:4) The plural form of *crisis* is *crises;* the plural form of *syllabus* is *syllabi.*

11. Choice (B) is correct. (1:2,3:4) A partner is required to tango; light is required to see.

12. Choice (A) is correct. (1:2,3:4) A bazooka fires a rocket; a pistol fires a round.

13. Choice (D) is correct. (1:2,3:4) *Plagiarism* and *originality* are antonyms; *denouement* and *beginning* are also antonyms.

14. Choice (B) is correct. (1:2,3:4) *Excellent* means "extremely great"; *atrocious* means "extremely poor."

15. Choice (C) is correct. (1:3,2:4) *Pig* is a name used to describe a glutton; *sheep* is a name to describe someone who is a follower.

16. Choice (A) is correct. (1:3,2:4) Members of a theater company act; members of an orchestra play.

17. Choice (D) is correct. (1:2,3:4) *Sinister* and *inauspicious* are synonyms; *veracious* and *credible* are also synonyms.

18. Choice (B) is correct. (1:2,3:4) With positions $(w, x) : (y, z)$, the numbers in positions w and z should be the same and have the same signs. The numbers in positions x and y should be the same and have opposite signs.

19. Choice (C) is correct. (1:3,2:4) People go to the seminary to become clergy; people go to the academy to become policemen.

20. Choice (A) is correct. (1:3,2:4) Castanets are a percussion instrument; the sousaphone is a brass instrument.

21. Choice (D) is correct. (1:3,2:4) Sashimi is a Japanese food; okroshka is a Russian food.

22. Choice (B) is correct. (1:2,3:4) *Saloon* and *labour* are words that, in British English, mean the same as *sedan* and *labor* in American English.

23. Choice (C) is correct. (1:2,3:4) Emus and ostriches are similar birds; talons are similar to claws.

24. Choice (A) is correct. (1:3,2:4) A bully displays baseness; an adulator displays flattery.

25. Choice (D) is correct. (1:2,3:4) One polishes something to make it shiny; one washes something to make it clean.

26. Choice (B) is correct. (1:2,3:4) "The real McCoy" is an idiom meaning "a genuine article"; *semblance* means "having the outward appearance of something." If a diamond is the genuine article, then rhinestones have the semblance of a diamond because rhinestones are used as diamond simulants.

27. Choice (C) is correct. (1:2,3:4) Anatomy is a subfield of biology; phonetics is a subfield of linguistics.

28. Choice (A) is correct. (1:2,3:4) Rage is a more intense form of anger; chagrin is a more intense form of annoyance.

29. Choice (D) is correct. (1:2,3:4) *Psychic* and *psychosis* have the same first five letters, the first of which is silent. *Wrong* and *write* have the same first two letters, the first of which is silent.

30. Choice (B) is correct. (1:3,2:4) 22 is an even number; 23 is a prime number.

31. Choice (A) is correct. (1:3,2:4) *Raw* and *frigid* are synonyms; *war* and *conflict* are also synonyms.

32. Choice (C) is correct. (1:2,3:4) One executes at a lynching; one celebrates at a party.

33. Choice (B) is correct. (1:3,2:4) Royal and straight are types of flushes in poker; love and deuce are types of scores in tennis.

34. Choice (B) is correct. (1:2,3:4) There are 180 degrees in a triangle and 360 degrees in a square.

35. Choice (D) is correct. (1:3,2:4). Silk comes from caterpillars; wool comes from sheep.

36. Choice (C) is correct. (1:3,2:4) A noologist studies intellect, and a dendrologist studies trees.

37. Choice (D) is correct. (1:2,3:4) There are four quarts in a gallon; there are four cups in a quart.

38. Choice (A) is correct. (1:2,3:4) Kelvin is a unit of temperature; ampere is a unit of electric current.

39. Choice (D) is correct. (1:2,3:4) Crimson is a shade of red; when a traffic light is red, one stops. Jade is a shade of green; when a traffic light is green, one goes.

40. Choice (C) is correct. (1:2,3:4) Mycology is the study of fungi; carcinology is the study of crustaceans.

41. Choice (B) is correct. (1:2,3:4) In phonology, *hiatus* and *diaeresis* are two different names for the same thing: two vowel sounds occurring in adjacent syllables. In geometry, a perfect quadrilateral is a square.

42. Choice (A) is correct. (1:2,3:4) In mathematics, an axis is part of a graph and a column is part of a matrix.

43. Choice (B) is correct. (1:2,3:4) An isosceles triangle has two sides and angles of the same measure; an equilateral triangle has three sides and angles of the same measure.

44. Choice (D) is correct. (1:2,3:4) A hexadecagon has 16 sides; the square root of 16 is 4. A nonagon has 9 sides; the square root of 9 is 3.

45. Choice (C) is correct. (1:2,3:4) A hop is a small jump; a leap is a large jump. A nap is a short sleep; slumber is a long sleep.

46. Choice (B) is correct. (1:3,2:4) A canvas is a fabric; to *canvass* means "to secure votes."

47. Choice (A) is correct. (1:2,3:4) Jay Gatsby is the protagonist in *The Great Gatsby,* by F. Scott Fitzgerald. Rick Blaine is the protagonist in *Casablanca,* directed by Michael Curtiz.

48. Choice (D) is correct. (1:2,3:4) A building is the result of construction; a product is the result of multiplication.

49. Choice (C) is correct. (1:3,2:4) Wine is made from grapes; mead is made from honey.

50. Choice (C) is correct. (1:2,3:4) The measurement 27 feet is the same as 9 yards; 3^3 is the same as 27.

51. Choice (B) is correct. (1:3,2:4) A section is a division of a newspaper; a book is a division of the Bible.

52. Choice (A) is correct. (1:3,2:4) In a democracy, the majority rules; the popular vote in an election reflects the majority's opinion. In a republic, elected leaders rule; an electoral college in an election reflects the electors' opinions.

53. Choice (D) is correct. (1:3,2:4) *Bizarre* means "strange"; a bazaar is a market.

54. Choice (C) is correct. (1:2,3:4) A faucet controls water flow; an amplifier controls volume.

55. Choice (A) is correct. (1:2,3:4) An Eagle Scout is a type of Boy Scout; a golden eagle is a type of eagle (bird).

56. Choice (B) is correct. (1:2,3:4) Bryology is a division of botany; positivism is a division of sociology.

57. Choice (C) is correct. (1:2,3:4) The gallbladder stores bile; the bladder stores urine.

58. Choice (D) is correct. (1:2,3:4) A Dachshund is a breed of dog; a Burmilla is a breed of cat.

59. Choice (B) is correct. (1:2,3:4) *Exasperation* and *pique* are synonyms; *vilification* and *calumny* are also synonyms.

60. Choice (A) is correct. (1:3,2:4) In architecture, a blueprint shows the design of a structure; in music, a score shows the design of a song.

61. Choice (C) is correct. (1:2,3:4) *Vespine* means "relating to wasps"; *bubaline* means "relating to buffalo."

62. Choice (B) is correct. (1:3,2:4) *Base* and *apex* mean the lowest point and highest point, respectively. The foundation is the lowest part of a building, and the spire is the highest part.

63. Choice (D) is correct. (1:2,3:4) *Hexahedron* is another name for a cube; 6 is equal to $\sqrt{36}$.

64. Choice (A) is correct. (1:3,2:4) If one trips, one might fall; if one gets cut, one might scar.

65. Choice (C) is correct. (1:3,2:4) A baby bird is a chick; a baby reptile is a hatchling.

66. Choice (B) is correct. (1:2,3:4) Limestone is a sedimentary rock; marble is a metaphoric rock (metamorphosed limestone).

67. Choice (D) is correct. (1:3,2:4) Kufi is a type of hat; brogue is a type of shoe.

68. Choice (A) is correct. (1:3,2:4) In baseball, a single is a type of hit; a sinker is a type of pitch.

69. Choice (C) is correct. (1:3,2:4) A cardinal is a religious figure of authority; a convocation is a council of religious authorities. A senator is a political figure of authority; parliament is a council of political authorities.

70. Choice (B) is correct. (1:2,3:4) In taxonomy, phyla make up kingdoms and orders make up classes.

71. Choice (D) is correct. (1:2,3:4) If one has an accomplishment, one might feel pride. If one makes a mistake, one might feel shame.

72. Choice (A) is correct. (1:2,3:4) The quill is an older writing utensil; the pen is a newer writing utensil. The sundial is an older timekeeping device; the watch is a newer timekeeping device.

73. Choice (C) is correct. (1:2,3:4) A line has an infinite length; a line segment has a finite length.

74. Choice (B) is correct. (1:2,3:4) Beehive, afro, mohawk, and bun are all hairstyles.

75. Choice (D) is correct. (1:3,2:4) Bebop is a style of music; jitterbug is a style of dance.

76. Choice (C) is correct. (1:3,2:4) A bungler blunders; a pundit lectures.

77. Choice (A) is correct. (1:2,3:4) A prince lives in a palace; a peon lives in a shack.

78. Choice (B) is correct. (1:2,3:4) If one is irascible, one lacks cheer; if one is disconsolate, one lacks joy.

79. Choice (D) is correct. (1:2,3:4) Water contains oxygen; ammonia contains nitrogen.

80. Choice (C) is correct. (1:2,3:4) A googol is 1 followed by 100 zeros; 100 is 1 followed by 2 zeros.

81. Choice (A) is correct. (1:2,3:4) A sloop is a type of boat. A rambutan is a type of fruit.

82. Choice (B) is correct. (1:2,3:4) Calcium carbonate is the scientific name for chalk; scapula is the scientific name for shoulder blade.

83. Choice (C) is correct. (1:2,3:4) *Despot* and *tyrant* are synonyms; *serf* and *vassal* are also synonyms.

84. Choice (D) is correct. (1:3,2:4) Sodium chloride is salt; a monosaccharide is sugar.

85. Choice (A) is correct. (1:2,3:4) An atoll is an island; a butte is a hill.

86. Choice (B) is correct. (1:3,2:4) Frequency is measured in hertz; pressure is measured in pascals.

87. Choice (C) is correct. (1:3,2:4) *Laze* is *blaze* without the *b; room* is *broom* without the *b.*

88. Choice (D) is correct. (1:3:2:4) *Encumbrance* and *relief* are antonyms; *onus* and *help* are also antonyms.

89. Choice (A) is correct. (1:2,3:4) Anatoly Karpov and Garry Kasparov were great chess rivals. Roger Federer and Rafael Nadal are great tennis rivals.

90. Choice (B) is correct. (1:3,2:4) *Piscine* means "relating to fish"; mackerel is a type of fish. *Lupine* means "relating to wolves"; the gray wolf is a type of wolf.

91. Choice (C) is correct. (1:3,2:4) Socrates was an ancient Greek philosopher; Hesiod was an ancient Greek poet.

92. Choice (D) is correct. (1:3,2:4) The formula for area of a square is s^2; the formula for area of a circle is πr^2.

93. Choice (B) is correct. (1:2,3:4) Iron is the most abundant element on Earth; hydrogen is the most abundant element in the sun.

94. Choice (A) is correct. (1:2,3:4) An alphabet is made up of letters; a bouquet is made up of flowers.

95. Choice (C) is correct. (1:2,3:4) Om is a major symbol in Hinduism; the crescent is a major symbol in Islam.

96. Choice (D) is correct. (1:3,2:4) *Convivial* and *mirthful* both mean "merry." *Staid* and *demure* both mean "reserved."

97. Choice (A) is correct. (1:2,3:4) Prospero is the main character in *The Tempest*. Viola is the main character in *Twelfth Night*.

98. Choice (B) is correct. (1:3,2:4) *Fly* and *abscond* are synonyms; *run* and *work* are also synonyms.

99. Choice (D) is correct. (1:2,3:4) *Data* is the plural of *data; foci* is the plural of *focus.*

100. Choice (C) is correct. (1:2,3:4) The number 64 is four times 16. The number 8 is four times 2.

101. Choice (A) is correct. (1:3,2:4) A mouse squeaks; a seal barks.

102. Choice (D) is correct. (1:2,3:4) The duodenum and ileum are parts of the intestine; the maxilla and mandible are parts of the skull.

103. Choice (B) is correct. (1:2,3:4) The Eucharist is kept in the tabernacle; animals are kept in the barn.

104. Choice (A) is correct. (1:2,3:4) In reasoning, a fallacy is an error and an axiom is a premise.

105. Choice (C) is correct. (1:2,3:4) *Obstreperous* and *quiet* are antonyms; *scintillating* and *dull* are also antonyms.

106. Choice (D) is correct. (1:2,3:4) *Epithet, appellation, sobriquet,* and *moniker* are all synonyms meaning "name."

107. Choice (B) is correct. (1:2,3:4) *Ersatz* and *bogus* are synonyms. *Erudite* and *educated* are also synonyms.

108. Choice (A) is correct. (1:2,3:4) A barometer measures pressure; a theodolite measures angles.

109. Choice (C) is correct. (1:2,3:4) There are 36 inches in 1 yard; there are 1728 cubic inches in 1 cubic foot.

110. Choice (D) is correct. (1:2,3:4) Henry Dearborn and George Prévost were conflicting commanders in the War of 1812. Winfield Scott and Mariano Arista were conflicting commanders in the Mexican–American War.

111. Choice (B) is correct. (1:3,2:4) The ballista and trebuchet were ancient siege engines. The mortar and cannon are more modern siege engines.

112. Choice (A) is correct. (1:2,3:4) *Spoilsport* and *killjoy* are names for a person who is a downer. *Pessimistic* and *cynical* are synonyms that describe a downer.

113. Choice (D) is correct. (1:2,3:4) The interpunct is a punctuation mark used for interword separation. The hyphen is a punctuation mark used for joining words.

114. Choice (C) is correct. (1:3,2:4) *Fireman* and *waterfall* are compound words.

115. Choice (B) is correct. (1:3,2:4) The pi symbol is π; the radical symbol is $\sqrt{}$.

116. Choice (D) is correct. (1:2,3:4) Spanish is an official language in Bolivia; Khmer is the official language in Cambodia.

117. Choice (A) is correct. (1:3,2:4) One jumps on a trampoline; one skates on ice.

118. Choice (C) is correct. (1:2,3:4) *Plot* and *lot* are synonyms; *dresser* and *bureau* are also synonyms.

119. Choice (B) is correct. (1:3,2:4) Alfred Adler and Nathaniel Branden are psychologists. Johannes Kepler and Edmond Halley are astronomers.

120. Choice (C) is correct. (1:2,3:4) The measure 9 inches is half of 1 foot, and the measure 7 inches is half of 1 foot, 2 inches.

Chapter 15

MAT Practice Test #4

....

*H*ere's the fourth MAT practice test. Like the other exams in this book, this one is modeled on authentic MAT questions, to help you get accustomed to the real test's style. Remember to use good technique throughout the test as you take it. If you want to make the experience realistic, don't just look through the test. Instead, take it all at once, timed strictly, in a room where you won't be interrupted for an hour.

As you take the test, it's a good idea to circle questions you guessed on — after all, if you get them right, it may just be luck. Review questions you guessed on as carefully as you review questions you got wrong. After taking the test, review your mistakes and guesses. Be your own coach: for any given question, what do you need to work on? Your term knowledge? Your analogy technique? Or did you simply not have enough time to spend on the question? Write down a quick corrective action for each mistake and follow through to improve your skills. Good luck!

1. LIZARD : _____ :: ARACHNID : SPIDER

    (A) wizard

    (B) iguana

    (C) scorpion

    (D) reptile

2. DISTRESS: _____ :: BELIE : PROVE

    (A) comfort

    (B) belly

    (C) disprove

    (D) unease

3. EVIL : LIVE :: GULP : _____

    (A) sip

    (B) good

    (C) plug

    (D) die

4. WATER : _____ :: LIGHT : WATT

    (A) volt

    (B) heavy

    (C) wind

    (D) fathom

5. ORCHESTRA : _____ :: VIRTUOSO : SOLO

    (A) symphony

    (B) duet

    (C) violin

    (D) virtuous

6. FENCE : PROPERTY :: FRET : _____

    (A) picket

    (B) guitar

    (C) worry

    (D) land

7. NIETZSCHE : NIHILISM :: _____ : OBJECTIVISM

    (A) Freud

    (B) Caesar

    (C) Rand

    (D) Aristotle

8. TUMULTUOUS : ORDERLY :: DEFICIENT : _____

    (A) nurse

    (B) lacking

    (C) confused

    (D) adequate

9. STIMULANT : CAFFEINE :: DEPRESSANT : _____

    (A) nicotine

    (B) heroin

    (C) anxiety

    (D) coffee

10. EMINENCE : CELEBRITY :: TRIVIALITY : _____

    (A) pettiness

    (B) famous

    (C) prominence

    (D) vitality

11. DAUBER : TROUBADOUR :: PAINTER : _____

    (A) carpenter

    (B) architect

    (C) singer

    (D) baker

12. SCALE : CHRONOGRAPH :: WEIGHT : _____

    (A) mass

    (B) lithograph

    (C) energy

    (D) time

13. _____ : WORDS :: CULINARIAN : STENOGRAPHER

    (A) climate

    (B) food

    (C) stencils

    (D) language

14. _____ : CONSPICUOUSNESS :: FAST : DISPATCH

    (A) obvious

    (B) obscure

    (C) slow

    (D) hastily

15. DIAGONAL : DIAMETER :: _____ : CIRCLE

    (A) circumvent

    (B) triangle

    (C) square

    (D) circumference

16. OLD GLORY : _____ :: UNION JACK : U.K.

    (A) UAE

    (B) Confederates

    (C) Civil War

    (D) USA

17. 2L + 2W : _____ :: πD : CIRCLE

    (A) radius

    (B) rectangle

    (C) triangle

    (D) π

18. REPRODUCTION : DNA :: _____ : ATP

    (A) metabolism

    (B) respiration

    (C) excretion

    (D) genetics

19. _____ : AFFLUENT :: DESTITUTE : OPULENT

    (A) cantankerous

    (B) maladroit

    (C) impecunious

    (D) purlieu

20. 3 DIMENSIONS : CUBE :: 4 DIMENSIONS : _____

    (A) parabola

    (B) hyperbola

    (C) octahedron

    (D) tesseract

21. EXOSPHERE : THERMOSPHERE :: _____ : STRATOSPHERE

    (A) mesosphere

    (B) troposphere

    (C) ionosphere

    (D) ozone layer

22. MENDELEEV : _____ :: GATLING : MACHINE GUN

    (A) chloroform

    (B) periodic table

    (C) waterproofing

    (D) microprocessor

23. FAIR : _____ :: PULCHRITUDINOUS : AMIABLE

    (A) just

    (B) light

    (C) warm

    (D) hot

24. _____ : DOPPLER :: CHEMISTRY : PAULING

    (A) anthropology

    (B) psychology

    (C) astrology

    (D) physics

25. _____ : GENETICS :: HAWKING : MENDEL

   (A) Singularities

   (B) Flight

   (C) Birds

   (D) Ionization

26. _____ : LEAD :: AU : GOLD

   (A) Sn

   (B) Pb

   (C) Ld

   (D) Le

27. EXOTHERMIC : ENDOTHERMIC :: _____ : SPONGE

   (A) reaction

   (B) Porifera

   (C) broom

   (D) faucet

28. PUP : POULT :: BAT : _____

   (A) crocodile

   (B) baboon

   (C) turkey

   (D) bison

29. MIEN : DEMEANOR :: _____ : INEXORABLE

   (A) harsh

   (B) soft

   (C) temperament

   (D) free

30. SOMME : 1916 :: _____ : 1944

   (A) Inchon

   (B) Saipan

   (C) Princeton

   (D) Coburg

31. DALAI LAMA : POPE :: _____ : CATHOLICISM

   (A) Taoism

   (B) Hinduism

   (C) Sikhism

   (D) Buddhism

32. CANONIZATION : _____ :: CORONATION : MONARCH

   (A) weapon

   (B) book

   (C) saint

   (D) king

33. SWARM : _____ :: BEE : LION

   (A) pride

   (B) mane

   (C) felid

   (D) lioness

34. SAKE : SOJU :: JAPAN : _____

   (A) Indonesia

   (B) Korea

   (C) China

   (D) Malaysia

35. CHARM : TAU :: : _____ : LEPTON

   (A) boson

   (B) atom

   (C) neutron

   (D) quark

36. ROTATE : AXIS :: REVOLVE : _____

   (A) sun

   (B) spin

   (C) hemisphere

   (D) stars

37. JAINISM : _____ :: ALTRUISM : WELFARE

    (A) conservative

    (B) equality

    (C) nonviolence

    (D) social security

38. COUTURE : FASHION :: LOUCHE : _____

    (A) cumbersome

    (B) disreputable

    (C) left

    (D) naïve

39. PIANO : _____ :: CLASSICAL : CHIPTUNE

    (A) forte

    (B) violin

    (C) baroque

    (D) synthesizer

40. AXE : _____ :: RAMP : INCLINED PLANE

    (A) wedge

    (B) screw

    (C) spear

    (D) wheelchair

41. SPRING : _____ :: HONEYCOMB : HEXAGONAL

    (A) summer

    (B) equinox

    (C) helix

    (D) octagonal

42. DIACRITIC : _____ :: LETTER : NUMBER

    (A) diabolic

    (B) exponent

    (C) count

    (D) numeral

43. DRAIN : DARK :: _____ : BARK

    (A) woof

    (B) tree

    (C) brain

    (D) empty

44. _____ : MORAL :: NEFARIOUS : IMMORAL

    (A) Meritorious

    (B) Rapacious

    (C) Impudent

    (D) Quintessence

45. AMORTIZATION : _____ :: DECREASING : INCREASING

    (A) mortgage

    (B) economics

    (C) accrual

    (D) mercantilism

46. FISH : GILL :: WHALE : _____

    (A) mammal

    (B) mouth

    (C) shark

    (D) blowhole

47. USA : SPAIN :: NAVAJO : _____

    (A) Sicilian

    (B) Catalan

    (C) Aboriginal

    (D) Cherokee

48. _____ : $\sqrt{3}$ :: INTEGER : $\sqrt{4}$

    (A) Inverse

    (B) Argand

    (C) Surd

    (D) Natural

49. MISSISSIPPI : _____ :: POTOMAC : OKEECHOBEE

    (A) Iliamna

    (B) Missouri

    (C) Florida

    (D) Victoria

50. _____ : GATES :: RED ARMY : MICROSOFT

    (A) Lenin

    (B) Stalin

    (C) Marx

    (D) Trotsky

51. _____ : MISBEHAVIOR :: APPROBATION : OBEDIENCE

    (A) Deference

    (B) Admonishment

    (C) Innuendo

    (D) Resolute

52. _____ : DAUNTLESS :: CAPRICIOUS : MERCURIAL

    (A) Disheveled

    (B) Rapturous

    (C) Stalwart

    (D) Daunting

53. SON : FARM :: NATIVE : _____

    (A) Animal

    (B) Dairy

    (C) House

    (D) Local

54. QUIXOTIC : ELASTIC :: _____ : RUBBER

    (A) grouch

    (B) dreamer

    (C) tire

    (D) duck

55. APPRAISE : APPRISE :: _____ : INFORM

    (A) prism

    (B) abreast

    (C) antique

    (D) assess

56. TACIT : _____ :: ATTIC : VEILS

    (A) lives

    (B) quiet

    (C) basement

    (D) bride

57. _____ : CERTAIN :: PART : LIKELY

    (A) Definite

    (B) Piece

    (C) Whole

    (D) Hair

58. 4^{-1} : QUARTER :: 1/20 : _____

    (A) dollar

    (B) nickel

    (C) dime

    (D) penny

59. TASTE : _____ :: PALATE : PALETTE

    (A) sight

    (B) toast

    (C) soft

    (D) colors

60. _____ : CHICANERY :: ABUNDANCE : ARTIFICE

    (A) Delusion

    (B) Ablution

    (C) Profusion

    (D) Confusion

61. SACCHARIN : SUGAR :: _____ : GRASS

    (A) AstroTurf

    (B) sucrose

    (C) meadow

    (D) graminoid

62. BATTLE : COMMUNION :: WAR : _____

    (A) accord

    (B) Mass

    (C) Tolstoy

    (D) violence

63. _____ : 4 :: 0.125 : 8

    (A) 32

    (B) 0.5

    (C) 0.25

    (D) 12

64. _____ : PEACE :: MOIETY : CONCILIATION

    (A) Piece

    (B) Harmony

    (C) Council

    (D) Dove

65. TAOISM : LAOZI :: THOMISM : _____

    (A) Wittgenstein

    (B) holism

    (C) opportunism

    (D) Aquinas

66. PHLEGMATIC : _____ :: TEMPESTUOUS : FIERCE

    (A) phlegm

    (B) pragmatic

    (C) unemotional

    (D) tempest

67. FORWARD : STICKY :: CONTRACTS : _____

    (A) retroactive

    (B) prices

    (C) agreements

    (D) awkward

68. CONE : COLOR :: ROD : _____

    (A) peripheral

    (B) orange

    (C) rodent

    (D) pulmonary

69. POMMEL : _____ :: BUTT : RIFLE

    (A) cigarette

    (B) pistol

    (C) horse

    (D) sword

70. 3 : 27 :: 0 : _____

    (A) 0

    (B) 1

    (C) 3

    (D) 9

71. _____ : SAMUEL WILSON :: SANTA CLAUS : UNCLE SAM

    (A) George Washington

    (B) Nathan Hale

    (C) St. Nicholas

    (D) Easter Bunny

72. REVIVER : MADAM :: DEIFIED : _____

    (A) worshipped

    (B) rotator

    (C) mister

    (D) vivify

73. NONFICTION : FACTS :: FICTION : _____

   (A) truths
   (B) biography
   (C) pacts
   (D) imagination

74. ELBRUS : RUSSIA :: _____ : CANADA

   (A) Logan
   (B) Charles
   (C) Peters
   (D) Preston

75. _____ : y − 5 :: 23% : 5 less than

   (A) 5%
   (B) 0.23%
   (C) 0.23y
   (D) 23y

76. NEOPHYTE : _____ :: FLEDGLING : CONNOISSEUR

   (A) hatchling
   (B) maven
   (C) neonate
   (D) wine

77. VORACIOUS : _____ :: QUIESCENT : ACTIVITY

   (A) hobby
   (B) quiet
   (C) understanding
   (D) generosity

78. _____ : C :: CANE : J

   (A) Crescent
   (B) See
   (C) Jay
   (D) Candy

79. METER : KILOMETER :: _____ : 100

   (A) 0.01
   (B) 0.1
   (C) 1
   (D) 10

80. _____ : GHRELIN :: OVARY : ESTRONE

   (A) Liver
   (B) Spleen
   (C) Stomach
   (D) Brain

81. ASSUME : _____ :: CERTIFY : SUBSTANTIATE

   (A) consort
   (B) rapport
   (C) confirm
   (D) purport

82. PASSWORD : COMPUTER :: _____ : DOOR

   (A) lock
   (B) knob
   (C) login
   (D) secret

83. VICTORIA : QUEENSLAND :: CHARLES : _____

   (A) West Virginia
   (B) Connecticut
   (C) North Carolina
   (D) North Dakota

84. JOCULAR : MOROSE :: JAUNTY : _____

   (A) juvenile
   (B) lethargic
   (C) muster
   (D) villainous

85. CAPITALIST : _____ :: DENTIST : ORTHODONTIST

    (A) doctor

    (B) communist

    (C) economy

    (D) entrepreneur

86. PHOTOTROPISM : LIGHT :: THIGMOTROPISM : _____

    (A) touch

    (B) water

    (C) sound

    (D) temperature

87. BOOK : BACK :: _____ : FIRE

    (A) magazine

    (B) quit

    (C) mark

    (D) water

88. MULL : MULLIGAN :: THINK : _____

    (A) thinly

    (B) self-evident

    (C) things

    (D) do-over

89. BRAZIL : GREECE :: CAIPIRINHA : _____

    (A) ouzo

    (B) absinthe

    (C) balsam

    (D) port

90. BACK : _____:: FRONT : BOW

    (A) behind

    (B) stern

    (C) ribbon

    (D) dorsal

91. _____ : DISCRETION :: ENCUMBRANCE : IMPEDIMENT

    (A) Profusion

    (B) Refection

    (C) Associate

    (D) Prerogative

92. COGITATE : ENVISAGE :: DEPICT : _____

    (A) penchant

    (B) predilection

    (C) delineate

    (D) dream

93. 183 : NATURAL :: _____ : INTEGER

    (A) –591

    (B) 0.5625

    (C) ¼

    (D) pi

94. _____ : BOCCE :: UNO : SNOOKER

    (A) rakes

    (B) spades

    (C) grass

    (D) court

95. VESTIBULAR SYSTEM : _____ :: BALANCE : HEARING

    (A) thoracic

    (B) pineal

    (C) adenoid

    (D) cochlea

96. TRAINEE : _____ :: INTERNEE : FREEDOM

    (A) experience

    (B) novice

    (C) liberty

    (D) secretary

97. _____ : SOCAGE :: KNIGHT : FARMER

    (A) Suffrage

    (B) Chain mail

    (C) Scutage

    (D) Birdcage

98. DUODENUM : JEJUNUM :: ILEUM : _____

    (A) alimentary

    (B) cecum

    (C) colon

    (D) intestine

99. TENACIOUS : LANGUID :: _____ : TORPID

    (A) loquacious

    (B) fallacious

    (C) pertinacious

    (D) gracious

100. _____ : NOTICE :: SOJOURN : VISIT

    (A) Stripe

    (B) Star

    (C) Speckle

    (D) Spot

101. CANTERBURY : PIERS :: TALES : _____

    (A) plowman

    (B) poltergeist

    (C) prefect

    (D) preferred

102. GASTRIC ACID : BLEACH :: _____ : TSUNAMI

    (A) sashimi

    (B) splash

    (C) vinegar

    (D) stomach

103. TENNIS : VOLLEYBALL :: _____ : SPIKE

    (A) net

    (B) racquet

    (C) smash

    (D) lob

104. _____ : ORIGINAL :: TRITE : INVENTIVE

    (A) Daunting

    (B) Nippy

    (C) Egregious

    (D) Hackneyed

105. 120 − 20% : 100 + 20% :: _____ : 120

    (A) 96

    (B) 100

    (C) 104

    (D) 92

106. PEANUT : LEGUME :: CUCUMBER : _____

    (A) silique

    (B) pepo

    (C) hesperidium

    (D) loment

107. SERBIAN : BUNJEVAC :: LUXEMBURGISH : _____

    (A) Dacian

    (B) Umbrian

    (C) Dutch

    (D) Hellenic

108. CAUSE : EFFECT :: AGENT : _____

    (A) doctor

    (B) affect

    (C) clause

    (D) patient

109. : THEREFORE :: : _____

(A) either

(B) because

(C) only

(D) until

110. FERRIC : FERRIAGE :: : TOLL

(A) iron

(B) boat

(C) untamed

(D) wheel

111. KONEV : POUND :: _____ : BROOKE

(A) Mathieu

(B) Harding

(C) Zhukov

(D) Phillips

112. FELIX : SYLVESTER :: BABE : _____

(A) Frederick

(B) Caesar

(C) Donald

(D) Napoleon

113. SOMNOLOGY : VEXILLOLOGY :: SLEEP : _____

(A) flags

(B) confusion

(C) dreams

(D) antiques

114. BOOM : DEPRESSION :: DEPRECIATION : _____

(A) interest

(B) appreciation

(C) recession

(D) gratitude

115. HEART : _____ :: LOVE : PEACE

(A) atrium

(B) war

(C) dove

(D) brain

116. 4 : 5 :: : _____ :: 11

(A) 8

(B) 21

(C) 2

(D) 6

117. RICIN : STRYCHNINE :: PROTEIN : _____

(A) plant

(B) carbohydrate

(C) sodium

(D) alkaloid

118. PIANO : FORTE :: _____ : BASS

(A) percussion

(B) contra

(C) pianissimo

(D) pike

119. PHOTON : STRANGE :: GLUON : _____

(A) muon

(B) light

(C) down

(D) weird

120. INTERDECILE RANGE : DISPERSION :: _____ : SCALE PARAMETER

(A) gamma distribution

(B) scale factor

(C) coefficient

(D) binomial theorem

Chapter 16

Answers to MAT Practice Test #4

- -

*Y*ou've completed another practice test — nice job! Remember, all this practice is going to pay off when you take the real MAT. Now, it's time to learn as much as you can from your mistakes. Make sure that you take the time to review any questions on which you guessed or struggled, as well as to review any incorrect answers. Your mistakes should be helpful in pointing you toward areas where you need to learn more content, and they may highlight places where you can use your technique more strictly.

1. Choice (B) is correct. (1:2,3:4) An iguana is a lizard, and a spider is an arachnid.

2. Choice (A) is correct. (1:2,3:4) *Distress* and *comfort* are antonyms; *belie* and *prove* are also antonyms.

3. Choice (C) is correct. (1:2,3:4) *Evil* spelled backward is *live; gulp* spelled backward is *plug*.

4. Choice (D) is correct. (1:2,3:4) Water depth can be measured in fathoms; the strength of light bulbs can be measured in watts.

5. Choice (A) is correct. (1:2,3:4) An orchestra performs a symphony; a virtuoso performs a solo.

6. Choice (B) is correct. (1:2,3:4) Fences divide property; frets divide guitar necks.

7. Choice (C) is correct. (1:2,3:4) Friedrich Nietzsche was known for his work in nihilism; Ayn Rand was known for her work in objectivism.

8. Choice (D) is correct. (1:2,3:4) *Tumultuous* and *orderly* are antonyms; *deficient* and *adequate* are also antonyms.

9. Choice (B) is correct. (1:2,3:4) Caffeine is a stimulant; heroin is a depressant.

10. Choice (A) is correct. (1:2,3:4) *Eminence* and *celebrity* are synonyms; *triviality* and *pettiness* are also synonyms.

11. Choice (C) is correct. (1:3,2:4) A dauber is a painter; a troubadour is a singer.

12. Choice (D) is correct. (1:3,2:4) Scales measure weight; chronographs measure time.

13. Choice (B) is correct. (1:3,2:4) A culinarian deals with food; a stenographer deals with words.

14. Choice (A) is correct. (1:2,3:4) *Obvious* is an adjective that relates synonymously to the noun *conspicuousness. Fast* is an adjective that relates synonymously to the noun *dispatch.*

15. Choice (C) is correct. (1:3,2:4) A diagonal passes through the center of a square from one point on the perimeter to the opposite point on the perimeter. A diameter passes through the center of a circle from one point on the circumference to the opposite point on the circumference.

16. Choice (D) is correct. (1:2,3:4) Old Glory is a nickname for the flag of the USA; Union Jack is a nickname for the flag of the U.K.

17. Choice (B) is correct. (1:2,3:4) 2L + 2W is the formula for the perimeter of a rectangle. πD is the formula for the circumference of a circle.

18. Choice (A) is correct. (1:2,3:4) DNA is a key molecule in the process of reproduction; ATP is a key molecule in the process of metabolism.

19. Choice (C) is correct. (1:3,2:4) *Impecunious* and *destitute* are synonyms; *affluent* and *opulent* are also synonyms.

20. Choice (D) is correct. (1:2,3:4) The tesseract is the four-dimensional equivalent of the three-dimensional cube.

21. Choice (A) is correct. (1:2,3:4) The four outermost layers of the atmosphere, starting from space and getting closer to Earth, are the exosphere, thermosphere, mesosphere, and stratosphere.

22. Choice (B) is correct. (1:2,3:4) Mendeleev created the first periodic table; Gatling created the first machine gun.

23. Choice (C) is correct. (1:3,2:4) *Fair* and *pulchritudinous* are synonyms; *warm* and *amiable* are also synonyms.

24. Choice (D) is correct. (1:2,3:4) Doppler was known for his work in physics; Pauling was known for his work in chemistry.

25. Choice (A) is correct. (1:3,2:4) Hawking is known for his contributions to the understanding of singularities; Mendel is known for his contributions to the understanding of genetics.

26. Choice (B) is correct. (1:2,3:4) Pb is the symbol for lead; Au is the symbol for gold.

27. Choice (D) is correct. (1:3,2:4) Exothermic is a type of reaction in which energy is released; a faucet releases water. Endothermic is a type of reaction in which energy is absorbed; a sponge absorbs water.

28. Choice (C) is correct. (1:3,2:4) A pup is a young bat; a poult is a young turkey.

29. Choice (A) is correct. (1:2,3:4) *Mien* and *demeanor* are synonyms; *harsh* and *inexorable* are also synonyms.

30. Choice (B) is correct. (1:2,3:4) The Battle of the Somme took place in 1916; the Battle of Saipan took place in 1944.

31. Choice (D) is correct. (1:3,2:4) The Dalai Lama is the primary religious leader in Buddhism; the Pope is the primary religious leader in Catholicism.

32. Choice (C) is correct. (1:2,3:4) Canonization is a process by which one becomes a saint; coronation is a process by which one becomes a monarch.

33. Choice (A) is correct. (1:3,2:4) A group of bees is a swarm; a group of lions is a pride.

34. Choice (B) is correct. (1:3,2:4) Sake is a drink that originated in Japan; soju is a drink that originated in Korea.

35. Choice (D) is correct. (1:3,2:4) Charm is a type of quark; tau is a type of lepton.

36. Choice (A) is correct. (1:2,3:4) Earth rotates on its axis and revolves around the sun.

37. Choice (C) is correct. (1:2,3:4) Jainism is a philosophy of nonviolence; altruism is concerned with the welfare of people.

38. Choice (B) is correct. (1:2,3:4) The French word "couture" means "fashion" in English; the French word "louche" means "disreputable" in English.

39. Choice (D) is correct. (1:3,2:4) The piano is an acoustic instrument that can be used to play classical music. The synthesizer is an electronic instrument that can be used to play chiptune music.

40. Choice (A) is correct. (1:2,3:4) An axe is an example of a wedge; a ramp is an example of an inclined plane.

41. Choice (C) is correct. (1:2,3:4) A spring has a helix shape; a honeycomb has a hexagonal shape.

42. Choice (B) is correct. (1:3,2:4) A diacritic modifies a letter; an exponent modifies a number.

43. Choice (C) is correct. (1:3,2:4) *Drain* and *brain* rhyme and are spelled the same, except for the first letter. *Dark* and *bark* are related in the same way.

44. Choice (A) is correct. (1:2,3:4) *Meritorious* and *moral* are synonyms; *nefarious* and *immoral* are also synonyms.

45. Choice (C) is correct. (1:3,2:4) In economics, *amortization* refers to the decreasing of an amount; *accrual* refers to the increasing of an amount.

46. Choice (D) is correct. (1:2,3:4) Fish take in oxygen through their gills; whales take in oxygen through their blowholes.

47. Choice (B) is correct. (1:3,2:4) The Navajo people are found in the USA; the Catalan people are found in Spain.

48. Choice (C) is correct. (1:2,3:4) $\sqrt{3}$ in decimal form is an example of a surd; $\sqrt{4}$ in decimal form is an example of an integer.

49. Choice (A) is correct. (1:3,2:4) The Mississippi and Potomac are both U.S. rivers; the Iliamna and Okeechobee are both U.S. lakes.

50. Choice (D) is correct. (1:3,2:4) Trotsky founded the Red Army; Gates founded Microsoft.

51. Choice (B) is correct. (1:2,3:4) One might receive admonishment for misbehavior; one might receive approbation for obedience.

52. Choice (C) is correct. (1:2,3:4) *Stalwart* and *dauntless* are synonyms; *capricious* and *mercurial* are also synonyms.

53. Choice (A) is correct. (1:3,2:4) *Native Son* and *Animal Farm* are both novels.

54. Choice (B) is correct. (1:3,2:4) A dreamer could be described as quixotic; rubber could be described as elastic.

55. Choice (D) is correct. (1:3,2:4) *Appraise* means "to assess"; *apprise* means "to inform."

56. Choice (A) is correct. (1:3,2:4) *Tacit* and *attic* are anagrams of each other; *lives* and *veils* are also anagrams of each other.

57. Choice (C) is correct. (1:3,2:4) The words *whole* and *certain* imply totality; the words *part* and *likely* imply a piece of totality.

58. Choice (B) is correct. (1:2,3:4) 4^{-1} is 1/4 or 0.25; $0.25 is a quarter. 1/20 is 0.05; $0.05 is a nickel.

59. Choice (D) is correct. (1:3,2:4) *Taste* and *palate* are synonyms; *colors* and *palette* are also synonyms.

60. Choice (C) is correct. (1:3,2:4) *Profusion* and *abundance* are synonyms; *chicanery* and *artifice* are also synonyms.

61. Choice (A) is correct. (1:2,3:4) Saccharin is an artificial sweetener used as a sugar substitute. AstroTurf is artificial grass.

62. Choice (B) is correct. (1:3,2:4) A battle is a part of a war; communion is a part of Mass.

63. Choice (C) is correct. (1:2,3:4) 0.25 multiplied by 4 equals 1; 0.125 multiplied by 8 equals 1.

64. Choice (A) is correct. (1:3,2:4) *Piece* and *moiety* are synonyms; *peace* and *conciliation* are also synonyms.

65. Choice (D) is correct. (1:2,3:4) Taoism is based on the teachings of Laozi; Thomism is based on the teachings of Aquinas.

66. Choice (C) is correct. (1:2,3:4) *Phlegmatic* and *unemotional* are synonyms; *tempestuous* and *fierce* are also synonyms.

67. Choice (B) is correct. (1:3,2:4) In economics, *forward contracts* and *sticky prices* are compounds.

68. Choice (A) is correct. (1:2,3:4) Cone cells are responsible for color vision; rod cells are responsible for peripheral vision.

69. Choice (D) is correct. (1:2,3:4) The pommel is the base of a sword; the butt is the base of a rifle.

70. Choice (A) is correct. (1:2,3:4) 3 to the third power is 27; 0 to the third power is 0.

71. Choice (C) is correct. (1:3,2:4) Santa Claus is based on St. Nicholas; Uncle Sam is based on Samuel Wilson.

72. Choice (B) is correct. (1:2,3:4) *Reviver, madam, deified,* and *rotator* are all palindromes.

73. Choice (D) is correct. (1:2,3:4) Nonfiction writing requires facts; fiction writing requires imagination.

74. Choice (A) is correct. (1:2,3:4) Mount Elbrus is the highest mountain in Russia; Mount Logan is the highest mountain in Canada.

75. Choice (C) is correct. (1:3,2:4) $0.23y$ is 23% of y; $y - 5$ is 5 less than y.

76. Choice (B) is correct. (1:3,2:4) *Neophyte* and *fledgling* are synonyms; *maven* and *connoisseur* are also synonyms. Both pairs of words are antonyms to each other.

77. Choice (D) is correct. (1:2,3:4) *Voracious* means "lacking generosity"; *quiescent* means "lacking activity."

78. Choice (A) is correct. (1:2,3:4) The letter *C* is shaped like a crescent; the letter *J* is shaped like a cane.

79. Choice (B) is correct. (1:2,3:4) A meter is 1/1000 of a kilometer. 0.1 is 1/1000 of 100.

80. Choice (C) is correct. (1:2,3:4) Ghrelin is a hormone produced in the stomach; estrone is a hormone produced in the ovaries.

81. Choice (D) is correct. (1:2,3:4) *Assume* and *purport* are synonyms; *certify* and *substantiate* are also synonyms.

82. Choice (A) is correct. (1:2,3:4) A password is a type of security system for computers; a lock is a type of security system for doors.

83. Choice (C) is correct. (1:2,3:4) Queensland, Australia, is named for Queen Victoria. North Carolina, USA, is named for King Charles.

84. Choice (B) is correct. (1:2,3:4) *Jocular* and *morose* are antonyms; *jaunty* and *lethargic* are also antonyms.

85. Choice (D) is correct. (1:2,3:4) A capitalist and an entrepreneur both believe in private business ownership; a dentist and an orthodontist both work on teeth.

86. Choice (A) is correct. (1:2,3:4) Phototropism is the movement of plants in response to light; thigmotropism is the movement of plants in response to touch.

87. Choice (C) is correct. (1:3,2:4) *Bookmark* and *backfire* are compounds.

88. Choice (D) is correct. (1:3,2:4) To mull is to think; a mulligan is a do-over.

89. Choice (A) is correct. (1:3,2:4) Caipirinha is the national alcoholic drink of Brazil; ouzo is the national alcoholic drink of Greece.

90. Choice (B) is correct. (1:2,3:4) The stern is the back part of a boat; the bow is the front part of a boat.

91. Choice (D) is correct. (1:2,3:4) *Prerogative* and *discretion* are synonyms; *encumbrance* and *impediment* are also synonyms.

92. Choice (C) is correct. (1:2,3:4) *Cogitate* and *envisage* are synonyms; *depict* and *delineate* are also synonyms.

93. Choice (A) is correct. (1:2,3:4) 183 is a natural number; –591 is an integer.

94. Choice (B) is correct. (1:3,2:4) Spades and Uno are card games; bocce and snooker are sports.

95. Choice (D) is correct. (1:3,2:4) In the inner ear, the vestibular system controls balance and the cochlea controls hearing.

96. Choice (A) is correct. (1:2,3:4) A trainee desires experience; an internee desires freedom.

97. Choice (C) is correct. (1:3,2:4) Scutage was a feudal tax that applied to knights; socage was a feudal tax that applied to farmers.

98. Choice (B) is correct. (1:2,3:4) Food travels through the duodenum, jejunum, ileum, and cecum, in that order.

99. Choice (C) is correct. (1:3,2:4) *Tenacious* and *pertinacious* are synonyms; *languid* and *torpid* are also synonyms.

100. Choice (D) is correct. (1:2,3:4) *Spot* and *notice* are synonyms; *sojourn* and *visit* are also synonyms.

101. Choice (A) is correct. (1:3,2:4) *The Canterbury Tales* and *Piers Plowman* are both examples of medieval literature.

102. Choice (B) is correct. (1:2,3:4) Gastric acid has a very low pH; bleach has a very high pH. A splash is a small amount of water; a tsunami is a large amount of water.

103. Choice (C) is correct. (1:3,2:4) A smash is an aggressive, offensive shot in tennis; a spike is an aggressive, offensive attack in volleyball.

104. Choice (D) is correct. (1:3,2:4) *Hackneyed* and *trite* are synonyms; *original* and *inventive* are also synonyms.

105. Choice (A) is correct. (1:3,2:4) $120 - 20\% = 120 - 24 = 96$. $100 + 20\% = 100 + 20 = 120$.

106. Choice (B) is correct. (1:2,3:4) A peanut is a legume; a cucumber is a pepo.

107. Choice (C) is correct. (1:2,3:4) Serbian and Bunjevac are Slavic languages; Luxemburgish and Dutch are Germanic languages.

108. Choice (D) is correct. (1:2,3:4) In grammar, the agent is the cause of an event, and the patient is the target of that event.

109. Choice (B) is correct. (1:2,3:4) In mathematical proofs, means "therefore," and means "because."

110. Choice (A) is correct. (1:3,2:4) *Ferric* refers to iron; *ferriage* is the toll to take a ferry.

111. Choice (C) is correct. (1:3,2:4) Konev and Zhukov were Russian commanders during World War II; Pound and Brooke were British commanders during World War II.

112. Choice (D) is correct. (1:2,3:4) Felix and Sylvester are fictional cats; Babe and Napoleon are fictional pigs.

113. Choice (A) is correct. (1:3,2:4) Somnology is the study of sleep; vexillology is the study of flags.

114. Choice (B) is correct. (1:2,3:4) In economics, *boom* and *depression* are opposites; *depreciation* and *appreciation* are also opposites.

115. Choice (C) is correct. (1:3,2:4) The heart is a symbol of love; the dove is a symbol of peace.

116. Choice (A) is correct. (1:2,3:4) When spelled, 4 and 5 both start with *f*, 8 and 11 both start with *e*.

117. Choice (D) is correct. (1:3,2:4) Ricin is a poisonous protein; strychnine is a poisonous alkaloid.

118. Choice (B) is correct. (1:2,3:4) The pianoforte and contrabass are both musical instruments.

119. Choice (C) is correct. (1:3,2:4) Photons and gluons are bosons; strange and down are types of quarks.

120. Choice (A) is correct. (1:2,3:4) In statistics, interdecile range is a type of dispersion; gamma distribution is a type of scale parameter.

Chapter 17

MAT Practice Test #5

• •

*W*elcome to the fifth MAT practice test! Just like the other exams in this book, this one is based on authentic MAT questions, to help you get used to the real test's style. Remember to use good technique throughout the test as you take it. If you want to make the experience realistic, don't just look through the test. Instead, take it all at once, timed strictly, in a room where you won't be interrupted for an hour.

As you take the test, it's a good idea to circle questions you guessed on — after all, if you get them right, it may just be luck. Review questions you guessed on as carefully as you review questions you got wrong. After taking the test, review your mistakes and guesses. Try to be your own coach. Ask yourself questions like: What made me get this question wrong? What do I need to do to fix the problem? and What will I do differently next time? The answers to those questions should be helpful in creating some corrective actions to improve your skills. Good luck!

1. ELUCIDATE : EXPLICATE :: _____ : ENJOIN

    (A) expedite

    (B) entreat

    (C) equip

    (D) extract

2. DOME : DOMESTIC :: VAULT : _____

    (A) household

    (B) foreign

    (C) bank

    (D) cupola

3. _____ : FROG :: CARNIVORA : DOG

    (A) aves

    (B) hibernation

    (C) anura

    (D) tiger

4. _____ : AQUEDUCT :: BATTERY : PIPELINE

    (A) arches

    (B) fresh water

    (C) electricity

    (D) voltaic pile

5. _____ : RESERVE :: DEMAND : WANT

    (A) supply

    (B) reprimand

    (C) container

    (D) reservation

6. -PATH : -LITH :: _____ : STONE

    (A) tree

    (B) disease

    (C) part

    (D) trail

7. _____ : ALTO :: DOUBLE BASS : BASS

    (A) cello

    (B) bow

    (C) viola

    (D) violin

8. IMPEACHED : FIRED :: _____ : DISMISSED

    (A) resigned

    (B) expelled

    (C) freed

    (D) denounced

9. POLITICIAN : _____ :: BRASS : CORNET

    (A) hornet

    (B) senator

    (C) trumpet

    (D) clergyman

10. BUSH : _____ :: SEPTEMBER 11 : APOLLO 11

    (A) Kennedy

    (B) Johnson

    (C) Nixon

    (D) Ford

11. ABATE : AMASS :: WANE : _____

    (A) garnish

    (B) garden

    (C) gander

    (D) garner

12. TREE : _____ :: CYPRESS : CIRRUS

    (A) cloud

    (B) tray

    (C) whistle

    (D) knife

13. RATIONAL : INTEGER :: 7/4 : _____
    (A) √2
    (B) π
    (C) 7
    (D) 7/0

14. _____ : 12π :: 17 : 34π
    (A) 6
    (B) 22π
    (C) 11
    (D) 6π

15. ONOMATOPOEIA : _____ ::
    CONSONANCE : REPEATS
    (A) clarifies
    (B) imitates
    (C) compares
    (D) narrows

16. RESISTOR : CURRENT :: _____ :
    TENSION
    (A) screw
    (B) conductor
    (C) spring
    (D) compression

17. _____ : AMOUNT OF SUBSTANCE ::
    cd : mol
    (A) electric current
    (B) thermodynamic temperature
    (C) energy/time
    (D) luminous intensity

18. PEDAL : PETAL :: _____ : FLOWER
    (A) bicycle
    (B) flour
    (C) stem
    (D) spoke

19. _____ : REPRIMAND ::
    ACCOMPLISHMENT : INFRACTION
    (A) scold
    (B) greet
    (C) congratulate
    (D) punish

20. _____ : SMALL :: FAMILY : LARGE
    (A) awkward
    (B) fun
    (C) clan
    (D) friend

21. ATTACK : RANSACK :: ENEMY :
    _____
    (A) house
    (B) sky
    (C) sea
    (D) steak

22. MORE : MOST :: _____ : BEST
    (A) good
    (B) well
    (C) less
    (D) better

23. DIURNALITY : _____ ::
    NOCTURNALITY : POSSUM
    (A) crepuscular
    (B) crypsis
    (C) squirrel
    (D) raccoon

24. SHUN : SHUNT :: _____ : SHIFT
    (A) skiff
    (B) ignore
    (C) shaft
    (D) praise

25. _____ : CELL :: ORGAN : ORGANELLE

    (A) cellblock

    (B) pipes

    (C) tissue

    (D) body

26. BROBDINGNAGIAN : _____ :: STENTORIAN : BLARING

    (A) gigantic

    (B) orotund

    (C) centenarian

    (D) preposterous

27. URINARY : KIDNEY :: REPRODUCTIVE : _____

    (A) jugular

    (B) epidermis

    (C) uterus

    (D) femur

28. BORE : BOARD :: _____ : SWORD

    (A) plank

    (B) soar

    (C) boar

    (D) dagger

29. _____ : PLATE :: CHALICE : PITCHER

    (A) catcher

    (B) mail

    (C) malice

    (D) saucer

30. EFFECT : CAUSE :: FLOODING : _____

    (A) brooding

    (B) affect

    (C) rain

    (D) sand

31. THIRD : _____ :: FIFTH : QUINARY

    (A) fourth

    (B) tertiary

    (C) primary

    (D) quintessence

32. TOO : FOR :: $(\sqrt{9} - 1)$: _____

    (A) $(\sqrt{25} - 1)$

    (B) $(\sqrt{36} - 3)$

    (C) $(\sqrt{16} + 1)$

    (D) $(\sqrt{4} + 4)$

33. IRASCIBLE : CHEERFUL :: IMPERIOUS : _____

    (A) vehement

    (B) teeming

    (C) servile

    (D) chummy

34. SEMIOTICS : ETHNOGRAPHY :: LINGUISTICS : _____

    (A) semantics

    (B) cartography

    (C) alchemy

    (D) anthropology

35. PHOBOS : _____ :: IO : EUROPA

    (A) Deimos

    (B) Triton

    (C) Titania

    (D) Charon

36. _____ : CARPENTER :: BOXER : ATHLETE

    (A) pugilist

    (B) cooper

    (C) wood

    (D) mason

37. BEAU : SMALL :: _____ : BAWL
    - (A) handsome
    - (B) behemoth
    - (C) dough
    - (D) cry

38. DUMAS : _____ :: TOLSTOY : RUSSIA
    - (A) Andorra
    - (B) Switzerland
    - (C) Belgium
    - (D) France

39. 37 : 31 :: 61: _____
    - (A) 59
    - (B) 63
    - (C) 53
    - (D) 67

40. ODYSSEUS : _____ :: ARES : HERMES
    - (A) Artemis
    - (B) Hector
    - (C) Demeter
    - (D) Hestia

41. _____ : EXPONENTIATION :: $n : b^n$
    - (A) matrix
    - (B) base
    - (C) power
    - (D) factor

42. ESCRITOIRE : DESK :: CHIFFONIER : _____
    - (A) table
    - (B) bed
    - (C) couch
    - (D) bureau

43. RHEUMATOLOGIST : HEMATOLOGIST :: _____ : BLOOD
    - (A) sinuses
    - (B arthritis
    - (C) nose
    - (D) AIDS

44. BIG : _____ :: DIPPER : MAJOR
    - (A) Ursa
    - (B) Canis
    - (C) Virgo
    - (D) Pegasus

45. IMPUGN : EULOGIZE :: CRITICIZE : _____
    - (A) condemn
    - (B) eulogy
    - (C) praise
    - (D) impunity

46. SECOND : _____ :: TIME : LUMINOUS INTENSITY
    - (A) candle
    - (B) candelabra
    - (C) candida
    - (D) candela

47. PHLOGISTAN : OXIDATION :: _____ : PHYSICS
    - (A) Copernican
    - (B) Aristotelian
    - (C) Mendelian
    - (D) Neptunism

48. BRAKE : _____ :: CAFFEINE : SLEEP
    - (A) motion
    - (B) wakefulness
    - (C) alcohol
    - (D) pedal

49. CONFINE : CONSTRAIN :: _____ : DEPRECATE

    (A) remand

    (B) prison

    (C) deplore

    (D) demonstrate

50. ASSIDUOUS : _____ : DILIGENT : SOUR

    (a) sweet

    (B) harmonious

    (C) base

    (D) acidic

51. _____ : RECORD :: DULL : SCRATCHED

    (A) blade

    (B) sharp

    (C) play

    (D) archive

52. HEAT : FAMINE :: SWEAT : _____

    (A) perspiration

    (B) hunger

    (C) thirst

    (D) cold

53. _____ : INFINITE :: ZERO : UNENDING

    (A) hull

    (B) full

    (C) null

    (D) mull

54. TIMOROUS : SAGACIOUS :: _____ : JUDICIOUS

    (A) judicial

    (B) extroverted

    (C) miniscule

    (D) afraid

55. OBJECT : PARTICLE :: _____ : WAVE

    (A) oscillation

    (B) vibration

    (C) stagnation

    (D) subject

56. _____ : IMITATE :: INVENTION : IMITATION

    (A) creation

    (B) invent

    (C) fake

    (D) innovate

57. WOW : DISAPPOINT :: AWE : _____

    (A) ennui

    (B) awesome

    (C) chagrin

    (D) triumph

58. 50 : USA :: _____ : CANADA

    (A) 13

    (B) 9

    (C) 15

    (D) 11

59. _____ : DROP :: INFERNO : SPARK

    (A) catch

    (B) blaze

    (C) infernal

    (D) flood

60. CONGRUENT : _____ :: GRADE : TILT

    (A) inclination

    (B) postulate

    (C) same

    (D) locus

61. SPADE : _____ :: TROWEL : MOP

    (A) broom

    (B) club

    (C) neutered

    (D) trough

62. DIAMOND : _____ :: GRAPHITE : CARBON

    (A) dysprosium

    (B) carbon

    (C) gold

    (D) platinum

63. REBELLIOUS : CONTUMACIOUS :: _____ : EMOLLIENT

    (A) grating

    (B) overflowing

    (C) sobering

    (D) soothing

64. TRIBE : _____ :: CLAN : PERFORMANCE

    (A) intersection

    (B) horse

    (C) jury

    (D) chieftain

65. SHILLELAGH : DRAISINE :: _____ : VEHICLE

    (A) club

    (B) sleigh

    (C) gondola

    (D) heart

66. DAWN : _____ :: DUSK : GLOAMING

    (A) stone

    (B) aurora

    (C) borealis

    (D) loaming

67. _____ : GUERNICA :: MONET : WATER LILIES

    (A) Pollock

    (B) Goya

    (C) Warhol

    (D) Picasso

68. COMPLICITY : _____ :: COMPLAIN : GRIPE

    (A) grape

    (B) complicated

    (C) collusion

    (D) duplicity

69. SHARP : COMBUSTIBLE :: CUT : _____

    (A) burn

    (B) scrape

    (C) dull

    (D) compostable

70. $x^2 + 8x + 16 : x + 4 :: x^2 + 12x + 36$: _____

    (A) $x + 12$

    (B) $x^2 + 6$

    (C) $x^2 + 12$

    (D) $x + 6$

71. FLEMING : PENICILLIN :: _____ : OXYGEN

    (A) Bunsen

    (B) Priestley

    (C) Bohr

    (D) Volta

72. MADELEINE : PIZZELLE :: CAKE : _____

    (A) cookie

    (B) pie

    (C) casserole

    (D) cocktail

73. BALM : BOMB :: MISSED : _____
    (A) blundered
    (B) lips
    (C) mist
    (D) explosive

74. NUCLEOLUS : TRANSCRIPTION :: RIBOSOME : _____
    (A) photosynthesis
    (B) protein synthesis
    (C) endoplasmic reticulum
    (D) support

75. $(4/3)\pi r^3$: _____ :: SPHERE : CUBE
    (A) s^3
    (B) πr^2
    (C) 1/2bh
    (D) a + b

76. LINCOLN : GARFIELD :: MCKINLEY : _____
    (A) Reagan
    (B) Carter
    (C) Truman
    (D) Kennedy

77. CYSTITIS : BLADDER :: MASTITIS : _____
    (A) disease
    (B) constriction
    (C) breast
    (D) nose

78. POLYTHEISM : MONOGAMY :: DEITIES : _____
    (A) demigod
    (B) spouse
    (C) wives
    (D) monotheism

79. _____ : HOOVER :: ACTOR : REAGAN
    (A) engineer
    (B) lawyer
    (C) soldier
    (D) tailor

80. QUEEN : EMPRESS :: JACK : _____
    (A) emperor
    (B) prince
    (C) bee
    (D) buck

81. ESCHEW : FORGO :: EXTOL : _____
    (A) wince
    (B) avail
    (C) laud
    (D) forgot

82. NOTE : 5.00 :: COIN : _____
    (A) 500.00
    (B) 0.05
    (C) 50.00
    (D) 0.005

83. MARLOWE : KLIMT :: PLAYWRIGHT : _____
    (A) author
    (B) sculptor
    (C) composer
    (D) painter

84. INNING : ROUND :: BASEBALL : _____
    (A) boxing
    (B) tennis
    (C) football
    (D) basketball

85. AKITA : _____ :: PERSIAN : SIAMESE
    (A) twin
    (B) altai
    (C) Husky
    (D) chunky

86. GILL : _____ :: PACE : LENGTH
    (A) weight
    (B) volume
    (C) time
    (D) area

87. THAILAND : SRI LANKA :: SIAM : _____
    (A) Ceylon
    (B) Azania
    (C) Belau
    (D) Hellas

88. CEPHALIC : BUCCAL :: HEAD : _____
    (A) brain
    (B) joints
    (C) throat
    (D) cheek

89. INDIGENT : POSH :: COMELY : _____
    (A) indignant
    (B) plush
    (C) homely
    (D) quickly

90. KEY : LOCK :: BOARD : _____
    (A) council
    (B) smith
    (C) summer
    (D) baker

91. TENANT : TENET :: RENTER : _____
    (A) belief
    (B) render
    (C) tent
    (D) classification

92. UNICORN : CHURCH :: HORN : _____
    (A) trumpet
    (B) bigfoot
    (C) buttress
    (D) spire

93. WHAM : WHIM :: WHACK : _____
    (A) whilst
    (B) impulse
    (C) smack
    (D) wisp

94. PRAISE : _____ :: EULOGY : ELEGY
    (A) compliment
    (B) complement
    (C) lament
    (D) emptiness

95. EON : ERA :: PERIOD : _____
    (A) age
    (B) chron
    (C) year
    (D) epoch

96. DEMURE : _____ :: OUTGOING : TIRELESS
    (A) effete
    (B) accede
    (C) prolific
    (D) abele

97. PRODIGIOUS : INFINITESIMAL :: PRIMEVAL : _____

    (A) finite

    (B) prestigious

    (C) modern

    (D) primordial

98. ACOUSTIC : _____ :: ELECTRIC : DIGITAL PIANO

    (A) tapboard

    (B) oboe

    (C) clavinet

    (D) kiboe

99. 212 : FAHRENHEIT :: _____ : KELVIN

    (A) 32

    (B) 100

    (C) 216.85

    (D) 373.15

100. SENSE : _____ :: PHYSIOLOGICAL : MENTAL

    (A) percept

    (B) sight

    (C) physical

    (D) corporeal

101. DRAIN : _____ :: DRINK : EAT

    (A) beverage

    (B) polish

    (C) sewer

    (D) edible

102. CIRCUMFERENCE : DIAMETER :: _____ : 1

    (A) area

    (B) $2\pi r$

    (C) π

    (D) radius

103. _____ : PRESSURE :: GRADUATED CYLINDER : VOLUME

    (A) Graduated prism

    (B) Tachymeter

    (C) Sonar

    (D) Barometer

104. GRAM : KILOGRAM :: YEAR : _____

    (A) day

    (B) decade

    (C) century

    (D) millennium

105. SARTRE : _____ :: EXISTENTIALISM : IDEALISM

    (A) Polignac

    (B) Hegel

    (C) Abejo

    (D) Castillo

106. BROOM : _____ :: SWEEP : EXCAVATE

    (A) dolabra

    (B) cadenza

    (C) caliper

    (D) mop

107. BOOKS : ARTIFACTS :: LIBRARY : _____

    (A) discotheque

    (B) librarian

    (C) veterinarian

    (D) museum

108. _____ : CON :: KICK : SORT

    (A) punch

    (B) start

    (C) side

    (D) edge

109. PUTRID : _____ :: FETID : FRAGRANT

    (A) aromatic

    (B) felid

    (C) frequent

    (D) pride

110. OPENING : INTRODUCTION :: RESOLUTION : _____

    (A) appendix

    (B) denouement

    (C) conflict

    (D) index

111. MEXICO : THAILAND :: PESO : _____

    (A) lev

    (B) birr

    (C) rial

    (D) baht

112. BAFFIN ISLAND : CANADA :: SUMATRA : _____

    (A) Myanmar

    (B) Papua New Guinea

    (C) Indonesia

    (D) Malaysia

113. _____ : CATAMOUNT :: HALITE : ROCK SALT

    (A) puma

    (B) tantamount

    (C) caterpillar

    (D) quartz

114. CHROMOSOME : GENE :: SYMPHONY : _____

    (A) violin

    (B) note

    (C) instrument

    (D) musician

115. CLOSE : NEAR :: SHUT : _____

    (A) open

    (B) far

    (C) there

    (D) seal

116. ONTOLOGY : VITALISM :: _____ : SOUL

    (A) geography

    (B) language

    (C) being

    (D) birds

117. ARM : _____ :: STRONG : RAD

    (A) lie

    (B) con

    (C) no

    (D) not

118. BEGGAR : MISER :: _____ : CHARITY

    (A) wealth

    (B) rags

    (C) foundation

    (D) stingy

119. MISOGAMY : ISOGAMY :: HATRED : _____

    (A) isolation

    (B) misogyny

    (C) reproduction

    (D) love

120. CHAMP : HURLING :: _____ : SPORT

    (A) drink

    (B) holiday

    (C) dance

    (D) dish

Chapter 18

Answers to MAT Practice Test #5

Now that you're done taking the fifth practice MAT, make sure that you take the time to review any questions on which you guessed or struggled, as well as to review any incorrect answers. If you did as well or better than you expected, now's a good time to reward yourself! If you didn't, keep your chin up. Your mistakes should be helpful in pointing you toward areas where you need to learn more content, and they may highlight places where you can use your technique more strictly. Ultimately, your mistakes will show you where to spend more of your time and energy to improve your skills and score.

1. Choice (B) is correct. (1:2,3:4) *Elucidate* and *explicate* are synonyms. *Entreat* and *enjoin* are also synonyms.

2. Choice (A) is correct. (1:3,2:4) A dome is a type of vault; *domestic* means "relating to the household."

3. Choice (C) is correct. (1:2,3:4) A frog belongs to the order *Anura*. A dog belongs to the order *Carnivora*.

4. Choice (D) is correct. (1:3,2:4) A voltaic pile was a precursor to the modern electric battery. An aqueduct was a precursor to the modern pipeline.

5. Choice (A) is correct. (1:2,3:4). In economics, a supply is a reserve of goods; demand is the want for those goods.

6. Choice (B) is correct. (1:3,2:4). *–path* is a suffix meaning "disease"; *–lith* is a suffix meaning "stone."

7. Choice (C) is correct. (1:2,3:4) The viola is the second-highest of the four instruments in the violin family. Alto is the second-highest of the four primary vocal parts. The double bass is the lowest of the four instruments in the violin family. Bass is the lowest of the four primary vocal parts.

8. Choice (D) is correct. (1:3,2:4) To be impeached is to be denounced; to be fired is to be dismissed.

9. Choice (B) is correct. (1:2,3:4) A senator is a kind of politician; a cornet is a type of brass instrument.

10. Choice (C) is correct. (1:3,2:4). George W. Bush was the president when the September 11 attacks occurred; Richard Nixon was the president when the Apollo 11 Moon landing occurred.

11. Choice (D) is correct. (1:3,2:4) *Abate* and *wane* are synonyms; *amass* and *garner* are also synonyms.

12. Choice (A) is correct. (1:3,2:4) A cypress is a type of tree; cirrus is a type of cloud.

13. Choice (C) is correct. (1:3,2:4) ¼ is a rational number; 7 is an integer.

14. Choice (A) is correct. (1:2,3:4) 6 times $2\pi = 12\pi$; 17 times $2\pi = 34\pi$.

15. Choice (B) is correct. (1:2,3:4) Onomatopoeia occurs when a word imitates the sound that it describes; consonance occurs when a consonant sound repeats.

16. Choice (C) is correct. (1:2,3:4) A resistor resists electric current; a spring resists tension.

17. Choice (D) is correct. (1:3,2:4) *cd* is the symbol for candela, which measures luminous intensity; *mol* is the symbol for mole, which measures amount of substance.

18. Choice (A) is correct. (1:3,2:4) A pedal is a part of a bicycle; a petal is a part of a flower.

19. Choice (C) is correct. (1:3,2:4) One is congratulated for an accomplishment and reprimanded for an infraction.

20. Choice (B) is correct. (1:2,3:4) *Fun* is a term used to describe a small food; *family* is a term used to describe a large food.

21. Choice (A) is correct. (1:3,2:4) One attacks an enemy and ransacks a house.

22. Choice (D) is correct. (1:2,3:4) Most is the superlative of the adjective more; best is the superlative of the adjective better.

23. Choice (C) is correct. (1:2,3:4) A squirrel is an animal that displays diurnality; a possum is an animal that displays nocturnality.

24. Choice (B) is correct. (1:3,2:4) *Shun* and *ignore* are synonyms; *shunt* and *shift* are also synonyms.

25. Choice (D) is correct. (1:3,2:4) Organs are parts of the body; organelles are parts of a cell.

26. Choice (A) is correct. (1:2,3:4) *Brobdingnagian* and *gigantic* are synonyms; *stentorian* and *blaring* are also synonyms.

27. Choice (C) is correct. (1:2,3:4) The kidneys are part of the urinary system; the uterus is part of the reproductive system.

28. Choice (B) is correct. (1:3,2:4) *Bore* and *soar* rhyme; *board* and *sword* rhyme. *Bore* and *board* begin with *b; soar* and *sword* begin with *s.*

29. Choice (D) is correct. (1:2,3:4) A saucer is a small dish; a plate is a larger dish. A chalice is a small vessel; a pitcher is a larger vessel.

30. Choice (C) is correct. (1:3,2:4) If flooding is the effect, then rain could be the cause.

31. Choice (B) is correct. (1:2,3:4) *Tertiary* means "third"; *quinary* means "fifth."

32. Choice (A) is correct. (1:3,2:4) *Too* sounds the same as *two;* two equals $(\sqrt{9} - 1)$. *For* sounds the same as *four;* four equals $(\sqrt{25} - 1)$.

33. Choice (C) is correct. (1:2,3:4) *Irascible* and *cheerful* are antonyms; *imperious* and *servile* are also antonyms.

34. Choice (D) is correct. (1:3,2:4) Semiotics is a subfield of linguistics; ethnography is a subfield of anthropology.

35. Choice (A) is correct. (1:2,3.4) Phobos and Deimos are moons of Mars; Io and Europa are moons of Jupiter.

36. Choice (B) is correct. (1:2,3:4) A cooper is a type of carpenter; a boxer is a type of athlete.

37. Choice (C) is correct. (1:3,2:4) *Beau* and *dough* rhyme; *small* and *bawl* also rhyme.

38. Choice (D) is correct. (1:2,3:4) Alexandre Dumas was a French writer; Leo Tolstoy was a Russian writer.

39. Choice (A) is correct. (1:2,3:4) 31 is the next-lowest prime after 37. 59 is the next-lowest prime after 61.

40. Choice (B) is correct. (1:2,3:4) Odysseus and Hector are mortal heroes in Greek mythology. Ares and Hermes are gods in Greek mythology.

41. Choice (C) is correct. (1:3,2:4) Exponentiation is written as b^n. In this expression, *n* is the power.

42. Choice (D) is correct. (1:2,3:4) An escritoire is a desk; a chiffonier is a bureau.

43. Choice (B) is correct. (1:3,2:4) A rheumatologist specializes in arthritis; a hematologist specializes in blood.

44. Choice (A) is correct. (1:3,2:4) The Big Dipper is an asterism that is a part of the constellation Ursa Major.

45. Choice (C) is correct. (1:3,2:4) *Impugn* and *criticize* are synonyms; *eulogize* and *praise* are also synonyms.

46. Choice (D) is correct. (1:3,2:4) The second is the SI base unit for time; the candela is the SI base unit for luminous intensity.

47. Choice (B) is correct. (1:2,3:4) The phlogiston theory is an obsolete theory regarding oxidation. Aristotelian physics were made obsolete by Newtonian physics.

48. Choice (A) is correct. (1:2,3:4) A brake inhibits motion; caffeine inhibits sleep.

49. Choice (C) is correct. (1:2,3:4) *Confine* and *constrain* are synonyms; *deplore* and *deprecate* are also synonyms.

50. Choice (D) is correct. (1:3,2:4) *Assiduous* and *diligent* are synonyms; *acidic* and *sour* are also synonyms.

51. Choice (A) is correct. (1:3,2:4) When a blade is dull, it does not work correctly; when a record is scratched, it does not work correctly.

52. Choice (B) is correct. (1:3,2:4) One sweats when there is heat; one hungers when there is famine.

53. Choice (C) is correct. (1:3,2:4) *Null* and *zero* are synonyms; *infinite* and *unending* are also synonyms.

54. Choice (D) is correct. (1:3,2:4) *Timorous* and *afraid* are synonyms; *sagacious* and *judicious* are also synonyms.

55. Choice (A) is correct. (1:2,3:4) A particle is an object; a wave is an oscillation.

56. Choice (B) is correct. (1:3,2:4) One invents to create an invention; one imitates to create an imitation.

57. Choice (C) is correct. (1:3,2:4) When one is wowed, one has awe; when one is disappointed, one feels chagrin.

58. Choice (A) is correct. (1:2,3:4) The USA has 50 states; Canada has a total of 13 provinces and territories.

59. Choice (D) is correct. (1:2,3:4) A drop is a tiny part of a flood; a spark is a tiny part of an inferno.

60. Choice (C) is correct. (1:2,3:4) *Congruent* means "same"; *grade* means "tilt."

61. Choice (A) is correct. (1:3,2:4) Spades and trowels are tools for digging; brooms and mops are tools for cleaning.

62. Choice (B) is correct. (1:2,3:4) Both diamonds and graphite are made of pure carbon.

63. Choice (D) is correct. (1:2,3:4) *Rebellious* and *contumacious* are synonyms; *soothing* and *emollient* are also synonyms.

64. Choice (C) is correct. (1:3,2:4) *Tribe* and *clan* are synonyms; *jury* and *performance* are also synonyms.

65. Choice (A) is correct. (1:3,2:4) A shillelagh is a type of club; a draisine is a type of vehicle.

66. Choice (B) is correct. (1:2,3:4) *Dawn* and *aurora* are synonyms; *dusk* and *gloaming* are also synonyms.

67. Choice (D) is correct. (1:2,3:4) *Guernica* is a painting by Picasso; *Water Lilies* is a series of paintings by Monet.

68. Choice (C) is correct. (1:2,3:4) *Complicity* and *collusion* are synonyms; *complain* and *gripe* are also synonyms.

69. Choice (A) is correct. (1:3,2:4) A sharp object could cut; a combustible object could burn.

70. Choice (D) is correct. (1:2,3:4) By squaring $(x + 4)$, one gets $x^2 + 8x + 16$. By squaring $(x + 6)$, one gets $x^2 + 12x + 36$.

71. Choice (B) is correct. (1:2,3:4) Fleming discovered penicillin; Priestley discovered oxygen.

72. Choice (A) is correct. (1:3,2:4) A madeleine is a cake; a pizzelle is a cookie.

73. Choice (C) is correct. (1:2,3:4) *Balm* and *bomb* sound the same; *missed* and *mist* also sound the same.

74. Choice (B) is correct. (1:2,3:4) In a cell, the nucleolus handles transcription; the ribosomes handle protein synthesis.

75. Choice (A) is correct. (1:3,2:4) $(\frac{4}{3})\pi r^3$ is the formula for the volume of a sphere; s^3 is the formula for the volume of a cube.

76. Choice (D) is correct. (1:2,3:4) Lincoln, Garfield, McKinley, and Kennedy were the four U.S. presidents to be assassinated.

77. Choice (C) is correct. (1:2,3:4) Cystitis is the inflammation of the bladder; mastitis is the inflammation of breast tissue.

78. Choice (B) is correct. (1:3,2:4) Polytheism is the belief in deities; monogamy is the practice of having one spouse.

79. Choice (A) is correct. (1:2,3:4) Before becoming president, Hoover was an engineer. Before becoming president, Reagan was an actor.

80. Choice (D) is correct. (1:2,3:4) *Queen* and *empress* are names for female animals; *jack* and *buck* are names for male animals.

81. Choice (C) is correct. (1:2,3:4) *Eschew* and *forgo* are synonyms; *extol* and *laud* are also synonyms.

82. Choice (B) is correct. (1:2,3:4) $5.00 is a denomination of a note; $0.05 is a denomination of a coin.

83. Choice (D) is correct. (1:3,2:4) Marlowe was a playwright; Klimt was a painter.

84. Choice (A) is correct. (1:3,2:4) Baseball games are divided into innings; boxing matches are divided into rounds.

85. Choice (C) is correct. (1:2,3:4) Akita and Husky are types of dogs; Persian and Siamese are types of cats.

86. Choice (B) is correct. (1:2,3:4) The gill is a unit of volume; the pace is a unit of length.

87. Choice (A) is correct. (1:3,2:4) Siam is the former name of Thailand; Ceylon is the former name of Sri Lanka.

88. Choice (D) is correct. (1:3,2:4) *Cephalic* means "relating to the head"; *buccal* means "relating to the cheek."

89. Choice (C) is correct. (1:2,3:4) *Indigent* and *posh* are antonyms; *comely* and *homely* are also antonyms.

90. Choice (B) is correct. (1:3,2:4) *Keyboard* and *locksmith* are compounds.

91. Choice (A) is correct. (1:3,2:4) A tenant is a renter; a tenet is a belief.

92. Choice (D) is correct. (1:3,2:4) The horn is the tapering conical part of a unicorn; the spire is the tapering conical part of a church.

93. Choice (B) is correct. (1:3,2:4) *Wham* and *whack* are synonyms; *whim* and *impulse* are also synonyms.

94. Choice (C) is correct. (1:3,2:4) A eulogy is an expression of praise; an elegy is an expression of lament.

95. Choice (D) is correct. (1:2,3:4) Eons are divided into eras; periods are divided into epochs.

96. Choice (A) is correct. (1:3,2:4) *Demure* and *outgoing* are antonyms; *effete* and *tireless* are also antonyms.

97. Choice (C) is correct. (1:2,3:4) *Prodigious* and *infinitesimal* are antonyms; *primeval* and *modern* are also antonyms.

98. Choice (B) is correct. (1:2,3:4) The oboe is an acoustic instrument; the digital piano is an electric instrument.

99. Choice (D) is correct. (1:2,3:4) Water boils at 212 degrees Fahrenheit and 373.15 degrees Kelvin.

100. Choice (A) is correct. (1:3,2:4) A sense is experienced by physiological means; a percept is experienced mentally.

101. Choice (B) is correct. (1:3,2:4) To drain is to drink something completely; to polish off is to eat something completely.

102. Choice (C) is correct. (1:2,3:4) The ratio of circumference to diameter is equal to π to 1.

103. Choice (D) is correct. (1:2,3:4) A barometer measures pressure; a graduated cylinder measures volume.

104. Choice (D) is correct. (1:2,3:4) There are 1,000 grams in a kilogram and 1,000 years in a millennium.

105. Choice (B) is correct. (1:3,2:4) Sartre was a figure in existentialism; Hegel was a figure in idealism.

106. Choice (A) is correct. (1:3,2:4) A broom is used to sweep; a dolabra is used to excavate.

107. Choice (D) is correct. (1:3,2:4) Libraries contain books; museums contain artifacts.

108. Choice (C) is correct. (1:3,2:4) *Sidekick* and *consort* are compounds and synonyms.

109. Choice (A) is correct. (1:3,2:4) *Putrid* and *fetid* are synonyms; *aromatic* and *fragrant* are also synonyms. Both pairs of words are antonyms to each other.

110. Choice (B) is correct. (1:2,3:4) *Opening* and *introduction* are synonyms; *resolution* and *denouement* are also synonyms.

111. Choice (D) is correct. (1:3,2:4) The currency of Mexico is the peso; the currency of Thailand is the baht.

112. Choice (C) is correct. (1:2,3:4) Baffin Island is an island in Canada; Sumatra is an island in Indonesia.

113. Choice (A) is correct. (1:2,3:4) *Puma* is another name for catamount; *halite* is another name for rock salt.

114. Choice (B) is correct. (1:2,3:4) Chromosomes are made up of genes; symphonies are made up of notes.

115. Choice (D) is correct. (1:2,3:4) *Close* and *near* are synonyms; *shut* and *seal* are also synonyms.

116. Choice (C) is correct. (1:3,2:4) Ontology is concerned with being; vitalism is concerned with the soul.

117. Choice (B) is correct. (1:3,2:4) Armstrong and Conrad have walked on the moon.

118. Choice (A) is correct. (1:3,2:4) A beggar lacks wealth; a miser lacks charity.

119. Choice (C) is correct. (1:3,2:4) Misogamy is a type of hatred; isogamy is a type of reproduction.

120. Choice (D) is correct. (1:3,2:4) Champ is an Irish dish; hurling is an Irish sport.

Chapter 19

MAT Practice Test #6

*H*ere's the sixth and last MAT practice test — if you've made it this far, congratulations! We closely imitated the real test's style to give you a realistic depiction of what you may encounter on your test day. Remember to use good technique throughout the test as you take it. If you want to make the experience realistic, don't just look through the test. Instead, take it all at once, timed strictly, in a room where you won't be interrupted for an hour. You'll have 60 minutes to answer the 120 questions, like usual.

As you take the test, it's a good idea to circle questions you guessed on — after all, if you get them right, it may just be luck. Review questions you guessed on as carefully as you review questions you got wrong. After taking the test, review your mistakes and guesses as best you can, focusing on figuring out the reason you missed the question so you learn as much as possible from the experience. In particular, if you knew the terms in the question and still picked the wrong choice, it's probably a good idea to review your step-by-step analogy-solving technique in Chapter 3. Good luck!

1. CETACEA : _____ :: CARNIVORA : TIGER

   (A) hawk

   (B) whale

   (C) earthworm

   (D) newt

2. PUBLIC : _____ :: ARDUOUS : FACILE

   (A) private

   (B) common

   (C) strenuous

   (D) faculty

3. ERGO : OGRE :: PAWS : _____

   (A) troll

   (B) therefore

   (C) swap

   (D) feet

4. RICHTER : _____ :: TNT EQUIVALENT : EXPLOSION

   (A) hurricane

   (B) tornado

   (C) wildfire

   (D) earthquake

5. BED : _____ :: EMU : MOB

   (A) clam

   (B) dolphin

   (C) nails

   (D) comforter

6. DOOR : DUMB :: KNOB : _____

   (A) handle

   (B) bell

   (C) know

   (D) stupid

7. _____ : UTILITARIANISM :: MARX : COMMUNISM

   (A) Locke

   (B) Rousseau

   (C) Bentham

   (D) Chomsky

8. CRAVEN : BRAVE :: FAIR : _____

   (A) light

   (B) just

   (C) crave

   (D) bigoted

9. DIPHENHYDRAMINE : ANTIHISTAMINE :: _____ : ANTI-INFLAMMATORY

   (A) methamphetamine

   (B) ibuprofen

   (C) paracetamol

   (D) acetaminophen

10. KNOLL : HUMMOCK :: ARROYO : _____

    (A) gully

    (B) gull

    (C) hammock

    (D) highway

11. LAWYER : COUNSEL :: POLITICIAN : _____

    (A) commander

    (B) physician

    (C) statesman

    (D) counselor

12. ANEMOMETER : HYGROMETER :: WIND SPEED : _____

    (A) germination

    (B) density

    (C) current

    (D) humidity

13. _____ : PERSUASION :: MAGICIAN : SALESMAN

    (A) courtship

    (B) illusion

    (C) envy

    (D) empiricism

14. _____ : VERACIOUS :: DISCREET : CAUTIOUS

    (A) truthful

    (B) scurrilous

    (C) pleasant

    (D) slippery

15. PERIMETER : CIRCUMFERENCE :: _____ : ELLIPSE

    (A) circle

    (B) prism

    (C) tetragon

    (D) polyhedron

16. THESAURUS : _____ :: DICTIONARY : DEFINITIONS

    (A) rhymes

    (B) analogies

    (C) anecdotes

    (D) synonyms

17. πr^2 : _____ :: $(n - 2)*180$: DEGREES

    (A) diameter

    (B) area

    (C) circumference

    (D) radians

18. MEIOSIS : REPRODUCTION :: _____ : SECRETION

    (A) mitosis

    (B) syngamy

    (C) glands

    (D) hairs

19. _____ : INEPT :: CANNY : MALADROIT

    (A) clumsy

    (B) inert

    (C) gauche

    (D) astute

20. VERTEX : VORTEX :: INTERSECTION : _____

    (A) spinning

    (B) interdiction

    (C) apex

    (D) jumping

21. WATER : BLOOD :: _____ : AIR

    (A) carbon

    (B) hydrogen

    (C) nitrogen

    (D) oxygen

22. FERMI : _____ :: MICHELIN : PNEUMATIC TIRE

    (A) microscope

    (B) nuclear reactor

    (C) FM radio

    (D) iron lung

23. COOL : _____ :: NEAT : LAME

    (A) square

    (B) cold

    (C) organized

    (D) warm

24. _____ : BRAUN :: CHEMISTRY : RAMSAY

    (A) biology

    (B) astronomy

    (C) psychology

    (D) physics

25. _____ : MICROBIOLOGY :: NEWTON : PASTEUR

    (A) biology

    (B) Quantum theory

    (C) gravitation

    (D) psychology

26. _____ : KIDNEYS :: PATHOLOGY : DISEASES

    (A) neonatology

    (B) nephrology

    (C) neurology

    (D) pneumology

27. F : ma :: p : _____

    (A) F/A

    (B) A/F

    (C) a/m

    (D) m/a

28. FILLY : GILT :: HORSE : _____

    (A) bear

    (B) frog

    (C) pig

    (D) cow

29. CALLOUS : OBDURATE :: _____ : HALCYON

    (A) plucky

    (B) calm

    (C) jealous

    (D) trusty

30. LIEGE : 1914 :: _____ : 1945

    (A) Midway

    (B) blitz

    (C) Normandy

    (D) Okinawa

31. OMAN : SAUDI ARABIA :: _____ : KING

    (A) sultan

    (B) president

    (C) supreme leader

    (D) prime minister

32. CELL : _____ :: TABERNACLE : CHURCH

    (A) library

    (B) holy water

    (C) prison

    (D) mitochondria

33. PACK : _____ :: WOLF : LEOPARD

    (A) spot

    (B) leap

    (C) herd

    (D) fang

34. HAGGIS : _____ :: SCOTLAND : SPAIN

    (A) couscous

    (B) curry

    (C) ceviche

    (D) paella

35. STRANGE : MUON :: _____ : LEPTON

    (A) quark

    (B) atom

    (C) bizarre

    (D) nucleus

36. NONAGON : 9 :: ENNEAGON : _____

    (A) 3

    (B) 9

    (C) 11

    (D) 19

37. CARTESIANISM : _____ ::
    NATURALISM : NATURE
    (A) physicalism
    (B) economy
    (C) dualism
    (D) community

38. INFLUENZA : DISEASE :: LIBRETTO :
    _____
    (A) barrette
    (B) valet
    (C) hay fever
    (D) text

39. RESERVOIR : _____ :: LAKE : RIVER
    (A) tributary
    (B) aqueduct
    (C) dam
    (D) ocean

40. TORQUE : _____ :: FORCE : PUSH
    (A) twist
    (B) pull
    (C) tension
    (D) spring

41. ANNULAR : _____ :: OCTAGONAL :
    STOP SIGN
    (A) crescent
    (B) yield
    (C) washer
    (D) screw

42. BEGINNING : _____ :: END : PERIOD
    (A) comma
    (B) hyphen
    (C) apostrophe
    (D) capital

43. GRAPE : GAZE :: _____ : DAZE
    (A) confuse
    (B) drape
    (C) fruit
    (D) raisin

44. _____ : TRUTHFUL :: MENDACIOUS
    : DISHONEST
    (A) ingenuous
    (B) mirthful
    (C) recondite
    (D) onerous

45. RAISE : INFLATION :: DECREASE :
    _____
    (A) disinflation
    (B) growth
    (C) deflation
    (D) dividend

46. DEER : ANTLERS :: ANTELOPE :
    _____
    (A) moose
    (B) tusks
    (C) gazelle
    (D) horns

47. USA : GERMANY :: CHEROKEE :
    _____
    (A) Saracens
    (B) Saxons
    (C) Tamoio
    (D) Anglicans

48. DIVISION : _____ ::
    MULTIPLICATION : TIMES
    (A) obeisant
    (B) obento
    (C) obelus
    (D) obelisk

49. YANGTZE : _____ :: YELLOW : SUPERIOR
    - (A) Baikal
    - (B) better
    - (C) Amazon
    - (D) sapphire

50. _____ : ROCKEFELLER :: APPLE : STANDARD OIL
    - (A) Macintosh
    - (B) Gates
    - (C) Carnegie
    - (D) Jobs

51. _____ : COMMENDATION :: LIE : DECEPTION
    - (A) jib
    - (B) compliment
    - (C) complement
    - (D) fib

52. _____ : CITE :: DERIDE : DETRACT
    - (A) allude
    - (B) desire
    - (C) adduce
    - (D) take

53. KARENINA : BOVARY :: ANNA : _____
    - (A) Madame
    - (B) Flaubert
    - (C) bovine
    - (D) Eliot

54. HECKLER : ARBITER :: BADGERS : _____
    - (A) pickles
    - (B) mediates
    - (C) escalates
    - (D) otters

55. COMPLAISANT : COMPLACENT :: _____ : SMUG
    - (A) smog
    - (B) menacing
    - (C) placid
    - (D) obliging

56. EMITS : _____ :: SMITE : TRIANGLE
    - (A) integral
    - (B) pentagon
    - (C) strike
    - (D) radiates

57. HOOD : LESS :: ARCH : _____
    - (A) dome
    - (B) bonnet
    - (C) post
    - (D) fewer

58. 2^{-3} : 0.25 :: 10 : _____
    - (A) 10
    - (B) 20
    - (C) 40
    - (D) 100

59. _____ : AGONIZING :: TORTUOUS : TORTUROUS
    - (A) organizing
    - (B) fortuitous
    - (C) painful
    - (D) twisted

60. _____ : SOLEMN :: FANDANGLE : SERIOUS
    - (A) contraption
    - (B) jovial
    - (C) frippery
    - (D) quiet

61. TOFURKEY : TURKEY :: _____ : LIMB

    (A) prosthesis

    (B) climber

    (C) leg

    (D) malarkey

62. SCENE : BOOKS : ACT : _____

    (A) novels

    (B) Torah

    (C) Abraham

    (D) pretend

63. _____ : 2 :: 0.2 : 5

    (A) 10

    (B) 1

    (C) 0.5

    (D). 0.25

64. _____ : STRAIGHT :: CHANNEL : DIRECT

    (A) volume

    (B) arrow

    (C) division

    (D) strait

65. PRAGMATISM : DEWEY :: NIHILISM : _____

    (A) Spinoza

    (B) Stirner

    (C) Mencius

    (D) Montesquieu

66. EQUIVOCATE : _____ :: ACCOST : BOTHER

    (A) dodge

    (B) equate

    (C) annoy

    (D) amass

67. ASYMMETRIC : MINIMUM :: SHOCK : _____

    (A) electrocute

    (B) symmetric

    (C) wage

    (D) maximum

68. BIRTHDAY : COCKTAIL :: DINNER : _____

    (A) fear

    (B) envy

    (C) gratitude

    (D) surprise

69. CAR : _____ :: WING : PLANE

    (A) train

    (B) boat

    (C) helicopter

    (D) wheel

70. $3/ (\frac{1}{4}) : 12 :: 6/ (\frac{2}{3}) :$ _____

    (A) 18

    (B) 6

    (C) 9

    (D) 12

71. MOUNT DOOM : MOUNT KILIMANJARO :: _____ : EAGLE

    (A) komodo

    (B) griffin

    (C) bald

    (D) hawk

72. RADAR : TENET :: REDDER : _____

    (A) reviver

    (B) tenant

    (C) bluer

    (D) belief

73. YEARNS : _____ :: AVOIDS : BANE
    (A) attracts
    (B) wane
    (C) yen
    (D) yarns

74. DE GAULLE : FRANCE :: _____ : USSR
    (A) Brodovitch
    (B) Brezhnev
    (C) Kravchuk
    (D) Dessoff

75. _____ : y – 9 :: 37% : 9 less than
    (A) 9%
    (B) 0.37%
    (C) 0.37y
    (D) 37y

76. ECONOMICAL : _____ :: STEEP : EXORBITANT
    (A) orbital
    (B) political
    (C) flat
    (D) nominal

77. LETHARGIC : _____ :: PEEVISH : CONTENTMENT
    (A) squeamish
    (B) animation
    (C) drowsiness
    (D) commitment

78. _____ : L :: ACUTE : V
    (A) Right
    (B) 5
    (C) Left
    (D) 50

79. INCH : YARD :: _____ : 72
    (A) 12
    (B) 6
    (C) 9
    (D) 2

80. _____ : DOPAMINE :: STOMACH : GASTRIN
    (A) heart
    (B) testes
    (C) hypothalamus
    (D) duodenum

81. PECULATE : _____ :: EXCULPATE : EXONERATE
    (A) forget
    (B) appropriate
    (C) forgive
    (D) excruciate

82. MOAT : CASTLE :: _____ : COMPUTER
    (A) firewall
    (B) trench
    (C) abacus
    (D) steam

83. CHRISTOPHER : COLOMBIA :: _____ : COOK ISLANDS
    (A) Harry
    (B) William
    (C) Peter
    (D) James

84. CHIPPER : CRESTFALLEN :: TACITURN : _____
    (A) cavernous
    (B) devout
    (C) talkative
    (D) sententious

85. HUMORIST : _____ :: CHAUVINIST : JINGOIST

    (A) luminist

    (B) comic

    (C) sexist

    (D) downer

86. METAL : FOUNDRY :: _____ : WOODSHOP

    (A) timber

    (B) stone

    (C) basketry

    (D) rock

87. SPEAR : HORSE : _____ : PLAY

    (A) sword

    (B) musical

    (C) mint

    (D) work

88. PULL : PULLOVER :: TUG : _____

    (A) infraction

    (B) tungsten

    (C) push

    (D) sweater

89. CUBA : SPAIN : MOJITO : _____

    (A) sangria

    (B) scotch

    (C) cognac

    (D) balsam

90. LOUD : _____ :: QUIET : MUTED

    (A) audacious

    (B) clamorous

    (C) deaf

    (D) bright

91. _____ : PREDILECTION :: PERFIDIOUS : UNSCRUPULOUS

    (A) agglutinative

    (B) uncouth

    (C) pasture

    (D) penchant

92. GALVANIZE : STIMULATE :: BELEAGUER : _____

    (A) simulate

    (B) behemoth

    (C) beset

    (D) inspire

93. 237 : NATURAL :: _____ : INTEGER

    (A) −898

    (B) 0.8475

    (C) ⅛

    (D) *e*

94. _____ : KICKBALL :: WAR : CURLING

    (A) peacetime

    (B) rummy

    (C) violence

    (D) baseball

95. NOSTRIL : _____ :: ORIFICE : FOSSA

    (A) nose

    (B) nasal septum

    (C) rhinitis

    (D) nasal cavity

96. DEVOTEE : _____ :: JUBILEE : ANNIVERSARY

    (A) follower

    (B) birthday

    (C) wedding

    (D) suffragist

97. _____ : CONSTABLE :: CANADA : U.K.
    - (A) Maple
    - (B) Quebec
    - (C) Mountie
    - (D) Province

98. LARYNX : TRACHEA :: BRONCHUS : _____
    - (A) stomach
    - (B) bronchiole
    - (C) pharynx
    - (D) esophagus

99. REMUNERATIVE : ANNULMENT :: _____ : DEFEASANCE
    - (A) divorce
    - (B) malfeasance
    - (C) remediation
    - (D) lucrative

100. _____ : TOAST :: MONEY : BREAD
    - (A) salute
    - (B) coin
    - (C) bacon
    - (D) insult

101. INVISIBLE : GULLIVER'S :: MAN : _____
    - (A) journeys
    - (B) treasure
    - (C) travels
    - (D) adventures

102. HYDROGEN : UNUNOCTIUM :: _____ : MOUNT EVEREST
    - (A) Bouvet
    - (B) Challenger Deep
    - (C) South Pole
    - (D) Chimborazo

103. GOAL : RUN :: HOCKEY : _____
    - (A) track
    - (B) puck
    - (C) keeper
    - (D) baseball

104. _____ : DISENCHANTING :: INVITING : DISGUSTING
    - (A) alluring
    - (B) inducting
    - (C) sorcery
    - (D) revolting

105. $130 - 30\%$: $100 + 30\%$ :: _____ : 130
    - (A) 95
    - (B) 100
    - (C) 91
    - (D) 113

106. DATE : APRICOT :: ORANGE : _____
    - (A) banana
    - (B) grapefruit
    - (C) watermelon
    - (D) grape

107. ENGLISH, FRENCH : CANADA :: CANTONESE, MANDARIN : _____
    - (A) China
    - (B) Spain
    - (C) Japan
    - (D) Portugal

108. CONJUNCTION : PREPOSITION :: _____ : RELATION
    - (A) greeting
    - (B) qualifies
    - (C) action
    - (D) connects

109. ≠ : NOT EQUAL TO :: : _____

   (A) direct sum

   (B) empty set

   (C) approximately

   (D) ideal

110. BASI : BASIC :: _____ : HIGH pH

   (A) whine

   (B) wine

   (C) low pH

   (D) acidic

111. BLAIR : PIERCE :: _____ : POLK

   (A) Thatcher

   (B) Jackson

   (C) Toulouse

   (D) Zimmer

112. KEHAAR : TWEETY :: TIGGER : _____

   (A) Aslan

   (B) Winnie

   (C) Sylvester

   (D) Shere Khan

113. OSTEOLOGY : HELIOLOGY :: BONES : _____

   (A) moon

   (B) helium

   (C) sun

   (D) muscles

114. IRIS : PUPIL :: PLANT : _____

   (A) larva

   (B) student

   (C) factory

   (D) medicine

115. ANKH : _____ :: LIFE : CHRISTIANITY

   (A) lauburu

   (B) tilaka

   (C) yantra

   (D) ichthys

116. 3 : 2 :: _____ : 7

   (A) 6

   (B) 1

   (C) 9

   (D) 14

117. ANTIMATTER : ANTIDOTE :: MATTER : _____

   (A) Whymper

   (B) poison

   (C) energy

   (D) Matterhorn

118. LEGATO : ARTICULATION :: _____ : DYNAMICS

   (A) adagio

   (B) gelato

   (C) fortissimo

   (D) fluid

119. ANION : NEGATIVE :: _____ : POSITIVE

   (A) onion

   (B) ion

   (C) electron

   (D) cation

120. MEAN : AVERAGE :: MODE : _____

   (A) common

   (B) mediocre

   (C) setting

   (D) middle

Chapter 20

Answers to MAT Practice Test #6

• •

*A*nother practice test done — great job! Now that you're done taking the sixth practice MAT, make sure that you take the time to review any questions on which you guessed or struggled, as well as to review any incorrect answers. Your mistakes should be helpful in pointing you toward areas where you need to learn more content, and they may highlight places where you can use your technique more strictly. Check Chapter 3 if you aren't sure about your step-by-step analogy solving method.

1. Choice (B) is correct. (1:2,3:4) A whale is a member of the order *Cetacea*. A tiger is a member of the order *Carnivora*.

2. Choice (A) is correct. (1:2,3:4) *Public* and *private* are antonyms; *arduous* and *facile* are also antonyms.

3. Choice (C) is correct. (1:2,3:4) *Ergo* spelled backward is *ogre*; *paws* spelled backward is *swap*.

4. Choice (D) is correct. (1:2,3:4) Earthquakes are measured with the Richter scale; explosions are measured using TNT equivalent.

5. Choice (A) is correct. (1:2,3:4) A group of clams is called a bed; a group of emus is called a mob.

6. Choice (B) is correct. (1:3,2:4) *Doorknob* and *dumbbell* are compounds.

7. Choice (C) is correct. (1:2,3:4) Bentham was a figure in utilitarianism; Marx was a figure in communism.

8. Choice (D) is correct. (1:2,3:4) *Craven* and *brave* are antonyms; *fair* and *bigoted* are also antonyms.

9. Choice (B) is correct. (1:2,3:4) Diphenhydramine is an antihistamine; ibuprofen is an anti-inflammatory.

10. Choice (A) is correct. (1:2,3:4) *Knoll* and *hummock* are synonyms; *arroyo* and *gully* are also synonyms.

11. Choice (C) is correct. (1:2,3:4) *Lawyer* is another name for *counsel*; *politician* is another name for *statesman*.

12. Choice (D) is correct. (1:3,2:4) An anemometer measures wind speed; a hygrometer measures humidity.

13. Choice (B) is correct. (1:3,2:4) A magician uses illusion to perform his craft; a salesman uses persuasion to perform his craft.

14. Choice (A) is correct. (1:2,3:4) *Truthful* and *veracious* are synonyms; *discreet* and *cautious* are also synonyms.

15. Choice (C) is correct. (1:3,2:4) A tetragon has a perimeter; an ellipse has a circumference.

16. Choice (D) is correct. (1:2,3:4) A thesaurus contains synonyms; a dictionary contains definitions.

17. Choice (B) is correct. (1:2,3:4) πr^2 is the formula for finding area of a circle; $(n-2)*180$ is the formula for finding the degrees of a regular polygon.

18. Choice (C) is correct. (1:2,3:4) Meiosis is an important component of the reproduction process; glands are an important part of the secretion process.

19. Choice (D) is correct. (1:3,2:4) *Astute* and *canny* are synonyms; *inept* and *maladroit* are also synonyms.

20. Choice (A) is correct. (1:3,2:4) In geometry, a vertex is an intersection of lines; a vortex is a spinning fluid.

21. Choice (C) is correct. (1:2,3:4) By volume, blood is comprised primarily of water; air is comprised primarily of nitrogen.

22. Choice (B) is correct. (1:2,3:4) Fermi invented the nuclear reactor; Michelin invented the pneumatic tire.

23. Choice (A) is correct. (1:3,2:4) *Cool* and *neat* are synonyms; *square* and *lame* are also synonyms.

24. Choice (D) is correct. (1:2,3:4) Braun was known for his work in physics; Ramsay was known for his work in chemistry.

25. Choice (C) is correct. (1:3,2:4) Newton was known for his contributions to the understanding of gravitation; Pasteur was known for his contributions to microbiology.

26. Choice (B) is correct. (1:2,3:4) Nephrology is the study of the kidneys; pathology is the study of diseases.

27. Choice (A) is correct. (1:2,3:4) The equation for force is $F = ma$ (force equals mass times acceleration). The equation for pressure is $p = F/A$ (pressure equals force per area).

28. Choice (C) is correct. (1:2,3:4) A filly is a young female horse. A gilt is a young female pig.

29. Choice (B) is correct. (1:2,3:4) *Callous* and *obdurate* are synonyms; *calm* and *halcyon* are also synonyms.

30. Choice (D) is correct. (1:2,3:4) The Battle of Liège was fought in 1914; the Battle of Okinawa was fought in 1945.

31. Choice (A) is correct. (1:3,2:4) The head of state and government in Oman is the sultan; the head of state and government in Saudi Arabia is the king.

32. Choice (C) is correct. (1:2,3:4) One would find a cell in a prison and a tabernacle in a church.

33. Choice (B) is correct. (1:3,2:4) A group of wolves is called a pack; a group of leopards is called a leap.

34. Choice (D) is correct. (1:3,2:4) Haggis is a traditional dish of Scotland; paella is a traditional dish of Spain.

35. Choice (A) is correct. (1:3,2:4) Strange is a type of quark; muon is a type of lepton.

36. Choice (B) is correct. (1:2,3:4) *Nonagon* and *enneagon* are both names for a polygon with nine sides.

37. Choice (C) is correct. (1:2,3:4) Cartesianism is based on the idea of dualism; naturalism is based on the laws of nature.

38. Choice (D) is correct. (1:2,3:4) Influenza is a disease; a libretto is a text. (*Influenza* and *libretto* are Italian words used in English.)

39. Choice (B) is correct. (1:3,2:4) A reservoir is an artificial lake; an aqueduct is like an artificial river.

40. Choice (A) is correct. (1:2,3:4) A force is a push to something; torque is a twist to something.

41. Choice (C) is correct. (1:2,3:4) A washer has an annular shape; a stop sign has an octagonal shape.

42. Choice (D) is correct. (1:2,3:4) A capital letter comes at the beginning of a sentence; a period comes at the end of a sentence.

43. Choice (B) is correct. (1:3,2:4) *Grape* and *drape* rhyme and are spelled the same except for the first letter. *Gaze* and *daze* are related in the same way.

44. Choice (A) is correct. (1:2,3:4) *Ingenuous* and *truthful* are synonyms; *mendacious* and *dishonest* are also synonyms.

45. Choice (C) is correct. (1:2,3:4) Inflation is an increase in the level of prices; deflation is a decrease in the level of prices.

46. Choice (D) is correct. (1:2,3:4) A deer has antlers; an antelope has horns.

47. Choice (B) is correct. (1:3,2:4) The Cherokee people are from the area that is now called the U.S.A.; the Saxons were from the area that is now called Germany.

48. Choice (C) is correct. (1:2,3:4) The obelus is the sign used for division; the times sign is used for multiplication.

49. Choice (A) is correct. (1:3,2:4) Yangtze and Yellow are rivers; Baikal and Superior are lakes.

50. Choice (D) is correct. (1:3,2:4) Apple was founded by Jobs; Standard Oil was founded by Rockefeller.

51. Choice (B) is correct. (1:2,3:4) If one compliments, one practices commendation. If one lies, one practices deception.

52. Choice (C) is correct. (1:2,3:4) *Adduce* and *cite* are synonyms; *deride* and *detract* are also synonyms.

53. Choice (A) is correct. (1:3,2:4) *Anna Karenina* and *Madame Bovary* are both novels.

54. Choice (B) is correct. (1:3,2:4) A heckler badgers; an arbiter mediates.

55. Choice (D) is correct. (1:3,2:4) *Complaisant* means "obliging"; *complacent* means "smug."

56. Choice (A) is correct. (1:3,2:4) *Emits* and *smite* are anagrams; *integral* and *triangle* are also anagrams.

57. Choice (C) is correct. (1:2,3:4) *Hood* and *less* are suffixes; *arch* and *post* are prefixes.

58. Choice (B) is correct. (1:2,3:4) $2^{-3} = 0.125$. $0.125 \times 2 = 0.25$. $10 \times 2 = 20$.

59. Choice (D) is correct. (1:3,2:4) *Twisted* and *tortuous* are synonyms; *agonizing* and *torturous* are also synonyms.

60. Choice (C) is correct. (1:3,2:4) *Frippery* and *fandangle* are synonyms; *solemn* and *serious* are also synonyms.

61. Choice (A) is correct. (1:2,3:4) Tofurkey is artificial turkey; a prosthesis is an artificial limb.

62. Choice (B) is correct. (1:3,2:4) Acts are divided into scenes; the Torah is divided into books.

63. Choice (C) is correct. (1:2,3:4) $0.5 \times 2 = 1$; $0.2 \times 5 = 1$.

64. Choice (D) is correct. (1:3,2:4) *Strait* and *channel* are synonyms; *straight* and *direct* are also synonyms.

65. Choice (B) is correct. (1:2,3:4) Dewey belonged to the school of pragmatism; Stirner belonged to the school of nihilism.

66. Choice (A) is correct. (1:2,3:4) *Equivocate* and *dodge* are synonyms; *accost* and *bother* are also synonyms.

67. Choice (C) is correct. (1:3,2:4) Asymmetric shock and minimum wage are terms used in economics.

68. Choice (D) is correct. (1:2,3:4) Birthday, cocktail, dinner, and surprise are all types of parties.

69. Choice (A) is correct. (1:2,3:4) A car is a part of a train; a wing is a part of a plane.

70. Choice (C) is correct. (1:2,3:4) $3/(1/4) = 12$; $6/(2/3) = 9$.

71. Choice (B) is correct. (1:2,3:4) Mount Doom is a fictional mountain; Mount Kilimanjaro is a real mountain. A griffin is a fictional animal; an eagle is a real animal.

72. Choice (A) is correct. (1:2,3:4) *Radar, tenet, redder,* and *reviver* are all palindromes.

73. Choice (C) is correct. (1:2,3:4) One yearns for something that is a yen; one avoids something that is a bane.

74. Choice (B) is correct. (1:2,3:4) De Gaulle was a leader of France; Brezhnev was a leader of the U.S.S.R.

75. Choice (C) is correct. (1:3,2:4) $0.37y$ is 37% of y; $y - 9$ is 9 less than y.

76. Choice (D) is correct. (1:2,3:4) *Economical* and *nominal* are synonyms; *steep* and *exorbitant* are also synonyms. Both pairs of words are antonyms.

77. Choice (B) is correct. (1:2,3:4) *Lethargic* means "lacking animation"; *peevish* means "lacking contentment."

78. Choice (A) is correct. (1:2,3:4) The letter *L* forms a right angle; the letter *V* forms an acute angle.

79. Choice (D) is correct. (1:2,3:4) An inch is 1/36 of a yard. 2 is 1/36 of 72.

80. Choice (C) is correct. (1:2,3:4) Dopamine is a hormone produced in the hypothalamus; gastrin is a hormone produced in the stomach.

81. Choice (B) is correct. (1:2,3:4) *Peculate* and *appropriate* are synonyms; *exculpate* and *exonerate* are also synonyms.

82. Choice (A) is correct. (1:2,3:4) A moat is a type of security for a castle; a firewall is a type of security for a computer.

83. Choice (D) is correct. (1:2,3:4) Colombia was named for Christopher Columbus; the Cook Islands were named for James Cook.

84. Choice (C) is correct. (1:2,3:4) *Chipper* and *crestfallen* are antonyms; *taciturn* and *talkative* are also antonyms.

85. Choice (B) is correct. (1:2,3:4) A humorist and a comic are both experts of comedy; a chauvinist and a jingoist are both extreme patriots.

86. Choice (A) is correct. (1:2,3:4) Metal products are made in a foundry; timber products are made in a woodshop.

87. Choice (C) is correct. (1:3,2:4) *Spearmint* and *horseplay* are compounds.

88. Choice (D) is correct. (1:3,2:4) To pull is to tug; a pullover is a sweater.

89. Choice (A) is correct. (1:3,2:4) The mojito is a traditional drink of Cuba; sangria is a traditional drink of Spain.

90. Choice (B) is correct. (1:2,3:4) *Loud* and *clamorous* are synonyms; *quiet* and *muted* are also synonyms.

91. Choice (D) is correct. (1:2,3:4) *Penchant* and *predilection* are synonyms; *perfidious* and *unscrupulous* are also synonyms.

92. Choice (C) is correct. (1:2,3:4) *Galvanize* and *stimulate* are synonyms; *beleaguer* and *beset* are also synonyms.

93. Choice (A) is correct. (1:2,3:4) 237 is a natural number; –898 is an integer.

94. Choice (B) is correct. (1:3,2:4) Rummy and War are card games; kickball and curling are sports.

95. Choice (D) is correct. (1:3,2:4) The nostril is an orifice; the nasal cavity is a fossa.

96. Choice (A) is correct. (1:2,3:4) A devotee is a follower; a jubilee is an anniversary.

97. Choice (C) is correct. (1:3,2:4) In Canada, *mountie* is a name for a police officer; in the U.K., *constable* is a name for a police officer.

98. Choice (B) is correct. (1:2,3:4) Air travels through the larynx, trachea, bronchus, and bronchiole, in that order.

99. Choice D is correct. (1:3,2:4) *Remunerative* and *lucrative* are synonyms; *annulment* and *defeasance* are also synonyms.

100. Choice (A) is correct. (1:2,3:4) *Salute* and *toast* are synonyms; *money* and *bread* are also synonyms.

101. Choice (C) is correct. (1:3,2:4) *Invisible Man* and *Gulliver's Travels* are novels.

102. Choice (B) is correct. (1:2,3:4) Hydrogen is the element with the lowest atomic number; ununoctium is the element with the highest atomic number. Challenger Deep is the lowest natural point on Earth; Mount Everest is the highest point on Earth.

103. Choice (D) is correct. (1:3,2:4) A goal is the unit of scoring in hockey; a run is the unit of scoring in baseball.

104. Choice (A) is correct. (1:3,2:4) *Alluring* and *inviting* are synonyms; *disenchanting* and *disgusting* are also synonyms. Both pairs of words are antonyms to each other.

105. Choice (C) is correct. (1:3,2:4) $130 - 30\% = 130 - 39 = 91$. $100 + 30\% = 100 + 30 = 130$.

106. Choice (B) is correct. (1:2,3:4) Dates and apricots are drupe fruits; oranges and grapefruits are citrus fruits.

107. Choice (A) is correct. (1:2,3:4) English and French are official languages of Canada; Cantonese and Mandarin are official languages of China.

108. Choice (D) is correct. (1:3,2:4) A conjunction connects; a preposition establishes relation.

109. Choice (C) is correct. (1:2,3:4) In mathematics, ≠ means not equal to; ≈ means approximately.

110. Choice (B) is correct. (1:3,2:4) Basi is a type of wine; *basic* refers to something with a high pH.

111. Choice (A) is correct. (1:3,2:4) Blair and Thatcher were prime ministers of the U.K.; Pierce and Polk were presidents of the U.S.A.

112. Choice (D) is correct. (1:2,3:4) Kehaar and Tweety are fictional birds; Tigger and Shere Khan are fictional tigers.

113. Choice (C) is correct. (1:3,2:4) Osteology is the study of bones; heliology is the study of the sun.

114. Choice (B) is correct. (1:3,2:4) An iris is a plant; a pupil is a student.

115. Choice (D) is correct. (1:3,2:4) The ankh is a symbol of life; the ichthys is a symbol of Christianity.

116. Choice (A) is correct. (1:2,3:4) When spelled, 3 and 2 both start with *T*; 6 and 7 both start with *S*.

117. Choice (B) is correct. (1:3,2:4) Antimatter and matter counteract each other; an antidote counteracts a poison.

118. Choice (C) is correct. (1:2,3:4) In music, legato is a mark of articulation; fortissimo is a mark of dynamics.

119. Choice (D) is correct. (1:2,3:4) An anion has a negative charge; a cation has a positive charge.

120. Choice (A) is correct. (1:2,3:4) In mathematics, the mean is the average of a set; the mode is the most common value of a set.

Part IV
Part of Tens

In this part . . .

✔ Read tips for preparing yourself the morning of the test—mentally and physically—by ensuring your well rested, well fed, and well stretched.

✔ Get organized ahead of time to be calm on test day—know where the test is being held and how much time you need to get there, and have your ID and anything else you need packed and ready to go.

✔ Look at simple, immediate ways to reduce stress and anxiety on test day, including giving yourself a little break, building your confidence with a pep talk, and allowing yourself to skip the occasional question.

Chapter 21
Ten Tried-and-True Test Tips

In This Chapter

▶ Getting in top shape for test day

▶ Preparing and showing up for the MAT

By the time test day nears, you will have — I hope — read through this book and gotten familiar with the different types of analogies and the structure of the MAT. You've completed practice tests and reviewed your answers. Ready to go, right?

This chapter provides some tips for what to do — and what not to do — in the final weeks and days before you take on the MAT. It's about more than hitting the books: Getting physically and mentally prepared and feeling organized on test day can go a long way toward your success with the MAT.

Exercise Your Body, Not Just Your Brain

Our bodies often function best when in motion, and exercising the day of the test, or the night before, can relieve pent-up stress, increase blood flow to the brain, and in general, make your body and mind function better. Do something you're used to — now is not the time to try a totally new exercise routine. Even a 20-minute jog will get your heart rate up enough to give you benefits that will last during the duration of the test. Stretching or yoga can be a great way to relieve stress as well.

Be Sure You Get Enough Sleep

Sleep is crucial for your body and mind to perform at their best. But a common misconception is that it's important to get a good night's sleep the night before the test. First, this can be difficult to do. If you're nervous and excited, you might not sleep well, and there's no magic trick to falling asleep in that condition. A better idea is to make sure you allow yourself enough time to sleep during the week leading up to the test. That way, the overall quantity of sleep you get will help compensate if you can't sleep well the night of the test.

Get Organized the Night Before

It's funny, but having to rush, even a little bit, to get to your MAT testing center can really affect your mood. One of the easiest ways you can prepare to have a smooth test day is to prepare everything the evening beforehand.

Make sure you have your directions, identification, and anything else you might need for the day of the test. Doing this will decrease your stress, and anything you can do to reduce your stress on the day of the test is worthwhile!

Be Well Fed

Even though the MAT is not a long test, it's a good idea to eat something before you leave the house. If you get hungry during the test, it can be a minor or even a major distraction. Also, if your blood sugar is low from not eating, you may find it more difficult to think clearly. Don't forget, the MAT will demand a lot of mental energy.

If you have a morning test appointment and you don't normally eat breakfast, you may want to get used to eating something small over the week leading up to the test, so eating is not a shock to your system on the day of the test. Watch out for foods that your body can process extremely quickly, like processed carbohydrates — these can lead to an energy crash if you don't combine them with foods containing fiber, protein, and/or fat.

On Test Day, Don't Study

You'll have enough to worry about on test day without adding studying to the mix. Even if you're worried about your performance, studying on test-day usually doesn't accomplish much.

Make sure you plan ahead enough to get your game plan down so that you don't have to worry about remembering it on test day. Studying the day of the test is also a great way to needlessly stress yourself out, so try not to do it.

Warm Up

Wait, I thought you just said "don't study the day of the test!" you may be thinking. But a warm up is different. The purpose of warming up, just like when you warm up before you exercise, is to get things moving before you face your first real MAT question. A good way to warm up is to review some practice questions you've already done and answered correctly.

Go through the motions, identifying the analogy types, making sentences, and choosing choices. This should help you hit the ground running. Not warming up is not a bad thing, but if you're a slow starter in the morning or you tend to struggle with initial questions on practice tests, warming up can be a great idea.

Arrive Early

On the day of the test, make sure you rise early enough to allow yourself plenty of time for your morning routine, as well as time to get to the MAT testing center. Arriving early is a good idea for many reasons. Checking in can take time, especially on a weekend test date — and you don't want to have to worry about being turned away because you're late for your appointment. Getting to the center early will also give you some time to chill out and relax instead of having to hustle into the test room without any time to collect yourself.

Review How Many Questions You Can Skip

Unless you're a super-genius and you're legitimately trying for a perfect score on the MAT, you probably will not be spending time on every question. Yes, you have to answer each question, but in order to pick up the maximum number of points that you possibly can, you need to know about how many questions you can skip.

To figure this out, you'll need to review your practice tests and determine the average number of wrong answers on the last two or three. That number is, more or less, the number of questions you'll be either skipping or spending a minimal amount of time on during the real MAT. This strategy is designed to employ your time where it will earn you the most points. The questions you'll be skipping should be ones you've identified as weak content areas of yours, and will be more likely to appear later in the test (because the order of difficulty increases as the test progresses).

Write It Down

During the real MAT, you may be tempted to forgo writing down your analogy structures and sentences because you're worried about timing. However, what's more important to you — finishing the test on time or getting the questions you work on right?

To ensure that you accurately answer MAT questions that you're capable of answering correctly, it's well worth it to write down the analogy's structural type and your sentence describing the presented relationship (assuming you can identify these things). It only takes a few extra seconds, and actually buys you more time in the long run because the analogy will now be easier and quicker to think about.

Don't Rush or Second Guess

On the day of the test, many test-takers either rush or second guess themselves to one degree or another. If you've identified which one of these camps you fall into (if any) by thinking about your practice test experiences, you have an advantage. Be aware of your tendency so that you can limit it during the real test. If you haven't identified any tendency, it's still a good idea to be aware.

If you do a question quickly, then get scared you made a mistake and go back and redo it, you're probably wasting valuable time. Or, if you're taking technique shortcuts and continually checking the time, you may be rushing and getting questions wrong that you could be getting right. Work carefully, but trust yourself.

Chapter 22

Ten Ways to Fight off Test-Related Anxiety

*N*o matter how much you've studied, no matter how many practice tests you've taken and aced, there's nothing quite like test-day jitters to make you feel suddenly unprepared and panicked.

It'd be unusual not to feel a little nervous — taking the MAT is an important step toward getting into the graduate program of your choice, and of course you want to do well. But you needn't let a little last-minute anxiety derail all the effort you've put into preparing for the test. There are simple ways to manage and conquer test stress, and this chapter describes ten of the best.

Breathe

When people get nervous, they often tense their muscles, consciously or unconsciously. Aside from increasing stress, this clenching can make it difficult to breathe deeply because the muscles around your rib cage are tight. To combat this tendency, make sure you take the time to breathe during the MAT. A good way to make sure you do this is to get in the habit now. After selecting a choice for each question, take a breath. More oxygen will get to your brain and make it easier for you to think clearly. Breathing might not immediately make you feel less anxious, but over the course of the test, you'll definitely feel less anxiety if you breathe deeply than if you don't. Also, breathing through your nose is usually more relaxing than mouth breathing.

Take a Break

The last thing you may want to do during the MAT is take a break. After all, the test is timed! But if you're panicking, taking a break may be one of the most helpful things you can do. Close your eyes and take deep breaths for about 15 seconds. Imagine, after you've completed the test, that you're lying on a beach or doing something else relaxing. Being nice to yourself like this can help your anxiety fade. This technique can also break the cycle if you're rushing or second-guessing yourself.

Stretch

If you're hunched over a computer for a long period of time, your muscles probably won't like it. And if you're anxious during the MAT, it may actually be a physical thing. Have you ever witnessed a small child fidgeting when he's told to sit still? Our bodies are meant to move. Try stretching your arms over your head, twisting back and forth, moving your legs — anything to get your body moving and your blood circulating so it can carry oxygen to your brain.

Move Your Pencil

Often, when people are anxious, they are actively imagining a negative possibility coming true. For instance, if you're scared of public speaking, you've probably imagined yourself giving a bad speech, or forgetting your speech entirely. It's obviously not a great idea to imagine yourself getting a low score on the MAT while you're taking it. Plus, why imagine something that hasn't even happened yet? If you do feel anxious, a good way to get yourself out of your head is as simple as moving your pencil. Write something — anything — down to help with the analogy in front of you. This simple action can move your attention from your anxiety to the concrete problem in front of you.

Slow Down

One of the main side effects of test-taking anxiety is rushing — and it's one of the worst things you can do on the MAT. To make matters worse, when you rush, you often know you're rushing, which can make you even more anxious. Even if you're worried about being behind on time, it's never a good idea to go faster than you're capable of going, because it will increase the likelihood that you'll make careless mistakes. Slowing down (by making sure you write down your technique and check every answer choice) can actually reduce anxiety, because it will make you a little bit more confident in your chosen answers.

Skip a Weakness

One source of anxiety on the MAT, not surprisingly, is the questions. When a bizarre-looking analogy term that you've never even heard of before pops up on your screen, it can be frightening. Or, you might panic when you see a question type that you know you're not that good at. But just because a question is in front of you doesn't mean you have to work on it. If you know a certain question is a weakness of yours, especially if you know the difficulty level is high, don't stress yourself out by working on it.

Skip it and come back to it if you have time. The time you save may help lower your anxiety, especially if you remember that you're (hopefully) not trying for a perfect score. Also, pick a letter (A, B, C, or D) ahead of time that you'll use for all your guesses, so you don't waste time thinking about which letter to choose randomly on questions you're truly guessing on.

Get Perspective

Anxiety is often the result of a mental focus on something unpleasant that might happen. If you're feeling anxious or panicky during the MAT, it might help to remember that, while you're still sitting in that chair, you are the one in control of the test's outcome. That's reality. It's also reality that your life is a lot more than the MAT and its result. It's unlikely that the MAT will make or break your chances of having a happy, successful life — and it can help to remind yourself of that fact if you're feeling nervous.

Be Goofy

It's pretty hard to feel anxious when you're laughing, smiling, or just remembering a funny moment. It can be a good idea to call to mind a joke or funny situation if you're feeling stressed out during the MAT. Even if you can make yourself smile a little bit, it will ease your tension somewhat. The simple act of smiling will also relax your facial muscles, calm you down, and put you in a slightly better mood. Or, make a goofy face at the computer — anything to break the pattern of anxiety and seriousness for a second or two.

Feel What You're Feeling

Have you ever been so stressed out from a traumatic event that you found it difficult to talk or even think? The more deeply you feel, the less clearly you think. The problem is that when many people feel something painful, they tense their muscles to avoid the painful feelings, constricting their breathing and thereby making it harder for their brains to get oxygen.

A way to avoid this is to let yourself feel whatever emotion you're experiencing during the test. Trying to shut off the emotion will just create more tension. Don't dwell on the emotion, just let yourself feel it, accept it's there, then go back to your technique. And definitely don't waste your energy by yelling at yourself for being nervous.

Use Positive Self-Talk

Most people have little conversations with themselves in their heads — that might sound a little crazy, but it's true. But problems can arise when your self-talk is negative or gloomy — like anxiety. Try purposefully thinking positive statements, like "I can do this!" or "I'm doing great so far." You might not completely believe yourself at the time, but positivity is going to be a lot better for your mental state than negativity. Plus, it will probably actually help you do better. Can you imagine if a baseball player told himself "I'm gonna strike out" before every at-bat, versus one who always told himself "I'm going to get a hit"? Make sure you use positive self-talk in practice, too. Finally, remember that you've prepared for the test and tell yourself that your preparation will pay off — which it certainly will!

Part V
The Appendixes

Understand the meanings of words, even words you haven't encountered before, by recognizing roots. Check out www.dummies.com/extras/mat.

In this part . . .

✔ Boost your vocabulary to impress your friends and triumph on test day with mnemonics that will help you identify and remember the meanings of words you may encounter on the MAT test.

✔ Understand what your test results mean and what schools and future employers will derive from the score you earn.

Appendix A

Graduate Level Vocabulary

● ●

*I*f you're studying for the MAT, you may be feeling a bit anxious — especially if you've taken a practice test and encountered words you didn't know (or maybe words you've never even seen)! Whether you have seven days or seven months to prepare for the test, you're going to want to boost your vocabulary. But it's not that simple — you've got to *remember* the words you learn. And on many MAT questions, getting the right answer comes down to knowing the precise definition of the words.

You can make vocabulary flashcards. You can look up words you don't know. You can read a book with lots of big words. But unless you give your brain a way to hold on to the words you learn, it will have a hard time remembering them when they appear on the test. Therein lies the problem with most vocabulary books: The definitions and sentences in the books aren't especially memorable.

This appendix is different. I've not only clearly defined the words, but I've also created sentences designed to help you remember the words through a variety of associations — using mnemonics.

How to Use This Appendix

There are several ways. You could look up the words you don't know, or just read it straight through. If you're an auditory learner, you might say all the definitions and sentences into a recorder and listen to them. If you're at all artistic, you might even draw sketches illustrating the sentences.

If your test date is within a few months, I recommend setting a goal to learn about ten new words a day. This schedule gets you through the whole appendix in a couple months. Here's another tip: Go back and review the words you've learned after 24 hours, review them again after 48 hours, and review them again after 96 hours, doubling the amount of time between reviews as you go.

The mnemonics

Abase (verb): To humiliate or degrade.

Think: Giving up A BASE.

Abate (verb): To reduce.

Think: REBATE.

It may be annoying to have to mail it in, but the REBATE on the new cellphone will ABATE its cost.

Abeyance (noun): Temporary inactivity.

Think: OBEY ENDS.

After the sergeant leaves, our desire to OBEY his command ENDS and we usually have an ABEYANCE of work.

Abridge (verb): To shorten.

Think: A BRIDGE.

A BRIDGE would ABRIDGE my commute, which involves driving around the canyon.

Abstemious (adjective): Sparing or moderate, especially with food and drink.

Think: STEAM VEGGIES.

If you follow an ABSTEMIOUS diet, STEAM your veggies instead of frying them.

Abstruse (adjective): Hard to comprehend.

Think: ABSTRACT and CONFUSE.

The ABSTRACT strudel directions will CONFUSE the new cook because they are ABSTRUSE.

Abysmal (adjective): Awful.

Think: PEPTO-BISMOL.

When I had food poisoning, my stomach felt so ABYSMAL that I had to drink a bottle of Pepto-BISMOL.

Accede (verb): To express approval.

Think: AGREED.

Since we all ACCEDE to the plan to seed the garden, it looks like we're AGREED.

Acerbic (adjective): Harsh; biting.

Think: ACIDIC.

The movie reviewer, a bitter old man, wrote reviews that were ACERBIC to the point of being ACIDIC.

Acidulous (adjective): Somewhat harsh.

Think: ACID-ISH.

I like Sour Patch Kids because their ACIDULOUS taste is ACID-ISH without being too painful.

Acrimonious (adjective): Bitter.

Think: A CRIME ON US.

Committing A CRIME ON US makes us ACRIMONIOUS.

Acumen (noun): Insightfulness.

Think: ACCURATE MEN.

In business, ACCURATE MEN often have ACUMEN.

Adorned (adjective): Decorated.

Think: ORNAMENT.

If you adore Christmas, your tree is probably ADORNED with ORNAMENTS.

Adroit (adjective): Skillful.

Think: A DROID.

A DROID is an ADROIT cellphone, since it can do so much.

Adulation (noun): Excessive admiration.

Think: ADORATION.

The goblin's ADORATION of a jewel was so intense that it could only be called ADULATION.

Aesthetic (adjective): Relating to beauty.

Think: ATHLETIC body.

If you're ATHLETIC, you're more likely to have a body that is AESTHETIC.

Affable (adjective): Friendly.

Think: LAUGHABLE.

Since they want tourists to feed them, zoo giraffes are so AFFABLE that it's LAUGHABLE.

Affectation (noun): An artificial way of behaving.

Think: A FAKE FICTION.

Madonna's phony English accent is an AFFECTATION; it is A FAKE FICTION.

Alleviate (verb): To soothe or lessen the severity of.

Think: ALEVE.

Phyllis's headache was so bad that she took four ALEVE pills to ALLEVIATE the pain.

Altruistic (adjective): Unselfish; generous.

Think: ALWAYS TRUE.

Those who pray at altars are usually more likely to be ALTRUISTIC and ALWAYS TRUE to others.

Amalgamate (verb): Unify; join parts into a whole.

Think: MALCOM'S GUM.

After breaking the vase, MALCOLM used GUM to AMALGAMATE the pieces back together.

Ameliorated (verb): Made better.

Think: EMILIO RATE.

EMILIO RATED my pasta as a 10 out of 10, which AMELIORATED my fears that I had ruined it.

Amenable (adjective): Willing; cooperative.

Think: AMEN-ABLE.

After she shouted, "AMEN!," I could tell she was AMENABLE to my plan.

Amicable (adjective): Friendly.

Think: HAMMOCK-ABLE.

When Amy said that her HAMMOCK was ABLE to hold two people, I knew that she was AMICABLE.

Anachronism (noun): A thing in the wrong time period.

Think: INACCURATE CHRONOMETER.

The B-movie had something INACCURATE: a caveman wearing a CHRONOMETER, a huge ANACHRONISM.

Anile (adjective): Senile.

Think: SENILE.

I knew my Aunt Ann was ANILE to the point of being SENILE when she asked to go swimming in the Nile.

Anodyne (noun): A pain reliever.

Think: NOT DYING.

When I had the flu, the doctor-prescribed ANODYNE finally made me feel like I was NOT DYING.

Antediluvian (adjective): Ancient; primitive.

Antithesis (noun): Opposite.

Think: ANTI-THESIS.

You got a D on your essay because your examples argued for the ANTITHESIS of your introduction's THESIS.

Apace (adjective): Quickly.

Think: Keep PACE.

The Indy 500 racer's pit crew changed his tires APACE so he could keep PACE with the leaders.

Apartheid (noun): The policy of separating groups based on race.

Think: APART TO HIDE.

In South Africa, APARTHEID kept blacks APART TO HIDE them from whites.

Aplomb (noun): Confidence.

Think: The BOMB.

If you have APLOMB, you think you're the BOMB.

Apocryphal (adjective): Of doubtful truthfulness.

Think: APOCALYPSE predictions.

The prediction that the APOCALYPSE is going to happen in 2012 is APOCRYPHAL.

Apothegm (noun): A short, wise remark.

Think: POCKET THE GEM.

"POCKET THE GEM!" is a good APOTHEGM to remember if you see a ruby lying in the grass.

Apposite (adjective): Appropriate.

Think: A POSITIVE SITE.

Wikipedia is A POSITIVE SITE because it's APPOSITE for all kinds of research.

Arch (adjective): Sassy.

Think: ARCHED EYEBROW.

Her playful, ARCH (adjective) comment made me ARCH (verb) my eyebrow.

Ardent (adjective): Passionately enthusiastic.

Think: Flame RETARDANT.

I'm so ARDENT and fired up about life that I have to wear clothes that are FLAME RETARDANT.

Arid (adjective): Very dry.

Think: ARRID Extra Dry.

Get a little closer; don't be shy! Get a little closer, with ARRID Extra Dry (which keeps your armpits ARID)!

Ashen (adjective): Very pale.

Think: ASH.

When he saw the ghost, his complexion became so ASHEN that his face was the color of ASH.

Aspersion (noun): A false claim intended to harm.

Think: ASP POISON.

Her ASPERSIONS about what I did last night felt like ASP POISON.

Assiduous (adjective): Hardworking; dedicated.

Think: ASSIST US.

Assuage: (verb): To make less severe.

Think: MASSAGE.

Getting a long MASSAGE will ASSUAGE those sore muscles.

August (adjective): Majestic.

Think: AUGUSTUS Caesar.

AUGUSTUS Caesar, the first Roman emperor, was so AUGUST that that they named a month after him.

Austere (adjective): Plain; strict; serious; cold.

Think: AUSTRIA STERN.

Life among the Alps in AUSTRIA is STERN and AUSTERE — it's hard to party when there's a windchill of –20.

Automaton (noun): One who acts in a robotic way.

Think: AUTOMATIC.

If doing your work is so AUTOMATIC that you feel like an AUTOMATON, it's time for a new job.

Avuncular (adjective): Like an uncle.

Think: UNCLE.

The AVUNCULAR professor was like an UNCLE to him, dispensing well-intentioned advice.

Beatific (adjective): Extremely happy.

Think: BEAUTIFUL! TERRIFIC!

If you feel BEATIFIC, you probably walk around exclaiming, "BEAUTIFUL! TERRIFIC!" all day.

Beatify (verb): To bless; to make happy.

Think: BEAUTIFY.

The makeover will BEAUTIFY your home and BEATIFY your family.

Beguile (verb): To trick.

Think: BE GULLIBLE.

BE GULLIBLE, and you'll be easy to BEGUILE.

Behemoth (noun): Something huge.

Think: BEAST MAMMOTH.

One really large BEAST was the woolly MAMMOTH, a BEHEMOTH that lived during the Ice Age.

Belied (verb): Contradicted.

Think: LIED.

The used car salesman's sweaty handshake BELIED his smooth manner and made me think, "He LIED!"

Belligerent (adjective): Warlike; hostile.

Think: Albert BELLE.

Albert BELLE, a former baseball player, was so BELLIGERENT that he once assaulted a fan who heckled him.

Bereft (adjective): Deprived or robbed of something.

Think: HE LEFT.

After HE LEFT her at the altar and crushed her dreams, she felt completely BEREFT.

Bespoke (adjective): Custom made.

Think: Kanye's BESPOKE suit.

Kanye's BESPOKE suit SPOKE volumes about his wealth.

Bifurcated (verb): Split in two.

Think: BY FORKING.

BY FORKING, the road BIFURCATED into the popular road and the road less traveled by.

Bloviated (verb): Wordy/windy when speaking.

Think: BLOW hot air.

Harry Potter's professor Gilderoy Lockhart BLOVIATED; he would BLOW a lot of hot air without much meaning.

Bootless (adjective): Useless.

Think: BOOTY-LESS.

A BOOTY-LESS pirate is probably a BOOTLESS pirate.

Bugbear (noun): Something to fear.

Think: BUG a BEAR.

If you BUG a BEAR, you'll soon have a very serious BUGBEAR.

Bumptious (adjective): Assertive in a loud, arrogant way.

Think: BUMP US.

You're the type of guy who would push past us in a crowd and BUMP US and not say you're sorry — you're BUMPTIOUS.

Burgeoning (adjective): Growing.

Think: BURGERS.

If you eat too many BURGERS, your waistline will be BURGEONING.

Buttress (noun): A support.

Think: BUTT REST.

The stone column is both a BUTTRESS and a BUTT REST for tired people to lean against.

Bygone (adjective): Past.

Think: BYE-GONE.

The BYGONE days of my childhood are days I've said BYE to because they're GONE.

Byzantine (adjective): Devious; complicated.

Think: BUSY ANT.

Only the most BUSY ANT will be able to make its way through the BYZANTINE maze you've created.

Cache (noun): A secure storage place or something in that place.

Think: CASH.

The drug dealer kept his CASH in a CACHE under the bed because he didn't trust banks.

Calamitous (adjective): Related to a terrible event.

Think: CALAMARI VOMIT.

It's CALAMITOUS when you eat undercooked CALAMARI, become VOMITOUS, and puke on your date.

Camaraderie (noun): Togetherness.

Think: COMRADES.

The Russian camera factory workers shared a sense of CAMARADERIE, calling each other COMRADES.

Capacious (adjective): Spacious.

Think: CAPE SPACIOUS.

Batman is a big guy, so his CAPE is SPACIOUS and CAPACIOUS.

Capricious (adjective): Impulsive; done without forethought.

Think: CAPRI PANTS.

At the mall, Jenny made the CAPRICIOUS decision to buy five pairs of CAPRI pants, which she later regretted when they went out of style.

Cardinal (adjective): Of main importance.

Think: CARDINAL bird.

You'd think the bright red male CARDINAL (noun) was the most CARDINAL (adjective) bird because of its vivid color.

Celerity (noun): Quickness.

Think: ACCELERATE.

After Cee Lo switched to an all-celery diet, he lost 40 pounds; his ability to ACCELERATE increased, as did his CELERITY.

Censure (verb): To criticize harshly.

Think: CENSOR.

If you really wanted to CENSURE the passage, you would CENSOR it completely.

Champion (verb): To fight for.

Think: CHAMPION (noun).

It's easy to CHAMPION (verb) the CHAMPION (noun) of the match, but not so easy to stick up for the loser.

Chicanery (noun): Trickery.

Think: CHICK-GAIN-ERY

Your frat brother's feigned interest in that cute girl's paintings was clearly CHICANERY; his motive was "CHICK-GAIN-ERY."

Chide (verb): To scold.

Think: CHILD SCOLD.

If you have a CHILD, you probably SCOLD and CHIDE him or her on a daily basis.

Choleric (adjective): Irritable.

Think: CHOLERA.

I'd be CHOLERIC, too, if someone's fecal matter made me get CHOLERA.

Circuitous (adjective): Roundabout; not direct.

Think: CIRCUIT-ISH.

The crooked cabdriver took a CIRCUITOUS route; his path was CIRCUIT-ISH to increase the fare.

Circumspect (adjective): Cautious.

Think: CIRCLE INSPECT.

When you rent a car, walk in a CIRCLE to INSPECT it for dents; if you're not CIRCUMSPECT now, they may charge you later.

Clandestine (adjective): Secret.

Think: CLAN.

The rebel CLAN assumed they were destined to be tracked by the Empire, so they held CLANDESTINE meetings.

Clemency (noun): Mercy.

Think: CLEMENS MERCY.

The pitcher Roger CLEMENS was shown MERCY by the jury and found not guilty — an act of CLEMENCY, since he was accused of taking steroids.

Cloying (adjective): Gross because it's too much.

Think: ANNOYING.

Always talking baby-talk to each other, the couple was so ANNOYING that they were CLOYING.

Cocksure (adjective): Overconfident.

Think: COCKY and SURE.

The baseball rookie was so COCKY and SURE that he'd hit a home run during his first at-bat that he was COCKSURE.

Cognizant (adjective): Aware; informed.

Think: RECOGNIZE.

If you're COGNIZANT of our theory, you must RECOGNIZE where our solution came from.

Complicit (adjective): Having helped with a crime.

Think: ACCOMPLICE.

Though I robbed the bank and my ACCOMPLICE just drove me there, he was considered COMPLICIT by the law.

Composure (noun): Calmness.

Think: CALM POSE.

Even though he was performing his music for kings and queens, the composer's CALM POSE showed his COMPOSURE.

Concord (noun): Harmony.

Think: CONQUERED.

After the uprising had been CONQUERED, the kingdom enjoyed a state of CONCORD for many years.

Concupiscence (noun): Strong desire, especially sexual desire.

Think: CUPID'S ESSENCE.

If you have CONCUPISCENCE, you have CUPID'S ESSENCE running through your veins.

Condign (adjective): Deserved; appropriate.

Think: I CAN DIG.

I CAN DIG the murderer's conviction because it was CONDIGN.

Conflagration (noun): A fire.

Think: FLAG NATION.

There is a debate about the FLAG in our NATION — is it legal to use the Stars and Stripes for a CONFLAGRATION?

Contumacious (adjective): Disobedient; rebellious.

Think: TUMS.

The kids were so CONTUMACIOUS that their babysitter always had a tummy ache and had to take TUMS.

Conundrum (noun): A difficult problem.

Think: NUN DRUM.

Building a NUN DRUM is a CONUNDRUM because nuns don't like loud noises.

Cordial (adjective): Affectionate.

Think: Alcoholic CORDIAL.

After drinking the alcoholic CORDIAL (noun), I became more CORDIAL (adjective).

Corroborate (verb): To support with evidence.

Think: CO-ROBBER.

When robbing a bank, use a CO-ROBBER who will CORROBORATE your story.

Coruscate (verb): Sparkle.

Think: CHORUS CATE.

When she was on stage during the musical, "CHORUS CATE" would CORUSCATE due to her breathtaking voice.

Cosmopolitan (adjective): Sophisticated.

Think: COSMO.

After reading the dating advice in *COSMO*, the 14-year-old thought she was quite COSMOPOLITAN.

Countenance (noun): Facial expression.

Think: ENCOUNTER US.

Your COUNTENANCE is the first part of you that will ENCOUNTER US, so make sure you're smiling.

Covert (adjective): Not openly shown.

Think: COVERED.

The CIA agent was on a COVERT mission, so he COVERED his true identity.

Cowed (adjective): Intimidated.

Think: COWARD.

The bully was at heart a COWARD; as soon as I stood up to him, he was COWED into silence.

Crepuscular (adjective): Related to twilight.

Think: CREEPY.

In the movie *Breaking Dawn*, CREEPY, muscular vampires prowl during the CREPUSCULAR hours of the day.

Culpable (adjective): Deserving blame.

Think: CULPRIT.

Unsurprisingly, the cop thought the CULPRIT was CULPABLE.

Cumbersome (adjective): Awkward due to large size.

Think: CUCUMBER.

It was CUMBERSOME to write with the pen made out of a giant CUCUMBER.

Cupidity (noun): Greedy desire for.

Think: CUPID.

After being shot by CUPID'S arrow, Sarah developed such a CUPIDITY for her valentine that she called him daily.

Curmudgeon (noun): A grumpy old man.

Think: CURSE MUD.

Only a CURMUDGEON would CURSE the MUD in the garden on this sunny spring day.

Cynosure (noun): Something that guides or stands out.

Think: SIGN to be SURE.

The North Star was a CYNOSURE for ancient sailors, a SIGN they could be SURE of.

Dearth (noun): Lack.

Think: DEAD EARTH.

Due to the DEAD EARTH of our farmland, there will be a DEARTH of food this winter.

Declaimed (verb): Spoke loudly and self-importantly.

Think: "I DECLARE!"

"Well, I DECLARE!" the Southern belle DECLAIMED.

Decorous (adjective): Well-behaved.

Think: THE CHORUS.

Kids in THE CHORUS are usually not rebels — they're often DECOROUS.

Decried (verb): Expressed strong disapproval about.

Think: CRIED.

After my boss DECRIED my work in front of everyone, I went home and CRIED.

Defenestrate (verb): To quickly throw out.

Think: DEFENSE DEMONSTRATE.

If you DEFENESTRATE a burglar through a plate-glass window, your home DEFENSE is DEMONSTRATED.

Defunct (adjective): No longer existing.

Think: DE-FUNCTION.

When I can fly in my dreams, the law of gravity seems to be DEFUNCT, like it has been "DE-FUNCTIONED."

Deleterious (adjective): Harmful.

Think: DELETES.

Using that old computer could be DELETERIOUS to your grade, since it randomly DELETES files.

Demagogue (noun): A leader who gains power by trickery.

Think: DEMIGOD.

The cult was led by a DEMAGOGUE; he manipulated followers into thinking he was a DEMIGOD.

Demarcate (verb): To define; to set apart.

Think: MARK IT.

If you want to DEMARCATE your side of the dorm room, MARK IT with a long piece of masking tape.

Denigrate (verb): To attack the reputation of or to put down.

Think: DENY I'M GREAT.

If you DENY I'm GREAT, you DENIGRATE me.

Desiccated (adjective): Dried out.

Think: DESERT-SICK.

The DESERT made me SICK because the dry heat DESICCATED my body.

Despoiled (verb): Stripped of value.

Think: SPOILED.

Desperate for oil, the U.S. drilled in Alaska and DESPOILED the land and SPOILED it for future generations.

Desuetude (noun): Disuse.

Think: DISUSE ATTITUDE.

The unnecessary security guard at the knitting store had an air of lazy DESUETUDE about him, kind of a DISUSE ATTITUDE.

Diaphanous (adjective): So flimsy as to be see-through.

Think: DIANA'S FAN.

Princess DIANA's delicate rice-paper FAN was DIAPHANOUS.

Diatribe (noun): An angry speech.

Think: DIE TRIBE.

I didn't understand the words of his DIATRIBE, but I guessed the native said I'd DIE from his TRIBE killing me.

Didactic (adjective): Designed to teach.

Think: DICTIONARY TACTIC.

The definitions in a DICTIONARY use the TACTIC of explaining words clearly in order to be DIDACTIC.

Dilatory (adjective): Tending to procrastinate.

Think: DELAY.

The DILATORY gator liked to DELAY things till later.

Dint (noun): Force; power.

Think: DENT.

The Incredible Hulk made a DENT in the car by DINT of his enormous strength.

Discomfit (verb): To embarrass or confuse.

Think: DISCOMFORT.

Realizing one's suit had been replaced with a too-tight Speedo would DISCOMFORT and DISCOMFIT anyone.

Discriminate (verb): To notice subtle variations.

Think: One meaning is criminal, one is neutral.

DISCRIMINATE so you'll know when *discriminate* is about prejudice and when it's about noticing.

Disgruntled (adjective): Displeased.

Think: GRUNTED.

The fat warthog GRUNTED to show he was DISGRUNTLED with his small dinner.

Disparage (verb): To insult or put down.

Think: DESPAIR and RAGE.

He felt DESPAIR and RAGE because the rapper liked to diss and DISPARAGE him.

Dispatch (noun): Speed; efficiency.

Think: Police DISPATCHER.

If you want a job as a DISPATCHER — using the radio to direct police — you'd better have DISPATCH.

Disputatious (adjective): Inclined to argue.

Think: DISPUTE.

After being pulled over, the DISPUTATIOUS lawyer unwisely DISPUTED the accuracy of the cop's radar gun.

Distension (noun): Swelling.

Think: STOMACH WITH NO TENSION.

A belly showing DISTENSION after a huge meal may be the result of weak abs with no muscle TENSION.

Divisive (adjective): Creating disunity.

Think: DIVIDE.

Yoko Ono had a DIVISIVE effect on The Beatles, DIVIDING the group into two parts.

Docile (adjective): Calm, even-tempered.

Think: DOCTOR.

The DOCILE DOCTOR remained calm even though his patient was clinging to life by a thread.

Doggedness (noun): Stubborn determination.

Think: DOG-NESS.

The fighter's DOGGEDNESS, even after he was knocked down, was like that of a fearless BULLDOG.

Doggerel (noun): Poorly written verse.

Think: DOG VERSE.

Most Valentine's Day card poems are such DOGGEREL that it seems as though DOGS wrote the VERSE.

Dogmatic (adjective): Stubborn; inflexible.

Think: DOG bath.

My DOG AUTOMATICALLY becomes DOGMATIC if you try to give him a bath, since he hates water.

Draconian (adjective): Cruelly strict.

Think: DRACO MALFOY.

If DRACO Malfoy taught the Gryffindor students, I'm sure he would have been a DRACONIAN instructor.

Droll (adjective): Funny.

Think: ROLL (with laughter).

DROLL humor makes me ROLL with laughter.

Dubious (adjective): Doubtful or suspect.

Think: DUBSTEP.

I am DUBIOUS as to whether the DUBSTEP music trend is going to last.

Dudgeon (noun): A tantrum caused by being offended.

Think: DUNGEON GRUDGE.

I was in high DUDGEON after they threw me in the DUNGEON for jaywalking, and I held a GRUDGE.

Dupe (verb): To trick.

Think: DOPE.

A DOPE is easy to DUPE.

Duplicitous (adjective): Deceptive.

Think: DUPLICATE-NESS.

You gave DUPLICATE excuses to each of us, but they don't quite match up — you're totally being DUPLICITOUS.

Dyspeptic (adjective): Grumpy.

Think: DISS PEPTO-BISMOL.

Don't DISS PEPTO-BISMOL — if you get indigestion and don't have any, you'll be DYSPEPTIC.

Ebullient (adjective): Excitedly enthusiastic.

Think: RED BULL.

After I chugged a giant RED BULL, I felt extremely EBULLIENT.

Eclectic (adjective): Varied.

Think: SELECTION COLLECTION.

If your musical tastes are ECLECTIC, I can probably name any style SELECTION and you'll say it's in your COLLECTION.

Effaced (verb): Made less visible.

Think: ERASED.

On old nickels, Thomas Jefferson's face is often EFFACED to the point of almost being ERASED.

Efficacious (adjective): Effective.

Think: EFFECTIVENESS.

If you have senioritis, a brief vacation is an EFFICACIOUS way to increase your EFFECTIVENESS.

Effusive (adjective): Extremely expressive.

Think: FUSS.

Imagine if Nicki Minaj was your grandma! She's so EFFUSIVE, she'd make a FUSS over your every accomplishment.

Egalitarian (adjective): Based on the belief in human equality.

Think: EQUAL EAGLE.

In the U.S., our EGALITARIAN belief that all men are created EQUAL is symbolized by the bald EAGLE.

Eldritch (adjective): Weird; eerie.

Think: ELF-WITCH. The ELF-WITCH was ELDRITCH with her ability to speak inside our heads.

Embroiled (verb): In a difficult situation.

Think: ON BROIL.

I was EMBROILED in a dangerous situation when I got locked in an oven set on BROIL.

Embryonic (adjective): In an early stage.

Think: EMBRYO.

It's pretty obvious that a human EMBYRO is EMBRYONIC when compared to an adult human.

Emollient (adjective): Soothing.

Think: EMO.

Listening to EMO music has an EMOLLIENT effect on my emotions because it's so sensitive.

Encomium (noun): Praise.

Think: IN COMIC-CON.

IN COMIC-CON, the entertainment convention, nerds give ENCOMIUM to the latest comic-book movies.

Encompass (verb): To include.

Think: COMPASS.

Use this COMPASS to draw a circle around the things you want to ENCOMPASS.

Enervating (adjective): Tiring.

Think: RENOVATING.

RENOVATING their kitchen by themselves not only got on the couple's nerves, but also was extremely ENERVATING.

Ensorcelled (adjective): Bewitched; enchanted.

Think: SORCERER.

The SORCERER ENSORCELLED the adventurers with a powerful spell that made them forget who they were.

Entreat (verb): To plead.

Think: TREAT.

I usually ENTREAT my dog to sit down by offering him a dog TREAT if he does.

Eradicate (verb): To wipe out.

Think: RADIATE.

You can RADIATE food to ERADICATE the bacteria in it.

Eschew (verb): To avoid.

Think: AH-CHOO.

ESCHEW people who say "AH-CHOO!" unless you want to catch their colds.

Estimable (adjective): Worthy.

Think: ESTEEM-able.

If someone is ESTIMABLE, he "ESTEEM-ABLE," so he's deserving of your positive regard.

Etiolated (verb): Made pale; weakened.

Think: TOILET-ED.

Keeping my goldfish in the bleach-containing TOILET tank violated his trust and ETIOLATED him so much that he turned white.

Evanescent (adjective): Fleeting; lasting only briefly.

Think: EVAN'S SCENT.

He puts on only a drop of cologne, so EVAN'S SCENT is EVANESCENT.

Evinced (verb): Revealed.

Think: EVIDENCE.

Vince EVINCED the villain by providing EVIDENCE.

Exacting (adjective): Requiring strict attention to detail.

Think: EXACT.

Our EXACTING architecture professor demanded that our model be drawn EXACTLY to scale.

Exculpated (verb): Freed from blame.

Think: EX-CULPRIT.

If you commit a crime but have a clever lawyer, you'll be EXCULPATED and be an EX-CULPRIT.

Exonerated (verb): Freed from blame.

Think: EXXON.

It made the environmentalist mad that EXXON was basically EXONERATED for its tanker's massive oil spill in Alaska.

Exorbitant (adjective): Excessive.

Think: EXTRA for ORBIT.

The fancy space hotel charged EXORBITANT fees due to the EXTRA costs needed to ORBIT Earth.

Expatriate (noun): One who has moved to a foreign county.

Think: EX-PATRIOT.

We said our EXPATRIATE friend was an anti-American EX-PATRIOT since he moved to France.

Expedient (adjective): Helpful in a practical way.

Think: SPEEDY.

To be SPEEDY, I booked my flight on Expedia.com; it was more EXPEDIENT than calling the airline.

Expunge (verb): To get rid of.

Think: EX with SPONGE.

The best way to make a spill an "EX-spill" is to use a SPONGE to EXPUNGE the mess.

Extant (adjective): Present or existing (opposite of *extinct*).

Think: EXISTING ANT.

Since he was about to get stepped on, "I EXIST!" exclaimed the ANT to the elephant.

Extirpate (verb): To get rid of completely.

Think: EXTERMINATE.

If you have pests in your house that you want to EXTIRPATE, call someone who will EXTERMINATE them.

Fastidious (adjective): Having very picky standards.

Think: FAST TO TIDY.

My roommate is FASTIDIOUS about cleaning; she gets mad if I am not FAST to TIDY UP the apartment.

Fatuous (adjective): Foolish.

Think: FAT TO US.

If we were already overweight, it would be FATUOUS to give FAT TO US.

Fawning (verb) Kissing up to.

Think: FAWN (baby deer).

The little FAWN's only hope to get the bear to spare its life was by using FAWNING behavior.

Feckless (adjective): Weak; worthless; irresponsible.

Think: F in CLASS.

If you get an F in CLASS, your study habits were probably FECKLESS.

Fecund (adjective): Fruitful; inventive.

Think: FECES UNDER.

Spreading manure, or FECES, UNDER your crops as fertilizer will make your harvest FECUND.

Fetid (adjective): Bad-smelling.

Think: FEET.

FEET often are FETID.

Filial (adjective): Like a son or daughter.

Think: AFFILIATED.

It was the son's FILIAL duty to care for his dying mother since he was AFFILIATED with her by blood.

Florid (adjective): Overly decorated; reddish.

Think: FLOWERED.

The 12-year-old girl's room was FLOWERED with hundreds of red-hued decorations — her style was FLORID.

Flouted (verb): Treated without respect.

Think: FLUNG OUT.

The rebel FLOUTED the rules so badly that he FLUNG them OUT the window.

Flummoxed (adjective): Confused.

Think: FLUME OX.

At the water park, I was completely FLUMMOXED when, in the FLUME ride, I saw an OX swimming along.

Foible (noun): A minor weakness of character.

Think: WOBBLE.

Santa Claus's only real FOIBLE is that he laughs hard enough to make his belly WOBBLE.

Forbearance (noun): Patience; tolerance.

Think: BEAR TOLERANCE.

I'm usually harsh on people who borrow my money, but for BEARS, I have more TOLERANCE and practice FORBEARANCE, since they scare me.

Fortitude (noun): Strength.

Think: FORTRESS.

The Bulgarian weightlifter's mental FORTITUDE during training gave him a body that looked like a FORTRESS.

Fracas (noun): A noisy brawl.

Think: FRAT RUCKUS.

The FRAT brothers often caused a RUCKUS by getting into a drunken FRACAS.

Fractious (adjective): Cranky.

Think: FRACTURE US.

The FRACTIOUS football player is best avoided: If his team loses, he gets mad enough to FRACTURE US.

Froward (adjective): Stubbornly disobedient.

Think: AFRO.

I try to straighten my hair, but it's FROWARD — after a few hours, it's a FRO again.

Fruition (noun): A productive result.

Think: FRUIT.

My plans to grow my own oranges came to FRUITION when my orange tree produced FRUIT.

Fuliginous (adjective): Obscure; murky; dark.

Think: FULL OF GIN.

After he was FULL OF GIN, Joyce composed poetry so moody and FULIGINOUS that few could appreciate it.

Fulsome (adjective): Abundant.

Think: FULL of SOME.

In the U.S., we are FULL of SOME crops — for instance, corn here is FULSOME.

Funereal (adjective): Like a funeral.

Think: FUNERAL.

Your gothic style is so FUNEREAL that it looks as though you're headed to a FUNERAL instead of the mall.

Furor (noun): An outburst of rage or excitement.

Think: FURIOUS.

The governor's use of the Fuhrer's (Hitler's) image in an ad made many FURIOUS and created a political FUROR.

Gaffe (noun): A social mistake.

Think: LAUGH.

It's definitely a GAFFE to bring your pet giraffe to the party — everyone will LAUGH.

Gainsay (verb): To deny.

Think: AGAINST SAY.

Those who GAINSAY us are AGAINST what we SAY.

Gambol (verb): To happily dance around; to frolic.

Think: GAMBLE.

If you GAMBLE and win, you'll GAMBOL all around the casino.

Gargantuan (adjective): Enormous.

Think: GIGANTIC.

The GARGANTUAN orangutan was so GIGANTIC that it needed a special enclosure at the zoo.

Garrulous (adjective): Annoyingly talkative.

Think: GORILLAZ.

The rapper in the band GORILLAZ is GARRULOUS, especially since he uses phrases like "chocolate attack."

Genial (adjective): Good-natured.

Think: GENIE.

If you sign up to be a GENIE and grant people wishes, you're probably GENIAL by nature.

Germinate (verb): To grow or to cause to grow.

Think: GERM IN NATE.

After entering his nose, the GERM IN NATE was able to GERMINATE into a cold because he was so tired.

Glacial (adjective): Slow and/or cold.

Think: GLACIER.

My answer had a GLACIAL (slow) pace, and the interviewer gave me a GLACIAL (cold) look that made me feel like I was on a GLACIER.

Glancing (adjective): Indirect.

Think: GLANCE.

The knight took a quick GLANCE at his opponent; as a result, his blow was GLANCING and didn't cause damage.

Glowered (verb): Looked at with anger.

Think: GLOW RRR.

The scary, frowning jack-o'-lantern GLOWERED at us; its GLOW seemed to say "RRRRRRRR!"

Grandiloquent (adjective): Loud; colorful; egotistical.

Think: GRAND ELOQUENT.

If you're GRANDILOQUENT, you're GRAND and ELOQUENT with your speech so that everyone notices you.

Gravitas (noun): Powerful seriousness.

Think: GRAVITY.

As the judge entered, his GRAVITAS was like GRAVITY, drawing everyone's eyes to him and silencing the room.

Grouse (verb): To complain.

Think: GROUCH.

Oscar the GROUCH likes to GROUSE about everyone else on Sesame Street.

Grovel (verb): To act like an unworthy servant by crawling or lowering oneself.

Think: Face in the GRAVEL.

GROVEL to his majesty by putting your face in the GRAVEL, slave!

Gumption (noun): Drive; initiative.

Think: Forrest GUMP.

Forrest GUMP showed GUMPTION by playing football, starting a shrimp business, and running across the country.

Hackneyed (adjective): Trite or overused.

Think: HACKED KNEES.

The veteran soccer player had HACKED KNEES; his knees were HACKNEYED from overuse.

Hallowed (adjective): Sacred.

Think: HALO-ED.

The cemetery where saints are buried is so HALLOWED, it's practically "HALO-ED."

Harangue (noun): A ranting lecture.

Think: HER EARS RANG.

HER EARS RANG so much after the loud HARANGUE that she joked she'd rather hang than listen to it again.

Hermetic (adjective): Protected from outside influence.

Think: HERMIT.

The HERMIT lived in a HERMETIC cave that was reachable only via a treacherous mountain path.

Heyday (noun): One's best time period.

Think: HEY DAY.

During my HEYDAY, when I was the starting quarterback and had a 4.0, all the girls said "HEY" to me every DAY.

Hiatus (noun): An interruption or break.

Think: HYATT.

The Hawaiian HYATT ad urged us to take a HIATUS from work to stay at its luxurious hotel for a few days.

Hidebound (adjective): Inflexible; ultra-conservative.

Think: Animal HIDE-BOUND.

Santorum's views are so HIDEBOUND that his underwear is probably made from animal HIDE BOUND around his waist.

Hirsute (adjective): Hairy.

Think: HAIR SUIT.

I saw an old guy in the locker room who was so HIRSUTE that he looked like he was wearing a HAIR SUIT.

Histrionic (adjective): Overly emotional for effect.

Think: HYSTERICAL.

Her HYSTERICAL laughter was designed to get attention and was therefore HISTRIONIC.

Holistic (adjective): Dealing with something as a whole.

Think: WHOLE LIST.

HOLISTIC medicine treats the WHOLE LIST of body issues instead of addressing just one symptom.

Husbandry (noun): Careful management.

Think: HUSBAND.

In the 1950s, a woman's HUSBAND usually practiced HUSBANDRY of their finances.

Iconoclast (noun): Someone who goes against society.

Think: CLASHED.

The ICONOCLAST had beliefs that CLASHED with most people's views.

Idiosyncrasy (noun): A weird trait.

Think: IDIOTIC 'N SYNC.

I might seem IDIOTIC to suggest an 'N SYNC-CRASY where 'N SYNC rules our nation, but it's just my IDIOSYNCRASY.

Illiberal (adjective): Narrow-minded.

Think: ILL LIBERAL.

Unlike his fellow open-minded Democrats, Jack was so ILLIBERAL that people thought he must be a mentally ILL LIBERAL.

Imbroglio (noun): Complicated situation.

Think: BRO IGLOO.

I knew my friend was in an IMBROGLIO after getting the text, "I just woke up and I'M IN AN IGLOO, BRO!"

Impeded (verb): Blocked.

Think: STAMPEDE.

As I walked across the fruited plain, a buffalo STAMPEDE IMPEDED my progress.

Imperious (adjective): Dominant in a kingly way.

Think: EMPEROR.

When we went out to dinner with the EMPEROR, he was so IMPERIOUS that he ordered all of our meals.

Impregnable (adjective): Unconquerable; impenetrable.

Think: IMPOSSIBLE to get PREGNANT.

Wearing IMPREGNABLE metal chastity belts in the Middle Ages made it IMPOSSIBLE for those women to get PREGNANT.

Impromptu (adjective): Without preparation.

Think: IMPROVISE.

If you forget your lines, I'm not going to prompt you, so just IMPROVISE and make some IMPROMPTU remarks.

Impugn (verb): To attack verbally.

Think: I'M A PUG.

If the insecure little dog talked, he might say, "I'M a PUG, and that's why I IMPUGN people by barking at them."

Inchoate (adjective): Incomplete; formless.

Think: INCOHERENT.

The INCHOATE paper received an F because it was INCOHERENT.

Incisive (adjective): Sharp; direct.

Think: INCISION.

Luckily, the surgeon was INCISIVE — she only had seconds to make an INCISION before the patient's appendix burst.

Incredulous (adjective): Extremely skeptical.

Think: INCREDIBLE.

I'm INCREDULOUS that a guy with no street cred could make the gangs agree on that INCREDIBLE truce.

Indigenous (adjective): Native to an area.

Think: INDIAN DIG.

The archaeologist found arrowheads on the INDIAN DIG and concluded that Native Americans were INDIGENOUS to the area.

Indomitable (adjective): Unconquerable.

Think: IN-DOMINATE-ABLE.

Spain's soccer team is so good that they're INDOMITABLE, or "IN-DOMINATE-ABLE" — they're unable to be dominated.

Inexorable (adjective): Unstoppable.

Think: UN-X-OUT-ABLE.

The fighter's INEXORABLE rise made it impossible to cross his name off the contender list; he was "UN-X-OUT-ABLE."

Ingenious (adjective): Extremely clever.

Think: GENIUS; there's an *I* for *intelligence* in the middle of both *ingenious* and *genius*.

Your plan to make cars run on garbage is INGENIOUS — you're a GENIUS!

Inimical (adjective): Unfriendly; hostile.

Think: ENEMY.

Of course the other beauty contestant hid your lipstick! She's your ENEMY; it's no surprise she'll be INIMICAL.

Innocuous (adjective): Harmless.

Think: INNOCENT.

My dog will bark at you once you come in, but it's INNOCENT — he's INNOCUOUS.

Insular (adjective): Narrow-minded.

Think: INSULATE.

The hick's outlook was so INSULAR that he might as well have been surrounded by INSULATION.

Inundated (adjective): Flooded.

Think: NUN DATE.

After the church allowed NUNS to DATE, they INUNDATED Match.com.

Invidious (adjective): Unpleasantly envious or causing envy.

Think: INVITE ENVIOUS.

My band rocks so hard that we basically INVITE you to be ENVIOUS; we're just INVIDIOUS.

Irascible (adjective): Easily angered.

Think: IRRITABLE RASCAL.

My grandfather is an IRRITABLE old RASCAL; he's so IRASCIBLE that he yells at every waiter we get.

Jejune (adjective): Dull; juvenile.

Think: JUVENILE.

My frat brothers' jokes are so JEJUNE that you could almost call them JUVENILE or "jejune-venile."

Jingoism (noun): Extreme nationalism, belligerent foreign policy.

Think: RINGO STARR.

My dad used to be guilty of American JINGOISM until he met RINGO Starr of the Beatles — then he liked England, too.

Jocose (adjective): Given to joking.

Think: JOKE COACH.

It was no surprise that the JOCOSE high school student grew up to be a JOKE COACH.

Juggernaut (noun): Something very powerful.

Think: JUGGLER KNOT.

That JUGGLER tied that huge KNOT by juggling six balls of yarn — it'll be a JUGGERNAUT to untie.

Kindle (verb): To start; to stir up.

Think: KINDLING.

You can't just light a log on fire — to KINDLE the campfire, you need some KINDLING (twigs, paper, dried grass, and so on).

Kismet (noun): Fate.

Think: KISS MET.

I knew it was KISMET that I'd marry her because we KISSED as soon as we MET each other.

Kowtow (verb): To kiss up to.

Think: COW TOES.

If you want to KOWTOW to a farmer, BOW and offer to give a pedicure to his COW's TOES.

Lachrymose (adjective): Tearful; mournful.

Think: LACK CHRISTMAS.

If you LACK CHRISTMAS presents, I don't blame you for being LACHRYMOSE.

Lackadaisical (adjective): Without energy or spirit.

Think: LACK DAZE.

LACKADAISICAL people LACK energy so much that they're in a constant DAZE.

Laconic (adjective): Using few words.

LACKING KICK.

His personality was LACKING KICK; he was so LACONIC that he barely even said hello to us.

Languid (adjective): Lazy; lacking energy.

Think: LAYING SQUID.

The LAYING SQUID was LANGUID because it just lay on the bottom of the ocean all day.

Lapidary (adjective): Precise; cutting.

Think: LAP your opponent.

If your track relay team can LAP its opponent, you're justified in making a LAPIDARY remark.

Largess (noun): Generosity.

Think: LARGE-NESS.

Due to his wealthy parents' LARGESS and the LARGE-NESS of their generosity, the college student lived pretty large and drove a Ferrari.

Lassitude (noun): Tiredness; laziness.

Think: LAZY ATTITUDE.

Your LASSITUDE is caused by your LAZY ATTITUDE and belief that Lassie will come save you if you need help.

Laudable (adjective): Worthy of praise.

Think: APPLAUDABLE.

Something that's LAUDABLE is APPLAUDABLE.

Lax (adjective): Loose; not strict.

Think: LACKS.

That student plays lacrosse because he is LAX; he LACKS the work ethic needed to make the football team.

Legerdemain (noun): Sleight of hand; a display of skill.

Think: Heath LEDGER.

Heath LEDGER's DOMAIN was the silver screen; his acting LEGERDEMAIN captivated audiences.

Levity (noun) Lightheartedness.

Think: LEVITATE.

The comedian's LEVITY made us laugh so hard that we felt as though we were LEVITATING above our chairs.

Licentious (adjective): Lacking restraint.

Think: LICENSE-ish.

Flappers were thought to be LICENTIOUS, since they acted as if they had a LICENSE to do whatever they wanted.

Lionized (verb): Treated with great interest.

Think: LION-ized.

The cute little meerkat was so LIONIZED by the zoo's visitors that he felt like a LION.

Listless (adjective): Having little interest or energy.

Think: To-do-LIST-LESS.

If you've never made a to-do LIST, you're LIST-LESS and probably LISTLESS.

Logorrhea (noun): Excessive wordiness.

Think: Word DIARRHEA.

I thought a long speech would help my grade, but my teacher said my LOGORRHEA was like verbal DIARRHEA.

Lovelorn (adjective): Without love.

Think: LOVE TORN.

After his wife died in an accident, the man felt LOVELORN, as though he'd had his LOVE TORN from him.

Lucre (noun): Money; profit.

Think: LUCRATIVE.

When you put in the years of training necessary to secure a LUCRATIVE career, LUCRE is your reward.

Lugubrious (adjective): Mournful or gloomy.

Think: LUG BRIAN.

I became LUGUBRIOUS when I realized I would have to LUG the unconscious BRIAN up the stairs.

Lurid (adjective): Sensational; shocking.

Think: LURE IN.

I'm trying to be more LURID to LURE IN more followers.

Macerate (verb): To weaken, break down, or make soft.

Think: MACE in the face.

Spraying someone in the face with MACE (tear gas) will usually MACERATE him.

Machination (noun): A crafty scheme.

Think: MACHINE NATION.

I don't trust this friendly-looking robot; I bet its MACHINATION is designed to create a MACHINE NATION in which we are slaves.

Maelstrom (noun): Violently powerful; like a whirlpool.

Think: MAIL STORM.

Reading your spam is like being drawn into a MAELSTROM; the MAIL STORM will suck up your time.

Magisterial (adjective): Having strong authority; kingly.

Think: MAJESTY.

If people are greeting you by saying "Your MAJESTY," you're probably looking MAGISTERIAL.

Magnanimous (adjective): Generous.

Think: MAGNET for ANIMALS.

The MAGNANIMOUS nanny was a MAGNET for ANIMALS because she always fed them.

Malinger (verb): To fake sickness to avoid working.

Think: LINGER.

Those who MALINGER often LINGER in bed, pretending to have the flu.

Malleable (adjective): Able to be shaped.

Think: MALLET-ABLE.

Twenty-four-karat gold is so MALLEABLE that you can dent it with a wooden hammer — it's MALLET-ABLE.

Mandate (noun): An order or command.

Think: MANDATORY.

The admiral's MANDATE was obviously MANDATORY.

Manifold (adjective): Diverse; varied.

Think: MANY FOLDS.

The surface of the brain is MANIFOLD because it has MANY FOLDS.

Maudlin (adjective): Overly sentimental.

Think: MAUDE's VIOLIN.

MAUDE played emotional VIOLIN music every time she made an entrance, so we called her MAUDLIN.

Mawkish (adjective): Overly sentimental.

Think: MA's AWKWARD KISS.

My MA is AWKWARD because she has to KISS us every time we leave the house — she's MAWKISH.

Menial (adjective): A task suitable to a servant.

Think: ME KNEEL.

Tasks that make ME KNEEL, like scrubbing the floor, are aptly called MENIAL.

Mercurial (adjective): Having rapidly changing moods.

Think: MERCURY.

Marie Curie was notorious for her MERCURIAL temper, which revolved as fast as the planet MERCURY.

Meshuga (adjective): Foolish.

Think: ME SHRUGS.

As a pirate captain, ME SHRUGS at me crew when their actions be MESHUGA.

Mettle (noun): Strength; stamina.

Think: METAL.

The gladiator was so full of METTLE that he may have been made of METAL.

Miasma (noun): An unhealthy atmosphere.

Think: MY ASTHMA.

The smog in Los Angeles is a MIASMA that worsens MY ASTHMA.

Milieu (noun): Setting or environment.

Think: MY LOO.

I prefer to use MY LOO in my own MILIEU — other people's bathrooms are gross!

Milquetoast (noun): A timid person.

Think: MILHOUSE.

MILHOUSE is a MILQUETOAST — he's about as tough as a piece of soggy, milky toast, since Bart Simpson bosses him around.

Minatory (adjective): Threatening.

Think: MINOTAUR.

The MINOTAUR, a creature that is half-man and half-bull, is MINATORY by nature.

Misanthrope (noun): One who hates people.

Think: MISTAKE ANTHROPOLOGIST.

It's a huge MISTAKE to be an ANTHROPOLOGIST and study people all day long if you're a MISANTHROPE.

Miscreant (noun): A person who behaves badly or in a way that breaks the law.

Think: MISTAKE of CREATION.

A MISCREANT is a MISTAKE of CREATION.

Miserly (adjective): Stingy or cheap with money.

Think: MISERABLE.

Scrooge was MISERABLE at making friends because he was too MISERLY to ever chip in for the dinner tab.

Mitigate (verb): To lessen or make less severe.

Think: MITT GATE.

The thief put an oven MITT on the spiked GATE of the mansion so he could climb over it.

Modish (adjective): Fashionable.

Think: MODEL-ISH.

MODISH brands like Burberry and Prada are MODEL-ISH because only models seem to actually wear them.

Morass (noun): A situation that makes you stuck.

Think: MOLASSES.

Don't tailgate a MOLASSES truck — if you run into it and it spills on you, you'll be in a MORASS.

Munificent (adjective): Generous or giving.

Think: MONEY SENT.

The MONEY SENT to us by our grandparents every year makes us consider them to be MUNIFICENT.

Nebulous (adjective): Vague.

Think: NEBULA.

The Horsehead NEBULA is so many light-years away that we have only a NEBULOUS idea of what it's like.

Nepotism (noun): Unfairly hiring family members.

Think: NEPHEW FAVORITISM.

They said I practiced NEPHEW FAVORITISM and accused me of NEPOTISM when I promoted my 22-year-old nephew to vice president of the company.

Noisome (adjective): Stinky.

Think: NOSE POISON.

The boys' locker room is NOISOME; going in there is like taking NOSE POISON.

Non sequitur (noun): Something unrelated.

Think: NOT SEQUENCE.

Bringing up koala bears after my girlfriend asked me about our relationship was a NON SEQUITUR; it was NOT in the right SEQUENCE.

Nondescript (adjective): Plain.

Think: NO DESCRIPTION.

The little desert island was so NONDESCRIPT that it had NO DESCRIPTION in our guidebook.

Nonpareil (adjective): Having no equal.

Think: NO PARALLEL.

The master parachutist had NONPAREIL skill; he truly had NO PARALLEL in the parachuting field.

Notorious (adjective): Famous for being bad.

Think: NOTORIOUS B.I.G.

The NOTORIOUS B.I.G. got away with calling himself NOTORIOUS because he'd sold drugs as a youth.

Nugatory (adjective): Unimportant.

Think: McNUGGETS.

Eating chicken McNUGGETS is NUGATORY for good health; their health benefits could be said to be negatory.

Numinous (adjective): Mysterious in a holy way.

Think: NUMBING US.

The NUMINOUS raising of Jesus from the dead made the apostles think, "This is so amazing, it's NUMBING US."

Obeisance (noun): A gesture to show respect.

Think: OBEY STANCE.

When the natives bowed to the conqueror in OBEISANCE, it was like an "OBEY STANCE."

Obfuscated (verb): Made unclear.

Think: OBSTACLES CONFUSED.

The professor barely spoke English: the OBSTACLES his speech created CONFUSED us and OBFUSCATED his message.

Obstreperous (adjective): Uncontrollably noisy.

Think: OBSTRUCTED STREP.

My desire to stay healthy was OBSTRUCTED by STREP throat; the illness gave me an OBSTREPEROUS cough.

Odious (adjective): Arousing or deserving hatred.

Think: ODOROUS ONIONS.

Only eating onions is ODIOUS because they make one's breath so ODOROUS.

Officious (adjective): Bossy.

Think: OFFICIAL is VICIOUS.

The OFFICIAL was VICIOUS enough to measure every fish we caught with a ruler to make sure it was legal.

Onus (noun): Burden; obligation.

Think: ON US.

Since we broke the vase, the ONUS is ON US to pay for it.

Openhanded (adjective): Generous.

Think: OPEN your HAND.

To be OPENHANDED, OPEN your HAND and share what you have with others instead of keeping it clenched in your fist.

Opprobrium (noun): Public disgrace.

Think: OPRAH OPPOSES.

Sometimes OPRAH brings people she OPPOSES on her show to cause them OPPROBRIUM — it's like "OPRAH-BRIUM."

Ostracized (verb): Excluded.

Think: OSTRICH.

The OSTRICH buried its head in the sand because the other birds OSTRACIZED it for its goofy looks.

Otiose (adjective): Useless; lazy.

Think: TORTOISE.

Playing fetch with this TORTOISE is OTIOSE.

Overweening (adjective): Arrogant.

Think: WEENIE.

The young actor's demands were so OVERWEENING that the movie crew started calling him a WEENIE behind his back.

Pacific (adjective): Soothing.

Think: PACIFIER.

The infant's PACIFIER had a PACIFIC effect, and the baby was soon asleep.

Painstaking (adjective): Careful.

Think: PAINS TAKING.

Some say I'm too careful, but I think I'm just PAINS TAKING to the point of being PAINSTAKING.

Palliate (verb): To reduce the severity of.

Think: PAL.

Hanging out with a PAL will PALLIATE your depression.

Pallid (adjective): Lacking color.

Think: PALE.

After playing video games in his mother's basement all winter, Al was so PALE that his friends described him as PALLID.

Panacea (noun): A cure-all.

Think: BANANA.

Eating a BANANA a day will improve your health, but it's not a PANACEA.

Pander: (verb): To appeal to someone's desire for selfish reasons.

Think: PANDA.

The American company that used a PANDA as its logo was accused of PANDERING to the Chinese market.

Paragon (noun): A model of excellence.

Think: ARAGORN.

If you're looking for a PARAGON in *The Lord of the Rings,* choose ARAGORN: He became the king.

Pariah (noun): An outcast.

Think: MARIAH'S ANTHEM.

MARIAH Carey became a PARIAH after butchering the national anthem in front of 80,000 fans.

Parley (verb): To talk.

Think: PARSLEY BREATH.

If you're going to PARLEY with someone you like, eat some PARSLEY — it's good for your breath.

Parochial (adjective): Narrow-minded.

Think: PARISH YOKEL.

Our church is led by a PARISH YOKEL who is so PAROCHIAL that he believes woman should be barefoot and pregnant.

Parsimonious (adjective): Stingy.

Think: PARSLEY MONEY.

My dad was so PARSIMONIOUS that he'd give us PARSLEY MONEY instead of lunch money.

Partisan (adjective): Biased toward one side.

Think: PARTY'S SON.

The chairman of the Democratic PARTY'S SON was understandably PARTISAN about politics.

Pastiche (noun): An imitation; something made of many things.

Think: PASTE EACH.

If you copy Wikipedia and PASTE EACH entry into your paper, it will be a PASTICHE.

Patent (adjective): Clear.

Think: PATENT (noun) on an invention.

I got a PATENT (noun) for my invention, so it would be PATENT (adjective) that no one could copy it.

Patois (noun): The speech/slang used by a certain group.

Think: PATIO SPEECH.

PATIO SPEECH during barbecues is more likely to contain PATOIS than speech in the office.

Paucity (noun): Lack of.

Think: POOR CITY.

In the POOR CITY, there was a PAUCITY of resources.

Pejorative (adjective): Having a negative meaning.

Think: PIGEON.

If I call a girl a PIGEON, it's a PEJORATIVE term, since pigeons are looked down on.

Penchant (noun): A liking for something.

Think: PENDANT ENCHANT.

If a girl wears a PENDANT to ENCHANT the boys, they'll soon have a PENCHANT for her.

Penitent (adjective): Being sorry for one's actions.

Think: REPENT.

The beggar's sign read, "REPENT! Do penance for your sins! Only the PENITENT will see God!"

Penurious (adjective): Stingy.

Think: PENNY FURIOUS.

The PENNY tip made the waiter FURIOUS; the customer must have been PENURIOUS.

Penury (noun): Severe poverty.

Think: PENALTY.

The court's PENALTY was so large that the defendant suffered from PENURY to the point of owning only one penny.

Peremptory (adjective): Bossy, prone to cutting others off.

Think: PRE-EMPTED.

The Emperor PRE-EMPTED Luke's replies so much that even Darth Vader called him PEREMPTORY.

Perfidy (noun): Treachery; treason.

Think: PERFORATED FIDELITY.

When I realized my friend had spread rumors about me, I felt like I had a PERFORATED FIDELITY because of his PERFIDY.

Perfunctory (adjective): Showing little interest.

Think: PER FUNCTION.

I know I won't get them right, so I spend only a PERFUNCTORY amount of time PER FUNCTION problem.

Permeated (verb): Spread through; penetrated.

Think: PERM HE ATE.

The PERM HE ATE will PERMEATE his stomach lining and prove that it's stupid to eat human hair.

Petulant (adjective): Rude; irritable.

Think: PETTY AUNT.

My PETTY AUNT is always whining about something or holding a grudge; she's PETULANT.

Phlegmatic (adjective): Sluggish; unresponsive.

Think: PHLEGM.

When I had the flu, I had so much PHLEGM clogging my lungs that I was completely PHLEGMATIC.

Physiological (adjective): Related to the body.

Think: PHYSICAL.

I knew I wasn't just imagining I was ill because my PHYSIOLOGICAL symptom, a fever of 103°, was PHYSICAL.

Picaresque (adjective): About someone's adventures.

Think: PIXAR-ESQUE.

Your novel is like *Wall-E* because of your hero's journey; it's both PICARESQUE and PIXAR-ESQUE.

Picayune (adjective): Unimportant; small-minded.

Think: PICKY ONE.

The PICAYUNE bridezilla was a PICKY ONE, worrying about every single detail of her wedding.

Picturesque (adjective): Lovely.

Think: PICTURES.

The Grand Canyon at sunrise is so PICTURESQUE that you can't help but take PICTURES.

Piebald (adjective): Many-colored; varied.

Think: PIES.

The horse's coat was PIEBALD, pebbled with blotches of so many colors that it looked like PIES had been thrown at it.

Pittance (noun): A very small amount.

Think: PIT ANTS.

PIT ANTS are known for eating even the PITTANCE of fruit that clings to discarded peach pits.

Platitude (noun): An overused expression.

Think: BLAH ATTITUDE.

Dude, she's giving you that BLAH ATTITUDE because your pickup line was a PLATITUDE.

Platonic (adjective): Not related to romance or sex.

Think: PLATO DATE.

If you talk to your date about only the philosopher PLATO, you'll end up as her PLATONIC friend.

Plaudits (noun): Approval.

Think: APPLAUD IT.

If you want to give PLAUDITS to his work, APPLAUD IT.

Plebeian (adjective): Common; low-class.

Think: FLEAS BE IN.

I don't stay in PLEBEIAN motels because FLEAS BE IN 'em.

Plenipotentiary (adjective): fully empowered.

Think: PLENTY of POTENCY.

If the candidate wins the election, he will be PLENIPOTENTIARY; being president will give him PLENTY of POTENCY.

Poignant (adjective): Sharply affecting.

Think: POINTED.

The Notebook was such a POIGNANT love story that watching it felt like something POINTED was piercing my heart.

Politesse (noun): Politeness.

Think: POLITENESS.

French maids are trained to show POLITENESS at all times; their POLITESSE is without equal.

Prattle (noun): Meaningless talk.

Think: RATTLE.

Her PRATTLE about reality TV was as exciting as listening to a baby shake its RATTLE.

Precocious (adjective): Very talented at a young age.

Think: PRE-COACHING.

Sadie was PRECOCIOUS at piano PRE-COACHING; she taught herself to play Mozart at the age of 2.

Pretentious (adjective): Self-important.

Think: PRETENDS.

He's really cool onscreen, but in real life, the actor is PRETENTIOUS; he PRETENDS he's better than everyone else.

Primordial (adjective): Original; existing since the beginning.

Think: PRIMARY ORDER.

The Big Bang is PRIMORDIAL because it has the PRIMARY position in the ORDER of events.

Pristine (adjective): Pure.

Think: LISTERINE.

LISTERINE mouthwash tastes bad, but it kills bacteria and makes your mouth PRISTINE.

Profligacy (noun): Reckless wastefulness.

Think: PROFITS FLING.

If your PROFITS FLING out the window, you're probably following a course of PROFLIGACY.

Prolific (adjective): Abundantly productive.

Think: PRO-LIFE.

PRO-LIFE couples don't consider abortion, so they're more likely to be PROLIFIC.

Prolix (adjective): Too long/wordy.

Think: PROLIFIC.

After writing dozens of 1,000-page books, the PROLIFIC author was often criticized for his PROLIX writing style.

Prominent (adjective): Well-known or standing out.

Think: PROM KING.

The PROM KING is usually not the shy boy no one knows; he's often a PROMINENT, popular kid.

Promulgate (verb): To make known.

Think: PROM DATE.

If you want a PROM DATE, don't be shy — PROMULGATE your intentions to the girl you want to take.

Prosaic (adjective): Dull or boring.

Think: PROS SAY "ICK."

I was going to watch the new Adam Sandler movie, but the movie critic PROS SAY, "ICK — the film is PROSAIC."

Prowess (noun): Exceptional bravery and/or skill.

Think: PROWL LIONESS.

While on the PROWL, the LIONESS displayed her PROWESS by bringing down a woolly mammoth.

Puerile (adjective): Childish.

Think: PUBERTY.

The high school freshman's PUERILE sense of humor was typical of a boy who was going through PUBERTY.

Punctilious (adjective): Marked by following the rules strictly.

Think: PUNCTUAL.

The teacher's pet was both PUNCTILIOUS and PUNCTUAL, but most wanted to punch him.

Pungent (adjective): Strongly scented.

Think: PUNCH SCENT.

The boxer's body odor was so PUNGENT that it was like getting hit by a PUNCH of SCENT.

Punitive (adjective): Involving punishment.

Think: PUNISH.

The PUNITIVE damages in the O. J. Simpson murder case were clearly designed to PUNISH the defendant.

Pusillanimous (adjective): Cowardly.

Think: PUSSYCAT.

The PUSSYCAT is an animal that is PUSILLANIMOUS when scared — hence the expression "scaredy cat."

Quagmire (noun): A difficult situation.

Think: QUICKSAND MIRE.

QUICKSAND can MIRE you if you step in it, and the more you struggle, the worse the QUAGMIRE becomes.

Quash (verb): To completely stop from happening.

Think: SQUASH.

The best way to QUASH an invasion of ants in your kitchen is simple: SQUASH them.

Querulous (adjective): Whiny; complaining.

Think: QUARREL US.

We'd invite you over more, but you're so QUERULOUS that you always end up in a QUARREL with US!

Quiescent (adjective): At rest.

Think: QUIET.

The hibernating bear was both QUIET and QUIESCENT.

Quixotic (adjective): Idealistic; impractical.

Think: QUICK EXOTIC.

It's QUIXOTIC to think that you should earn some QUICK cash by becoming an EXOTIC dancer.

Quotidian (adjective): Daily.

Think: QUOTA.

The meter maid met her QUOTA of parking tickets by her QUOTIDIAN patrolling of the streets.

Rancorous (adjective): Hateful.

Think: *Star Wars* RANCOR.

In *Return of the Jedi*, the RANCOR under Jabba the Hutt's palace is undoubtedly RANCOROUS for having been imprisoned.

Rapturous (adjective): Full of wonderful feelings; ecstatic.

Think: RAPTOR US.

The RAPTOR saw US being lowered into his cage and felt RAPTUROUS since he was hungry.

Raucous (adjective): Noisy; disorderly.

Think: ROCKS US.

The Beastie Boys's RAUCOUS track "Fight For Your Right to Party" ROCKS US.

Raze (verb): To completely destroy.

Think: RAYS BLAZE.

The powerful laser's RAYS are making a BLAZE that will RAZE the old building to make room for the new one.

Recalcitrant (adjective): Difficult to manage or change.

Think: CALC RANT.

The CALC worksheet made Alex RANT because it was so RECALCITRANT.

Recapitulated (verb): Summarized.

Think: RECAP.

His RECAP of the news nicely RECAPITULATED the day's events.

Recidivist (noun): Someone who relapsed into crime.

Think: SID's DIVISION.

Sid had two sides to his personality: the law-abiding side and the RECIDIVIST.

Recrudescent (adjective): Reactivating.

Think: RECRUITS SENT.

The conflict in Afghanistan must be RECRUDESCENT, since more RECRUITS are SENT there daily.

Rectitude (noun): Extreme integrity.

Think: CORRECT ATTITUDE.

Since he was a church rector, Paul considered the CORRECT ATTITUDE to be RECTITUDE.

Redress: To set right.

Think: RE-DRESS Lady Gaga.

Lady Gaga's fashion choices are so wrong that the only way to REDRESS her style is to literally RE-DRESS her.

Reductive (adjective): Related to making something smaller or simpler.

Think: REDUCE.

REDUCTIVE CliffsNotes REDUCE brilliant works of literature into basic summaries.

Refracted (verb): Distorted or changed from an initial direction.

Think: REFLECTED FRACTURED.

The prism REFRACTED the white light and REFLECTED it FRACTURED into a rainbow of colors.

Refractory (adjective): Stubborn; unmanageable.

Think: RE-FRACTURE.

The REFRACTORY athlete insisted on playing despite his broken toe; unsurprisingly, he RE-FRACTURED it.

Rejuvenated (verb): Gave new life to.

Think: RE-JUVENILE.

His plans for the new year REJUVENATED the middle-aged man so much that he felt like a JUVENILE again.

Relish (verb): To enjoy; to savor.

Think: DELISH.

I RELISH (verb) eating hot dogs with RELISH (noun) because they taste DELISH.

Remedial (adjective): Intended to correct at a basic level.

Think: REMEDY.

If you are terrible at math, the only REMEDY might be to take a REMEDIAL arithmetic class.

Remiss (adjective): Careless.

Think: RE-MISS.

If you are REMISS in your study technique, you'll miss the point the first time you read and then RE-MISS it the second time.

Replete (adjective): Full.

Think: REPLACE COMPLETE.

REPLACE carbs to COMPLETE your workout so that your body stays REPLETE with energy.

Reprehensible (adjective): Deserving blame.

Think: PRETEND HENS.

You sold me PRETEND HENS instead of real ones — that's REPREHENSIBLE.

Repugnant (adjective): Gross.

Think: UGLY PUG.

Although some people think PUGS's upturned faces and wheezing are cute, many find them to be REPUGNANT.

Requisite (adjective): Necessary.

Think: REQUIRES IT.

If you fail English, your school REQUIRES IT to be retaken; it's REQUISITE that you have four years of English.

Resigned (adjective): Reluctantly accepting of a bad situation.

Think: RESIGNATION from office.

After being implicated in Watergate, Nixon was RESIGNED and offered his RESIGNATION from office.

Resplendent (adjective): Shining brilliantly.

Think: SPLENDID.

Cinderella was RESPLENDENT in a sequined white ball gown; she looked absolutely SPLENDID.

Restive (adjective): Stubborn.

Think: RESIST-IVE.

When I try to get my dog into the bathtub, he's "RESIST-IVE" and RESTIVE because he hates being washed.

Reticent (adjective): Reserved, shy, or quiet.

Think: REST IN TENT.

If you're RETICENT, on camping trips, you probably REST IN the TENT while the others are toasting marshmallows.

Retiring (adjective): Shy.

Think: RETIRE.

The shy girl was so RETIRING that she decided that she would RETIRE from going to parties.

Retrenchment (noun): A reduction.

Think: RETURN to TRENCH.

For a World War I soldier, a RETRENCHMENT of his duty meant he could RETURN to his TRENCH and lay low for a while.

Revanche (noun): Revenge.

Think: REVENGE.

Motivated by REVENGE, the French monarch ordered her general to take REVANCHE on those who had captured the island.

Reverent (adjective): Having deep respect for.

Think: REVEREND.

During church, the REVEREND reminded them to be REVERENT to Jesus.

Rickety (adjective): Weak.

Think: RICKETS.

RICKETS, a disease that weakens the bones, makes its sufferers RICKETY.

Riposte (noun): A comeback.

Think: RIP POST.

After being mocked, the blogger would RIP into his critic's POST with a brutal RIPOSTE.

Risible (adjective): Funny; inclined to laugh.

Think: Get a RISE.

If you like to get a RISE out of people by being a class clown, you're probably RISIBLE.

Risque (adjective): Almost improper or indecent.

Think: RISKY.

Making a RISQUE joke the first time you meet your girlfriend's parents is RISKY.

Riveting (adjective): Fascinating.

Think: RIVETS.

Watching the footage of a UFO was so RIVETING that I felt like steel RIVETS had fastened me to my chair.

Roborant (noun): An invigorating drug.

Think: ROBO-ANT.

After I gave him a ROBORANT, my ant felt as strong as a ROBO-ANT.

Rudimentary (adjective): Basic; primitive.

Think: RUDE ELEMENTARY.

RUDE ELEMENTARY school kids are impolite only because their knowledge of social graces is RUDIMENTARY.

Ruffian (noun): A brutal person.

Think: ROUGH.

The club hired a RUFFIAN as a bouncer because he was strong enough to be ROUGH with misbehaving drunks.

Ruminate (verb): To carefully reflect on.

Think: RAMEN MARINATE.

To RUMINATE means to think about something for at least as long as it takes your top RAMEN to MARINATE.

Saccharine (adjective): Sweet in a fake way.

Think: SACCHARIN.

The beauty contestant's personality was so SACCHARINE that there must have been Sweet'N Low (SACCHARIN) in her veins.

Sacrosanct (adjective): Holy.

Think: SACRED SANCTUARY.

The temple was a SACRED SANCTUARY and was declared SACROSANCT to protect it from real estate developers.

Salutary (adjective): Beneficial.

Think: SALUTE.

Sal's cooking has such a SALUTARY effect on me that I SALUTE him.

Sanguine (adjective): Optimistic.

Think: SANG WIN.

The penguin SANG that he would WIN; he was SANGUINE.

Sapid (adjective): Flavorful.

Think: SAP.

We make maple syrup from the SAP of maple trees because their SAP is naturally SAPID.

Satiated (adjective): Satisfied.

Think: SAY SHE ATE.

If you SAY SHE ATE, she must be SATIATED.

Scapegoat (noun): One who takes the blame.

Think: ESCAPED GOAT.

Even though the dog ate some of the vegetables in the garden, the ESCAPED GOAT became the SCAPEGOAT.

Scathing (adjective): Sharply critical.

Think: SCYTHE.

Getting killed by the Grim Reaper's sharp, hooked SCYTHE is as about as SCATHING a criticism as one can get.

Schadenfreude (noun): Enjoyment from others' troubles.

Think: SHADY FREUD.

If your psychologist giggles about your divorce, he has SCHADENFREUDE and is a SHADY FREUD.

Scintillating (adjective): Sparkling; brilliant.

Think: SQUINT.

Her sequined shirt was so SCINTILLATING that I had to SQUINT to see it.

Scurrilous (adjective): Obscenely abusive.

Think: SCURVY CURSES.

After the pirate developed SCURVY, his CURSES became even more SCURRILOUS.

Scuttle (verb): To destroy; to scrap.

Think: IT'S CUT.

SCUTTLE the launch of that space shuttle! IT'S CUT from the space program as of 2011.

Secretes (verb): Forms and gives off.

Think: SEA CREATURE SECRET.

The octopus is a SEA CREATURE that stays SECRET when it SECRETES an inky cloud.

Sedentary (adjective): Inactive; lazy.

Think: SOFA DENT.

SEDENTARY people make SOFA DENTS because they sit on the cushions for hours at a time.

Sedulous (adjective): Careful; hardworking; diligent.

Think: SCHEDULE US.

Our SEDULOUS hairstylist is always able to SCHEDULE US, since she's so efficient.

Seminal (adjective): Important; original.

Think: SEMINAR.

If a book is SEMINAL, you're probably gonna have to read it in your freshman year literature SEMINAR.

Sere (adjective): Dried; withered.

Think: SEAR.

If you SEAR those vegetables on the grill too long, they'll become SERE.

Serendipity (noun): Luck.

Think: SARA ENDED PITY.

After winning the lottery, SARA ENDED her PITY toward herself because of her amazing SERENDIPITY.

Servile (adjective): Submissive.

Think: SERVANT.

The SERVANT was so SERVILE that he wouldn't make eye contact.

Shard (noun): A broken piece of something fragile.

Think: SHARP.

Be careful of the SHARD of glass on the floor; it's really SHARP.

Simper (verb): To smile in a silly way.

Think: SMILE CHIMP.

Have you ever seen a SMILE on a CHIMP? They SIMPER in a way that cracks me up.

Simulacrum (noun): An image or representation of something.

Think: SIMULATION.

Coachella audiences saw a SIMULACRUM of Tupac: a hologram that was an incredible SIMULATION of him.

Sinuous (adjective): Having many curves.

Think: SINE WAVE.

Unsurprisingly, if you graph a SINE wave on your calculator, it's going to look SINUOUS.

Skittish (adjective): Restless; easily frightened.

Think: SKITTLE-ISH.

After I ate a 54-oz. bag of SKITTLES by myself, the sugar high made me SKITTISH.

Skulk (verb): To hide or be stealthy.

Think: SKUNKS LURK.

SKUNKS LURK and SKULK until it's dark enough for them to eat from your garbage cans.

Skullduggery (noun): Tricky or sneaky behavior.

Think: SKULL HE DUG.

The SKULL he DUG up from the local cemetery proved he was a witch doctor who practiced SKULLDUGGERY.

Slake (verb): To quench or satisfy.

Think: LAKE.

If you're a zebra, you probably can't operate a water fountain: SLAKE your thirst at the LAKE.

Solecism (noun): A blunder.

Think: SOLE IS IN.

If you put your foot in your mouth — such as ask a woman her age — it's a SOLECISM; your SOLE IS IN your mouth.

Solicitous (adjective): Concerned for.

Think: SOLELY LISTENED.

I knew the man was SOLICITOUS because he SOLELY LISTENED to us.

Solipsistic (adjective): Being extremely self-centered.

Think: SOLD LIPSTICK.

The model whose image SOLD LIPSTICK became SOLIPSISTIC due to all the compliments she received.

Somnolent (adjective): Sleepy.

Think: INSOMNIA.

If you have INSOMNIA, you're probably SOMNOLENT from lack of sleep.

Sonorous (adjective): Having a deep, rich sound.

Think: TYRANNO-SONOROUS REX.

TYRANNOSAURUS Rex had a SONOROUS roar that could be heard for miles.

Sophistry (noun): Deceptive reasoning.

Think: SOPHISTICATED TRICKERY.

Sophocles's SOPHISTRY was so SOPHISTICATED that his TRICKERY made his character Oedipus kill his dad and marry his mom.

Sophomoric (adjective): Immature.

Think: SOPHOMORE-ONIC.

SOPHOMORES act MORONIC, since they're immature and are more SOPHOMORIC than seniors.

Sovereign (adjective): Having supreme power.

Think: LADY SOVEREIGN REIGNS.

Lady SOVEREIGN is SOVEREIGN when she raps; she REIGNS over the mic.

Spendthrift (noun): Someone who spends wastefully.

Think: SPENDING before THRIFTY.

SPENDTHRIFT means someone for whom SPENDING comes before being THRIFTY.

Spurious (adjective): False.

Think: SPUR CURIOUS.

His SPUR-of-the-moment explanation made me CURIOUS whether his story was SPURIOUS.

Statuesque (adjective): Attractively tall.

Think: STATUE.

The model was so STATUESQUE that the sculptor asked her if he could make a STATUE of her.

Steadfast (adjective): Loyal; immovable.

Think: STAYED FASTENED.

The fallen soldier's dog was so STEADFAST that it STAYED FASTENED to the ground near his grave.

Stentorian (adjective): Loud.

Think: STAND AUTHORITY.

If you STAND with AUTHORITY while giving a speech, it will help your voice become more STENTORIAN.

Stigmas (noun): Marks of shame.

Think: STICK-MAS.

They used to make unfaithful mothers wear branches strapped to their backs as STIGMAS; they called the women STICK-MAS.

Stilted (adjective): Overly formal; stiff.

Think: STILTS.

The soldier's manner of walking was so STILTED that it looked like his legs were actually wooden STILTS.

Stolid (adjective): Unemotional.

Think: SOLID.

The STOLID butler was as SOLID and expressionless as a block of wood.

Stratagem (noun): A clever scheme.

Think: STRATEGY GEM.

The general's battlefield STRATEGY was such a GEM that most historians call it a STRATAGEM.

Streamlined (adjective): Simplified; modernized.

Think: STREAM LINE.

The STREAMLINED shape of a trout lets it swim through even a rushing STREAM in a straight LINE.

Strenuous: (adjective): Requiring lots of energy.

Think: STRAIN ON US.

The STRENUOUS hike up Denali was a STRAIN ON US.

Strident (adjective): Harsh; loud.

Think: STRIDEX.

STRIDEX commercials are as STRIDENT as the harsh, acne-drying acid in the pads, in an effort to hold teens' interest.

Stultify (verb): To make ineffective.

Think: STUPID DOLT.

If you STULTIFY yourself by punching yourself in the skull, you'll become a STUPID DOLT.

Stupefied (adjective): Stunned.

Think: STUPID.

Hermione cast the STUPEFY spell on Crabbe, who became so STUPEFIED that he looked STUPID.

Sublime (adjective): Awesome.

Think: The band SUBLIME.

The band SUBLIME has spawned several cover bands, a good sign that it made SUBLIME music.

Subversive (adjective): Seeking to undermine or disturb.

Think: SUBVERSIVE VERSES.

The poet was detained by government officials for what they called her "SUBVERSIVE VERSES."

Subvert (verb): To weaken or ruin.

Think: SUBMARINE.

In naval warfare, a SUBMARINE can SUBVERT a battleship by attacking it from below.

Succor (noun): Aid.

Think: SUPPER.

If you're starving and stranded in a snowstorm, hopefully your SUCCOR will include some SUPPER.

Succumb (verb): To give in to a superior force.

Think: SUCK UNDER.

Do not SUCCUMB to the deadly pull of the quicksand, or it will SUCK you UNDER.

Suffrage (noun): The right to vote.

Think: SUFFER-RAGE.

American women SUFFERED and often RAGED at a sexist system before they won SUFFRAGE in 1920.

Sumptuary (adjective): Made to prevent overindulgence.

Think: CONSUMPTION-ARY.

CONSUMPTION of harmful things, like cigarettes or alcohol, can be limited with a SUMPTUARY tax.

Superfluous (adjective): Unnecessary.

Think: SUPER FLU US.

We wanted to catch your cold so we could stay home from school, but it was SUPERFLUOUS of you to give the SUPER FLU to US.

Supplant (verb): Replace.

Think: UP PLANT.

After you pull UP a PLANT out of the soil, you should SUPPLANT it with another one to help preserve the environment.

Surmise (verb): To guess.

Think: SUMMARIZE.

Since a police report will only SUMMARIZE what happened, one usually has to SURMISE the actual events of a crime.

Surpassing (adjective): Really, really great.

Think: SUPER PASS.

If you're SUPER at running, you'll PASS everyone due to your SURPASSING speed.

Surreptitious (adjective): Sneaky or stealthy.

Think: REPTILES.

REPTILES like snakes are good at camouflage because they're SURREPTITIOUS.

Sycophant (noun): One who flatters for self-gain.

Think: SICK OF ELEPHANT.

The animals were SICK of the ELEPHANT because he was a SYCOPHANT who kissed up to the zookeeper.

Synergy (noun): Combined action that produces mutually helpful results.

Think: 'N SYNC ENERGY.

By forming a boy band and using SYNERGY, 'N SYNC created more ENERGY than if they'd all gone solo.

Synoptic (adjective): Giving a summary.

Think: SYNOPSIS.

The SYNOPTIC nature of Spark Notes provides a SYNOPSIS of a novel's plot at the expense of the novel's beauty.

Tacit (adjective): Understood without needing to be said.

Think: TASSELED.

It's rude to openly make fun of someone's TASSELED clothing, so just make your disapproval TACIT by frowning.

Taciturn (adjective): Not talkative.

Think: TAKES HIS TURN.

If he's passive and TACITURN at the debate and just politely TAKES HIS TURN when speaking, he'll never win.

Temerity (noun): Recklessness.

Think: TEAM ERROR.

If you have TEMERITY, maybe you should join TEAM ERROR, because I bet you make a lot of mistakes.

Temperance (noun): Moderation.

Think: TEMPER ANTS.

At the picnic, I didn't lose my TEMPER over the ANTS because I possess the quality of TEMPERANCE.

Tempestuous (adjective): Stormy.

Think: TEMPERS.

Our hot TEMPERS make US have a TEMPESTUOUS relationship.

Tenable (adjective): Able to be defended; workable.

Think: TEN ABLE.

The scientist's theory was TENABLE because it was "TEN-ABLE," worthy of being rated a 10 our of 10.

Tenuous (adjective): Lacking substance or strength.

Think: TENTATIVE.

At the debate, the TENTATIVE speaker's argument was unsurprisingly judged to be TENUOUS.

Terse (adjective): Brief and abrupt.

Think: TERSE VERSE.

Haikus are VERSES / That are as TERSE as the lives / Of gentle fruit flies.

Timorous (adjective): Fearful.

Think: TIMID OF US.

Tim felt TIMID around US, since he was TIMOROUS.

Tirade (noun): A long, angry speech.

Think: TIRED of RAGE.

If someone gives you a TIRADE, you'll probably be TIRED of the RAGE after a few minutes.

Titular (adjective): Relating to a title.

Think: TITLE.

The TITULAR character is Harry Potter because his name is also in the TITLE of the book.

Tonic (noun): Something helpful.

Think: GIN AND TONIC.

Drinking a pitcher of GIN AND TONIC before my date was a TONIC for my anxiety, but then I threw up on her shoes.

Toothsome (adjective): Tasty; appealing.

Think: TOOTH SOME.

The food looked so TOOTHSOME that I wanted to give my TOOTH SOME.

Torpid (adjective): Sluggish.

Think: TAR PIT.

After I walked into the sticky TAR PIT, my pace became TORPID.

Tortuous (adjective): Winding.

Think: TORTOISE.

The streets of Boston are so TORTUOUS that you have to drive at a TORTOISE'S speed.

Touted (verb): Praised publicly.

Think: SHOUTED.

Guinness Stout is highly TOUTED; I know this because the guy drinking it next to me SHOUTED its praises in my ear.

Tranquil (adjective): Calm.

Think: TRANQUILIZE.

The bear became very TRANQUIL after I shot him with a TRANQUILIZER dart.

Tremulous (adjective): Fearful.

Think: TREMBLE.

I felt so TREMULOUS when I saw a shark swim underneath me that I began to TREMBLE.

Trepidation (noun): Fear.

Think: TRAP.

The haunted house filled me with TREPIDATION; I feared a TRAP would be sprung on me at any moment.

Trite (adjective): Not original.

Think: TRITE-AID.

They should call the drugstore RITE-AID TRITE-aid, since it just copies everything CVS does.

Truculent (adjective): Ready to fight.

Think: TRUCE YOU LENT.

The armies should write their own peace treaty because they're still TRUCULENT after that TRUCE YOU LENT them.

Truncated (adjective): Shortened.

Think: TRUNK ATE.

The elephant's TRUNK ATE so many branches that the tree was TRUNCATED.

Tumid (adjective): Swollen.

Think: TUMOR-ED.

The cancer patient's large TUMOR caused his abdomen to be TUMID.

Tumultuous (adjective): Disorderly; like a riot.

Think: TUMBLED US.

The mosh pit was so TUMULTUOUS that it TUMBLED US around like a dryer.

Turbid (adjective): Stirred up and made unclear or muddy.

Think: TAR BED.

The lake became TURBID when storms disturbed particles from the TAR BED underneath its waters.

Turgid (adjective): Swollen.

Think: TURKEY IN.

After Thanksgiving dinner, my belly was so TURGID that it looked like I had eaten the whole TURKEY.

Turpitude (noun): Vile or immoral behavior.

Think: TAR PIT ATTITUDE.

His TAR PIT ATTITUDE made him engage in TURPITUDE.

Umbrage (noun): Offense; annoyance.

Think: UMBRELLA RAGE.

Someone who takes UMBRAGE at his UMBRELLA probably felt RAGE when it broke during a storm.

Unassuming (adjective): Modest.

Think: UN-ASSUME.

The millionaire's UNASSUMING car definitely didn't make us ASSUME he was wealthy.

Unbridled (adjective): Not restrained.

Think: UN-BRIDLE.

After I took off my horse's BRIDLE, he became so UNBRIDLED that I had no control over him.

Unctuous (adjective): Smooth in a fake way.

Think: SKUNK-TOUS.

Pepe Le Pew, the smooth-talking, playboy SKUNK, acts UNCTUOUS to charm the ladies.

Undermine (verb): To weaken in a sneaky way.

Think: UNDER MINE.

UNDER the ground lay a land MINE designed to UNDERMINE the army's advance.

Unsavory (adjective): Unpleasant, especially morally unpleasant.

Think: UN-SAVOR.

The icky memory of the UNSAVORY used car salesman was not one I wanted to SAVE or SAVOR.

Upbraided (verb): Criticized severely.

Think: UPSIDE BRAID.

The hippie UPBRAIDED me so much that I was afraid she was going to slap me UPSIDE the head with her giant BRAID.

Urbane (adjective): Sophisticated; polite and polished.

Think: URBAN.

The farm boy moved to a hip URBAN city and became so URBANE that he threw away his straw hat.

Usury (noun): Charging a high interest rate to take advantage of someone.

Think: YOU SORRY.

YOU will be SORRY if you borrow money from a bank that engages in USURY.

Utilitarian (adjective): Useful.

Think: UTILIZE.

The military likes to buy UTILITARIAN tools that can be UTILIZED for many different tasks.

Vacuous (adjective): Stupid.

Think: VACUUM.

The beauty pageant contestant's answer was so VACUOUS that the judges thought her brain had been VACUUMED out of her head.

Vapid (adjective): Dull; air-headed.

Think: VAPOR.

All VAPOR and no substance, MTV is so VAPID that it makes me want to take a nap.

Variegated (adjective): Varied.

Think: VARIED.

The autumn leaves in Vermont are known for their VARIEGATED colors; last year, they VARIED from red to yellow, to orange.

Vaunted (adjective): Widely praised.

Think: VAULTED.

The gymnast VAULTED so well that she was VAUNTED by the judges.

Vehement (adjective): Strongly emotional.

Think: HE MEANT IT.

His warning was so VEHEMENT that we knew HE MEANT it.

Verbose (adjective): Wordy.

Think: VERB BOSS.

They call me a VERB BOSS, since I am VERBOSE and know a zillion different words.

Verboten (adjective): Forbidden.

Think: VERB EATIN'.

In North Korea, VERB EATIN' — instead of speaking one's mind — is common since many topics are VERBOTEN.

Verisimilar (adjective): Seeming to be true.

Think: VERY SIMILAR.

The conman's VERISIMILAR story almost tricked me, since it was VERY SIMILAR to the truth.

Vernacular (noun): The way a certain group uses language.

Think: VERN'S KNACK.

Since he was a good old boy, VERN had a KNACK for the deep South's VERNACULAR.

Vex (verb): To annoy.

Think: HEX.

At Hogwarts, casting a HEX, or spell designed to cause pain, on someone will definitely VEX him.

Vigilant (adjective): Watchful; alert.

Think: VIGILANTE.

If you want some street justice, hire a VIGILANTE — they are VIGILANT by nature.

Vilify (verb): To speak ill of.

Think: VILLAIN-FY.

The dumpee decided to VILIFY her ex-boyfriend so that the other girls would think he was a VILLAIN.

Vindictive (adjective): Wanting revenge.

Think: VIN DIESEL.

VIN DIESEL often plays VINDICTIVE characters, since he has been typecast as a tough guy.

Virtuoso (noun): Someone highly skilled at something.

Think: VIRTUE.

VIRTUES? I have OH SO many because I'm a VIRTUOSO.

Viscous (adjective): Syrupy.

Think: STICKS TO US.

The VISCOUS BISQUICK pancake batter STICKS TO US.

Vitiate (verb): To impair or degrade.

Think: WISH YOU ATE.

If you eat Taco Bell, it will VITIATE your stomach and make you WISH YOU ATE something else.

Vituperated (verb): Criticized harshly.

Think: VIPER.

He was VITUPERATED so badly that he felt like he had been bitten by a VIPER.

Vivacious (adjective): Lively.

Think: VIVA LA VIDA.

The Coldplay song "VIVA LA VIDA" means "Long Live Life" and makes me want to be VIVACIOUS.

Vociferous (adjective): Loud.

Think: VOICE FOR US.

The announcer's loud VOICE, FOR US, was too VOCIFEROUS.

Volition (noun): A conscious choice.

Think: VOLUNTEER.

No one forced him to VOLUNTEER for the mission; he did it of his own VOLITION.

Waffle (verb): To go back and forth.

Think: Deciding about WAFFLES.

When I go out to brunch, I WAFFLE (verb) between getting WAFFLES (noun) and getting eggs.

Wan (adjective): Sick-looking.

Think: OBI-WAN.

In *Star Wars,* Obi-WAN Kenobi looked WAN even though he was a Jedi master because he was old.

Whet (verb): To sharpen; to make more intense.

Think: WET MOUTH.

If you're starving and I show you a picture of a cheeseburger, it will WHET your appetite, and your mouth will water and get WET.

Willful (adjective): Stubborn, insistent.

Think: WILL-FULL.

The WILLFUL horse was so WILL-FULL that he refused to be trained or ridden.

Wily (adjective): Clever; sly.

Think: WILE E. COYOTE.

WILE E. Coyote was not quite WILY enough to catch the Roadrunner, despite his clever traps.

Winsome (adjective): Charming and pleasing.

Think: WIN SOME.

She'll probably WIN SOME hearts at the dance, due to her WINSOME manner.

Wistful (adjective): Sadly wishing for.

Think: WISHFUL.

The "Forever Alone" meme guy feels WISTFUL because he is still alone after weeks of being WISTFUL for a girlfriend.

Wizened (adjective): Shrunken and wrinkled, usually due to age.

Think: WIZARD.

WIZARDS like Gandalf and Dumbledore are usually WIZENED, since they're really old.

Zealous (adjective): Passionate.

Think: JEALOUS.

Zoe was so ZEALOUS about her first boyfriend that she became JEALOUS of every other girl he knew.

Zenith (noun): The highest point.

Think: BENEATH.

When you reach the ZENITH, everything else is BENEATH.

Zephyr (noun): A gentle breeze.

Think: ZEBRA FUR.

The summer evening ZEPHYR was as soft as ZEBRA FUR.

Appendix B

Making the MAT Work for You

A good way to think of the MAT is as one of several tools in your graduate school admissions toolbox. It's not the whole picture. The real function of your results is to show schools how you compare to other MAT takers. Try not to view the scores as a measure of your intelligence or a grade. But when you have them, it's time to think about the big picture — getting into your desired program.

Putting Your Scores to Work

After you finish the MAT, your unofficial score appears on the screen, from 200 to 600. Whether the number is higher than, lower than, or exactly what you'd hoped, don't worry about it too much yet — it's just another piece in the graduate school admissions puzzle.

When you receive your official score report in the mail, you'll have your official score and see your percentile rank, both overall and in your specific graduate school discipline. If you selected a school (or schools) to receive your three free test result transcripts, they'll receive the same information. If you didn't specify any schools, you have to request a transcript report, for an additional fee.

Unless you're really short on cash, you may want to forego specifying any schools when you register, just in case you don't do well. You'll have to pay a fee to get the transcripts sent later, but paying a fee is better than risking rejection from your desired program.

Retaking the MAT

If you're really not happy with your score, you can retake the MAT. Just keep in mind that schools will know how many times you've taken the test overall. If you didn't select any schools to receive scores for your first MAT attempt and you then decide to send the scores of your second MAT attempt to schools, they will know you've taken the test twice. It probably isn't a big deal — schools mostly want to know your best MAT score and don't care that much if you took the test two or three times. If you take the MAT more than three times, though, it can be a bit of a turn-off.

Some students take an official MAT test as a "practice test." That practice is unnecessary and potentially detrimental since it will show up on your official transcript. Instead, practice using the practice tests available at MillerAnalogies.com.

Gearing Up for Graduate Admissions

Of course, the main reason you're taking the MAT is probably to get into graduate school. Here's a quick primer on graduate school admissions to keep in mind.

Be early and organized. Some programs have rolling admissions, which means that when the school starts receiving applications, it accepts good candidates until its program is full. In the beginning of this process, since more spots in the program are available, the school can be less selective. Later in the process, when most of the spots are full, the program can be more critical. Generally, applying early works to your advantage.

To get your application in early, start working on components like your MAT prep and your application essays soon, if not now. Essays, in particular, often benefit from careful rewrites and long-term meditation on what to write about. Don't forget your recommendations — ask your professors early, before they get deluged with requests from all your classmates.

Presenting Your GPA

Your GPA, especially in your major, if you're applying to a relevant graduate school, is crucial. Even if your GPA isn't stellar right now, graduate schools like to see a trend of improvement. Do what you can to raise your grades; they're one of the factors over which you have the most control.

If there's a valid reason that your GPA doesn't represent your best abilities (such as illness), it's worth explaining. Some graduate school applications have a section in which you can offer any other information relevant to your application. If you feel that you need to explain your GPA, make use of that part of the application to do so. Be plain and brief. If your program's application does not include a section to explain any other factors that should be considered in evaluating your application, include a brief explanation as either part of your personal statement (if your program requests one), or as an additional note to the admissions committee.

Be sure that if you're explaining a low GPA that you have a valid, believable reason. And, don't over-explain.

If you have a legitimate reason, such as illness, that your MAT score doesn't show your best work, include a note or add a statement to your application explaining why.

Writing Your Essays

Application essays are a great way to show schools your unique background and personality, especially since most students make the mistake of writing what they think the admissions committee wants to hear. Don't do this — be yourself. To show your unique qualities, it's often a good idea to tell one to three specific stories in your essay, with the goal of *showing* the reader one of your outstanding qualities (instead of just *telling* the reader you have the quality). For example, if you want the admissions committee to know you were an intellectually curious student, you may tell a story about reading all of Henry David Thoreau's works while you were in high school instead of just saying, "I love learning."

Avoid writing an essay that tries to cover everything and is essentially an expanded resume. The essay is your chance to showcase something about you that the admissions committee can't find out from the rest of your application.

Speaking of qualities that you may want to showcase, here are a few to think about: maturity, leadership, integrity, vulnerability, creativity, curiosity, and perseverance.

Preparing Your Resume

Many graduate programs ask for a resume or curriculum vitae (same thing). If so, here are a few tips for yours:

- ✔ Keep it to one page. Even if you've had a storied, 30-year career spanning several industries, not many people want to wade through a long resume. Just pick your biggest accomplishments.

- ✔ Tailor it. Make sure your resume highlights the most volunteer work and experience that's most relevant to the program to which you're applying. When in doubt, leave off points that don't apply.

- ✔ Be specific. The most memorable bullet points on a resume are specific, concrete, and interesting. "Improved SAT scores by an average of 254 points" is more interesting than "Helped students improve SAT scores."

Choosing Your Referrals

Recommendations have to be there, but they usually don't make or break an application because most applications have good recommendations. Obviously, students usually ask professors to write recommendations if they think the professors will write good ones. You, however, can stand out by making sure that the person who writes you a recommendation knows you well. Even if a recommendation is very positive, it won't stand out unless it's specific, detailed, and forthright. If you don't really know the person whom you're asking for a recommendation, make sure you *get* to know him or her. And give your professors plenty of time to get your recommendations done.

Preparing for Interviews

If your desired graduate program offers you the chance to interview, take it! Meeting someone in the admissions committee in person gives you the chance to make a memorable personal impression. An interview also gives you a chance to ask questions about the program. Here are a few quick tips on how to make a graduate school interview work for you.

- ✔ **Practice!** Have a friend ask you typical interview questions (do some research and find some online or in an admissions advice book), and respond as you would if it were a real interview. Even if you're used to thinking on your feet, practicing your responses can improve their quality.

- ✔ **Look professional.** Dress neatly and formally.

✔ **Be lively.** Ask questions, be responsive, smile, make eye contact, avoid one-word answers, and be yourself. If the interview turns into a conversation, that's good. After all, your interviewer is most likely a nice person who wants to get to know you. Prepare a few questions to ask your interviewer — so he knows you're interested in the program — and make sure they're questions without obvious answers — if you can find the answer on the program's website, it's not a good question. For example, you could ask if there are any courses the program is considering adding in the future.

✔ **Say thanks.** Everyone likes getting cards in the mail, so send your interviewer a thank-you note. Make sure you get a business card or the correct spelling of their name. Sending a note is another way to help your interviewer remember you.

As a final note, make sure you give yourself more than one option. It's tough to keep everything in perspective if you're applying only to your dream program. Unless you're truly interested in only one program, apply to a few schools you'd like to attend. And keep in mind that even if you don't get into any programs, you can almost always try again later. Remember the big picture when the application process becomes overwhelming or stressful. Life offers lots of options.

Index

• Numerics •

1:2,3:4 analogy, 25–26, 29–30
1:3,2:4 analogy, 26–27
1:4,2:3 analogy, 27
2:1,4:3 analogy, 29
38th parallel north, 97
1970s energy crisis, 103
1984 (Orwell), 88

• A •

a cappella, 79
a priori, 67
a tempo, 79
abase, 257
abate, 257
abeyance, 258
abolitionism, 100
Abraham Lincoln assassination, 104
abridge, 258
abscission, 117
absolute zero, 120
abstemious, 258
abstruse, 258
abysmal, 258
academic environment, 16–17
accede, 258
accelerando, 79
acceleration, 122
accent, musical, 79
accept/except, 64
acclimatization, 117
accommodations, for testing, 12
acerbic, 258
acid, 120
acid rain, 125
acidulous, 258
acoustics, 122
acrimonious, 258
act, literary, 83
actinide, 128
action steps, making a list of, 43
action theory, 110
activation energy, 120
acumen, 259
acute angle, 131
acute stress reaction, 108
ad hoc, 67
ad nauseum, 67

adagio, 79
Adam, 93
adapt/adopt, 64–65
addition, 130
ADHD (attention deficit-hyperactivity disorder), 108
adhesion, 122
adjective, 36
Adler, Alfred, 109
adopt/adapt, 64–65
adoption, 110
adorned, 259
Adriatic Sea, 97
adroit, 259
adulation, 259
Adventures of Huckleberry Finn, The (Twain), 89
Adventures of Tom Sawyer, The (Twain), 89
advice/advise, 65
Aegean Sea, 97
Aeineid, The (Virgil), 89
aeration, 120
aerobic organism, 117
aerodynamics, 122
Aeschylus, 85
Aesop, 85
aesthetic, 259
affable, 259
affectation, 259
affect/effect, 65
affirmative action, 110
agnosticism, 92
alcoholism, 108
Alcott, Louisa May, 85
Aldrich, John, 107
Alexander's Feast (Dryden), 86
alfresco, 67
algebra, 131
Alger, Horatio, 85
Alice in Wonderland (Caroll), 86
Alighieri, Dante, 85
alkali metal, 128
alkaline earth metal, 128
Allah, 93
allegory, 83
allegretto, 79
allegro, 79
alleviate, 259
Allies, 100
Allison, Graham, 107

alliteration, 83
alloy, 122
allusion, 83
allusion/illusion, 65
alology, 61
Alps, 97
altar/alter, 65
alter ego, 67
alternate meanings, analogies with, 37
alternating current, 122
altissimo, 79
alto, 79
altruistic, 259
Alzheimer's disease, 108
amalgamate, 260
Amazing Grace (Newton), 83
Amazon river, 97
amber, 125
ameliorated, 260
amenable, 260
amendment, 106
America (Smith), 83
America the Beautiful (Ward and Lee), 83
American Civil War, 103
American Gothic (Wood), 76
American Revolution, 104
amicable, 260
amino acid, 117
ampere, 122, 129
Ampere, Andre-Marie, 124
amphitheatre, 77
anachronism, 83, 260
anagrams, 23
analogical thinking, 15–17
analogies. *See also* solving analogies; structural types
  alternate meanings for, 37
  described, 8, 15
  description analogies, 18–19
  parts analogies, 20
  playful, 22–23
  similar/different, 21–22
  tough questions, 33–40
  type analogies, 19–20
analogy traps
  category traps, 38
  direction traps, 38–39
  distractor traps, 39
  tips for, 37–38

anatomy, 117
andante, 79
Andersen, Hans Christian, 86
Andes, 98
Andromeda galaxy, 125
Angelico, Fra, 74
Angelou, Maya, 86
angle, 131
angstrom, 123
anile, 260
Animal Farm (Orwell), 88
animalia kingdom, 127
animals, 127–128
anion, 120
Anna Karenina (Tolstoy), 89
anodyne, 260
anorexia nervosa, 108
antagonist, 83
Antarctic Circle, 98
antediluvian, 260
Anthony, Susan B., 102
anthropocentrism (AKA humanocentrism), 112
anthropology, 61, 112–113
antihero, 84
antipositivism, 110
antisemitism, 110
antithesis, 260
anxiety, dealing with, 49–50, 251–253
apace, 261
Apartheid, 100, 261
Aphrodite/Venus, 92
aplomb, 261
apocryphal, 261
Apollo, 92
Apollo 11, 104
apostrophe, 84
apothegm, 261
Appalachian Mountains, 98
Appearance and Reality (Bradley), 90, 91
appoggiatura, 79
apposite, 261
appraise/apprise, 65
aqueduct, 77
Arabian Sea, 98
arachnology, 117
arc, 132
arch, 261
archaeology, 61
archetype, 108
Archimedes, 124
architects, 78
architecture, 77–78
arctic circle, 98

ardent, 261
area, 132
Ares/Mars, 93
arid, 261
aristocracy, 106
Aristophanes, 86
Aristotle, 90, 91
arithmetic, 130–131
Armageddon, 92
Armstrong, Louis, 82
arpeggio, 79
art, 73–76
art deco, 73
Art of War, The (Tzu), 91
artists and works, 74–76
As I Lay Dying (Faulkner), 87
ascent/assent, 65
asceticism, 92
Asgard, 94
ashen, 262
aspersion, 262
Assassination of Abraham Lincoln, 104
assiduous, 262
assimilation, 110
assonance, 84
assuage, 262
asteroid, 125
astrology, 61
astronomical unit, 123
astronomy, 125
atheism, 92
Athena/Minerva, 93
Atlas Mountains, 98
atom, 120
atomic mass, 128
atomic number, 120, 128
atrium, 77
Attack on Pearl Harbor, 104
attention deficit-hyperactivity disorder (ADHD), 108
audio edition tests, 12
august, 262
Auld Lang Syne, 83
Austen, Jane, 86
austere, 262
authoritarianism, 106
authors/writers, 85–89
autocracy, 106
automaton, 262
average, 130
Avogadro, Amedeo, 122
avuncular, 262
axiology, 61
Axis, 100

• B •

Bacchus/Dionysus, 93
Bach, Johann Sebastian, 82
background radiation, 123
backward, working, 35–36
Bacon, Francis, 90
bacteria, 117
bacteriology, 61
bacteriophage, 117
balanced reciprocity, 112
ballad, 84
Balzac, Honoré de, 86
Bandaranaike, Sirimavo, 102
bankruptcy, 104
barometer, 120
baroque, 73
Barzun, Jacques, 111
base, 120
bas-relief, 77
bass, 79
Baudelaire, Charles, 86
bauhaus, 73
Bay of Pigs Invasion, 104
bear, 127
beat, musical, 79
beatific, 262
beatify, 262
beaufort, 129
Beckett, Samuel, 86
Becquerel, Antoine Henri, 124
bee, 127
Beethoven, Ludwig van, 82
beguile, 263
behaviorism, 108
behemoth, 263
belied, 263
Bell, Alexander Graham, 126
Bell Jar, The (Plath), 88
belligerent, 263
Bellow, Saul, 86
Beloved (Morrison), 88
bend, 79
Benedict, Ruth, 113
bereft, 263
Berlin, Irving, 83
Berlin Wall, fall of, 104
Bernoulli, Daniel, 124
bespoke, 263
bête noire, 67
Beyond Good and Evil (Nietzsche), 90, 91
Bible, 94
bifurcated, 263
big bang, 123

bildungsroman, 84
Bill of Rights, 100
Billy the Kid (Copland), 82
binary star, 123
Binet, Alfred, 109
biochemistry, 117, 120
biology, 61, 117–119
Birth of Venus, The (Botticelli), 74
bit, 129
Bizet, Georges (*Carmen*), 83
black hole, 123
Black Paintings (Goya), 75
Black Power, 110
Black Sea, 98
Blake, William, 86
bloviated, 263
Boas, Franz, 113
body and mind, preparing, 50
Bohr, Niels, 124
boiling, 120
bona fide, 67
Bonaparte, Napoleon, 102
bond, 120
bootless, 263
Bosch, Hieronymus, 74
boson, 123
botany, 118
Botticelli, Sandro, 74
bourgeoisie, 100
Bradbury, Ray, 86
Bradley, Herbert Francis, 90, 91
Brahms, Johannes, 82
brass, 79
Brave New World (Huxley), 87
breaks, taking, 251
breathing, during MAT test, 251
bridge, musical, 79
British Museum, 76
Brontë, Charlotte, 86
Brontë, Emily, 86
Buddha, Gautama, 93
Buddhism, 92
bugbear, 264
bulimia, 108
bumptious, 264
buoyancy, 123
burgeoning, 264
Burr, Aaron, 102
buttress, 264
bygone, 264
Byron, Lord George, 86
byte, 129
byzantine, 264

• *C* •

cabinet, 106
cache, 264
cadenza, 79
calamitous, 264
Calder, Alexander, 74
caliber, 129
Call of the Wild, The (London), 88
Calling of Saint Matthew (Caravaggio), 74
camaraderie, 264
cameo, 77
Camus, Albert, 86
Candidate Information Booklet, 7
Candide (Voltaire), 91
canon, musical, 79
Canterbury Tales, The (Chaucer), 86
canto, 84
capacious, 265
capital/capitol, 65
capitalism, 104
Capitol, building, 78
capricious, 265
carat, 129
Caravaggio, 74
Card Players, The (Cezanne), 74
cardinal, 265
cardiology, 61
caricature, 73
Carmen (Bizet), 83
Carnegie, Andrew, 102
carol, 79
Caroll, Lewis, 86
carpe diem, 67
carte blanche, 68
cartography, 98
Caruso, Enrico, 82
carving, 73
Caspian Sea, 98
caste, 100, 112
Castro, Fidel, 102
casus belli, 68
cat, 127
Cat in the Hat, The (Seuss), 88
catacombs, 77
catalyst, 120
categories, relationship. *See also* analogies
  description analogies, 18–19
  parts analogies, 20

playful analogies, 22–23
similar/different analogies, 21–22
type analogies, 19–20
categories, word
  collective nouns, 62–64
  commonly confused, 64–67
  foreign words, 67–69
  -ology words, 61–62
category traps, 38
Cather, Willa, 86
cation, 120
cattle, 127
caveat emptor, 68
celebration, scheduling, 44
celerity, 265
cell, 26–27
cell membrane, 118
cell nucleus, 118
celsius, 123, 129
censure, 265
centi-, 129
centrifuge, 120
centripetal force, 123
Cervantes, Miguel de, 86
Cezanne, Paul, 74
Chagell, Marc, 74
champion, 265
Charlemagne, 102
Chaucer, Geoffrey, 86
Chekov, Anton Pavlovich, 86
chemical reaction, 120
chemical symbol, 128
chemistry
  figures, 122
  periodic table, 128–129
  terms, 120–122
Chernobyl disaster, 104
Cherry Orchard, The (Checkov), 86
Chesapeake Bay, 98
chicanery, 265
chicken, 127
chide, 265
chloroplast, 118
choice overload (overchoice), 110
choleric, 265
Chop Suey (Hopper), 75
Chopin, Frederic, 82
chord, musical, 79
Christianity, 92
Christina's World (Wyeth), 76
Christmas, 94

Christmas Carol, A (Dickens), 86
chromosome, 118
church, 94
Churchill, Winston, 102
circle, 132
circuitous, 266
circumference, 132
circumspect, 266
cite/site, 65
clan, 112
clandestine, 266
Clash of Civilizations
    (Huntington), 107
class, 127
classical conditioning (Pavlovian
    conditioning), 108
classicism, 73
classification, of living things,
    127–128
clemency, 266
Cleopatra, 102
cliché, 84
climax, 84
Clouds, The (Aristophanes), 86
cloying, 266
cocksure, 266
coda, 79
cognizant, 266
cohabitation, 110
cohesion, 123
Cold War, 100
Coleman, James, 111
Coleridge, Samuel Taylor, 86
collective nouns, 62–64
colloid, 120
coloratura, 80
Colosseum, 78
Columbus, Christopher, 102
combustion, 120
comet, 125
comme il faut, 68
Common Sense (Paine), 88
communism, 101, 105
Communist Manifesto, The
    (Marx and Engels), 90, 91
complement/compliment, 65
complicit, 266
composers and musicians, 82
composure, 266
compound, 120
computer-based MAT, 11
Comte, Auguste, 111
concord, 267
"Concord Hymn" (Emerson), 87
concupiscence, 267

condensation, 120
condign, 267
conductor, 120
Confederate States of America,
    101
confidant/confident, 65
confirmation, 92
conflagration, 267
confused words, common, 64–67
congruent, 132
Conrad, Joseph, 86
conservative, 106
constellation, 125
constitutionalism, 106
Consumer Price Index (CPI), 105
Controlled Testing Centers
    (CTCs), 11
contumacious, 267
conundrum, 267
coordinates, 98, 131
Copernicus, Nicolaus, 126
Copland, Aaron, 82
cord, 129
cordial, 267
Corinthian Order, 77
corpus delicti, 68
corroborate, 267
coruscate, 267
cosmology, 61
cosmopolitan, 268
costs, 9, 11
council/counsel, 65
countenance, 268
countertenor, 80
coup de grace, 68
couplet, 84
covert, 268
cowed, 268
CPI (Consumer Price Index), 105
credit, 105
crepuscular, 268
crescendo, 80
Crick, Francis, 119
Crime and Punishment
    (Dostoevsky), 86
Critique of Pure Reason (Kant),
    90, 91
Crucible, The (Miller), 88
Crusades, 104
cryptology, 61
cubism, 73
culpable, 268
cultural literacy, measuring, 10
cultural materialism, 112

cultural relativism, 110
Cultural Revolution, 101
cumbersome, 268
cummings, e. e., 86
cupidity, 268
curie, 129
Curie, Marie, 122
curmudgeon, 268
currant/current, 65
currency, 38
curriculum vitae (resume),
    preparing, 321
cynosure, 269
cytology, 61
cytoplasm, 118
czar (tsar), 101

• *D* •

da Vinci, Leonardo, 74, 75
dada, 74
Dali, Salvador, 75
Darwin, Charles, 119
Daumier, Honoré, 75
David (Michelangelo), 75
David Copperfield (Dickens), 86
de facto, 68
de jure, 68
de Kooning, Willem, 75
deadlines for study, setting,
    43–44
dearth, 269
"Death Be Not Proud"
    (Donne), 86
Death Comes for the Archbishop
    (Cather), 86
Death Valley, 98
debt, 105
Debussy, Claude, 82
decelerando, 80
deci-, 129
decibel, 129
deciduous, 118
decimal point, 131
declaimed, 269
decorous, 269
decrescendo, 80
decried, 269
deer, 127
defenestrate, 269
Defoe, Daniel, 86
defunct, 269
Degas, Edgar, 75
degree, 132
déjà vu, 68

deleterious, 269
demagogue, 269
demarcate, 270
democracy, 106
demography, 110
denigrate, 270
denominator, 131
denouement, 84
density, 123
deontology, 61
dependant/dependent, 65
deposition, 120
Deposition of Christ (Angelico), 74
Depression, economic, 105
Descartes, René, 90
description analogies, 18–19
desert/dessert, 65
desiccated, 270
despoiled, 270
desuetude, 270
détente, 106
deus ex machina, 68
dew point, 123
Dewey, John, 90
diameter, 132
diaphanous, 270
diatribe, 270
Dickens, Charles, 86
Dickinson, Emily, 86
dictator, 106
dictionary definitions, remembering, 38
didactic, 270
Diesel, Rudolf, 126
difference, 131
different/similar analogies, 21–22
difficulty level, noticing, 34, 37, 46, 49
diffusion, 110, 112
dilatory, 270
dint, 271
Dionysus/Bacchus, 93
direction traps, 38–39
dirge, 80
discomfit, 271
discreet/discrete, 66
discriminate, 37, 271
disgruntled, 271
disparage, 271
dispatch, 271
displacement, 123
disputatious, 271
distension, 271
distillation, 125
distinguish, 37

distractor traps, 39
dividend, 131
Divine Comedy, The (Alighieri), 85
division, 131
divisive, 271
divisor, 131
DNA, 118
docile, 272
doggedness, 272
doggerel, 84, 272
dogmatic, 272
Doll's House, A (Ibsen), 87
domino theory, 106
Don Giovanni (Mozart), 83
Don Juan (Byron), 86
Don Quixote (Cervantes), 86
Donatello, 75
Donne, John, 86
doppelgänger, 68
doppler effect, 123
Doric Order, 77
Dostoevsky, Fyodor, 86
Douglass, Frederick, 102
Dr. Faustus (Marlowe), 88
draconian, 272
drag, 123
droll, 272
Dryden, John, 86
dubious, 272
Dubois, W. E. B., 111
dudgeon, 272
dupe, 272
duplicitous, 273
Durkheim, Émile, 111
dynamics, 80
dyspeptic, 273

• *E* •

Easter, 94
Easter Monday (De Kooning), 75
Easter Rising, 104
ebullient, 273
eclectic, 273
ecology, 118, 125
economics, 104–106
ecosystem, 118
Edison, Thomas, 126
educated guess, making, 37
effaced, 273
effect/affect, 65
efficacious, 273
effusive, 273
egalitarian, 273
egg, 118
ego, 108

Eid al-Adha, 94
Eid ul-Fitr, 94
Einstein, Albert, 124
Ekman, Paul, 109
El Niño–Southern Oscillation, 98
elasticity, 123
eldritch, 273
election, 107
electoral college, 107
electrolyte, 120
electron, 120
elegy, 84
elicit/illicit, 66
elimination, process of, 34–35
Eliot, George, 86
Eliot, T. S., 87
Ellington, Duke, 82
ellipse, 132
Ellison, Ralph, 87
Emancipation Proclamation, 101
embroiled, 274
embryo, 118
embryonic, 274
Emerson, Ralph Waldo, 87
eminent/imminent, 66
emollient, 274
empiricism, 89
encomium, 274
encompass, 274
encore, 80
endemism, 118
endogamy, 110
endothermic, 123
energy, 125
energy crisis, 1970s, 103
enervating, 274
enfant terrible, 68
Engels, Friedrich, 90, 91
English Channel, 98
enology, 61
ensorcelled, 274
ensure/insure, 66
entomology, 61
entreat, 274
entropy, 121
environment, for testing, 46
enzyme, 118
epic, 84
epidemiology, 61
epiphany, 84
epistemology, 61
equation, 131
equator, 98
equilateral triangle, 132
equilibrium, 123
eradicate, 274
Erie Canal, 98

Erikson, Erik, 109
eschatology, 61
eschew, 60, 275
essay, 84
Essay Concerning Human Understanding, An (Locke), 90, 91
essays, writing, 320–321
estimable, 275
etching, 74
Ethan Frome (Wharton), 89
ethics, 89
ethnocentrism, 112
ethology, 61, 118
etiolated, 275
etiology, 61
Euripedes, 87
evanescent, 275
Eve, 93
everglades, 98
evinced, 275
ex cathedra, 68
exacting, 275
except/accept, 64
exculpated, 275
exercise, 247
existentialism, 90
exonerated, 275
exorbitant, 275
exothermic, 123
expansion, economic, 105
expatriate, 276
expedient, 276
experimental questions, 12, 34
exponent, 131
expressionism, 74
expunge, 276
extant, 276
extirpate, 276

• F •

fable, 84
façade, 77
factor, 131
Faerie Queen, The (Spenser), 89
Fahrenheit, 129
faint/feint, 66
fait accompli, 68
Fall of the Berlin Wall, 104
falling behind in the test, 48
falsetto, 80
family, 127
farad, 123
Faraday, Michael, 124
farther/further, 66

fascism, 107
fastidious, 276
fathom, 129
fatuous, 276
Faulkner, William, 87
Faust (Goëthe), 87
faux pas, 68
fawning, 276
feckless, 276
fecund, 277
Federal Deposit Insurance Corporation (FDIC), 105
Federal Reserve Board of Governors, 105
Federal Trade Commission (FTC), 105
federalism, 107
feeling what you're feeling, 253
feint/faint, 66
fermata, 80
Fermi, Enrico, 124
ferret, 127
festivals/holidays, 94
fetid, 277
fiasco, 68
figures
  anthropologists, 113
  architects, 78
  artists, 74–76
  authors, 85–89
  biologists, 119
  chemists, 122
  economists, 106
  historical, 102–103
  musicians and composers, 82
  philosophers, 90–91
  physicists, 124–125
  political scientists, 107–108
  psychologists, 109
  religious, 93
  scientists, 126
  sociologists, 111
filial, 277
fine, 80
Firebird, The (Stravinsky), 82
fission, 123
Fitzgerald, F. Scott, 26, 87
flat, 80
Flaubert, Gustave, 87
Fleming, Alexander, 119
florid, 277
flouted, 277
flummoxed, 277
focal vocabulary, 112
focus during test, maintaining, 49–50

foible, 277
following through with plans, 42
food, 248
foot, 84
For Whom the Bell Tolls (Hemingway), 87
forbearance, 277
force, 123
foreign words, 67–69
foreshadowing, 84
foreword/forward, 66
forte, 80
fortissimo, 80
fortitude, 277
Fourteen Points, 101
fox, 128
fracas, 278
fraction, 131
fractious, 278
Frankenstein (Shelley), 88
Franklin, Benjamin, 126
freezing, 121
frequency, 121
Frère Jacques, 83
fresco, 74
Freud, Sigmund, 109
friction, 123
Frost, Robert, 87
froward, 278
fruition, 278
FTC (Federal Trade Commission), 105
fuliginous, 278
fulsome, 278
functionalism, 110
funereal, 278
fungi kingdom, 127
furlong, 129
furor, 278
further/farther, 66
fusion, 123

• G •

gaffe, 278
gainsay, 279
galaxy, 125
Galileo, 125
gambol, 279
gamma ray, 123
Gandhi, Indira, 102
Gandhi, Mahatma, 90, 102
Garden of Earthly Delights, The (Bosch), 74
gargantuan, 279
gargoyle, 77

garrulous, 279
Garvey, Marcus, 102
gas, 121
Gaudi, Antoni, 78
Gaugin, Paul, 75
Gaza Strip, 98
Geertz, Clifford, 113
Gehry, Frank, 78
gemeinschaft and gesellschaft, 110
gene, 118
genealogy, 112
general relativity, 123
generalized reciprocity, 112
genetics, 118
Geneva Conventions, 101
genial, 279
genre, 84
gentrification, 110
genus, 127
geochemistry, 121
geography, 97–100
geology, 61
geometry, 131–133
germinate, 279
gerontology, 62
Gershwin, George, 82
Giacometti, Alberto, 75
Gibson, James, 109
gift economy, 105
Gilbert and Sullivan, 82
Ginsberg, Allen, 87
glacial, 279
glancing, 279
Glasnost, 101
glowered, 279
GNP (Gross National Product), 105
goal score. *See also* score
   achieving, 47
   setting, 42–43
   timing each question and, 48
goals
   long-term, 45
   setting, 42–43
goat, 128
God Bless America (Berlin), 83
gods, 92–93
Goëthe, Johann Wolfgang von, 87
Golding, William, 87
Goodall, Jane, 119
goofy, being, 253
goose, 128
Gorbachev, Mikhail, 102
gothic architecture, 77
Goya, Francisco, 75

GPA, presenting, 320
graduate level vocabulary, 257–318
graduate school
   admission procedure, 320–322
   interviews, 321–322
   MAT score's role in, 10, 13
   referrals and resume for, 321
   sending score report to, 11–12, 319
graffiti, 74
grammar change analogies, 22–23
grandiloquent, 280
Grant, Ulysses S., 102
Grapes of Wrath, The (Steinbeck), 89
gravitas, 280
gravitation, 125
GRE test, 10–11
GRE vocabulary book, 59
Great Depression, 101
Great Gatsby, The (Fitzgerald), 87
Great Lakes, 98
Great Salt Lake, 98
Great Sphinx, 78
Greek/Roman gods, 92–93
greenhouse effect, 125
Greensleeves, 83
Grimm Brothers, 87
grisly/grizzly, 66
Gross National Product (GNP), 105
grouse, 280
grovel, 280
Guernica (Picasso), 75, 93
guessing
   benefits of, 46, 48
   educated, 37
   second guessing, 249, 251
Guevara, Che, 102
Guggenheim, 76
Gulliver's Travels (Swift), 89
gumption, 280

• H •

habeas corpus, 107
hackneyed, 280
Hades, 93, 94
Hagia Sophia, 78
hagiology, 62
haiku, 84
hajj, 92
half-life, 125
hallowed, 280

halogen, 128
Hamilton, Alexander, 102
Handel, George Frideric, 82, 83
Hanukkah, 94
harangue, 280
Hardy, Thomas, 87
harmony, 80
Hartz, Louis, 107
Hawthorne, Nathaniel, 87
Haydn, Joseph, 82
Haystacks (Monet), 75
Heart of Darkness (Conrad), 86
hectare, 129
Heisenberg, Werner, 125
heliocentric, 125
Hemingway, Ernest, 87
Henry VIII, 102
Hera/Juno, 93
Hermes/Mercury, 93
hermetic, 280
Hermitage Museum, 76
herpetology, 62, 118
hertz, 123, 129
Herzog (Bellow), 86
Hesse, Herman, 87
heterodox economics, 105
hexagon, 132
heyday, 281
hiatus, 281
hidden curriculum, 110
hidebound, 281
hieroglyphs, 77
Himalayas, 98
Hinduism, 92
Hippocrates, 119
hirsute, 281
histology, 62, 118
historical events, 103–104
history, 100–104
histrionic, 281
Hitler, Adolf, 102
Ho Chi Minh, 102
hoard/horde, 66
Hobbes, Thomas, 90, 91
Hobbit, The (Tolkien), 89
holidays/festivals, 94
holistic, 281
Holocaust, 104
Homer, 87
Homer, Winslow, 75
Hopper, Edward, 75
horology, 62
horse, 128
Howl (Ginsberg), 87
Hudson River, 98
Hughes, Langston, 87
Hugo, Victor, 87

human example, 127
humanism, 112
humanities
  architecture, 77–78
  art, 73–76
  literature, 83–89
  music, 79–83
  philosophy, 89–91
  practice test, 95–96
  religion/mythology, 92–95
humanocentrism (anthropo-
    centrism), 112
Hume, David, 90
Hundred Years' War, 104
Huntington, Samuel P., 107
Hurston, Zora Neale, 87, 113
husbandry, 281
Huxley, Aldous, 87
hymn, 80
hyperbole, 84
hypotenuse, 132

• I •

Iberian peninsula, 98
Ibsen, Henrik, 87
ichthyology, 62, 118
iconoclast, 281
icons used in this book, 3
id, 108
idealism, 90
idée fixe, 68
idiom, 84
idiosyncrasy, 281
igneous rock, 125
ignoring/skipping test
    questions
  benefits of, 252
  determining before the test,
    46, 249
  experimental questions, not
    counted toward score,
    12, 34
  tough questions and, 33
Iliad (Homer), 87
illiberal, 282
illicit/elicit, 66
illusion/allusion, 65
imagery, 84
imbroglio, 282
imminent/eminent, 66
impeachment, 107
impeded, 282
Imperialism, 101
imperious, 282
impregnable, 282

impressionism, 74
impromptu, 282
impugn, 282
in extremis, 68
in loco parentis, 68
in vino veritas, 68
inchoate, 282
incisive, 283
incite/insight, 66
incredulous, 283
indicator, 121
indigenous, 112, 283
indomitable, 283
inertia, 123
inexorable, 283
inflation, 105
ingenuous/ingenious, 66
inimical, 283
innocuous, 283
inorganic compound, 121
insight/incite, 66
instinct, 108
institutional racism, 110
instrumental conditioning
    (Operant Conditioning),
    108
insular, 284
insulator, 121
insulin, 118
insure/ensure, 66
intaglio, 77
Intelligence Quotient (IQ), 108
interest, 105
International Date Line, 98
interviews, preparing for,
    321–322
intro, 80
inundated, 284
invertebrate, 118
invidious, 284
Invisible Man, The (Ellison), 87
ion, 121
ionic order, 77
ionization, 121
ipso facto, 68
IQ (Intelligence Quotient), 108
irascible, 284
irony, 84
Isis, 93
Islam, 92
isosceles triangle, 132
isotope, 128
Italian Symphony
    (Mendelssohn), 82
itinerant (nomad), 112
Ivanhoe (Scott), 88

• J •

James, Henry, 87
James, William, 90
Jane Eyre (Bronte), 86
Jefferson, Thomas, 78, 102
jejune, 284
Jerusalem, 94
Jesus, 93
JFK (John Fitzgerald Kennedy),
    103
jingoism, 284
Joan of Arc, 103
Job, 93
jocose, 284
John the Baptist, 93
Johns, Jasper, 75
joie de vivre, 68
joint family, 112
joule, 123, 129
Joyce, James, 87
Judaism, 92
juggernaut, 284
Jung, Carl, 109
Jungle, The (Sinclair), 88
Jungle Book, The (Kipling), 87
Juno/Hera, 93
Jupiter/Zeus, 93
jury, 107

• K •

Kafka, Franz, 87
Kalahari Desert, 98
kangaroo, 128
Kant, Immanuel, 90, 91
Keats, John, 87
Kelvin, 129
Kennedy, John Fitzgerald (JFK),
    103
Kennedy, Robert Francis (RFK),
    103
Kepler, Johannes, 126
Kerouac, Jack, 87
key, musical, 80
kilo-, 129
kindle, 284
kinesics, 112
kinesiology, 62
kinetics, 121
King, Martin Luther, 103
kingdom, 127
Kipling, Rudyard, 87
kismet, 285
Kiss, The (Klimt), 75
kitsch, 84

Klee, Paul, 75
Klimt, Gustav, 75
knot, 129
knowing where you currently
    stand, 42
Korotayev, Andrey, 113
kowtow, 285
Krantz, Grover, 113
Krebs cycle, 118
Kremlin, 99
Kübler-Ross, Elisabeth, 109

• L •

La Bohème (Puccini), 82
La Comédie Humaine (Balzac),
    86
La Danse (Matisse), 75
La Niña, 99
La Traviata (Verdi), 83
labeling theory, 110
labor union, 105
lachrymose, 285
lackadaisical, 285
laconic, 285
Lady Chatterley's Lover
    (Lawrence), 87
Laissez-faire capitalism, 101
Lake Titicaca, 99
Lake Victoria, 99
Lamarck, Jean-Baptiste, 119
lampoon, 84
language and words
  collective nouns, 62–64
  commonly confused words,
    64–67
  foreign words, 67–69
  -ology words, 61–62
  practice test, 69–71
  unknown words, solving
    analogies and, 34
  vocabulary, 15, 59–60,
    257–318
  word prefixes, 56–58
  word roots, 53–56
  word suffixes, 58–59
languid, 285
lanthanide, 128
lapidary, 285
largess, 285
largo, 80
larva, 118
Lascaux, 76
lassitude, 285
Last supper, The (da Vinci), 74
latitude, 99

lattice, 121
laudable, 286
Lavoisier, Antoine, 122
Lawrence, D. H., 87
lax, 286
lay/lie, 66
Le Corbusier, 78
Leach, Edmund, 113
Leaf, Murray, 113
league, 129
Leaves of Grass (Whitman), 89
Lee, Katharine, 83
Lee, Robert E., 103
legato, 80
legerdemain, 286
Leibnitz, Gottfried, 90
Lenin, Vladimir, 103
Les Fleurs du Mal
    (Baudelaire), 86
Les Misérables (Hugo), 87
leukocyte, 118
lever, 124
Leviathan (Hobbes), 90, 91
levirate marriage, 112
Lévi-Strauss, Claude, 113
levity, 286
Lewis, Gilbert, 122
Lewis, Sinclair, 88
liberal, 107
licentious, 286
Lichtenstein, Roy, 75
lie/lay, 66
ligament, 118
light, 124
Light in August (Faulkner), 87
light-year, 125
limerick, 84
limnology, 62
Lincoln, Abraham (assassina-
    tion), 104
linguistic relativity (Sapir-
    Whort hypothesis), 112
lion, 128
lionized, 286
lipids, 118
liquid, 121
Lister, Joseph, 119
listless, 286
literature, 83–89
Little House on the Prairie
    (Wilder), 89
Little Women (Alcott), 85
locations, religious, 94
Locke, John, 90, 91
logic, 90
logical positivism, 90

logorrhea, 286
Lolita (Nobokov), 88
London, Jack, 88
Long Day's Journey into Night, A
    (O'Neill), 88
Longfellow, Henry
    Wadsworth, 88
longitude, 99
long-term goals, visualizing, 45
loose/lose, 66
Lorax, The (Seuss), 88
Lord of the Flies, The
    (Golding), 87
Lord of the Rings, The
    (Tolkien), 89
lose/loose, 66
Louis XIV, 103
Louisiana Purchase, 99, 104
Louvre, 76
lovelorn, 286
lucre, 287
lugubrious, 287
lunar eclipse, 125
lurid, 287

• M •

MacBeth (Shakespeare), 88
macerate, 287
Macfarlane, Alan, 113
Machiavelli, Nicolò, 90, 91, 108
machination, 287
macrostructure, 110
Madame Bovary (Flaubert), 87
Madame Butterfly (Puccini), 83
maelstrom, 287
Magellan, Ferdinand, 103
Magic Flute, The (Mozart), 82
Magic Mountain, The (Mann), 88
magisterial, 287
Magna Carta, 101
magnanimous, 287
Main Street (Lewis), 88
Malcolm X, 103
malinger, 287
Malinowski, Bronislaw, 113
malleable, 288
mammalogy, 62, 118
mandate, 288
Mandela, Nelson, 103
mandir, 94
Manet, Edouard, 75
Manhattan Project, 104
Manifest Destiny, 101
manifold, 288
Mann, Thomas, 88

marcato, 80
Marconi, Guglielmo, 126
marine biology, 118
market, 105
Marlowe, Christopher, 88
Mars/Ares, 93
Martian Chronicles, The
    (Bradbury), 86
Marx, Karl, 90, 91, 103
Mary, 93
Maslow, Abraham, 109
mass, 124
Mass in B Minor (Bach), 82
mass number, 128
mass production, 105
MAT (Miller Analogies Test).
    See also score report
  overview, 1, 7–11
  registering for, 11–12, 47
  retaking, 13, 319
  score report, 11–12
  scoring procedure, 12
  subjects covered by, 9
MAT Practice Test #1
  answers, 149–154
  questions, 137–147
MAT Practice Test #2
  answers, 167–172
  questions, 155–165
MAT Practice Test #3
  answers, 185–190
  questions, 173–183
MAT Practice Test #4
  answers, 203–208
  questions, 191–201
MAT Practice Test #5
  answers, 221–226
  questions, 209–219
MAT Practice Test #6
  answers, 239–244
  questions, 227–237
mathematics
  algebra, 131
  arithmetic, 130–131
  geometry, 131–133
  roman numerals, 130
Matisse, Henri, 75
matriarchy, 112
matter, 124
maudlin, 288
Mauss, Marcel, 113
mawkish, 288
Mayflower Compact, 101
McMillan, Edwin, 122
mea culpa, 68

Mead, Margaret, 113
measure, musical, 80
measurement, 129–130
Mecca, 94
Mediterranean Sea, 99
medley, 80
meiosis, 119
Meir, Golda, 103
melisma, 80
melting, 121
Melville, Herman, 88
memory device
  for learning word roots, 53–54
  mnemonics, 53, 60, 257
Mendel, Gregor, 119
Mendeleev, Dmitri, 122
Mendelssohn, Felix, 82
menial, 288
mercurial, 288
Mercury/Hermes, 93
meshuga, 288
Mesopotamia, 99
Messiah, The (Handel), 82, 83
metal, 128
metalloid, 128
metamorphic rock, 125
Metamorphoses (Ovid), 88
Metamorphosis, The (Kafka), 87
metaphor, 84
meteor, 126
meteorite, 126
meteoroid, 126
meter, 80, 84
meticulous, 39
metronome, 80
Metropolitan Museum of Art,
    The, 76
mettle, 288
mezzo-forte, 80
mezzo-piano, 80
miasma, 289
Michelangelo, 75
microbiology, 119
Middlemarch (Eliot), 86
Mies van der Rohe, Ludwig, 78
milieu, 289
Milky Way, 126
Mill, John Stuart, 90
Miller, Arthur, 88
milli-, 129
Mills, Robert, 78
milquetoast, 289
Milton, John, 88
minatory, 289
Minerva/Athena, 93

Miró, Joan, 75
misanthrope, 289
miscreant, 289
miserly, 289
Mississippi River, 99
Missouri River, 99
mitigate, 289
mitosis, 119
mnemonics, 53, 60, 257
Moby Dick (Melville), 88
modish, 289
modus operandi, 68
Mohr, Karl Friedrich, 122
mole, 121
molecule, 121
MOMA, 76
momentum, 124
Mona Lisa (da Vinci), 75
Mondrian, Piet, 75
monera kingdom, 127
Monet, Claude, 26, 74, 75
monopoly, 105
morass, 290
More, Thomas, 90, 91
morphology, 62
Morrison, Toni, 88
Morse, Samuel, 126
mosaic, 74
Moses, 93
mosque, 94
Mother Teresa, 103
motif, 74, 80, 84
motivation, maximizing, 44–45
Mount Everest, 99
Mount Kilimanjaro, 99
Mount McKinley, 99
Mount Olympus, 94
Mount Rushmore, 99
Mozart, Wolfgang Amadeus, 82
Mrs. Dalloway (Woolf), 89
Muhammad, 93
multiculturalism, 112
multiple meanings, words
    with, 63
multiplication, 131
multitasking, 45
Munch, Edvard, 75
munificent, 290
mural, 74
museums, 76
music, 79–83
musicians and composers, 82
mycology, 62, 119
mythology/religion, 92–95

• N •

Nabokov, Vladimir, 88
Nast, Thomas, 75
nationalism, 107
NATO (North Atlantic Treaty
    Organization), 101
natural, 81
nebulous, 290
negative reciprocity, 112
neoplatonism, 90
nepotism, 290
Neptune/Poseidon, 93
neurobiology, 119
neutrino, 124
neutron, 121
New Deal, 101
Newton, Isaac, 125
Newton, John, 83
Niagara Falls, 99
Nietzsche, Friedrich, 90, 91
Nile, 99
1984 (Orwell), 88
1970s energy crisis, 103
Noah, 93
Nobel, Alfred, 122
noble gas, 128
noblesse oblige, 68
noisome, 290
nom de plume, 68
nomad (itinerant), 112
non sequitur, 68, 290
nondescript, 290
nonmetal, 128
nono contendere, 68
nonpareil, 290
norm, 110
North Atlantic Treaty
    Organization (NATO), 101
"no-score" option, choosing, 12
notorious, 290
Notre Dame, 78
noun, 36
nouns, collective, 62–64
nucleus, 121
nugatory, 291
numerals, roman, 130
numerator, 131
numinous, 291
numismatology, 62

• O •

OASDI (Old-Age, Survivors, and
    Disability Insurance), 105
obeisance, 291

obfuscated, 291
obstreperous, 291
obtuse angle, 132
Oceania, 99
octagon, 132
octave, 81
"Ode on a Grecian Urn"
    (Keats), 87
odeon, 77
odious, 291
Odyssey (Homer), 87
Oedipus Rex (Sophocles), 89
officious, 291
ohm, 124, 130
O'Keeffe, Georgia, 75
Old Man and the Sea, The
    (Hemingway), 87
Old-Age, Survivors, and
    Disability Insurance
    (OASDI), 105
oligarchy, 113
Oliver Twist (Dickens), 86
-ology words, 61–62
Olympia (Manet), 75
On the Road (Kerouac), 87
oncology, 62, 119
*One Day in the Life of
    Ivan Denisovich*
    (Solzhenitsyn), 88
1:4,2:3 analogy, 27
O'Neill Eugene, 88
1:3,2:4 analogy, 26–27, 29
1:2,3:4 analogy, 25–26, 29–30
onomatopoeia, 85
ontology, 62
onus, 291
openhanded, 291
Operant Conditioning
    (instrumental condition-
    ing), 108
ophthalmology, 62
opprobrium, 292
oratorio, 81
orbit, 126
order, 127
Oregon Trail, 99
organic chemistry, 121
original sin, 92
ornithology, 62, 119
Orwell, George, 88
Osiris, 93
osmosis, 119
ostracized, 292
otiose, 292
Our Town (Wilder), 89
overchoice (choice overload),
    110

overweening, 292
Ovid, 88
ownership, taking, 43
oxymoron, 85

• P •

pacific, 292
Pacific Ring of Fire, 99
pacing, for test questions, 48
pagoda, 77
Paine, Thomas, 88
painstaking, 292
palate/palette, 66
paleontology, 62
palindromes, 23
palliate, 292
pallid, 292
panacea, 292
Panama Canal, 99
pancreas, 26–27
pander, 293
Pangaea, 99
Pantheon, 78
paper mache, 74
parable, 85
parabola, 131
Paradise Lost (Milton), 88
paradox, 85
paragon, 293
parallel, 132
Parallel Lives, The (Plutarch), 88
parallelogram, 132
parasitology, 119
pariah, 293
parley, 293
parochial, 293
parody, 85
parsimonious, 293
Parsons, Talcott, 111
Parthenon, 78
partisan, 293
parts analogies, 20
parts of speech, 36
Pascal, Blaise, 126
passed/past, 66–67
Pasteur, Louis, 119
pastiche, 293
patent, 293
pathology, 62
pathos, 85
patois, 294
patriarchy, 113
paucity, 294
Paul Revere's Ride
    (Longfellow), 88

Pauling, Linus, 122
Pavlov, Ivan, 109, 119
Pavlovian conditioning (classical conditioning), 108
Pearl Harbor attack, 104
Pei, I. M., 78
Peirce, Charles Sanders, 91
pejorative, 294
penchant, 294
pencil, moving, 252
pencil-and-paper MAT, 11
pendulum, 124
penitent, 294
pentagon, 132
penurious, 294
penury, 294
people. *See* figures
per se, 69
percussion, 81
peremptory, 294
Perestroika, 101
perfidy, 294
perfunctory, 295
Pergamon, 76
perimeter, 132
periodic table, 128–129
permeated, 295
perpendicular, 132
persecute/prosecute, 67
Persian Gulf, 99
Persistence of Memory, The (Dali), 75
persona non grata, 69
personification, 85
Peter the Great, 103
Petrarch, 88
petulant, 295
pH, 121, 130
philology, 62
philosophers, 90–91
philosophy, 89–91
phlegmatic, 295
phoenix, 92
photon, 124
phylum, 127
physics, 122–125
physiological, 295
physiology, 62, 119
phytopathology, 119
Pi, 132
pianissimo, 81
piano, 81
picaresque, 295
Picasso, Pablo, 75, 93
picayune, 295

Picture of Dorian Gray, The (Wilde), 89
picturesque, 295
piebald, 295
pig, 128
Pirates of Penzance, The (Gilbert and Sullivan), 82
pitch, musical, 81
pittance, 296
places of worship, 94–95
Planck, Max, 125
planetary, 38
planning. *See* preparation plan; study plan
plantae kingdom, 127
plasma, 121
plate tectonics, 126
Plath, Sylvia, 88
platitude, 296
Plato, 91
platonic, 296
plaudits, 296
playful analogies
  grammar change, 22–23
  "sounds like," 23
  wordplay, 22
plebeian, 296
plenipotentiary, 296
plot, 85
pluralism, 107
Plutarch, 88
Pluto/Hades, 93
pneumatics, 124
poco, 81
Poe, Edgar Allan, 88
Poetics (Aristotle), 90, 91
poignant, 296
pointillism, 74
politesse, 296
political science, 106–108
Pollock, Jackson, 75
polygon, 132
Pompidou Centre, 76
ponerology, 111
pore/pour, 67
Porgy and Bess (Gershwin), 82
portrait, 74
Portrait of Madame X (Sargent), 76
Portrait of the Artist As a Young Man, A (Joyce), 87
Poseidon/Neptune, 93
positive self-talk, using, 49, 253
positive thinking, focus on, 45
positivism, 111
post-transition metal, 128

Pound, Ezra, 88
pour/pore, 67
practice tests. *See also* preparation plan; *specific MAT Practice Tests*
  benefits and cost, 9
  environment for, 46
  humanities, 95–96
  identifying analogy structural type, 28–29
  language and words, 69–71
  pacing yourself, 48
  purchasing, 9
  science and math, 133–134
  social sciences, 114–116
  strategy for solving analogies, 32–33
  taking several tests, 46–47
  timing, 45–46
  tough questions, 39–40
Prado, 76
pragmatism, 90
prattle, 296
precipitate, 121
precocious, 297
prefixes, word, 56–58
prejudice, 37
prelude, 81
preparation plan. *See also* practice tests; study plan
  action steps, making a list of, 43
  creating your MAT study plan, 41–43
  dealing with test anxiety, 49–50, 251–253
  duplicating the test environment, 46
  following through with, 42
  for graduate school admissions, 320
  knowing when you're ready to register, 47
  knowing where you currently stand, 42
  maximizing your motivation, 44–45
  procrastination, avoiding, 45
  quality vs. quantity, 45, 47
  setting a deadline and mapping a schedule, 43–44
  setting a score goal, 42–43
  study materials, choosing, 44
  tackling MAT timing, 47–49
  test day preparations, 247–249
pressure, 124

presto, 81
pretentious, 297
Pride and Prejudice (Austen), 86
prima facie, 69
primary colors, 74
prime meridian, 99
prime number, 131
primordial, 297
Prince, The (Machiavelli), 90, 91, 108
principal/principle, 67
pristine, 297
pro bono, 69
pro forma, 69
process of elimination, 34–35
procrastination, avoiding, 45
product, 131
profligacy, 297
Prohibition, 101
proletariat, 101
prolific, 297
prolix, 297
Prometheus Bound (Aeschylus), 85
Prometheus Unbound (Shelley), 88
prominent, 297
promulgate, 297
propaganda, 107
prosaic, 298
prose, 85
prosecute/persecute, 67
protectionism, 105
protista kingdom, 127
proton, 121
Proust, Marcel, 88
prowess, 298
psychiatrist, 109
psychoanalysis, 109
psychologist, 109
psychology, 62, 108–109
Ptolemy, 126
Puccini, Giacomo, 82, 83
puerile, 298
pulley, 124
pulsar, 126
pun, 85
punctilious, 298
pungent, 298
punitive, 298
Purcell, Henry, 82
pusillanimous, 298
Pygmalion (Shaw), 88

• Q •

quagmire, 298
quality vs. quantity, 45, 47
quantum mechanics, 124
quark, 121
quasar, 126
quash, 298
Queen of Spades, The (Tchaikovsky), 82
querulous, 299
quid pro quo, 69
quiescent, 299
quixotic, 299
quotidian, 299
quotient, 131
Quran, 94

• R •

Ra, 93
Rabbit, Run (Updike), 89
Races of Humankind, The (Benedict), 111
Radcliffe-Brown, Alfred, 113
radius, 132
raison d'être, 69
Ramadan, 92
rancorous, 299
rapturous, 299
rara avis, 69
rare earth element, 129
rationalism, 90
raucous, 299
"Raven, The" (Poe), 88
raze, 299
reagent, 121
realism, 74
reasoning ability, measuring, 10
recalcitrant, 299
recapitulated, 300
recession, 105
recidivist, 300
recrudescent, 300
rectangle, 132
rectitude, 300
Red Scare, 107
redistribution, 113
redress, 300
reductive, 300
referrals, choosing, 321
refracted, 300
refractory, 300

registering for the MAT
knowing when you're ready, 47
procedure for, 11–12
Reichel-Dolmatoff, Gerardo, 113
rejuvenated, 300
relationship categories. *See also* analogies
description analogies, 18–19
parts analogies, 20
playful analogies, 22–23
similar/different analogies, 21–22
type analogies, 19–20
religion/mythology, 92–95
religious cosmology, 113
religious figures, 93
relish, 301
Rembrandt, 76
remedial, 301
Remembrance of Things Past (Proust), 88
remiss, 301
Renoir, Pierre-Auguste, 76
replete, 301
reprehensible, 301
republic, 101
Republic, The (Plato), 91
repugnant, 301
requisite, 301
resigned, 301
resplendent, 301
rest, 81
restive, 302
resume (curriculum vitae), preparing, 321
retaking the MAT, 13, 319
reticent, 302
retiring, 302
retrenchment, 302
revanche, 302
reverent, 302
RFK (Kennedy, Robert Francis), 103
rhetoric, 85
rhetorical question, 85
rhombus, 132
ribosome, 26–27
Richter, 130
rickety, 302
right angle, 132
right triangle, 132
Rigoletto (Verdi), 82
Rijksmuseum, 76

Rime of the Ancient Mariner
    (Coleridge), 86
riposte, 302
risible, 302
risque, 303
ritard, 81
River Thames, 100
riveting, 303
"Road Not Taken, The"
    (Frost), 87
Robinson Crusoe (Defoe), 86
roborant, 303
Rockefeller, J. D., 103
rococo, 77
Rodin, Auguste, 76
Rogers, Carl, 109
role homogeneity, 111
roman numerals, 130
rondo, 81
Rontgen, Wilhelm, 126
Roosevelt, Franklin D., 103
roots, word, 53–56
Rosh Hashanah, 94
Rousseau, Jean-Jacques, 91
rubato, 81
Rubens, Peter Paul, 76
rudimentary, 303
ruffian, 303
ruminate, 303
Rushdie, Salman, 88
rushing, 46, 47, 249, 252
Russian Revolution, 104

● *S* ●

Sabin, Albert, 119
saccharine, 303
sacrosanct, 303
Sahara, 100
St. Peter's Basilica, 78
Salk, Jonas, 119
Salome (Strauss), 82
salutary, 303
sangfroid, 69
sanguine, 304
sapid, 304
Sapir-Whort hypothesis (lin-
    guistic relativity), 112
sarcasm, 85
Sargent, John Singer, 76
Sartori, Giovanni, 108
Satan, 93
Satanic Verses, The
    (Rushdie), 88
satellite, 126

satiated, 304
satire, 85
saturine, 38
scale, 81
scalene triangle, 132
Scandinavia, 100
scapegoat, 111, 304
Scarlet Letter, The
    (Hawthorne), 87
scathing, 304
scene, 85
schadenfreude, 69, 304
schedule, mapping, 44
Schopenhauer, Arthur, 91
Schubert, Franz, 82
science and math
    biology, 117–119
    chemistry, 120–122
    classification, 127–128
    mathematics, 130–133
    measurement, 129–130
    other sciences, 125–126
    periodic table, 128–129
    physics, 122–125
    practice test, 133–134
scintillating, 304
score. *See also* score report
    goal for, 42–43, 47, 48
    measurement, 130
    "no-score" option, 12
    procedure for scoring, 12
    questions not counted
        toward, 12, 34
    role in graduate school appli-
        cation, 10, 13
    timing each question and, 48
score report
    preliminary and official score,
        13, 319
    sending, 11–12, 319
    when to receive, 11
Scott, Dred, 108
Scott, Sir Walter, 88
Scott Key, Francis, 83
Scream, The (Munch), 75
sculpture, 74
scurrilous, 304
scuttle, 304
second guessing, 249, 251
secretes, 305
sedentary, 305
sedimentary rock, 126
sedulous, 305
seismometer, 126
self-talk, positive, 49

seminal, 305
semitone, 81
sentences
    building, 30–31
    writing down, 249
separation of powers, 107
September 11 attacks, 104
sere, 305
serendipity, 305
servile, 305
Seuss, Dr., 88
seven deadly sins, 92
sforzando, 81
Shakespeare, William, 88
shard, 305
sharia, 92
sharp, 81
Shaw, George Bernard, 88
sheep, 128
Shelley, Mary, 88
Shelley, Percy Bysshe, 88
Siberia, 100
Siddhartha (Hesse), 87
Sikhism, 92
Silverstein, Shel, 88
similar/different analogies,
    21–22
simile, 85
Simmel, Georg, 111
Simon, Théodore, 109
simper, 305
simulacrum, 306
Sinan, Mimar, 78
Sinclair, Upton, 88
sine qua non, 69
sinuous, 306
Sistine Chapel, 75
site/cite, 65
Skinner, B. F., 109
skipping/ignoring test
    questions
    benefits of, 252
    determining before the test,
        46, 249
    experimental questions, not
        counted toward score,
        12, 34
    tough questions and, 33
skittish, 306
skulk, 306
skullduggery, 306
slake, 306
Slaughterhouse-Five
    (Vonnegut), 89
sleep, 247

slowing down, during test, 252
Smith, Adam, 91
Smith, Samuel Francis, 83
social capital, 111
Social Contract, The (Rousseau), 91
social sciences
  anthropology, 112–113
  economics, 104–106
  geography, 97–100
  history, 100–104
  political science, 106–108
  practice test, 114–116
  psychology, 108–109
  sociology, 109–111
social stigma, 111
socialism, 105
sociology, 109–111
Socrates, 91
sol, 121
solar eclipse, 126
solar system, 126
solecism, 306
solicitous, 306
solid, 121
solipsistic, 306
solute, 121
solvent, 121
solving analogies. *See also* analogies; skipping/ignoring test questions; tough questions; traps to avoid
  building sentences, 30–31, 249
  checking the choices, 31–32
  identifying the structural type, 25, 28–30
  practice tests, 32–33
Solzhenitsyn, Aleksander, 88
somnolent, 307
Songs of Innocence (Blake), 86
sonnet, 85
sonorous, 307
sophistry, 307
Sophocles, 89
sophomoric, 307
soprano, 81
Sound and the Fury, The (Faulkner), 87
"sounds like" analogies, 23
Sousa, John Philip, 82
sovereign, 307
species, 127
speech, parts of, 36
speed, tips on, 46
Spencer, Herbert, 111

spendthrift, 307
Spenser, Edmund, 89
spurious, 307
square, 132
square root, 131
staccato, 81
staff, musical, 81
Stalin, Joseph, 103
stanza, 85
Starry Night (Van Gogh), 76
Stars and Stripes Forever, The (Sousa), 82
Star-Spangled Banner, The (Scott Key), 83
stationary/stationery, 67
statuesque, 307
status quo, 69
steadfast, 307
Steinbeck, John, 89
stentorian, 308
Stevenson, Robert Louis, 89
stigmas, 308
still life, 74
stilted, 308
stolid, 308
stone, measurement, 130
Stonehenge, 78
Stowe, Harriet Beecher, 89
Strait of Magellan, 100
Stranger, The (Camus), 86
stratagem, 308
strategy for solving analogies. *See also* analogies; tough questions; traps to avoid
  building sentences, 30–31
  checking the choices, 31–32
  identifying the structural type, 25, 28–30
  practice tests, 32–33
Strauss, Richard, 82
Stravinsky, Igor, 82
streamlined, 308
Streetcar Named Desire, A (Williams), 89
strenuous, 308
stretching, 252
strident, 308
structural types. *See also* analogies
  described, 23
  identifying, 25, 28–30
  1:2,3:4 analogies, 25–26
  1:3,2:4 analogies, 26–27
  1:4,2:3 analogies, 27
  writing down during tests, 249

structuralism, 113
study plan. *See also* preparation plan
  creating, 41–43
  deadlines for study, setting, 43–44
  quality vs. quantity, 45, 47
  study materials, choosing, 44
  test day preparations, 248
stultify, 309
stupefied, 309
Styx, 94
subito, 81
subjects
  humanities, 73–96
  overview, 9
  science and math, 117–134
  social sciences, 97–116
  words and language, 53–71
sublimation, 121
sublime, 309
subsidy, 105
subtraction, 131
subversive, 309
subvert, 309
succor, 309
succumb, 309
Suez Canal, 100
suffixes, 58–59
suffrage, 101, 309
sui generis, 69
Sullivan, Louis, 78
sum, 131
sumptuary, 310
sunspot, 126
super-ego, 109
superfluous, 310
supernova, 124
supplant, 310
supply and demand, 105
surmise, 310
surpassing, 310
surrealism, 74
surreptitious, 310
swan, 128
Swan Lake (Tchaikovsky), 83
Swift, Jonathan, 89
sycophant, 310
symbol, 85
synagogue, 95
syncopation, 81
synergy, 310
synonyms, 21
synoptic, 311

• T •

table, periodic, 128–129
tacet, 81
tacit, 311
taciturn, 311
Taj Mahal, 78
Tale of Two Cities (Dickens), 86
Tate Modern, 76
Tchaikovsky, Pyotr Ilyich, 82, 83
teleology, 62
temerity, 311
tempera, 74
temperance, 311
temperature, 124
Tempest, The (Shakespeare), 88
tempestuous, 311
tempo, 81
Ten Commandments, 94
tenable, 311
tenor, 81
tenuous, 311
tenuto, 81
terms
   animals, 127–128
   anthropology, 112–113
   architecture, 77
   art, 73–74
   biology, 117–119
   chemistry, 120–122
   classification, of living things, 127
   dictionary definitions, remembering, 38
   economic, 104–106
   geographical, 97–100
   historical, 100–101
   literature, 83–85
   music, 79–82
   other sciences, 125–126
   philosophy, 89–90
   physics, 122–124
   political science, 106–107
   psychology, 108–109
   religion/mythology, 92
   sociology, 110–111
   words, multiple words, letters, or numbers, 18
terse, 312
tertius gaudens, 111
Tesla, Nikola, 125
Tess of the D'Urbervilles (Hardy), 87
tessitura, 81

test anxiety, dealing with, 49–50, 251–253
test day preparations, 247–249
test environment, 46
test takers, types of, 41
testing center
   accommodations, special, 12
   arriving at, 248
   checking in with, 47
   finding, 11
tests. *See* MAT (Miller Analogies Test); practice tests
tête-à-tête, 69
thanatology, 62
Thatcher, Margaret, 103
Their Eyes Were Watching God (Hurston), 87
theme, 85
Theory of the Leisure Class, The (Veblen), 111
thermodynamics, 126
Thinker, The (Rodin), 76
Third World, 113
Thirty Years' War, 104
38th parallel north, 97
Thor, 93
Thoreau, Henry David, 89
Three Flags (Johns), 75
Tibet, 100
tibia, 31
time
   pacing yourself, 48
   recovering when you've fallen behind, 48
   rushing, 46, 47, 249, 252
   setting a deadline and mapping a schedule, 43–44
   tackling MAT timing, 47–49
   timing each question, 48
   timing the practice tests, 45–46
timorous, 312
tirade, 312
Titian, 76
titular, 312
Tolkien, J. R. R., 89
Tolstoy, Leo, 89
tone, 85
tonic, 312
Tönnies, Ferdinand, 111
toothsome, 312
Torah, 94
torpid, 312
torque, 124
tortuous, 312

totalitarianism, 107
tough questions. *See also* analogies; solving analogies
   analogy traps to avoid, 37–39
   considering parts of speech, 36
   making educated guesses, 37
   noticing difficulty level, 34, 37, 46, 49
   practice tests, 39–40
   process of elimination, applying, 34–35
   skipping/ignoring, 33
   solving when don't know the words, 34
   working backward, 35–36
touted, 312
tranquil, 313
transcendentalism, 90
transcription, 119
transducer, 124
transition metal, 129
trapezoid, 133
traps to avoid. *See also* analogies; solving analogies
   category traps, 38
   direction traps, 38–39
   distractor traps, 39
   tips for, 37–38
Treasure Island (Stevenson), 89
treble, 81
tremulous, 313
trepidation, 313
triangle, 133
trill, 81
trinity, 101
triple point, 122
trite, 313
Tropic of Cancer, 100
Tropic of Capricorn, 100
truculent, 313
truncated, 313
tsar (czar), 101
tumid, 313
tumultuous, 313
turbid, 313
turgid, 314
Turn of the Screw, The (James), 87
turpitude, 314
tutor, working with, 44
tutti, 82
Twain, Mark, 89
Twittering Machine (Klee), 75
2:1,4:3 analogy, 29
type analogies, 19–20
Tzu, Sun, 91

• U •

Uffizi, 76
umbrage, 314
unassuming, 314
unbridled, 314
uncertainty principle, 124
Uncle Tom's Cabin (Stowe), 89
unctuous, 314
underclass, 111
undermine, 314
unsavory, 314
upbraided, 314
Updike, John, 89
urbane, 315
urbanization, 113
usury, 315
utilitarian, 315
Utopia (More), 90, 91

• V •

vacuole, 119
vacuous, 315
vacuum, 124
vain/vane, 67
valence electron, 122
Valhalla, 94
Van Gogh, Vincent, 76
vapid, 315
vaporization, 122
variegated, 315
Vatican City, 94
Vatican Museums, 76
vaunted, 315
Veblen, Thorstein, 111
vehement, 315
venal/venial, 67
veni, vidi, vici, 69
Venus de Milo, 76
Venus/Aphrodite, 92
verb, 36
verbose, 315
verboten, 69, 316
Verdi, Giuseppe, 82, 83
verisimilar, 316
vernacular, 316
Versailles, 78
verse, 85
vertical mobility, 111
vex, 316
vibrato, 82
vigilant, 316
vihara, 95

vilify, 316
vindictive, 316
Virgil, 89
virology, 62, 119
virtuoso, 316
vis-à-vis, 69
viscosity, 122
viscous, 316
vitiate, 317
vituperated, 317
vivacious, 317
Vivaldi, Antonio, 82
vocabulary. *See also* words
  graduate level, 257–318
  improving, 59–60
  testing, 15
vociferous, 317
Volga, 100
volition, 317
volt, 130
Voltaire (*Candide*), 91
Vonnegut, Kurt, 89

• W •

waffle, 317
Waiting for Godot (Beckett), 86
Walden (Thoreau), 89
wan, 317
Ward, Samuel A., 83
Warhol, Andy, 76
warming up for the test, 248
Wars Powers Resolution, 107
Washington, George, 103
Wason, James, 119
"Waste Land, The" (Eliot), 87
Watson, John B., 109
watt, 124, 130
Weber, Max, 111
weltschmerz, 69
westernization, 113
Wharton, Edith, 89
Where the Sidewalk Ends
  (Silverstein), 88
whet, 317
Whitman, Walt, 89
whittling, 74
Why Parties? The Origin and
  Transformation of Political
  Parties in America
  (Aldrich), 107
Wilde, Oscar, 89
Wilder, Laura Ingalls, 89
Wilder, Thornton, 89

willful, 317
Williams, Tennessee, 89
wily, 318
Winding Stair, The (Yeats), 89
winsome, 318
wistful, 318
wizened, 318
Wood, Grant, 76
Woodward, Robert Burns, 122
woodwinds, 82
Woolf, Virginia, 89
wordplay analogies, 22
words. *See also* terms
  collective nouns, 62–64
  commonly confused, 64–67
  dictionary definitions for, 38
  foreign, 67–69
  -ology words, 61–62
  practice test, 69–71
  prefixes, 56–58
  suffixes, 58–59
  unknown, solving analogies
    and, 34
  word roots, 53–56
Wordsworth, William, 89
working backward, to solve
  analogy questions, 35–36
workplace, analogical thinking
  in, 17
works
  architecture, 78
  art, 74–76
  music, 83
  philosophy, 91
  religious, 94
World as Will and
  Representation, The
  (Schopenhauer), 91
worship, places of, 94–95
wreathe/wreath, 67
Wren, Christopher, 78
Wright, Frank Lloyd, 78
writers/authors, 85–89
writing
  essays, 320–321
  structure and sentences, 249
Wuthering Heights (Bronte), 86
Wyeth, Andrew (*Christina's
  World*), 76

• X •

xenocentrism, 111
xenophobia, 111

• Y •

Yeats, William Butler, 89
yield, 122
Yom Kippur, 94

• Z •

zealous, 318
Zedong, Mao, 91

zeitgeist, 69
zenith, 318
zephyr, 318
Zeus/Jupiter, 93
ziggurat, 77
zoology, 62, 119
Zoroaster, 93

Math & Science

Algebra I For Dummies,
2nd Edition
978-0-470-55964-2

Anatomy and Physiology
For Dummies,
2nd Edition
978-0-470-92326-9

Astronomy For Dummies,
3rd Edition
978-1-118-37697-3

Biology For Dummies,
2nd Edition
978-0-470-59875-7

Chemistry For Dummies,
2nd Edition
978-1-1180-0730-3

Pre-Algebra Essentials
For Dummies
978-0-470-61838-7

Microsoft Office

Excel 2013 For Dummies
978-1-118-51012-4

Office 2013 All-in-One
For Dummies
978-1-118-51636-2

PowerPoint 2013
For Dummies
978-1-118-50253-2

Word 2013 For Dummies
978-1-118-49123-2

Music

Blues Harmonica
For Dummies
978-1-118-25269-7

Guitar For Dummies,
3rd Edition
978-1-118-11554-1

iPod & iTunes
For Dummies,
10th Edition
978-1-118-50864-0

Programming

Android Application
Development For Dummies,
2nd Edition
978-1-118-38710-8

iOS 6 Application
Development For Dummies
978-1-118-50880-0

Java For Dummies,
5th Edition
978-0-470-37173-2

Religion & Inspiration

The Bible For Dummies
978-0-7645-5296-0

Buddhism For Dummies,
2nd Edition
978-1-118-02379-2

Catholicism For Dummies,
2nd Edition
978-1-118-07778-8

Self-Help & Relationships

Bipolar Disorder
For Dummies,
2nd Edition
978-1-118-33882-7

Meditation For Dummies,
3rd Edition
978-1-118-29144-3

Seniors

Computers For Seniors
For Dummies,
3rd Edition
978-1-118-11553-4

iPad For Seniors
For Dummies,
5th Edition
978-1-118-49708-1

Social Security
For Dummies
978-1-118-20573-0

Smartphones & Tablets

Android Phones
For Dummies
978-1-118-16952-0

Kindle Fire HD
For Dummies
978-1-118-42223-6

NOOK HD For Dummies,
Portable Edition
978-1-118-39498-4

Surface For Dummies
978-1-118-49634-3

Test Prep

ACT For Dummies,
5th Edition
978-1-118-01259-8

ASVAB For Dummies,
3rd Edition
978-0-470-63760-9

GRE For Dummies,
7th Edition
978-0-470-88921-3

Officer Candidate Tests,
For Dummies
978-0-470-59876-4

Physician's Assistant Exam
For Dummies
978-1-118-11556-5

Series 7 Exam
For Dummies
978-0-470-09932-2

Windows 8

Windows 8 For Dummies
978-1-118-13461-0

Windows 8 For Dummies,
Book + DVD Bundle
978-1-118-27167-4

Windows 8 All-in-One
For Dummies
978-1-118-11920-4

 **Available in print and e-book formats.**

Take Dummies with you everywhere you go!

Whether you're excited about e-books, want more from the web, must have your mobile apps, or swept up in social media, Dummies makes everything easier .

Dummies products make life easier!

- DIY
- Consumer Electronics
- Crafts

- Software
- Cookware
- Hobbies

- Videos
- Music
- Games
- and More!

For more information, go to **Dummies.com**® and search the store by category

FOR
DUMMIES
A Wiley Brand